BODY CLOCK

BODY CLOCK

The effects of time on human health

Edited by Dr Martin Hughes

CONTRIBUTORS

Devised & produced by
Andromeda Oxford Ltd
11–15 The Vineyard
Abingdon
Oxfordshire OX14 3PX

Copyright © 1989
Andromeda Oxford Ltd
Reprinted 1991, 1992

**The National Library
of Australia**
Cataloguing-in-Publication
data
Bodyclock:time and your
health

Includes index
ISBN 0 86438 107 7

1. Life cycle, Human.
2. Biological rhythms.
3. Health. I. Hughes, Martin.
II. Keynes, Milo.
612

Originated by Scantrans,
Singapore

Printed and bound in Spain

VOLUME EDITOR

Martin Hughes PhD MB BChir
Family Practitioner; Affiliated
Lecturer, Department of
Clinical Pharmacology,
University of Cambridge

ADVISORY EDITOR

Milo Keynes MD BChir FRCS
Consultant Surgeon; Formerly
Lecturer in Surgery
Universities of Cambridge,
Oxford, London, Harvard

KEY TO AUTHORS

AER   Anthony Reading PhD
Director of Psychological
Studies, Division of
Reproductive Medicine, UCLA
School of Medicine

**AS   Alan Stevens MD
FRCPath** Senior Lecturer in
Pathology; Consultant
Pathologist, Queen's Medical
Centre, Nottingham, England

**ATS   Andrew T Stanway MB
MRCP** Psychosexual and
Marital Physician, Surrey,
England

**CS   Colin Shapiro MB BCh
PhD; MRCPysch,** Lecturer in
Psychiatry, University of
Edinburgh

**DD   Professor David Denison
PhD FRCP** Director, Depart-
ment of Clinical Physiology,
Brompton Hospital, London
Director, National Heart and
Lung Institute, London, England

DW   Douglas Wilson PhD
Tenovus Institute for Cancer
Research, Cardiff, Wales

**EM   Professor Elwin Marg OD
PhD** Professor of Physiological
Optics and Optometry,
University of California,
Berkeley

IMM   Isobel Madden BDS
Dental Surgeon; Clinical
Assistant in Oral Surgery,
Addenbrooke's Hospital,
Cambridge, England

**JC   Professor James
Christensen MD,** Department of
Internal Medicine, University
of Iowa Hospital

**LB   Leszek K Borysiewicz PhD
FRCP,** Lecturer in Medicine
Honorary Consultant Physician
(Infectious Diseases)
Department of Medicine,
Addenbrooke's Hospital,
University of Cambridge

**MH   Martin Hughes PhD MB
BChir** Family Practitioner
Affiliated Lecturer, Department
of Clinical Pharmacology,
University of Cambridge

MJ   Martin Johnson MA PhD
University Lecturer in
Anatomy, University of
Cambridge

NC   Nicholas Coni MD FRCP
Consultant Physician Lecturer
in Gerontology, University of
Cambridge

NR   Neil Rushton MD FRCS
Director, Orthopedic Research
Unit, University of Cambridge
Honorary Consultant
Orthopedic Surgeon,
Addenbrooke's Hospital,
Cambridge, England

**PB   Peter Braude MA PhD
MRCOG DPMSA,** Consultant
Lecturer, Department of
Obstetrics and Gynecology,
University of Cambridge

**PM   Paul Mooney MB ChB
MRCOG** Research Registrar,
Department of Obstetrics and
Gynecology, University of
Cambridge

PW   Paul Ward MB MRCP
Senior Registrar, Department of
Pediatrics, Addenbrooke's
Hospital, Cambridge, England

**SM   Susan Mitchell MB BS
MRCOG,** Research Registrar
Department of Obstetrics and
Gynecology, University of
Cambridge

**SS   Professor Steven K Smith
MB BS MD MRCOG,**
Consultant Obstetrician
Head of Department of
Obstetrics and Gynecology,
University of Cambridge

**VN   Vizvan Navaratnam MB
BS PhD,** Director of Medical
Studies, Christ's College,
University of Cambridge

Peter Davis of the Dunn
Nutrition Unit, Cambridge,
kindly provided data on body
composition for Part One

Height and weight chart on
page 30 reproduced from Diem,
K and Lentner, C (eds) 1970 7th
edn *Geigy Scientific Tables*
Ciba-Geigy, Basle, p712

DISTINGUISHED
CONSULTANTS

John T Potts Jr MD
Jackson Professor of Clinical
Medicine, Harvard University
Medical School
Chief of Medical Services,
Massachusetts General Hospital

Lord Butterfield MD FRCP
Chairman of the Health
Promotion Research Trust
Emeritus Regius Professor of
Physic, University of Cambridge

Norman E Shumway MD
Professor and Chairman
Department of Cardiovascular
Surgery, Stanford School of
Medicine

PROJECT EDITOR
Stuart McCready

TEXT

Assistant Project Editor
Joanne Lightfoot

Editors
Paul Barnett
Fiona Mullan

Indexer
Kate Mertes

Typesetting
Reina Foster-de Wit
Nicola Whale

PICTURES

Research coordinator
Thérèse Maitland

Researchers
Celia Dearing
Susanne Williams
Linda Proud

ART

Art editor
Chris Munday

**Assistant art editor
and layout designer**
Martin Anderson

Additional layout design
Kevin Hinton

Artists
Martin Cox
Simon Driver
Mary Ann Le May
Alan Hollingbery
Trevor Mason
Graham Rosewarne
Taurus Graphics

CONTENTS

INTRODUCTION

BODYCLOCK explores the relationship between your body and time. It examines how your body's needs and capabilities change at different times of the day, of the month, of the year, and of your life, and it explains how awareness of the relationship between time and health can help you to achieve maximum well-being.

An important part of what it means to be in good health is that your body keeps in rhythm — achieving a complex synchrony of repeating biological cycles. Health suffers when one body system or another fails to keep time with the others — when the heart, for example, beats too fast or too slow, or groups of cells divide at the wrong rate. Bodyclock explains the major cycles that make up good health, focusing on what can be done to prevent their disruption.

One biological cycle encompasses all of the others — the life cycle, which an individual experiences only once, and only by living long enough. The picture of normal body rhythms changes dramatically from one part of this cycle to another.

Part One of the book, the Bodyclock Lifespan Chart, outlines the changes that affect us across the life cycle and explains what should be done to monitor your health and screen for disease at each stage. It explains how self-screening for some diseases is possible, before going on to consider how doctors tackle the same task. It describes screening before birth, close monitoring during birth, developmental assessment during childhood, self-screening and medical checking during adulthood. At each point the reader is referred to those sections in Part Two, the major part of the book, which explain in detail the normal events of the body in relation to time — be it seconds, or days or years.

Our bodies alter throughout the continuing process of maturity and aging. We each start our existence as a single cell — the fertilized egg. From that moment on there are constant, irrevocable changes, and continuous activity. The single cell divides and becomes two. The two cells divide, and *then the four, and so on. Cells become different, develop and move, until what was one cell becomes a being with millions of cells and many different parts. After birth, development and growth continue. In the early weeks and years the changes are massive: bodies grow; we achieve both language and mobility; the process of learning continues every day. Eventually we reach physical maturity and the being that started as a single fertilized egg is capable of producing or fertilizing a new single egg that will, in turn, become a person.*

At different times in a lifespan — the time between fertilization and birth, birth and puberty, puberty and maturity, maturity and aging, aging and bodily decline — our bodies function in different ways. The child's heart rate is not the same as the adult's. Sleep patterns vary. Both shape and physical abilities change. These changes impose differing demands on our metabolism, and differing demands require adjustments in nutritional support, which also necessarily varies throughout our lifespan.

There are other differences too: vulnerability to disease changes over time; as infants we are more susceptible to infections, while adults are more at risk of conditions like arthritis. Our mental abilities change, as does the perceptiveness of our senses, and a host of other factors. Some changes are more apparent and immediate than others — the onset of menstruation in puberty, for example. Others are more subtle. It takes a determined effort over a period of time to improve our level of physical fitness, but when the effort stops it slips away unnoticed in no time at all.

We ask at any point in time: what should my physical abilities be? Am I putting myself — or my child — at risk of harm or disease? What can I do to stay well and fit?

Over recent years many of us have become more concerned, and curious, about our health and how we can maintain it. Besides offering you a basic knowledge of how your body works, Bodyclock helps you judge the level at which you should be able to function at any given period, and how you might monitor your health and improve it. The best of health to you!
Martin Hughes

Part One
LIFESPAN HEALTH CHART

WHEN people are asked who is responsible for their health and well-being, they often reply with the name of their doctor. But in fact the maintenance of health is a responsibility shared between doctor and patient: often doctors can do little for patients who have not taken care of themselves and who have neglected adequate precautions in terms of diet, exercise and health checks.

The Bodyclock Lifespan Chart is designed to help you to fulfill your share of the responsibility, and to understand what doctors are doing when they fulfill theirs. The chart shows which concerns feature largely at each different time of life. It tells you how to monitor your own and your children's health, itemizes the main health complaints at different ages, and details appropriate checks, screenings and immunizations. It gives a detailed account of the main elements in monitoring the health of a newborn baby, an infant, a child and an adolescent before explaining the procedures that adults of every age should use to keep a check on their health. Special attention is given to the early years of life and to the young adult years when child-bearing is most likely to occur.

No part of this chart should be regarded as a substitute for a qualified medical judgment – one of its major aims is to make you more aware of when to ask for help. If you are concerned about any aspect of your own or your children's health, you should seek medical advice.

Before Birth

In most cases conception does not lead to birth. The vast majority of fertilized ova do not survive the first 10 days; even if they do, the chances are high that they will be spontaneously miscarried during the first few weeks. In general, such early miscarriages go unnoticed.

Once a pregnancy is established, the doctor will give the mother periodic prenatal checks. Many women, understandably, find some of the more intimate examinations embarrassing. Most doctors are sympathetic. Their concern is solely the well-being of the mother and the success of the pregnancy.

At about 12 weeks the mother's blood group and hemoglobin level are tested. The basic checks – which continue throughout pregnancy – include regular monitoring of:
◆ weight
◆ blood pressure
◆ size of the womb
◆ levels of glucose and protein in the urine

If there is any doubt as to the viability of the pregnancy – for example, if there has been vaginal bleeding or severe period-type pain – the fetus may be surveyed using an ultrasound scan at around 8 weeks. The presence of a fetal heartbeat will confirm that the pregnancy is continuing.

In a normal pregnancy the ultrasound scan is performed at 16-18 weeks. One purpose of this is to measure the size of the fetus's skull in order to check the exact stage of fetal development. Skilled operators can also check that the spine has fused (if not, there is a risk that the child may be born with spina bifida). The site of the placenta is located, giving doctors advance warning of various potential problems – for example, placenta previa, where the placenta lies across the exit from the womb.

At the same stage of the pregnancy the level of a certain protein (alpha-feto-protein, or AFP) in the blood may be measured. A high level of AFP may indicate that the fetus is affected by spina bifida or some other problem connected with the development of the nervous system.

Weight change in pregnancy is important: too much might indicate that the mother is retaining too much fluid – too little that the placenta is not working effectively. In either case the doctor will organize more frequent or intensive tests.

At 32 weeks it is usual to test the mother's blood again, both to check hemoglobin levels and to make sure that her body is not producing antibodies against the fetus. (Antibodies are the body's guardians against invasion by "foreign" living cells). This can arise if the mother's and the fetus's blood groups are incompatible. Usually this incompatibility causes no problem, because there is no mixing of the mother's and the fetus's blood; difficulties only arise if there is some leakage. The baby may be affected. Even when leakage does not occur, incompatibility of rhesus blood groups can cause difficulties in future pregnancies. This is because, at birth, some of the baby's blood may enter the mother's circulation. If the mother starts to produce antibodies she will continue to do so, and these may pass from her bloodstream into future fetuses and there destroy red blood cells. As a result of modern medical techniques, problems are now fortunately very rare.

Pregnancy at risk

For pregnancies where there may be a risk of inherited disorders such as Down's syndrome, two other screening tests are available. At about 8 weeks it is possible to sample a portion of the "chorion" – a membrane which surrounds the fetus and which, in part, produces the placenta. Chorion cells are derived from the fetus. These cells can be examined to determine whether the fetus is affected by the inherited disease. The test involves a small risk (1-2

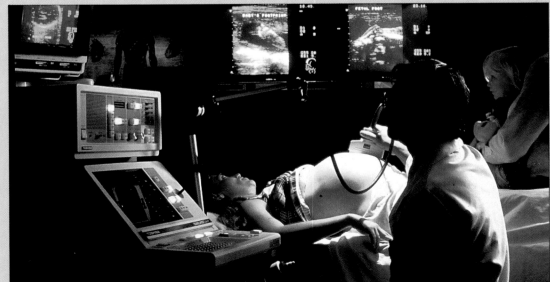

An ultrasound scan *allows doctors to screen the baby before it is born. High frequency soundwaves produce an image of the fetus on a monitor, enabling experts to diagnose conditions like heart or spinal defects, stunted growth or hydrocephaly (abnormal enlargement of the skull and atrophy of the brain). In some cases a scan may show up a problem that can be corrected by surgery. Here they reassure the whole family that the baby is healthy; they can just make out its foot on the far right.*

percent) of miscarriage. If the fetus is found to be affected, the parents may decide to terminate the pregnancy.

Alternatively, at 17-18 weeks gestation, parents may choose "amniocentesis." In this procedure a sample of the fluid surrounding the fetus (the "amniotic" fluid) is drawn off through a needle. The fluid contains cells shed by the fetus. These can be cultured (over a period of 2-3 weeks) and their genetic component analyzed. Again there is a risk of miscarriage of about 1-2 percent. Fetuses affected by inherited disease can be terminated. The difference between amniocentesis and chorion sampling is that with amniocentesis the mother of an affected fetus may have to undergo a very late (21 weeks) termination.

Late death in the womb

Death of a fetus after 28 weeks is very rare. Often the cause is unknown, but there are some conditions which increase the risk of late loss of a pregnancy. In one of these, known as "preeclampsia," the mother retains too much fluid, her blood pressure rises and she develops protein in the urine. The condition may progress to eclampsia, where the mother develops epileptic fits. Preeclampsia puts the fetus at risk; eclampsia threatens both the fetus and the mother. (This is one reason why the doctor monitors blood pressure, weight and urine throughout pregnancy). The cause is not known; fortunately it is an uncommon complication of pregnancy, and becomes less likely with second and subsequent babies.

Another cause of late death in the womb is diabetes – happily now much more easily controlled – and a third is separation of the placenta from the wall of the uterus, occasionally caused by trauma. These cases cannot be predicted, or prevented, but they are relatively rare.

Growth and development in weeks 3-5 of pregnancy

The pre-embryonic phase begins the first day of the 3rd week following the start of the last period (see pp140-143)
Day 1: conception; genetic material from mother fuses with genetic material from father in a single fertilized egg-cell – the microscopic package of genes, forming the nucleus of this cell, together with environmental influences, will control the pace and timing of growth and development up to adulthood, and the timing and rhythms of body functions throughout life.
Day 2: original cell divides to become two
Day 3-4: division to 12-cell stage; journey through fallopian tube complete (see p142)
Day 5-6: after further cell division the pre-embryo implants in the lining of the uterus
Day 14-18: pre-embryo separates into cells that will form part of the placenta and cells that will form the embryo

Main threats to life and health in the pre-embryonic phase

- chromosomal disorders
- failure to implant in uterine lining
- abnormal progress through the fallopian tube
- failure of corpus luteum

Risk of spontaneous abortion in pre-embryonic phase: 90 percent (see p141)

Growth and development in weeks 4-10 of pregnancy

The embryonic phase (see pp142-146)
4-5 weeks: mother misses period; three layers of cells form as embryonic disk (see pp142,143)
5-6 weeks: embryonic disk folds into a tube (see pp142, 144) risk of miscarriage slightly higher now than later
7-8 weeks: limb buds form; beginnings of internal organs, facial features
9-10 weeks: external sex organs appear
10-11 weeks: a human-like form with rudimentary limbs in place; risk of miscarriage slightly higher now than in earlier and later weeks.

Length at end of embryonic development: 30mm (1.2 in)

At the end of embryonic development the body composition is 90 percent water.

Main threats to life and health in embryonic phase

- infections to which mother is not immune (see p179)
- radioactivity (see p144)
- excess alcohol in mother's bloodstream
- products of tobacco smoke in mother's bloodstream
- other drugs in mother's bloodstream
- failure of the corpus luteum

Risk of spontaneous abortion in pre-embryonic phase: 15-25 percent (see p145)

Growth and development in weeks 11-42 of pregnancy

The fetal stage (see pp146-147)
18 weeks: the brain has most of its cells; first movements may be clearly felt
22-34 weeks: increasing strength and frequency of movement
34-38 weeks: brainwaves become like those of newborn baby

Weight at birth

Girls 2.5-4 kg (5.5-9lb)
Boys 2.5-4.5kg (5.5-10lb)

Length at birth

Girls 47-54cm (18-21in)
Boys 46-55cm (18-22in)

Body composition at birth

Lean body mass (muscle, nerves, bone) 10 percent
Fat: 10 percent
Water: 80 percent

Main threats to life and health in fetal phase

- infections to which mother is not immune (see p179)
- excess alcohol in mother's bloodstream
- products of tobacco smoke in bloodstream
- premature birth
- mother's diabetes
- eclampsia
- placental insufficiency
- trauma

Risk of spontaneous abortion in fetal phase: 1 in 150

The First Six Weeks

Health screening, begun while the baby is still in the womb, starts a new cycle from birth itself. Within the first minute after birth a baby is given an "Apgar test" (named after the doctor who devised it). Five indicators of health are checked:
◆ color
◆ heart rate
◆ respiration
◆ muscle tone
◆ response to stimuli such as the touch of a towel, or a catheter placed in a nostril.

Apgar Scores

Each indicator is allotted a score of 0, 1 or 2, so that if a baby has a score of 10 it is regarded as perfectly healthy. If the score is low, the baby may require immediate but usually short-term help. The test is repeated 5 minutes after birth. If the score is still low, especially if the baby is small, help may be required throughout the first month of life.

Examination at 30 minutes

After about 30 minutes, once the mother has had a chance to cuddle the baby to her breast, the doctor or midwife will take it away for a top-to-toe examination to check for congenital diseases and developmental faults. The baby is screened for the following problems:
● major limb deformities
● eyes too large or too small; cataracts (a possible consequence of rubella)
● hare lip; cleft palate
● fontanelles (the membrane-covered spaces between the bones) of greater than normal size
● abnormalities in heart rate and heart sound; is the heart on the correct side of the body?
● abnormalities in sound of breathing; do both sides move equally during breathing?
● abnormal swellings in the stomach (can be caused by enlarged kidneys); does the umbilical cord have the correct number of blood vessels (two arteries and one vein); can both femoral pulses (pulses at the top of the leg) be found?
● in boys, are both testicles present? Aperture of penis should be at tip, not on shaft
● congenital dislocation of hips (can often be corrected easily during early months of life; if left until later, surgery may be required, and there may be permanent walking difficulties)
● spina bifida (a cleft of the spinal column)
● abnormalities of the anus – it may be closed off (in which case surgery is needed), or wrongly sited
● abnormal "simian" creasing of palms (indicates Down's syndrome); abnormal fingers
● abnormal toes; clubfoot

Within 24 hours of birth, the baby will receive a further full-scale screening, with particular attention to the working of the heart.

The first blood test

Within the first week the baby receives its first blood test. The heel is pricked to produce a spot of blood, which is absorbed on filter paper. This spot is then tested for
◆ phenylketonuria (PKU) – a body-chemistry disorder that results in some proteins being poisonous to the sufferer's nervous system; a special diet is necessary up to 10-12 years old
◆ failure of the thyroid gland – untreated it causes cretinism
◆ cystic fibrosis – a life-threatening condition that affects the lungs and/or bowels. Formerly always fatal by early adolescence, this condition can now be managed much more successfully (see p68).

The six-week check

At various stages during the first year of life your baby will benefit from further screening. At about 6 weeks the doctor will have a standard checklist:

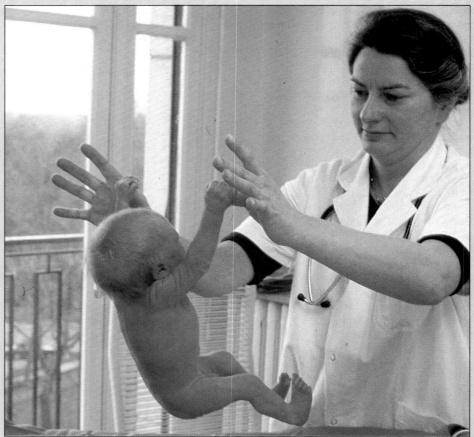

Checking a young baby's grip reflex.

Physical well-being

- is weight gain normal?
- is the head increasing in size at a normal rate?
- are there any abnormalities in the sound of the heart?
- are the hips normal, or do they dislocate?
- are there any signs of inguinal hernias (places where a small loop of intestine breaks through the wall of the abdomen)?
- in boys, are the testicles present and do they reach the bottom of the scrotum?

Development

- vision – will the baby's gaze follow moving objects?
- movement and coordination – can the baby hold its head up momentarily?
- hearing – is the baby alert to sounds?
- awareness – does the baby smile back at its mother?

The doctor will also ask you a number of questions to find out how much the baby cries, whether its sleeping pattern has stabilized, and so on. Do not be too concerned if your baby "fails" one of the tests: babies, just like adults, are individuals. Some develop at different rates. Sometimes, too, the test results can be misleading; for example, the baby's gaze may not follow a moving object simply because the baby is not interested in that particular object.

Sudden infant death syndrome (SIDS)

A small number of young babies die suddenly and without any clearly defined cause. These incidents are often grouped together and known as cot or crib deaths, but they cannot be explained by any single factor. Experts believe that there is no evidence to suggest that incidents are triggered by any inherited weakness, but there are certain patterns.

Poverty and overcrowding increase the risk, and babies of single parents are more likely to be affected than others. Parents who

Life expectancy: how many years is a newborn baby likely to have?
Girls almost 80
Boys more than 70

Developmental and health checks:
At 1 minute: first Apgar test (see OPPOSITE)
At 5 minutes: second Apgar test
At 30 minutes: first examination
Within 24 hours: second examination
Within 1 week: blood test
At 6 weeks: developmental check

Rate of growth: very rapid (see p152)

Weight: up to 10 percent lost in first few days, then irregular weight gains, averaging about 190-200g (6-7oz) per week; birthweight regained by second week
Girls at birth 2.5-4kg (5.5-9lb)
Boys at birth 2.5-4.5kg (5.5- 10lb)
Girls at six weeks 3.5-5.5kg (7.5-12lb)
Boys at six weeks 3.5-6kg (7.5-13lb)

Length: up to 1cm (0.4in) per week
Girls at birth 47-54cm (18-21in)
Boys at birth 46-55cm (18-22in)
Girls at six weeks 49-59cm(19-23in)
Boys at six weeks 51-60cm (20-24in)

Head circumference may decrease in first few days then rapidly increases - up to 5-8mm (0.2-0.3in) per week
Girls at birth 32.5-37cm (12.5-14.5in)
Boys at birth 33-38cm (13-15in)
Girls at six weeks 35-40cm (13.5-15.5in)
Boys at six weeks 36-41cm (14-16in)

Body composition at birth:
Lean body mass
  Girls 10 percent; Boys 10 percent
Fat
  Girls 10 percent; Boys 10 percent
Water
  Girls 80 percent; Boys 80 percent

Nutrition: breast feeding recommended, but not essential (see p154)

Normal heart rate at birth: 120-140 beats per minute (see pp50, 149)

Daily hours of sleep: highly variable, typically 16-17 (see p78)

Vision: may focus on close objects

Hearing: startled by sudden loud noises

Immunization: temporary immunity through antibodies acquired in womb from mother (see p180)

Main serious threats to life and health:
- congenital malformations
- premature birth
- accidents
- infection
- birth trauma

Risk of dying at birth: 1 in 500 for both girls and boys
Risk of dying between birth and six weeks:
Girls 1.6 in 500; Boys 2 in 500

drink heavily or take narcotics are also more likely to lose a child through SIDS. Fewer breast-fed babies are affected, but this may be because they are less likely to be in the high-risk categories anyway. In addition, many of these deaths are often thought to be caused by the following factors:

1 Chest infection.
 Occasionally an infection can strike quickly and there is no time to observe and treat it. Acute respiratory failure can kill a small baby before parents have time to react.

2 Allergy.
 Some experts believe that an allergic reaction to cow's milk could cause sudden death through a buildup of antibodies in the baby's blood. Although breast-fed babies are less at risk

from SIDS, there is no substantial proof for the allergy theory.

3 Overheating or suffocation.
 Heavy bedclothes, the wrong kind of bedding, or dangerous pillows have all been suggested as possible causes of death, often because no other explanation could be found. Pillows should not be used until the baby is a year old, but on the whole, bedding will usually allow babies to breathe. Mothers who sleep beside their infants have often been blamed, or blamed themselves, for rolling on them during the night, but this theory is often the result of exaggerated fear or excessive guilt, and babies can normally sleep safely beside their mothers.

Six Weeks to One Year

Screening tests may be carried out every three months or so during the first year of life. A full-scale hearing test often takes place when the baby is about 8 months. At 7-10 months the doctor's standard checklist will be something like this:

Physical development
- are the hips functioning properly (not dislocated)?
- is weight gain normal?
- is the head increasing in size at a normal rate?
- are there any abnormalities in the sounds of the heart?
- in boys, are the testes present and normal?
- is the baby in good general physical condition?

Development
◆ vision and fine movement – can the baby
- pass a toy block from hand to hand and also hold it in both hands?
- use its fingers in a pincer grip?
- use its hand to grasp objects?
◆ movement and coordination – can the baby
- lift its head?
- sit unsupported?
- take its weight on its feet when given support to keep it upright?
- roll over from front to back and/or from back to front?
- crawl?
- keep its head under control when pulled up to a sitting position?
◆ hearing and speech – does the baby
- babble constantly?
- imitate sounds?
- become distracted by unexpected sounds?
◆ feeding behavior – is the baby
- breast-fed?
- bottle-fed?
- cup-fed?
- able to chew?
◆ awareness and social behavior – does the baby
- behave in an uneasy or a friendly way with strangers?
- look around for a dropped toy that has fallen out of sight?
- laugh?
- cry a lot?
- sleep regularly and well?
- make eye contact with adults?
- show signs of alertness?

Taking the baby to a doctor
Whenever you are concerned about your baby's well-being you should seek medical advice. Most likely the condition will not be serious – but the visit to the doctor will have the important benefit of reassuring you, the parent. First babies, particularly, are frightening for parents. Generally, doctors will respect your concern for your child, and will help you to learn which minor ailments you can manage yourself. Gradually you should become more confident about handling routine conditions, and will only need medical

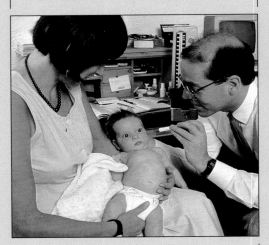

help if the problem persists or worsens.

The commonest reasons why parents call on the doctor are
● "snuffles"
● coughs and colds
● vomiting and diarrhea
● feeding difficulties
● raised temperature
● irritability
● sleeping difficulties
● rashes
● ear infections

The doctor will ask you for details of the severity and duration and then examine the baby. The standard checklist for the examination is:
◆ is the temperature (as recorded in the armpit or rectum) raised?
◆ what is the pulse rate?
◆ what is the rate of breathing?
◆ are the sounds of the chest, as heard through a stethoscope, normal?
◆ do the fontanelles feel normal?
◆ does the skin feel normal?
◆ are there any signs of swollen glands in the neck?
◆ are the ears normal?
◆ is the stomach swollen?
◆ are there any swellings or bulges in the stomach or groin? (These could indicate hernias)
◆ can the baby be "rolled into a ball," so that the head touches the knees?
◆ are there any signs of infection on the skin?
◆ is the throat sore?

Serious disease of babies is comparatively rare, but even common ailments can lead to grave problems. For example, prolonged diarrhea and vomiting can cause major dehydration, and a high temperature can induce fits (see Ch4). Dehydration can normally be prevented if the child is given copious amounts of clear liquids; similarly, a hot baby can be cooled using paracetamol and by sponging with tepid water.

When should you call the doctor?
You may feel that a single symptom does not normally justify a trip to see the doctor. However, a combination of a number of symptoms may make it important – or even urgent – that you get medical advice. By itself, none of the following symptoms should cause concern, but should your baby display several of them, or should any one of them persist for more than 24 hours, you ought to get medical advice.
● mild vomiting (do not be concerned about posseting – bringing up small amounts of milk immediately after feeding)
● taking up to 50 percent less fluid than usual
● passing less urine than usual
● showing tiny specks of blood in the feces
● being sleepier than usual
● crying in an unusual way
● being floppier, droopier or weaker than usual

- paying less attention to things going on nearby, including what you are saying directly to them
- looking pale
- slightly sucking in the chest or upper stomach when breathing in
- a slight rash that covers much of the body. A small sore area on the skin
- making a gentle whistling noise in the chest when breathing out
- bluish fingertips and/or toes (a sign of poor blood circulation)
- toes that take more than a few seconds to revert to their original color after having been pinched firmly for a couple of seconds (another sign of poor blood circulation)
- having a slightly raised temperature

Symptoms that require immediate attention

Some symptoms are serious enough in themselves to warrant action as soon as they appear. If your baby's feces are colored red because of the amount of blood being passed with them, you should certainly seek urgent medical help, as you should for repeated projectile vomiting (vomit that is ejected with force) or vomit flecked with green. Other single symptoms which are serious enough to warrant immediate medical attention, even if in the middle of the night, include:

- a fit or convulsion (keep the baby cool and lying on its side until the doctor arrives)
- drowsiness and irritability associated with a markedly raised temperature
- a bulging in the groin region associated with vomiting
- distressed breathing – noticeable sucking in of the chest or upper stomach as the baby breathes in, a fast breathing rate, "grunting" noises as the baby breathes
- persistent, severe vomiting with or without diarrhea

It should be stressed again that a combination of individually mild symptoms may indicate a serious illness, so contact your doctor if any symptom, or group of symptoms, suddenly worsens.

Developmental checks: At 6 weeks, then at intervals of about three months

Rates of growth: very rapid (see p153)

Weight:
Girls at six weeks 3.5-5.5kg (7.5-12lb)
Boys at six weeks 3.5-6kg (7.5-13lb)
Girls at one year 7.5-11.5kg (17-25lb)
Boys at one year 8-12kg (18-26.5lb)

Length: 25-30cm (10-12in) added to birth-length by one year
Girls at six weeks 49-59cm (19-23in)
Boys at six weeks 51-60cm (20-24in)
Girls at one year 69-79cm (27-31in)
Boys at one year 71-81cm (27-32in)

Head circumference up to 5-8mm (0.2-0.3in) per week
Girls at six weeks 35-40cm (13.5-15.5in)
Boys at six weeks 36-41cm (14-16in)
Girls at one year 43-49cm (16.5-19in)
Boys at one year 45-49cm (17.5-19in)

Body composition at 6 weeks
Lean body mass
  Girls 16 percent; Boys 19 percent
Fat
  Girls 16 percent; Boys 13 percent
Water
  Girls 68 percent; Boys 68 percent

Body composition at 1 year
Lean body mass, muscle, nerves, bones
  Girls 21 percent; Boys 23 percent
Fat
  Girls 19 percent; Boys 17 percent
Water
  Girls 60 percent; Boys 60 percent

Nutrition
3-6 months: weaning to solids begins; vitamin supplements recommended after weaning (see pp154-155)
7 months: may begin drinking from training beaker

Normal heart rate at 1 year: 100-110 beats per minute (see p50)

Daily hours of sleep: highly variable, typically 13-14 (see p78)

Vision
3 months: will move head to see better
4-6 months: may gaze intently at objects and people who are near
6 months: will look for dropped toy
After 6 months: persisting cross-eye should have medical attention (see p84)

Hearing: untreated middle-ear infection can cause permanent damage
6 months: can identify source of sound
8 months: doctor checks hearing

Teeth: teething discomfort (see p110)
Around 6 months: two lower central incisors
6-7 months: two upper central incisors
8-9 months: two upper lateral incisors
Around one year: two lower lateral incisors, four first molars

Communication
Around 6 weeks: smiling, gurgling and murmuring
3-4 months: begins to play at talking
6-9 months: first recognizable word sounds
Around one year: meaningful use of a few words

Dexterity and mobility
7-8 weeks: head drops back less than previously when baby is pulled to a sitting position
Around 4 months: no head lag when baby pulled to sitting position
Around 6 months: can sit for a moment without support; uses hand like a scoop
Around 9 months: can reach forward, twist around to reach toy; uses fingers and thumb
Around 11 months: learns to drop objects on purpose
Around 1 year: achieves pincer grip with thumb and forefinger; can stand with support; may walk while supported

Immunization
8-12 weeks: triple vaccination against diphtheria, tetanus and whooping cough; oral polio vaccine
16-18 weeks: boosters against diphtheria, tetanus, whooping cough and polio
6-11 months: boosters against diphtheria, tetanus, whooping cough and polio

Most common problems brought to the doctor
- snuffly cold
- difficulty with sleeping or feeding
- cough and temperature
- vomiting and diarrhea
- eye inflammation
- eczema
- nonspecific virus infection

Main threats to life and health
- congenital malformations
- accidents
- infections
- crib deaths (sudden infant death syndrome – mainly 2-6 months)

Risk of dying between 1 and 5
Girls 0.8 in 1,000; Boys 1.2 in 1,000

From Age One to Age Five

The common illnesses of children aged 1-5 years are, in general, much the same as those suffered in the first year. Often, though, they have a much smaller impact because the child is larger and more developed. Feeding difficulties almost always disappear by the end of this age range, although children may display faddiness. By five – and generally long before – most children are continent; persistent bedwetting may, on rare occasions, have a physiological or psychological cause that needs attention.

Conditions that become more common during these years are:
- ear infections
- tonsillitis
- mumps
- measles
- chickenpox
- asthma ("wheezy bronchitis")
- chest infections

What will the doctor look for in an 18-month-old child?

Throughout the early years children should receive regular medical examinations to ensure that, both physically and behaviorally, they are developing normally and are not missing medical help that they may need. At 18 months the doctor's checklist may be like this:

Physical well-being
- are immunizations up-to-date?
- is the child's growth satisfactory?
- has the child been hospitalized, and if so what for?
- does the child suffer from frequent chest or upper-respiratory-tract infections?
- what other illnesses has the child suffered?
- does the child show any signs of neglect or ill treatment?

Development
● vision and fine movement – can the child
- hold things in the fingers using a neat pincer grip?
- hold a pencil correctly?
- throw a ball in approximately the intended direction?
- build a tower of three wooden bricks?
- turn the pages of a book?
● movement and coordination – can the child
- walk if supported?
- walk a little when unsupported?
- walk confidently?
- climb?
● hearing and speech – is the child
- talkative or quiet?
- able to use 6-20 words correctly?
- fond of singing games?
- able to understand simple instructions?
- in the habit of prattling away when alone?
● feeding behavior – is the child
- able to use a cup competently?
- able to use a spoon competently?
- confident about chewing solids?
- causing the parents any problems through feeding habits?
● awareness and social behavior – does the child
- dribble at the mouth?
- play contentedly alone?
- have difficulty sleeping?
- cry frequently enough that the parents are concerned?

What will the doctor look for in a child of two and a half years?

By the time children have reached two and a half they will probably cooperate actively in a medical examination (unless they deliberate-

---

IMMUNIZATION UPDATE

At 13 months your child should be immunized against measles, mumps and rubella.

At 18 months your child should receive a booster against polio (oral booster).

At 4-5 years your child should receive boosters against diphtheria, tetanus and polio (oral booster).

---

ly choose not to) and enjoy joining in the game. The doctor's concerns about physical matters will be much the same as before. In terms of development the doctor's checklist might look like this:
● vision and fine movement – does the child
- tend to use one hand rather than the other (right or left)?
- hold a pencil like a screwdriver or a teaspoon, or as an adult does?
- confidently build towers of toy blocks?
● movement and coordination – can the child
- walk well?
- run well?
- stop and start walking (or especially running) without particular difficulty?
- throw a ball with reasonable accuracy?
- kick a ball with reasonable accuracy?
● hearing and speech – can the child
- point to eyes, nose and mouth on request?
- use and understand phrases of two or more words?
- speak simple sentences?
- use its own name?
- listen and answer appropriately (in other words, hold simple conversations)?
● feeding behavior – can the child
- lift, use and replace a cup with only occasional accidents?
- use a spoon for feeding?
- use a fork for feeding?
- eat the same foods as the parents?
- eat and drink without dribbling?
● awareness and social behavior – does the child
- join in with nursery rhymes?
- play contentedly alone?
- play contentedly with other children?
- make good eye contact with adults and other children?
- suffer from either urinary or bowel incontinence by day?
- suffer from either urinary or bowel incontinence by night?

What will the doctor look for in a child of three and a half years?

The physical checks the doctor will carry out during the fourth year are much the same as in previous years, with the likely addition of an "orthoptic screen," to make sure the child is not suffering from a long-term difficulty in coordinating eye movements – for example, crosseye (squint). By this time, feeding behavior is of interest only if it is causing problems; otherwise, although the child will probably still be quite messy when eating, feeding behavior should be much like an adult's. It should be well established whether the child is left- or right-handed. The doctor will also ask you about your child's social behavior.

● vision and fine movement – can the child
- build tall towers using toy blocks?
- build a bridge using whatever materials come to hand?
- hold a pencil in a mature fashion?
● movement and coordination – how well can the child
- stand on one foot?
- walk on tiptoe?
- run?
- skip?
- throw, catch and kick a ball?
● hearing and speech – can the child
- spontaneously use sentences of more than three words?
- give its name on being asked?
- say whether it is a boy or girl on being asked?
- use pronouns and plurals appropriately?
- identify and name different colors?
- count up to 3 or 4?
- talk freely with a parent?
- talk freely with strangers?
- talk about things that have happened in the past?
- correctly obey two-stage instructions?
- speak clearly enough to be understood by strangers or just by the parents?
● awareness and social behavior – does the child
- play well with other children?
- play contentedly alone for extended periods (five minutes or longer)?
- play constructively or destructively?
- have any problems in terms of general behavior and discipline?
- have any sleeping problems?
- suffer from either urinary or bowel incontinence by day?
- suffer from either urinary or bowel incontinence by night?

Growth: slowing after about 18 months (see p152)

Weight
Girls at one year 7.5-11.5kg (17-25lb)
Boys at one year 8-12kg (18-26.5lb)
Girls at five years 14-22kg (31-48lb)
Boys at five years 15-23kg (33-50.5lb)

Height
Girls at one year 69-79cm (27-31in)
Boys at one year 71-81cm (27-32in)
Girls at five years 100-116cm (39-45.5in)
Boys at five years 102-117cm (40-46in)

Head circumference: rapid growth - up to 1cm (0.4in) per week –continues until about 18 months
Girls at one year 43-49cm (16.5-19in)
Boys at one year 45-49cm (17.5-19in)
Girls at two years 45.5-50cm (18-19.5in)
Boys at two years 47-52cm (18-20.5in)

Body composition at 3
Lean body mass
  Girls 21 percent; Boys 22 percent
Fat
  Girls 19 percent; Boys 60 percent
Water
  Girls 60 percent; Boys 60 percent

Nutrition
Recommended daily calorie intake
  1-3 years 1300 Calories
  4-6 years 1700 Calories
Recommended daily protein intake
  1-3 years 23g (0.8oz)
  4-6 years 30g (1oz)

Normal heart rate at 5: 90-100 beats per minute (see p50)

Daily hours of sleep: highly variable, typically 13-14 hours at 1, falling to 10 hours at 5 (see p78)

Vision: cross-eye and lazy eye must be corrected before 5-6 years

Hearing: can be threatened by untreated middle-ear infection, mumps, meningitis

Teeth: teething complete during third year (see p111)
Around 1 year: two lower lateral incisors, four first molars
Around 18 months: four canines
2 years: first visit to dentist, then every six months
2-3 years: four second molars

Communication
Around 1 year: meaningful use of a few words
Around 18 months: first use of sentences

Dexterity and mobility: rapid development (see p98)
Around 1 year: achieves pincer grip with thumb and forefinger; can stand with support: may walk while supported
Around 15 months: self-feeding
Around 18 months: walking alone
Around 2 years: walks up and down stairs
2-4 years: increasingly agile at running, skipping, jumping
4-5 years: can dress and undress

Toilet training
Around 2 years: now able to begin controlling self; training should not be attempted earlier
5 years: about 10 percent still sometimes wet bed (see p116)

Immunization
13 months: measles, mumps, rubella (German measles)
18 months: oral polio vaccine booster
4 years: diphtheria, tetanus and oral polio vaccine boosters

Most common problems brought to the doctor
- common cold
- sore throat and raised temperature
- vomiting and diarrhea
- ear infection
- cough
- eye inflammation
- rash and raised temperature
- eczema
- cuts and bruises

Main threats to life and health
- accidents
- childhood cancers
- infections

Risk of dying between 1 and 5
Girls 0.8 in 1,000; Boys 1.2 in 1,000

From Age Five to Age Ten

Hearing and vision

During these years it is important that your child's hearing be regularly checked, since many children suffer an impairment of hearing as a result of ear infections. A common problem is "glue ear," in which the middle ear becomes filled with mucus. This and other conditions can cause educational problems, because the child cannot hear much of what the teacher is saying. Some children with hearing difficulties become adept lipreaders, and do not realize that this is not the way that everybody else interprets speech. Whisper to your child from behind: if the child hears you there is almost certainly no problem.

Checking the child's vision is not something that can be done so simply. It is wise to take your child to an optician every 2-3 years. If the child has frequent headaches, this may be a sign of difficulty in focusing. However, some children who require spectacles do not suffer headaches, so it is worth checking with the optician anyway. By this stage children who suffer from cross-eye (squint) should have been treated – a "lazy eye" will have been detected by much earlier screening (from six months onward) and made to work by covering the good eye for a period each day (see p85). Occasionally surgical treatment may be necessary at this age to achieve a cosmetically acceptable result. Once your child begins school any difficulty with vision is likely to be more noticeable. Do they have difficulty seeing what the teacher is doing from the back of the classroom, or do they hold reading material very close to their faces to make it out?

By the age of five your child should have achieved adequate movement, verbal and social skills; unless there is something wrong your doctor will no longer suggest routine developmental screening. Any abnormalities in development after this age should be obvious to you: if you are at all worried, consult your doctor. In particular, children who do not follow instructions may not be being deliberately disobedient: they may be suffering from other problems of hearing, understanding, or concentrating.

Physical parameters – height, weight and heartbeat – are likely to be checked regularly at your child's school. The common medical problems of this age-group are: coughs, colds, vomiting and diarrhea, chest infections, recurrent asthma, tonsillitis, ear infections, measles, mumps, chickenpox and in girls, infections of the urinary tract.

It is during these years too that children first develop allergies – particularly hay fever. Some children will only sneeze in the early summer, some all summer and some unfortunates all year. There are now excellent treatments available to ease these distressing symptoms. You should not hesitate to see your doctor.

Other less frequent problems may include: bedwetting, appendicitis and "childhood migraine" – often associated with stomach ache and vomiting.

Why is your child disobedient?

All children are disobedient some of the time, and some of them seem to be disobedient all of the time. It is worth considering if your child is suffering from some physical or mental problem that prevents them understanding and carrying out instructions. If you tell them to do two things, for example, they may fail to do the second because they have forgotten the instruction. Other symptoms are inability to tell the time, failure to report recent events, and problems in understanding time-related words like "before" and "after." Children with these problems require understanding and extra help, not just discipline. Age-related tests can help establish whether your child is suffering such difficulties. If you suspect that something is wrong, consult a doctor.

Emotional well-being

You should remember that during these years – childhood to pre-adolescence – an enormous number of physical and mental develop-

ments are taking place. Children acquire many physical skills, become increasingly involved in sporting activities around school and at home, and achieve a greater degree of independence. It is important that such development occurs in an atmosphere of love and security. This is best achieved by the parents and the children spending time together. An hour a day spent reading with a five-year-old will help both the child and the parent. Time spent playing games as the children grow is rewarding both at the time and in the future: the improved relationship will help during the difficult years of adolescence.

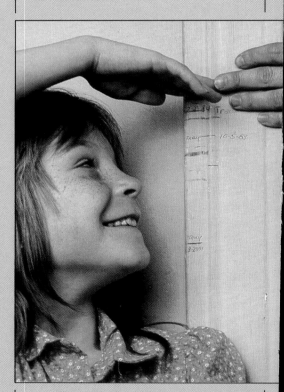

▲ **Height increases slowly but steadily** during childhood as the bones of the legs lengthen. With the onset of puberty a growth spurt begins (see Ch17).

▶ **Six-monthly dental visits** are particularly important for children, enabling the dentist to check that the teeth are developing correctly (see p111).

Many parents suffer terrible anxieties as their children become more independent: at what age should they climb trees? When can they walk to school with a friend rather than a parent? Should they ride their bicycle on the road? The anxieties will never entirely disappear, but they can be eased by a commonsense approach. The child should be aware of what is allowed, and reasons why rules are made should be explained whenever possible. It helps the child – and the parent – if guidelines are strictly adhered to: if a child is allowed to do something one day, and not the next, it causes confusion and needless unhappiness. Provided the child is aware of the limitations, and rules are eased as they grow, they will remain happy and confident. Children develop at different rates, and achieve skills – both physical and social – at different times. The constant factor should be the love and support of the parents. Be open with your children and honest about the dangers that surround them: warnings about talking to or accepting lifts from strangers cannot be given too often or too soon.

Is your child developing a weight problem?

In rare instances a child's abnormal weight gain is a result of

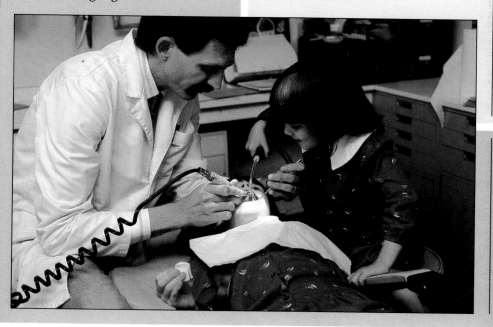

Growth: slow, then girls begin spurt around 10, boys begin later

Weight
Girls at five years 14-22kg (31-48lb)
Boys at five years 15-23kg (33-50.5lb)
Girls at ten years 24-47kg (53-104lb)
Boys at ten years 24-45kg (53-99lb)

Height
Girls at five years 100-116cm (33-50.5in)
Boys at five years 102-117cm (40-46in)
Girls at ten years 127-150cm (50-59in)
Boys at ten years 127-148cm (50-58in)

Body composition at 10
Lean body mass (muscle, nerves, bone)
  Girls 21 percent;   Boys 22 percent
Fat
  Girls 19 percent; Boys 18 percent
Water
  Girls 60 percent; Boys 60 percent

Nutrition 7-10 years
Recommended daily calorie intake
  2400 Kcal
Recommended daily protein intake
  34g

Pubertal development (see pp160-163)
Girls 8-9 breast budding in early developers
Boys 9-10 testicular enlargement in early developers

Normal heart rate at 10: 70-110 beats per minute (see p50)

Normal blood pressure at 10
Systolic 90; Diastolic 60

Daily hours of sleep: 9-10

Vision: some children may suffer hereditary nearsightedness or farsightedness (see p85); parents should arrange eye tests if not provided at school

Hearing: untreated middle ear infections can permanently damage hearing; some children become adept at lipreading to disguise problems; hearing checks essential

Teeth: decay may develop with poor care (see p110); six-monthly visits recommended
Around 6 four adult first molars appear in gap behind milk teeth
7-10 milk-teeth incisors replaced by permanent incisors
9-10 crowding may develop, orthodontal attention may be necessary

Immunization: check that preschool immunizations were performed (see p16); tetanus should be updated every five years, polio every ten years; consult doctor about immunizations needed for travel to other countries

Most common problems brought to the doctor
- sore throat with raised temperature
- common cold
- ear infection
- cough
- rash and raised temperature
- diarrhea and vomiting
- eye irritation
- sprains, cuts, bruises
- chickenpox
- hay fever

Main threats to life and health
- accidents (especially boys)
- childhood cancers

Risk of dying between 5 and 10
Girls 0.8 in 1,000; Boys 1.2 in 1,000

disease, but usually it is simply a matter of diet. What is important is not the weight itself but the rate of weight gain. If your child's rate of weight gain approximates to one of the curves in this chart, there is probably little to worry about, but if it diverges acutely you should pay attention to dietary factors and, if this has no effect, consult a doctor. During puberty there may be extreme but short-term divergences.

Early Adolescence

The years of adolescence are difficult for all concerned – children, parents, other family members and family friends. For hormonal and other reasons the adolescent may have to struggle with problems of self-identity, uncontrollable anger, resentment (especially toward the parents), anxiety and depression. Sexuality, sexual attractiveness and sexual adequacy are prime concerns, whether or not the adolescent has any sexual contact: girls often worry about the size of their breasts and boys about the size of their penis. Such anxieties are not helped by the frequent incidence of acne during these years.

What are the health problems of adolescence?

Common health problems during this stage of life include migraines, glandular fever, acne and, in girls, dysmenorrhea (menstrual difficulties). The common infections of youth – measles, mumps, chicken pox – are less frequent than in earlier years, largely because most young people have already had them and so are now immune. Some diseases of youth – for example, diabetes, rheumatoid arthritis – are more frequent at this stage than they were in earlier years; but it should be stressed that they are still rare.

In early adolescence medical examinations will usually focus on:
◆ blood pressure
◆ stage of sexual development
◆ height and weight
◆ distorted development of the spine
◆ goiter (a swelling in the neck due to enlargement of the thyroid gland)
◆ hearing and vision
◆ hereditary and congenital diseases that may not have been detected earlier

In girls:
● vaginal discharge
● breast tumors
● pregnancy (if appropriate)
● infections of the urinary tract (girls are 25 times more likely to suffer this than boys)

In boys:
● gynecomastia (swelling of the breasts due to hormone imbalance)
● urethral discharge
● tumor of the testicles

If there is any suggestion that the boy or girl is sexually active, then attention will be paid to the possibility of sexually transmitted disease. Contraception should be discussed if appropriate; self-examination of the breast or testicle (see page 22) should be described.

Adolescent worries

The main problems are psychological, and physiological conditions like acne and painful periods can contribute to these. Adolescents are also particularly vulnerable to the temptation to adopt health-destroying habits like smoking, alcohol and solvent-sniffing, either through curiosity or in an attempt to achieve peer-group approval. Real or imagined sexual underdevelopment can loom large in the adolescent's life and can, paradoxically, lead to precocious sexual experimentation (as can many other factors): the results can be unwanted pregnancy and sexually-transmitted diseases, including AIDS.

When dealing with adolescent children it is wise to be realistic. Talk about problems before they occur, rather than after. For example, do not worry that you are telling your children about sex too early: they have probably heard a lot about it from their peer group already, and may have acquired profound misunderstandings which are best corrected now in case they cause difficulties later. Likewise, although you may not wish your child to become sexually active at this age, your wishes are of secondary importance to an adolescent; you should therefore discuss contraception, and in particular the use of condoms to help prevent against AIDS. Girls should be warned that menarche (the onset of menstruation) is on its way, and equipped both practically and psychologically to cope with it. Advance guidance can be given about emotional relationships (in particular the agonies of young love), and also about dealing with

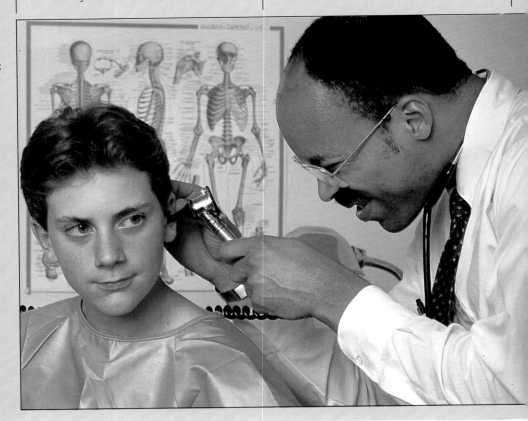

pressures from peers, especially pressure or temptation to do something foolish, like smoking or experimenting with drugs, just because "everyone else" does. This is also a good time to offer guidance about the dangers of becoming involved with quasi-religious cults, to talk about the importance of eating a balanced diet instead of depending on junk foods, to warn about the abuse of alcohol, to re-emphasize road safety and to discuss any other relevant psychological or physical hazards.

Dieting and eating disorders

Preoccupation with physical appearance sometimes causes girls, and more rarely boys, to develop eating disorders. Anorexia nervosa, deliberate severe self-starvation, is the most well-known of these. It may also be accompanied by bulimia, bingeing on food, then purging the body with vomiting or laxatives. These forms of extreme self-denial or self-indulgence are often an outlet for repressed anger or conflict as well as a desperate attempt to conform to sexual stereotypes. The problems are usually tackled by counseling, either by the parents or by professionals. Advice and guidance can be difficult to give, since a common condition of adolescence is a state of perpetual rebellion against everything and everyone regarded as part of the establishment.

Immunization update

At age 11 girls should be immunized against rubella (German measles) if this has not already been done. Between the ages of 11 and 14 children should be tested to see if they are already naturally immune to tuberculosis (TB) and, if not, vaccinated with the BCG vaccine. At age 14 they should receive tetanus and polio booster shots, to be repeated every five years afterward for tetanus, and every 10 years afterward for polio.

Growth: rapid, with girls peaking around 12, boys around 14 (see p162)

Weight
Girls at 10 years 24-47kg (53-104lb)
Boys at 10 years 24-45kg (53-99lb)
Girls at 15 years 41-78kg (90-170lb)
Boys at 15 years 43-80kg (95-176lb)

Height
Girls at 10 years 127-150cm (50-59in)
Boys at 10 years 127-148cm (50-58in)
Girls at 15 years 150-173cm (59-68in)
Boys at 15 years 155-182cm (61-72in)

Body composition at 13
Lean body mass (muscle, nerves, bone)
Girls 21.5 percent; Boys 21.5 percent
Fat
Girls 20.5 percent; Boys 18.5 percent
Water
Girls 58 percent; Boys 60 percent

Nutrition
Recommended daily calorie intake
Girls 11-14 2,200 Kcal; Boys 11-14 2,700 Kcal
Recommended daily protein intake
Girls 11-14 46g; Boys 11-14 45g

Pubertal development (see pp160-163)
Girls 10-11: breast budding for most early developers with first pubic hair and first menstruation
Boys 10-11: penis growth in early developers
Girls 11-12: most developing pubic hair
Boys 11-12: most with testicular enlargement
Boys 12-13: most now with pubic hair and penis growth
Girls at 13: first menstruation for most
Girls 14-15: most late developers with pubic hair

Normal heart rate at 13: 60-100 beats per minute (see p50)

Normal blood pressure at 13
Systolic 110; Diastolic 65

Daily hours of sleep: typically dropping from about 9 at 10 years to 8 by 15 years

Vision: parents should arrange eye tests if not provided at school

Hearing: excessively loud music can permanently damage

Teeth: dietary habits may lead to decay; risk of acute gum disease; six-monthly check-ups recommended (see p111)
9-12 years: adult canines appear, followed by first and second premolars; crowding may develop, orthodontal attention may be necessary
11-13 years: second molars appear

Immunization: tetanus should be updated every five years, polio every ten years; consult doctor about immunizations needed for travel to other countries
10-13 years: BCG (tuberculosis); girls should be immunized against rubella (German measles – see p180)

Most common problems brought to the doctor
- sore throat with raised temperature
- common cold
- hay fever
- sprains, cuts, bruises
- cough
- warts and verrucae
- diarrhea and vomiting
- ear infection
- acne
- mononucleosis (glandular fever)

Fertile menstrual cycles at 13: 10 percent of the average menstruating girl's cycles

Main threats to life and health
- accidents (especially boys)
- childhood cancers

Risk of dying between 10 and 15
Girls 1 in 1,000; Boys 2.5 in 1,000

Later Adolescence 15-18

This is the period in which young people usually begin to take responsibility for their own health and well-being. Becoming aware of the symptoms of any illness and what they might mean is an important part of being able to make your own decisions about when to contact a doctor and when to deal with any condition yourself. Young women, in particular, should be aware of what they can do to protect themselves by making regular gynecological checks.

Women and cancer

Two forms of cancer particularly affect women, and both can be fatal if not detected early enough. After puberty, every woman should check herself monthly for signs of breast cancer, and should immediately see a doctor if she has any cause for concern. All sexually active women should be screened at least every three years for cervical cancer.

Some women deliberately avoid all such tests: terrified of cancer, their reaction is that they "would rather not know." They are gambling with their lives. The earlier any form of cancer is discovered, the more likely it can be completely cured – often without major surgery. Most of the women who are cured of cancer of the breast discover it themselves, so the importance of self-examination cannot be overestimated.

Testing for breast cancer

Most breast problems are not due to cancer – usually they are due to other conditions such as the lumpiness (called dysplasia) which occurs before periods. The simple checks described here will help you to detect any problems which may develop; they should be performed monthly; a good time is just after the end of each period. The tests fall into two categories, looking and feeling. Ideally, instruction in how to perform them should be given by a doctor or a trained nurse.

The first time you check your breasts, study them carefully in the mirror, noting their size and shape and the position of the nipples. Then feel them to see what they are normally like. (Note that they may be naturally lumpy, especially just before a period). In future checks you will be looking for *changes* in the appearance or feel, so it is worth taking time to memorize the normal condition.

HOW TO LOOK

1 With your hands at your sides or on your hips, study the overall appearance of your breasts. Turn from side to side, and hold them up to look in the fold underneath.

2 Put your hands on your head and look for anything unusual, especially around the nipples.

3 Stretch your arms above your head and have another look, again concentrating on the area around the nipples.

HOW TO FEEL

1 Lie on a flat surface, your head on a pillow and the left shoulder slightly raised by a folded towel. Keeping them together, use the flat of the fingers of your right hand to feel the left breast.

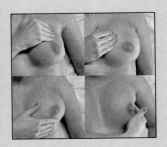

2 Press the breast gently and firmly in toward your body and feel every part of it. Work in a spiral, circling slowly outward from the nipple.

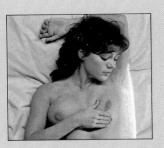

3 With your left arm above your head and the elbow bent, repeat the spiral carefully. Pay particular attention to the outer part of the breast.

Each month you should check that:
◆ the size and shape of your breasts are normal
◆ the position of the nipples is normal
◆ neither nipple
- has turned inward on itself
- is pointing upward or outward at an unaccustomed angle
- is bleeding or weeping
◆ there is no unusual swelling or dimpling
◆ the veins are not standing out more than usual
◆ the skin is not puckered
◆ there is no unusual rash or coloring when you feel your breasts
◆ there is no unusual lump or thickening.

If you detect any of these signs – or even if you just think you might have – see your doctor at once.

4 Finally, with your hands on your hips, press inward until your chest muscles tighten. This time look especially for any dimpling of the skin of your breasts.

4 Finally, still in the same position, feel the tail of the breast (the part closest to the armpit). Now repeat the whole process for the right breast.

Growth: a girl is likely to grow only another 4cm (1.5in) after first menstruation (see p163)

Weight
Girls at 15 years 41-78kg (90-170lb)
Boys at 15 years 43-80kg (95-176lb)
Girls at 18 years 45-86kg (100-180lb)
Boys at 18 years 54-96kg (119-210lb)

Height
Girls at 15 years 150-173cm (59-68in)
Boys at 15 years 155-182cm (61-72in)
Girls at 18 years 153-174cm (60.5-68.5in)
Boys at 18 years 166-188cm (65-74in)

Body composition at 18
Lean body mass (muscle, nerves, bone)
  Girls 21.5 percent; Boys 21.5 percent
Fat
  Girls 21.5 percent; Boys 18.5 percent
Water
  Girls 57 percent; Boys 60 percent

Nutrition
Recommended daily calorie intake
  Girls 15-18 2,100 Kcal; Boys 15-18 2,800 Kcal
Recommended daily protein intake
  Girls 15-18 46g; Boys 15-18 56g

Pubertal development (see pp160-163)
Girls 15-16: breast development well advanced for most; many late developers' first menstruation
Boys 15-16: most late developers with pubic hair
Boys 16-17: penis growth and testicular enlargement in late developers

Normal heart rate at 18: 60-100 beats per minute (see p50)

Normal blood pressure at 18
Systolic 100; Diastolic 65

Daily hours of sleep: about 8

Vision: many teenagers suffer hereditary nearsightedness or farsightedness; parents should arrange eye tests if not provided at school

Hearing: excessively loud music can permanently damage hearing

Teeth: dietary habits may lead to decay; risk of acute gum disease; six-monthly check-ups recommended (see p111)
After 17: third molars and wisdom teeth; inadequate space for wisdom teeth may necessitate their removal

Immunization: tetanus should be updated every five years, polio every ten years; consult doctor about immunizations needed for travel to other countries

Most common problems brought to the doctor
Girls:
- period problems (painful, irregular or absent)
- acne
- urinary tract infections
- viral infections
- vaginal discharge
- contraception
- asthma, chest infections
- hay fever
Boys:
- acne
- glandular fever
- sprains and strains
- viral infections
- asthma, bronchitis
- hay fever

Fertile menstrual cycles at 18: 30 percent of the average girl's cycles

Recommended contraception: contraceptive pill; slight risk of infection with coil or loop makes it a threat to future fertility (see p125); condoms should also be used to lower the risk of sexually transmitted disease

Main threats to life and health
- accidents (especially boys)

Risk of dying between 15 and 20
Girls 2.5 in 1,000; Boys 6 in 1,000

Young Adulthood 18-25

Between the ages of 20 and 30 you are likely to form the pattern of behavior you will follow for the rest of your life. Your health in later life will probably depend on your habits during these years, so it is worth paying some attention to what you are doing today. One good habit to get into is that of regular health screening.

Screening for cervical cancer

Every three years each sexually active woman should be tested for disease of the cervix (the narrow passage between the vagina and the womb), especially for the early signs of cervical cancer. Progress from the first appearances of changes in the cells of the cervix that herald cancer and the onset of the disease usually requires a number of years, so any condition discovered during a three-yearly check can be completely cured. If there is a particular cause for concern, the testing may be done more frequently.

Usually the test involves taking a cervical smear. A wooden spatula or plastic "cyto-brush" is used to take a scraping of cells from the neck of the womb. These are spread on a microscope slide, treated with preservative, stained with a dye and examined. There is a problem with cervical smears: by their very nature, the sample they take is small and randomly chosen, so that a negative result provides no absolute guarantee that there is no disease. However, if there are any suspicious signs a further investigation will be made.

One technique used to examine the whole cervix is known as "colposcopy." Acetic acid (pure vinegar) is painted onto the cervix to act as a staining agent. A special instrument, the colposcope, is then inserted. Using this instrument the doctor can survey the whole of the vagina and cervix. The acetic-acid staining shows up any areas of abnormal cell development. Small samples (biopsies) can be taken from these areas for analysis.

Colposcopy is expensive and time-consuming, requiring hospital services. Soon a different technique, named "cervicography," should be available in doctors' consulting rooms. This uses a special camera to produce a detailed picture of the cervix; the photograph is then enlarged and examined by a gynecologist. The ease of this technique means that, in future, screening for cervical cancer could contain the disease more effectively than at the moment.

There is, however, one proviso in such an optimistic prediction: women themselves must insist on regular testing. Some find the experience embarrassing, even humiliating; none find it pleasant. Bear in mind that it is a fate distinctly better than death, which is the inevitable result should cervical cancer progress too far before detection. You owe it not just to yourself but also to your loved ones to ensure that you are screened at appropriate intervals.

Testicular self-examination

Testicular cancer is still relatively rare, but if it does develop it is one of the fastest spreading cancers, and it is on the increase. Men between the ages of 20 and 40 are most at risk. If found early most cancers of the testicles can be cured; all can be treated if you seek medical help.

A simple examination once a month is the best way to stay alert for any early signs. Choose a date that you will remember like the first of the month or the date of your birthday. The best time is after a warm bath or shower when you will be most relaxed.
1 Hold the scrotum in the palms of the hands so that you can use the thumb and fingers of both your hands to feel the testicles.
2 Examine each side in turn using very gentle pressure. First examine the epididymis (where the spermatic cord joins the testicle) which should feel soft and slightly tender to the touch.
3 Next examine the spermatic cord which goes out from the top of the epididymis and then behind the testicle. It should feel like a firm, smooth tube.
4 Then feel the testicle itself. It should be smooth with no lumps or swellings. The most likely places for these to form are on the front or sides of the testicle. Remember to examine each in the same way.

If you feel any lumps, hardness or swelling in the scrotal sac, remember that it is not necessarily cancer. You should consult your doctor, who may recommend a small operation to find the cause. If cancer is found, X-ray treatment

or drugs may be prescribed. Details will vary according to diagnosis.

Immunization update

During adulthood you should remember to get your boosters against polio and tetanus. If you plan to travel abroad you should check (with your doctor) which immunizations you need for basic safety and (with the relevant authorities) which you require by law. You should certainly check if you need to be immunized against: typhoid fever, cholera, yellow fever, meningitis and hepatitis.

Some of these shots are painful and their immediate results distressing. You may be tempted to take a chance and avoid them. Remember, though, that if you catch any of these diseases, the outcome will be very much more painful and distressing – and quite possibly fatal.

Do you drink too much?

Many of us drink too much, often thinking that the advantages outweigh the disadvantages. However, even people who drink only a moderate amount of alcohol each day may be suffering from a dependency that can, over the years, damage the liver, brain and other vital organs. If you answer "yes" to more than a few of the questions here, think hard about your alcohol consumption.

- When pouring out drinks for a group of people, do you normally give yourself a larger measure?
- Do you ever drink on your own, either at home or in a bar?
- At parties, when your glass is empty, do you go for a refill rather than wait until one is offered?
- Do you feel bad if you do not have at least one drink per day?
- Do you have a regular schedule of drinking – do you find that, for example, you are seriously unhappy if you cannot have a drink at lunchtime?

Average height and weight for women 20-25
1.6m (5ft 2in): 52kg (114lb)
1.7m (5ft 6in): 59kg (130lb)
1.8m (5ft 10in): 65kg (144lb)

Average height and weight for men 20-25
1.7m (5ft 6in): 64kg (141lb)
1.8m (5ft 10in): 71kg (156lb)
1.9m (6ft 2in): 79kg (174lb)

Body composition at 22
Lean body mass (muscle, nerves, bone)
    Women 22.5 percent; Men 24 percent
Fat
    Women 22.5 percent; Men 16 percent
Water
    Women 55 percent; Men 60 percent

Nutrition
Recommended daily calorie intake
    Women 2,150 Kcal; Men 2,900 Kcal
Recommended daily protein intake
    Women 54g; Men 72g

Normal heart rate at 22: 50-100 beats per minute (see pp39, 50)

Normal blood pressure at 22
Systolic 110; Diastolic 75

Daily hours of sleep: about 7

Vision: regular eye checks advised

Hearing: loud music and industrial noise can cause permanent damage

Teeth: decay less common than during teens; wear on teeth and gum disease; six-monthly check-ups recommended

Immunization: tetanus should be updated every five years, polio every ten years; you should consult your doctor

about immunizations needed if you are traveling to another country

Most common problems brought to the doctor
Women:
- contraception
- cervical smear
- breast screen
- period problems (painful, irregular or absent)
- acne
- urinary tract infections
- viral infections
- vaginal discharge
- asthma, chest infections
- hay fever
- allergies
- antenatal care
Men:
- Sprains, strains
- viral infections
- asthma, hay fever allergies

Fertile menstrual cycles at 22: 60 percent of the average woman's cycles

Recommended contraception: contraceptive pill (see p125); slight risk of infection makes coil or loop a threat to future fertility: condoms should be used to lower risk of sexually transmitted disease if you have more than one sexual partner

Risk of bearing Down's syndrome child, mother aged 22: 1 in 1600

Main threats to life and health
- accidents (especially in men)
- cancer

Risk of dying between 18 and 24
Women 2.8 in 1,000; Men 7 in 1,000

- Does your drinking ever cause family quarrels?
- Do you take a stiff drink to settle your nerves when you get bad news or are under pressure?
- When your spouse asks you how much you have been drinking, do you lie?
- Do you often want a drink in the morning?
- Does your drinking ever cause you to miss an appointment or a deadline?

- Do you sometimes wake up unable to remember going to bed the night before?

Consider your answers according to habit rather than any isolated occasion. For example, most people have once or twice experienced the sensation of waking up unable to recall the night before. But if this happens to you frequently you probably have a drink problem.

Do you smoke too much? If you smoke at all, you do.

Young Adulthood 25-30

It is usually during these years that permanent or semi-permanent relationships are established, and couples begin to plan their families. Pregnancy, childbirth and parenthood can be made much more joyful by prudent attention to health.

Before pregnancy

Any woman planning to have a child should see her doctor or attend a clinic to be given a pre-pregnancy screen. Much of the session will be given over to counseling and advice. Also, in order to safeguard the health of the mother and to enhance the likelihood that the baby will suffer no physical or mental defects, your doctor will check that:
◆ you are neither under- nor over-weight
◆ your blood pressure is normal
◆ your breasts are normal – particularly that the nipples are not inverted
◆ your heart and lungs are functioning properly
◆ you are immune to rubella (German measles) – if necessary you can be immunized
◆ your urine is normal – some infections of the urinary tract show no obvious symptoms but can endanger a successful pregnancy
◆ your blood has an adequate count of hemoglobin (the chemical in the red blood cells that enables them to transport oxygen to all the different parts of the body)

If you are at all at risk your doctor will also check to see if you are suffering from, or are a carrier of, various viral diseases, notably vaginal herpes, AIDS (the HIV virus) and hepatitis B (one form of infectious jaundice).

How can your medical history affect your decision?

Your doctor will also inquire about your personal and family medical history. You will be asked if you or your family has a history of diabetes or high blood pressure (this affects the risk of you developing either during the pregnancy) as well as about various hereditary diseases such as:

● cystic fibrosis – a disease which affects certain of the body's glands and causes intestinal and lung difficulties
● hemophilia – a condition in which the blood clots very slowly, so that even the most minor wound can be a serious danger; the defect is sex-linked: it is carried by women and affects men
● Huntington's chorea – a progressive, incurable but fortunately rare disease affecting the brain cells
● mental subnormality – often a result of inherited weakness of the X chromosomes (fragile-X syndrome)
● thalassemia – a disease affecting the hemoglobin molecules, so that the red blood cells cannot function properly
● phenylketonuria – a defect (which can be detected early and controlled by dietary means) in the body's ability to process certain proteins, leading to brain damage
● Down's syndrome – a genetic (chromosomal) disorder characterized by mental retardation and physical deficiencies

The areas on which the doctor will focus when asking you about your own health history and current habits are:
◆ previous difficulties (if any) in pregnancy and childbirth – high blood pressure (hypertension), diabetes, delivery problems, congenital abnormalities, stillbirth and so on
◆ exposure to sexually transmitted diseases
◆ smoking – not just the mother's habit but also the father's
◆ use of alcohol
◆ use of drugs (whether prescribed or illicit)
◆ diet
◆ mental stability – many women become stressed when trying to conceive (especially if a few months go by before success); stress is also common during pregnancy and in the first year or so after the baby's birth
◆ kidney disease
◆ high blood pressure
◆ diabetes

The last three factors will involve simple tests. Diabetes is important because the high levels of glucose in the mother's blood mean that the fetus is overnourished, leading to a baby that is oversized and whose adrenal glands (which produce adrenaline) are underdeveloped. The mother's diabetes can be controlled during pregnancy through attention to diet, with or without insulin. High blood pressure can make pregnant mothers more likely to suffer preeclampsia (see p11).

Genetic counseling

Genetic counseling is the process whereby experts in inherited diseases assess whether a couple are likely to give birth to a baby with such a disease. It is only offered to those known to be at risk.

Two of the factors that can increase risk – family and personal medical history – have already been discussed. A third factor is race: certain hereditary medical conditions are quite strictly confined to people of specific racial backgrounds. For example:
● thalassemia is found only in people whose families come from Africa or the Middle or Far East
● Tay-Sachs disease is commonest in Ashkenazic Jews (Jews of eastern European extraction)
● sickle-cell disease (which involves the production of abnormal hemoglobin) is confined to people of African descent
● cystic fibrosis is commonest among people of Caucasian stock

Overt defects and disabilities in a child generally arise because of a flaw in a single gene: normally, if several genes are affected, the embryo or fetus is so disabled that the pregnancy does not come to term.

The number of single-gene defects is estimated to be about 4,500, of which the commonest (although all are rare) are cystic fibrosis, Down's syndrome, fragile-X syndrome, fructose intolerance, hemophilia, sickle-cell disease, Duchenne muscular dystrophy, Huntington's chorea, Tay-Sachs disease and thalassemia.

Multi-gene traits include susceptibility to heart disease.

If genetic screening is called for it must be applied to both parents. With many diseases (but not the sex-linked diseases such as hemophilia), if only one parent is suffering from the relevant genetic defect, the chances of the child suffering abnormality are fairly small (although the tendency may well be transmitted to the grandchildren).

However, if both parents possess the trait, the chance of its being transmitted to the child leap to 25 percent. In such instances many couples decide not to have children. Others proceed in the knowledge that tests early in the pregnancy will indicate whether or not the fetus is affected, so that the parents have the option of abortion.

How does pregnancy testing work?

Pregnancy tests are carried out by examining a sample of the mother's urine. The fertilized egg (or "pre-embryo") produces a hormone called human chorionic gonadotrophin – hCG – and by about the time of the first missed period there should be enough of this in the mother's urine to be detectable. However, a negative result so early does not exclude pregnancy, and so a further test should be carried out two weeks later.

HCG is present in still greater quantities in the mother's blood, so it is possible to test for pregnancy even earlier, within a week of conception. However, this is difficult and therefore expensive, and is justifiable only in rare cases. One such instance is where ova have been fertilized outside the woman's body and then artificially implanted in the womb.

Average height and weight for women 25-30
1.6m (5ft 2in): 54kg (119lb)
1.7m (5ft 6in): 60kg (132lb)
1.8m (5ft 10in): 67kg (147lb)

Average height and weight for men 25-30
1.7m (5ft 6in): 67kg (147lb)
1.8m (5ft 10in): 74kg (163lb)
1.9m (6ft 2in): 83kg (183lb)

Body composition at 25
Lean body mass (muscle, nerves, bone)
   Women 22.5 percent; Men 24 percent
Fat
   Women 22.5 percent; Men 16 percent
Water
   Women 55 percent; Men 60 percent

Nutrition
Recommended daily calorie intake
   Women 2,150 Kcal; Men 2,900 Kcal
Recommended daily protein intake
   Women 54g; Men 72g

Normal heart rate at 25: 50-100 beats per minute (see pp39, 50)

Normal blood pressure at 25
Systolic 120; Diastolic 80

Daily hours of sleep: 7-8

Vision: regular eye checks advised

Hearing: loud music and industrial noise can cause permanent damage

Teeth: decay less common than during teens; wear on teeth and gum disease; six-monthly check-ups recommended

Immunization: tetanus should be updated every five years, polio every ten years; consult your doctor about immunizations needed if you are traveling to another country

Most common problems brought to the doctor
Women:
- contraception
- antenatal care
- cervical/breast screening
- urinary tract infections
- period problems
- viral infections
- vaginal discharge
- asthma
- chest infection, hay fever
Men:
- aches and sprains
- viral infections
- asthma
- allergies
- hay fever
- high blood pressure

Fertile menstrual cycles at 28: 85 percent of the average woman's cycles

Recommended contraception: contraceptive pill; slight risk of infection with coil or loop makes it a threat to future fertility (see p124); condoms should be used to reduce the risk of sexually transmitted disease if you have more than one sexual partner

Risk of bearing Down's syndrome child, mother aged 28: one in 1000

Main threats to life and health
- accidents (especially men)

Risk of dying between 25 and 30
Women 4.2 in 1,000; Men 8 in 1,000

How early can pregnancy be detected?

Modern hormonal tests for pregnancy are extremely sensitive, so that it is sometimes possible to establish within a week whether or not conception has occurred. However, prospective parents should not form their expectations on this basis, since there is still a very high chance of an early miscarriage. Also, when such a test is done in the first few weeks, a negative result may be misleading. **PM**

Over 30

Screening your own health

A full health screening requires the involvement of a doctor. However, you can perform many checks on yourself. For example, you can find out if anyone closely related to you has suffered from:

◆ high blood pressure (hypertension)
◆ heart attack
◆ stroke
◆ angina
◆ diabetes mellitus
◆ cancer of the bowel
◆ cancer of the breast

If relatives of yours, especially close ones, have suffered from any of these problems, there is an increased likelihood that you might, too. Awareness of this can help you adjust your behavior so as to reduce the risk, and certainly should make you readier to consult your doctor should you have the slightest suspicion that you might be suffering from any of these conditions.

Then you can ask yourself about your habits. How many cigarettes do you smoke? How much alcohol do you drink? Smoking is likely to shorten your life through heart disease, chronic bronchitis, lung cancer and other ailments: if you find it impossible to give up completely, at least you can cut down. Excessive alcohol consumption affects your heart, kidneys, stomach and liver – as well as your brain. Consult the questionnaire on page 25.

What about your sex life? If you are promiscuous you run a heightened risk of:

● gonorrhea
● syphilis
● in women, cancer of the cervix
● AIDS

The first two of these diseases are unpleasant but fortunately curable. Cancer of the cervix is curable if discovered early enough (see p24). In terms of current medical science, AIDS is not curable – and neither is it completely preventable, since even the use of condoms can do no more than reduce the risk.

Ideally you should establish a permanent relationship with a single partner, indulging in regular sex only when both of you have been thoroughly screened. In addition, you can arrange to be screened between partners – and, if you think there is any possibility that you might be carrying an infection (especially AIDS), you should forgo sex altogether until you are certain one way or the other.

Women can also check their breasts for early signs of tumors (see p22) and people of either sex can examine any moles for changes. If a mole grows larger or darker, changes shape, itches or bleeds – you should consult a doctor at once. There is a possibility that it has become the site of a melanoma, a type of cancer that can spread swiftly, particularly to the liver and the lymph nodes.

Pregnancy in later life

As both mother and father grow older, the risk of conceiving a child with a genetic defect increases. At all ages the most frequent result is Down's syndrome, especially when the mother is 35-40 and the father much older. After both members of the couple have reached their late forties, the risk of their having a defective child has become extremely high.

Balanced translocation

Some parents are at increased risk of having a defective child because one or other carries a genetic abnormality called a balanced translocation. The number of chromosomes in the person's genes is the standard 46, and so the person suffers no ill-effects.

However, a section of one chromosome has become translocated onto another. The chromosome with the added section may be involved in the process of conception, so that the resulting child suffers from any or all of the ailments associated with an extra chromosome (see pp26-27). The risk is the same for each pregnancy, and is independent of the age of the parents.

Parental age and Down's syndrome

Women over the age of 35 are more likely to bear a Down's syndrome child, and this risk continues to increase as the woman grows older. Also, for a mother over 35, the age of the father likewise affects the chances of the baby suffering from Down's syndrome. This is because Down's syndrome is a product of a specific abnormality of the chromosomes, and such abnormalities are much more likely to occur in older than in younger parents. The effect of the father's age should not be underestimated. For example, if a mother is aged 35-40, her risk of bearing a Down's syndrome baby is about five times as great (2 percent) if the father is 47 or over than if he is under 34 (0.4 percent). When deciding whether or not it is too late to have a child you should therefore think about the ages of both potential parents, not just the woman.

Fitness

How fit are you? If you hardly ever take exercise – sports, jogging or even just walking – it is likely that you are very unfit and possibly overweight. Both unfitness and overweight shorten your life expectancy, so it is worth testing your fitness and checking your weight against the table on page 30.

Fitness is commonly estimated in terms of heart rate (pulse). When you are seated, having rested for at least five minutes, your pulse rate should be between 50 and 90 beats per minute (bpm). If you then stand up, the rate will increase: it should not do so by more than 24bpm, and after two minutes it should be no more than 12bpm above the resting rate. If you exceed these figures you should consult a doctor.

Your recovery rate after exercise is also important. This can be tested by stepping up and down two steps at a rate of 25 steps per minute for a period of three minutes; afterward you should sit down and rest for 10 seconds before taking your pulse for one minute:

more than 120bpm shows your recovery is poor,
95-110bpm shows your recovery is average,
80-95bpm shows your recovery is good,
under 80bpm shows your recovery is excellent.

How can I make myself fitter?

NOTE: You should *never* undergo training or vigorous exercise if you have the slightest concern about your health or general physical condition. People have died through trying to play sports while suffering no more than a dose of flu. If you are in any doubt at all, consult your doctor before you start.

You can improve your fitness by training regularly – for at least 15 minutes, three times per week. Start gradually: going straight from a sedentary lifestyle to playing squash is a recipe for a heart attack. For the first few months confine yourself to brisk walking or gentle jogging.

The level of exercise you can sensibly take depends upon your recovery rate, as indicated above. First calculate your theoretical maximum heart rate (mhr) by subtracting your age (in years) from 220. For example, if you are aged 50, your mhr is 170bpm.

The level of exercise you undertake should raise your heart rate as follows:
if you have poor recovery: 55 percent of mhr,
if you have average recovery: 70 percent of mhr,
if you have good or excellent recovery: 85 percent of mhr.

As you continue to train, your recovery rate will naturally improve. Check it each week and adjust your level of exercise accordingly.

Getting fit takes time. Do not be disappointed when you fail to get immediate results. You may have spent years becoming unfit, so you can hardly expect to reverse the situation overnight.

Average height and weight for women; 30-40
1.6m (5ft 2in): 57kg (125lb)
1.7m (5ft 6in): 63kg (139lb)
1.8m (5ft 10in): 70kg (154lb)

Average height and weight for men; 30-40
1.7m (5ft 6in): 70kg (154lb)
1.8m (5ft 10in): 77kg (169lb)
1.9m (6ft 2in): 85kg (187lb)

Body composition at 35
Lean body mass (muscle, nerves, bone)
Women 20.5 percent; Men 23 percent
Fat
Women 23.5 percent; Men 17 percent
Water
Women 55 percent; Men 60 percent

Nutrition
Recommended daily energy allowance
Women 2,150 Kcal; Men 2,750 Kcal
Recommended daily protein allowance
Women 54g; Men 69g

Normal heart rate at 35: 50-100 beats per minute (see pp39, 50)

Normal blood pressure at 35
Systolic 130; Diastolic 85

Daily hours of sleep: about 7

Vision: regular eye tests recommended

Hearing
Over age 30 we begin to lose sensitivity to high-pitched sounds (see p89)

Teeth: gum disease and wear on teeth are greater problems than decay; six-monthly check-ups recommended

Immunization: tetanus should be updated every five years, polio every ten years; consult your doctor about immunizations needed if you are traveling to another country

Most common problems brought to the doctor
Women:
- contraception
- screening for cancer of breast and cervix
- menstrual problems
- obesity
- high blood pressure
Men:
- high blood pressure
- sprains and strains
- obesity
- contraception (vasectomy)

Fertile menstrual cycles at 35: 82 percent of the average woman's cycles

Recommended contraception: diaphragm, coil or loop, condoms; over 30 there are slight risks to health in using contraceptive pills containing estrogen; if family not yet complete, avoid coil or loop - slight risk of infection makes it a threat to future fertility (see p124); condoms should be used to reduce the risk of sexually transmitted disease if you have more than one sexual partner. Sterilization or vasectomy if family complete.

Risk of bearing Down's syndrome child, mother aged 35-40
Father aged up to 35: one in 250
Father 35-40: one in 170
Father 41-46: one in 80
Father 47 or over: one in 50

Main threats to life and health
Women:
- cancer
- heart disease
- accidents
Men:
- heart disease
- accidents
- cancer

Risk of dying between 30 and 40
Women 10.2 in 1,000; Men 13.9 in 1,000

How to measure your own pulse
As the heart beats, successive waves of pressure pass through the arteries. Where arteries lie close to the skin it is possible to feel these waves with the fingers or thumb. The artery usually used for this purpose is the one just below the wrist.

Set a watch or clock with a second hand in front of you and feel with the tip of the index or middle finger for your pulse. Once you have found it (this becomes easier with practice), start to count the beats. When at rest you should count for a full minute. However, if you are measuring your rate of recovery from exercise, you are best to count for 10 seconds and then multiply by six to get an estimate of your heart rate in bpm.

Over 40

How your weight affects your lifespan

The more overweight or underweight you are, the less your life expectancy. Women are marginally more at risk from being underweight than men, but men are very much more at risk from being overweight than women. People in their forties often begin to lead a more sedentary lifestyle while continuing to eat the same kind of diet as they did when they were younger (see p167). Steady weight gain in these years should be guarded against. As a guide to recommended weight see the chart below.

Height		Weight range	
ft in	cm	lb	kg
MEN			
5 2	157.5	118-129	53.5-58.5
5 3	160	121-133	54.9-60.3
5 4	162.6	124-136	56.2-61.7
5 5	165.1	127-139	57.6-63
5 6	167.6	130-143	59 -64.9
5 7	170.2	134-147	60.8-66.7
5 8	172.7	138-152	62.6-68.9
5 9	175.3	142-156	64.4-70.8
5 10	177.8	146-160	66.2-72.6
5 11	180.3	150-165	68 -74.8
6 0	182.9	154-170	69.9-77.1
6 1	185.4	158-175	71.7-79.4
6 2	188	162-180	73.5-81.6
6 3	190.5	167-185	75.7-83.5
6 4	193	172-190	78.1-86.2
WOMEN			
4 10	147.3	96-107	43.5-48.5
4 11	149.9	98-110	44.5-49.9
5 0	152.4	101-113	45.8-51.3
5 1	154.9	104-116	47.2-52.6
5 2	157.5	107-119	48.5-54
5 3	160	110-122	49.9-55.3
5 4	162.6	113-126	51.3-57.2
5 5	165.1	116-130	49 -59
5 6	167.6	120-135	54.4-61.2
5 7	170.2	124-139	56.2-63
5 8	172.7	128-143	58.1-64.9
5 9	175.3	132-147	59.9-66.7
5 10	177.8	136-151	61.7-68.5
5 11	180.3	140-155	63.5-70.3
6 0	182.9	144-159	65.3-72.1

Are you overweight? This chart shows desirable weights (in indoor clothing) according to height for adults in their prime. The figures are based on average weights associated with lowest mortality in the United States for medium-framed men and women. If you have a small frame, the lower figure could be up to 7lb (3kg) less. If you have a large frame, the upper figure could be up to 14lb (6kg) more. As a general rule if you are more than 10 percent overweight you are likely to die younger than you should. If you are too heavy you can make changes to improve your life expectancy. Cut down on foods rich in saturated fats and sugar, and increase your intake of wholemeal bread and vegetables.

Medical checks during middle age

Between the ages of 30 and 60 you should have regular health checks, perhaps as often as once a year. The screening focuses on:
- personal and family medical history
- general physical assessment
- specific tests of:
  urine
  heartbeat
  respiration
  chest
  blood

Major health insurance groups often offer "well person" screening to people in this age range, and in many companies senior employees are required to undergo such checks.

When discussing your medical history the doctor will ask you not only about the ailments you yourself have suffered in the past but also about illnesses – such as heart disease – that have afflicted close relatives. This is because such conditions may run in the family. You will also be asked about any symptoms of malaise you might be experiencing and about your social habits, especially:
- how much do you smoke (if at all)?
- how much alcohol do you drink (if at all)?
- how much exercise do you take (if at all)?

Executives concerned that their promotion chances may be affected by the results of their medical checks are tempted to lie when answering these questions. To do so is foolish: your health is more important than your salary. In particular, if you have a drink problem, many companies will now give you time off and pay for you to receive treatment.

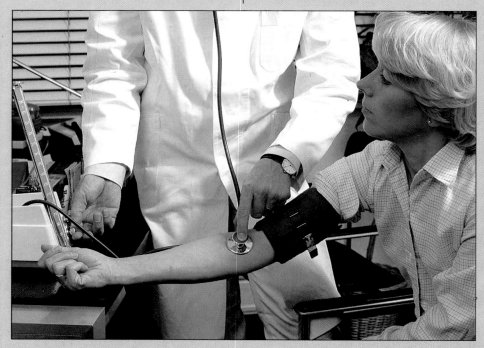

Your doctor will take your blood pressure as part of any routine health check.

Increasingly, computers are being used for this section of the medical check. Often they can be more thorough, more accurate and certainly more patient when questioning people than any human doctor could be.

The physical examination will focus on:
◆ height
◆ weight – if you are seriously overweight or underweight you will be given advice on diet and exercise
◆ blood pressure – if it is too high, you may be prescribed medication and certainly will be given advice on how to change your lifestyle so as to lower it
◆ vision – perhaps you need glasses, or a change of glasses?
◆ hearing – you may not be aware that your hearing is deteriorating
◆ reflexes – there may be something wrong with your nervous system.

If the doctor finds any abnormalities in any of these areas you will probably be asked to undergo further tests and, if necessary, treatment.

The remainder of the full examination consists of a battery of tests:
● The urine will be examined for the presence of blood and protein, which may indicate kidney problems, and of sugar, which can show that you are suffering from diabetes mellitus.
● The electrical activity of your heart will be checked using an electrocardiogram (ECG). This helps the doctor to find out if there is any evidence of coronary artery disease, if there is some problem with the conduction of electric impulses within the heart muscle, or if there is a possibility that the heart muscle has thickened as a result of high blood pressure (hypertension). Should the doctor suspect some abnormality, you may be asked to perform some physical exercise so that the readings can be taken again, with the heart this time under stress.
● Efficient respiration is measured by three factors:

OVER 40

Average height and weight for women 40-50
1.6m (5ft 2in): 60kg (132lb)
1.7m (5ft 6in): 67kg (147lb)
1.8m (5ft 10in): 75kg (163lb)

Average height and weight for men 40-50
1.7m (5ft 6in): 71kg (156lb)
1.8m (5ft 10in): 79kg (174lb)
1.9m (6ft 2in): 87kg (191lb)

Body composition at 45
Lean body mass (muscle, nerves, bone)
Women 19.5 percent; Men 21 percent
Fat
Women 25.5 percent; Men 19 percent
Water
Women 55 percent; Men 60 percent

Nutrition
Recommended daily calorie intake
Women 2,150 Kcal; Men 2,750 Kcal
Recommended daily protein intake
Women 54g; Men 69g

Normal heart rate at 45: 60-100 beats per minute (see pp39, 50)

Normal blood pressure at 45
Systolic 140; Diastolic 90

Daily hours of sleep: 6-7

Vision: oldsight (inflexibility of lens – see pp85, 86) may begin to cause difficulty in focusing on close objects; in the nearsighted it may begin to make distant objects easier to see

Hearing: sensitivity to high-frequency sounds may deteriorate (see p89)

Teeth: gum disease and wear on teeth are greater problems than decay; six-monthly check-ups recommended

Immunization: tetanus should be updated every five years, polio every 10 years; consult your doctor about immunizations needed if you are traveling to another country

Most common problems brought to the doctor
Women:
- checks for breast and cervical cancer
- high blood pressure
- menstrual problems
- menopausal symptoms
- arthritis
- infection
Men:
- high blood pressure
- arthritis
- bronchitis
- infection

Fertile menstrual cycles at 40: 65 percent of the average woman's cycles

Contraception: diaphragm, coil or loop, condoms; over 30 there are slight risks to health in using contraceptive pills containing estrogen; if family not yet complete, avoid coil or loop – slight risk of infection makes it a threat to future fertility (see p124); unless risk of sexually transmitted disease absent, condoms should be used. Sterilization if family complete

Risk of bearing Down's syndrome child, mother aged 41-46
Father aged up to 35: one in 125
Father 35-40: one in 85
Father 41-46: one in 35
Father 47 or over: one in 25

Main threats to life and health
women: cancer, cardiovascular disease
men: cardiovascular disease, cancer

Risk of dying between 40 and 50
Women 21.3 in 1,000; Men 32.5 in 1,000

1 the peak expiratory flow rate (PEFR) – the rate at which you can blow out, as measured by a meter
2 the forced vital capacity (FVC) – the maximum volume of air you can blow out in a single breath
3 the forced expiratory volume (FEV) – the maximum amount of air you can blow out in a second.

These three readings – whose values are affected by age and height – tell the doctor whether or not you have any tendency to breathing disorders like asthma and chronic bronchitis.

The chest is X-rayed to check for any of the following:
◆ major abnormalities, like lung tumors or cancers
◆ chronic bronchitis
◆ asthma [continued]

The relative size of the heart is also recorded, a useful piece of information when considering abnormal blood pressure or the likelihood of heart failure.

● Blood tests are carried out to look for early warning of trouble ahead (see below).

● The feces may be tested for "occult" blood – that is, blood that is present but not in such quantities that it is visible to the naked eye. Many cases of early cancer of the bowel have been discovered and cured because of such examinations.

What's in a blood test?

Blood tests fall into two categories. The first is concerned with the blood cells, both red and white, the second with the chemistry of the blood.

The blood-cell (hematology) profile includes measures of the level of hemoglobin (the iron-based chemical that transports oxygen about the body) in the blood. If this is too low we are either losing it, because of heavy periods or through the bowel, or are failing to produce enough, because of poor diet or (more rarely) because disease is adversely affecting our body's ability to absorb iron. Sometimes the level can be too high. This is usually a response of the body to the fact that it is being deprived of sufficient oxygen, perhaps because of chronic lung disease or heart failure. On rare occasions it may be because the cells responsible for creating our red blood cells are slowly beginning to malfunction.

The average size of the red blood cells and the number of them in a unit volume of blood, as well as the amount of hemoglobin contained in each, provide useful indicators of the state of balance between our iron intake and iron loss. The figures are lower for women than for men because of monthly loss through menstruation.

There are several different kinds of blood cells, including:

◆ neutrophils, which fight bacteria
◆ lymphocytes, which fight viruses
◆ monocytes, which serve numerous functions and are involved in a number of disease processes

◆ eosinophils, whose function is not well understood but which are involved in allergic responses
◆ basophils, whose function is likewise not well understood.

The presence of too many white cells of any or all of these kinds may indicate disease. In particular, if there are more eosinophils than normal it may be that you are suffering a chronic allergic condition like asthma. Tests on the blood chemistry focus primarily on:

● the function of the liver
- has the liver been damaged (for example, through excessive intake of alcohol)?
- is the person suffering from chronic hepatitis?

● the function of the kidneys
- are the kidneys cleaning the blood quickly enough?
● the level of blood sugar
- is it possible that the person has unsuspected diabetes?
- is the level of blood cholesterol too high? (This varies according to diet, genetic makeup, medication and alcohol intake).
- is the person eating a diet that is too rich (too high in fat)?
- is the person at an increased risk of heart attack?
- is the level of triglyceride too high? (This is affected by a person's alcohol intake and family history). Too much can produce disease.

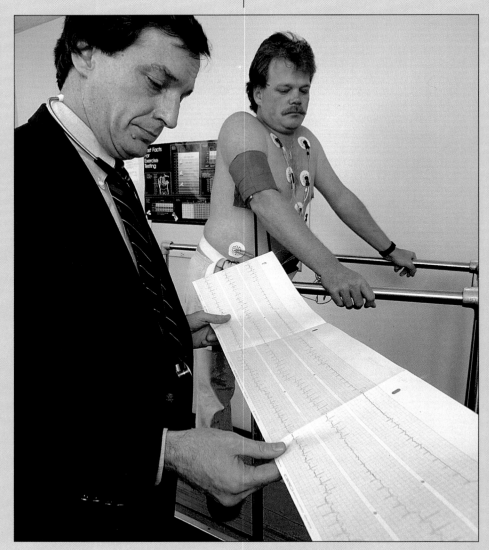

Fitness of the heart can be tested during exercise and recovery.

- what is the level of the hormones produced by the thyroid gland? Is the person at risk of any of the diseases caused by overproduction or underproduction? Potential blood donors receive other blood tests. Their hemoglobin level is checked to make sure they are not anemic. Also, they are screened in case their blood contains either or both of the viruses Hepatitis B and HIV (the AIDS virus), both of which could fatally infect recipients of the blood.

What can you find in a liter of blood?

Levels of hemoglobin and numbers of red blood cells differ between men and women because of menstruation. The blood of a healthy male contains 130-180 grams per liter (2-3oz/pt); that of a healthy female 115-165 grams per liter (1.9-2.75oz/pt). In a healthy male each liter of blood contains 4,500-6,500 billion red blood cells (2,100-3,100 billion per pint); the blood of a healthy female contains 3,800-5,800 billion red blood cells per liter (1,800-2,750 billion per pint). For healthy members of either sex, other values are:
platelets: 150-400 billion per liter (71-190 billion per pint)
white blood cells: 4-11 billion per liter (1.9-5.2 billion per pint).

The numbers of the different kinds of white blood cells are typically:
neutrophils: 2-7.5 billion per liter (0.9-3.5 billion per pint)
lymphocytes: 1.5-4 billion per liter (0.7-1.9 billion per pint)
monocytes: 200-800 million per liter (95-380 million per pint)
eosinophils: 40-400 million per liter (19-190 million per pint)
basophils: less than 100 million per liter (47 million per pint).

Breast cancer in the older woman

After the menopause, all women should be screened every three years (or more frequently) for early signs of breast tumors. This is advisable also for younger women. A screening program for all women over the age of 45 has recently been instituted in Britain, and is already in operation in other countries. It may be that younger women would also benefit. The technique used is called "mammography," and involves examination of the breasts using X-rays. At the very least, subjecting yourself to such an examination can give you reassurance.

Deteriorating vision

After 50 "oldsight" often develops and you may find you have difficulty focusing on near objects. After the mid-sixties, this condition does not usually worsen. Cataracts impair vision in 5 percent of older people and by the age of 90 most people suffer from them to some extent. In general, by the time we reach 70 we need 3 times as much illumination as the younger eye if we are to register an image as clearly. Chapter 7 describes how vision and other senses may become less acute as time passes.

OVER 50

Average height and weight for women 50-60
1.6m (5ft 2in): 62kg (136lb)
1.7m (5ft 6in): 69kg (152lb)
1.8m (5ft 10in): 77kg (172lb)

Average height and weight for men 50-60
1.7m (5ft 6in): 71kg (156lb)
1.8m (5ft 10in): 80kg (176lb)
1.9m (6ft 2in): 88kg (194lb)

Body composition at 55
Lean body mass (muscle, nerves, bone)
   Women 18.5 percent; Men 19 percent
Fat
   Women 26.5 percent; Men 21 percent
Water
   Women 55 percent; Men 60 percent

Nutrition
Recommended daily calorie intake
   Women 1,900 Kcal; Men 2,750 Kcal
Recommended daily protein intake
   Women 47g; Men 69g

Normal heart rate at 55: 70-100 beats per minute (see pp39, 50)

Normal blood pressure at 55
Systolic 145; Diastolic 95

Daily hours of sleep: 6-7

Vision: oldsight (inflexibility of lens - see p85-86) may begin to cause difficulty in focusing on close objects; in the near-sighted it may begin to make distant objects easier to see

Hearing: for the effects of age on hearing see p89

Teeth: gum disease and wear on teeth are greater problems than decay; six-monthly check-ups recommended

Immunization: tetanus should be updated every five years, polio every ten years; consult your doctor about immunizations needed if you are traveling to another country

Most common problems brought to the doctor
Women:
- menopause
- checks for breast and cervical cancer
- hormone replacement therapy
- arthritis
- high blood pressure
- heart disease
Men:
- high blood pressure
- heart disease
- arthritis
- bronchitis (acute and chronic)

Fertile menstrual cycles at 50: 40 percent of the average menstruating woman's cycles

Menopause
Average age when periods stop: 51
Most women have had the menopause by 58

Recommended contraception: none required after menopause; condoms should be used to reduce the risk of sexually transmitted disease

Main threats to life and health
women: cancer, cardiovascular disease
men: cardiovascular disease, cancer

Risk of dying between 50 and 60
Women 61.1 in 1,000; Men 94.7 in 1,000

33

60 Plus

Health in later life

"There are so few who can grow old with a good grace," wrote an essayist in the 18th century. Today, however, more and more people are able to "grow old with a good grace" – partly because of improved medical technology but largely because of personal attention to health and fitness both in earlier life and in old age itself.

Chapter 18 explains the main physical changes (both inside and outside the body) that occur as we grow older. After 55 people become more susceptible to cardiovascular disease (see *Ch 2*) and to cancers of the lung, bowel, stomach and skin. Being aware of any of the persistent symptoms listed on page 171 can help you and your doctor detect these before they become too far advanced. Maintaining a good level of health and fitness is important not just for a general feeling of well-being but because many bodily processes – those involved in healing, for example (see *Ch 21*) – become less efficient if health deteriorates. The younger people around you may not notice that it is deteriorating – you may not notice it yourself – so it is wise to continue with the regular medical checks you underwent in earlier years. Your doctor should pay particular attention to:

◆ Weight – as you age, your lifestyle will probably become less active and your body will start to replace muscle with fat (see p167). Being overweight can have dangerous consequences in later life; it can increase your chances of developing diabetes, for example. 10 percent of people over 70 have insulin-independent diabetes (see p167).

Keeping fit and active not only prevents weight gain, but can have other important health benefits. It may retard osteoporosis, the gradual loss of bone mass. This particularly affects women after the menopause, leaving their bones brittle and easily broken (see p101). Exercise also helps prevent constipation which can be a problem in later life (see p167).

◆ Blood pressure – it is important to have this checked regularly. In the developed countries blood pressure tends to rise until people reach their seventies, when it levels off or declines. Raised blood pressure may be an early warning symptom of other problems in the heart and surrounding arteries. Turn to page 40 for an explanation of how doctors monitor blood pressure. Page 54 explains why blood pressure may increase with age and pages 58-9 suggest ways of combating this. You can take steps to lower your blood pressure through diet, prescribed drugs and relaxation.

◆ Heart – aging can have significant effects on the heart: it generally pumps less blood per minute and is less well able to cope with the demands of physical exertion (see p56); in particular, the risk of heart disease increases in the over 60s (see p53).

◆ Arthritis – this can be severely debilitating. Those in their fifties and sixties are often victims of osteoarthritis or rheumatoid arthritis. Turn to pages 99-100 for advice on what the symptoms are and how exercise can help to prevent them.

◆ Lungs – chronic lung diseases such as bronchitis, emphysema and lung cancer are common in later life. People over 75 who suffer from lung diseases need to be wary of pneumonia (see p69).

Monitoring your own health in later life

You should ask yourself:

● Is your nutrition adequate? Page 167 explains how your nutritional needs change with age. If you are over 60 you may find you are suffering more from digestive disorders, for example, indigestion during or after eating. Nearly one-third of people over 60 have diverticular disease (sacs in the walls of the colon). You can avoid this by including more fiber in your diet (see p109).

● Is the heating in your home adequate?

● Do you ever find that your thinking is hazy or muddled? Though people over 70 often find they have difficulty remembering things (see p168), there is no reason why your intellectual abilities should decline, especially if you have plenty of interests and can keep socially active.

● Do you ever feel dizzy? Vertigo on turning the head suddenly or moving the head up or down often affects the elderly (see p91).

● Do you drink more than you did when you were younger? Old age can bring loneliness and it is easy to fall into the trap of drinking too much alcohol. The negative effects of drinking, however, can be more serious in old age (see p167).

● Do you suffer from urinary problems? Some men in their later sixties and most men over 85 develop some difficulty with their prostate gland. The gland increases in size and begins to obstruct the flow of urine from the bladder. Early symptoms include difficulty in urinating and a need to urinate very frequently (see pp116, 117). **MH**

OVER 60

Average height and weight for women 60-70
1.6m (5ft 2in): 62kg (136lb)
1.7m (5ft 6in): 70kg (154lb)
1.8m (5ft 10in): 78kg (172lb)

Average height and weight for men 60-70
1.7m (5ft 6in): 70kg (154lb)
1.8m (5ft 10in): 79kg (174lb)
1.9m (6ft 2in): 88kg (194lb)

Body composition at 65
Lean body mass (muscle, nerves, bone)
    Women 18 percent; Men 18 percent
Fat
    Women 28 percent; Men 24 percent
Water
    Women 54 percent; Men 58 percent

Nutrition
Recommended daily calorie intake
    Women 1,900 Kcal; Men 2,400 Kcal
Recommended daily protein intake
    Women 47g; Men 60g

Normal heart rate at 65: 70-100 beats per minute (see p50)

Normal blood pressure at 65
Systolic 150; Diastolic 95

Daily hours of sleep: 6-7

Vision: oldsight unlikely to become worse after 65 (see p87)

Hearing: most people over 60 have difficulty hearing sounds pitched above 1,000 cycles per second; 30 percent over 65 have difficulty with both soft and intense sound (see p89)

Teeth: gum disease and wear on teeth are greater problems than decay; six-monthly check-ups recommended

Immunization: tetanus should be updated every five years, polio every 10 years; consult your doctor about immunizations needed if you are traveling to another country

Most common problems brought to the doctor
Women:
- screening for cancer of breast and cervix
- heart disease
- high blood pressure
- arthritis, bronchitis

Men:
- heart disease
- high blood pressure
- arthritis
- bronchitis
- cancer

Recommended contraception: none required after menopause; with new sexual partners condoms should be used to reduce the risk of sexually transmitted disease

Main threats to life and health
Women:
- cardiovascular disease
- cancer
- respiratory disease
Men:
- cardiovascular disease
- cancer
- respiratory disease

Risk of dying between 60 and 70
Women 143 in 1,000; Men 193 in 1,000

OVER 70

Life expectancy: How many years is a 70-year-old likely still to have?
Women almost 15; Men more than 10

Average height and weight for men and women 70-80
By age 65 most people begin to shrink — height may reduce by 1in and weight by 10 percent

Body composition at 75
Lean body mass (muscle, nerves, bone)
    Women 18 percent; Men 18 percent
Fat
    Women 28 percent; Men 24 percent
Water
    Women 54 percent; Men 58 percent

Nutrition
Recommended daily calorie intake
    Women 1,650 Kcal; Men 2,150 Kcal
Recommended daily protein intake
    Women 42g; Men 54g

Normal heart rate at 75: 80-110 beats per minute
Normal heart rate at 85: 90-115 beats per minute (see p50)

Normal blood pressure at 75
Systolic 150; Diastolic 100

Normal blood pressure at 85
Systolic 160; Diastolic 110

Daily hours of sleep: about 6

Vision: night vision difficult for many; about 5 percent of people over 70 suffer from cataracts; most people over 90 show some signs of cataracts; regular checks for glaucoma

Hearing: much loss of hearing in higher frequencies; 60 percent of people over 80 have difficulty hearing both soft and intense sounds (see p89)

Teeth: gum disease and wear on teeth are greater problems than decay; six-monthly check-ups recommended

Immunization: tetanus should be updated every five years, polio every ten years; consult your doctor about immunizations needed if you are traveling to another country

Most common problems brought to the doctor
- all female screening stops now, most problems are the same for both sexes
- high blood pressure
- heart disease
- stroke
- cancer
- arthritis
- bronchitis
- Parkinson's disease
- in women (rarely) post-menopausal bleeding

Recommended contraception: none required after menopause; unless risk of sexually transmitted disease is absent, condoms should be used

Main threats to life and health
Women:
- cardiovascular disease
- cancer
- respiratory disease
Men:
- cardiovascular disease
- cancer
- respiratory disease

Risk of dying between 70 and 80
There are no useful figures available. The risk is roughly 1 in 2.

Part Two

TIME AND HEALTH

IF TIME could stand still, we would fall into a state of suspended animation – our bodies would not be living bodies, for living means constantly changing with time: living a life means growing, maturing and aging; even living from one minute to the next means passing through several complex cycles of bodily changes with each beat of the heart and each breath that we draw in and expel.

Part Two, *Time and Health*, details the key cycles of timed changes in the body that underlie good health, and the changes that are normal across the lifespan. It examines the irregularities of rhythm that we should be alert to and the opportunities that are open to us to foster healthy functioning and prevent disruption.

The first three chapters explain how the heart and lungs maintain the circulatory and respiratory rhythms that keep us alive from minute to minute. These systems change over the lifespan, and some of the most common changes for the worst are preventable. Special features focus on minimizing the risk of heart attacks and the risk of lung disease.

Chapter 4 examines the changing brainwave patterns that underlie different forms of brain activity, and Chapter 5 probes the world of body chemistry and its rhythms. Insights from both of these chapters are applied in Chapter 6 to questions about the daily cycle of waking, sleeping and dreaming.

Chapter 7 considers why our senses become less acute as we get older. It also draws attention to the critical points in childhood when neglecting problems with hearing and vision can put future healthy functioning at risk.

Heart, lungs, nervous system, body chemistry and senses work in harmony to put our muscles effectively to work for us. Across the lifespan, the physical abilities that result develop and decline. Chapter 8 explains how physical ability is achieved and how it can be maintained. None of our systems can work rhythmically if we do not take food into the body, absorb nutrients from it, and dispose efficiently of the waste. Chapter 9 examines how timing mechanisms in the digestive system keep us regular, and how good dietary practice can promote effective working of the system in the short run and fight disease in the long run.

About three-quarters of our body composition is fluids. Chapter 10 focuses on the processes by which we keep these fluids at the right levels and free of wastes – chiefly through the rhythmic action of the kidneys and the urinary system.

Chapters 11-16 trace the time elements in fertility and reproduction. How can an understanding of cycles of fertility be used to promote reproduction when a pregnancy is wanted, and prevent it at other times? What is the pattern of a normal menstrual cycle, and what can be done about problems? How important is it for a couple to synchronize their cycle of sexual arousal? What are the stages and intervals of a normal pregnancy and birth?

Chapter 17 explains what changes to expect, and when, as infants, children and adolescents grow and mature. Chapter 18 examines the aging process: many aspects of it – such as brain cell loss – are under way even as children grow.

Even after we have reached our full growth, many of the different kinds of cells in our bodies continue a cycle of division and renewal to maintain those of our tissues that constantly lose large numbers of cells. Chapter 19 focuses on cancer – a major threat to life and long-term health that arises when the cycle of tissue renewal goes out of control. What causes cancers? How long do they take to develop? When can treatment be effective?

Infection, the topic of Chapter 20, is another common threat. This chapter considers when we are most vulnerable and gives details about times of incubation of common viral and bacterial diseases.

Any disease or injury – a cancer, an infection or a wound – destroys cells that we need. Chapter 21 explains how the body uses the time that healing takes.

1 THE BEATING HEART

Before you reach the age of 70, your heart will probably beat for the 5 billionth time. When healthy, its rate of contraction may vary, from one moment to the next, between 50 and 200 beats per minute – finely tuned regulators ensure that the heart keeps pace with your body's changing needs.

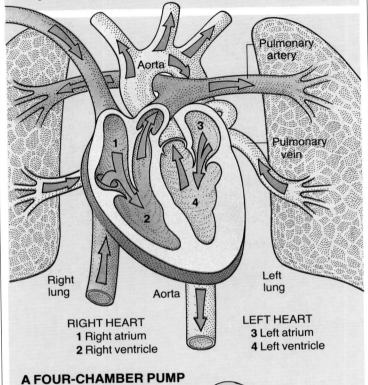

Aorta

Pulmonary artery

Pulmonary vein

1

3

2

4

Right lung

Aorta

Left lung

RIGHT HEART
1 Right atrium
2 Right ventricle

LEFT HEART
3 Left atrium
4 Left ventricle

A FOUR-CHAMBER PUMP

■ *The heart has a right side (seen on the left in diagrams) that pumps used blood from the body to the lungs – and a left side that pumps oxygen-rich blood from the lungs to the body.*

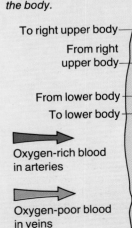

From head
To head
To left upper body
From left upper body

To right upper body
From right upper body

From lower body
To lower body

➡ Oxygen-rich blood in arteries

➡ Oxygen-poor blood in veins

DURING one minute of rest, a complete blood supply of about five liters (nine US pints, 8 Imperial pints) may circulate around the body of an average adult. In that minute about 250cc (15 cubic inches) of badly needed oxygen are picked up from the lungs and transported by the blood to the tissues. There the blood picks up and clears away carbon dioxide and other waste products.

When you want your body to work hard – to run or to jump – the blood circulates even faster. It can deliver up to 1,000cc (60 cubic inches) of oxygen per minute to the tissues, meeting the heightened demands of hard-pressed muscles and an aroused nervous system.

This rapid circulation is made possible by a pump: your heart. Its ability to keep rhythmically in time with the body's needs is a crucial aspect of good health.

How does the heart work?

The heart is two side-by-side pumps made mainly of muscle tissue. The side of your heart that lies on *your* left is conventionally called the "left heart," even when it appears in diagrams, as in this book, on the viewer's right. The left heart fills with oxygen-rich blood from the lungs (about 33ml – 1 fluid ounce – at a time) and pumps it in spurts through arteries and smaller arterioles, both with sealed walls, to tiny capillaries, whose permeable walls allow oxygen to escape into the tissues. The spurts raise the pressure in the arteries, causing them to dilate, and so heartbeats are felt as beats of your pulse wherever you can find an artery near the surface – for example, the radial artery in your wrist. Getting blood to the capillaries is the hardest work that the heart does – thus the left heart is larger and more muscular than the right.

Carbon dioxide seeps from the tissues into the capillaries. The blood becomes oxygen-poor, and capillaries become venules then veins (the vessels that look blue beneath your skin). Waste-removing blood flows through the veins in steady streams to the *right* heart. One of the forces that keep blood flowing in the veins is the suction you create in your chest cavity every time you draw a breath. A system of valves keeps the blood from flowing backward when you breath out. Suction is created too when, every few fractions of a second, the heart muscles relax and the chambers of the heart expand. Also, muscles in the limbs squeeze on larger veins, forcing blood toward the heart – it is good for your circulation when you keep on the move.

The right heart alternates between filling with incoming blood and forcing it in spurts into the lungs, where the blood loses carbon-dioxide and picks up oxygen (see *Ch 3*) before flowing into the left heart.

The two sides of the heart work in parallel – that is, they both fill at the same time and both squeeze at the same time. Each side consists of two pumping chambers

■ **(A) Relaxed and (B) contracting**, *the ventricles (lower chambers of the heart)* BELOW, *in horizontal section.* RIGHT *Computer images of the left side of the heart in vertical section:* **(A)** *blood (red) is concentrated in the contracting atrium (upper chamber) as it fills the relaxed ventricle;* **(B)** *the relaxed atrium fills as the ventricle forces blood into the aorta, seen in cross section, lower right.*

A

B

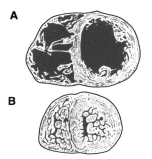

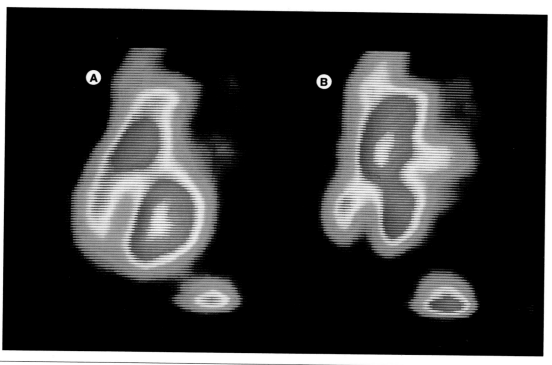

WHAT CREATES THE SOUND OF A BEATING HEART?

50-59 beats per minute

7%

60-69

28%

70-79

50%

80-89

9%

90-100

6%

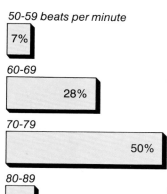

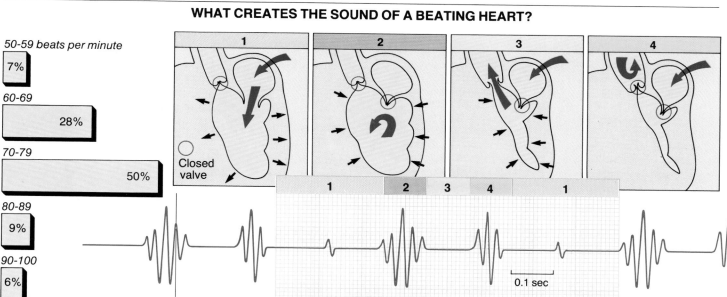

0.1 sec

▲ **People with normal heart rates.** *You are normal if your pulse is regular and beats between 50 and 100 times per minute when you are resting. About 50 percent of the normal population has a resting rate of 70-79 beats per minute. A rate of 40 beats would be dangerously low in the unfit, but a sign of super-fitness in an athlete.*

■ If you put your ear to someone's chest, or listen to their chest through a stethoscope, you will hear a "dub-dub" as the heart beats. These paired sounds occur as blood collides with two valves in the left heart when they close. (Pressures are much lower in the right heart, which does not contribute significantly to the sounds.)

1 The mitral valve between the atrium and the relaxed ventricle is open and the ventricle fills TOP. A sonogram BOTTOM registers little noise. In a heart pumping at about 75 beats per minute this may take half a second.
2 The mitral valve shuts as pressure builds in the contracting ventricle. For about a tenth of a second the sono-

gram registers a heart noise as blood hits the valve.
3 The aortic valve opens and blood empties into the aorta. For about a tenth of a second, the sonogram registers little noise.
4 The aortic valve closes under back pressure from the aorta. For a tenth of a second, the sonogram registers the second heart sound.

HOW IS HEART RATE RELATED TO BLOOD PRESSURE?

■ The contraction phase in a rhythm of contraction and relaxation is called "systole," and so the pressure in the arteries when the left ventricle contracts and ejects blood into them is called "systolic blood pressure." This pressure is created by the strength of the heart's contraction, and since the heart usually contracts more strongly when it beats faster, systolic blood pressure goes up with increasing heart rate.

Diastolic pressure

During "diastole," when the chambers of the heart relax and fill with blood, the pressure in the ventricles drops almost to zero. The pressure in the aorta and the other arteries does not drop nearly as much.

There are two reasons for this. First, when the pressure in the ventricles drops, the valve between the heart and the aorta – the aortic valve – closes, so that the blood is prevented from flowing back into the heart. Second, the arteries are flexible only to a limited degree.

The pressure of the blood during the phase when the ventricles are relaxed is called the "diastolic blood pressure." It depends mainly on the resistance of the arteries – if you suffer from hardening of the arteries (see p57) your arteries will dilate little and your diastolic blood pressure will be higher. Your systolic blood pressure is also likely to be raised – as the heart has to contract more strongly to force blood through inflexible arteries.

Testing blood pressure

Blood pressure is normally measured using a device called a sphygmomanometer. A cuff is wrapped around your arm just above the elbow, and a rubber bag inside the cuff is inflated until one of the arte-

ries in the arm – the brachial artery – is flattened, so that blood cannot flow through it. The nurse or doctor then slowly lowers the pressure in the bag until the blood can just squeeze through the artery. The pressure is read from a meter attached to the cuff – a column of mercury lifted by the air pressure inside the rubber bag. Next the bag is deflated until the blood is able to flow freely through the artery even between contractions; again, the pressure can be read off the meter.

The first measurement shows your systolic blood pressure, the second your diastolic blood pressure. When describing your blood pressure, the doctor will give it in terms of "systolic over diastolic" – in a healthy adult blood pressure should be about 120/80mm of mercury on the scale.

Blood-pressure control

The major organs involved in controlling changes of blood pressure are the brain, the heart and the kidney. The pressure is monitored by "baroreceptors" – these are specialized cells found in the carotid artery in the neck, in the aorta, and elsewhere in the heart and blood vessels. The baroreceptors send information about changes in blood pressure along nerves to special centers in the brain. These centers, in turn, affect the activity of the nervous system.

If the pressure drops – for example, when we stand up from a lying position – chemical messages from the nervous system increase the heart rate and also constrict the blood vessels. These effects act together to increase the blood pressure to its normal level. When blood pressure, for whatever reason, suddenly rises, the nervous system acts to

produce the opposite effect. Both responses return the blood pressure to its normal level within seconds. Even so, the delay can be long enough to be felt – for example, you can feel lightheaded for a little while if you jump out of bed too quickly in the morning.

What you are doing at any particular moment affects your blood pressure. Exercise not only increases the heart rate and the strength of the heart's contractions, thereby raising the systolic pressure; it also increases the levels of adrenaline in the blood, so that the blood vessels relax and the diastolic pressure drops. The "systolic over diastolic" ratio changes considerably.

During sleep your blood pressure can drop to very low levels – as you realize only too well if you have to get up to answer the telephone at 4am.

Action by the kidneys to control the total quantity of fluid in the body (see Ch9) also has a very important effect in controlling blood pressure.

The more blood there is to pump, the harder the heart has to contract and the more resistance there will be in the arteries. Since blood volume changes much more slowly than levels of body-chemicals such as adrenaline, this aspect of blood-pressure regulation takes days not minutes. **MH**

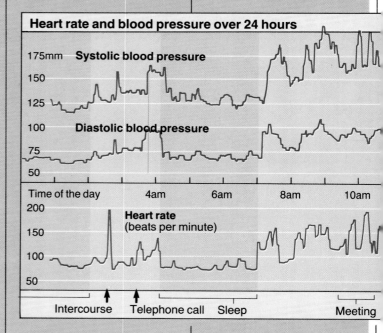

Heart rate and blood pressure over 24 hours

175mm **Systolic blood pressure**
150
125

100 **Diastolic blood pressure**
75
50

Time of the day   4am   6am   8am   10am
200

150 **Heart rate**
(beats per minute)
100

50

Intercourse   Telephone call   Sleep   Meeting

▲ **Heart rate and blood pressure** reflect activity and emotional states. Systolic blood pressure corresponds to the surge of blood in the arteries as the left ventricle of the heart contracts; the diastolic pressure occurs as the heart relaxes and fills.

■ **During sleep** your blood pressure can drop to very low

levels. Heart rate mostly remains near its resting level but responds to changing activity levels in the brain during dreams (see Ch4).

■ **Sexual arousal** (see Ch13) rises through stages of excitement and increasing pelvic muscular tension. Heart rate may reach 200 beats per minute at climax,

– an *atrium* (the upper chamber) and a *ventricle* (the lower one). The two chambers work in series – one after the other. The atrium becomes relaxed and open, collecting in-bound blood, while the ventricle is still contracting, forcing blood into the arteries. After it has emptied, blood flows for a fraction of a second from a relaxed atrium into a relaxed ventricle. Then a comparatively weak contraction of the atrium squeezes blood out of it to complete the filling of the still-relaxed ventricle. The ventricle contracts strongly to force the blood on its way, while in-coming blood again begins to fill the atrium.

How does the heart keep time?

Unlike the skeletal muscles by which we voluntarily control our movements, heart muscle does not require a nervous impulse in order to start a contraction: electrically, the cells switch on and off (and mechanically they contract and relax) rhythmically on their own. Activity of the heart muscle cells is coordinated, however, by a *cardiac impulse* that travels through the heart muscle over-riding the rhythms of individual cells.

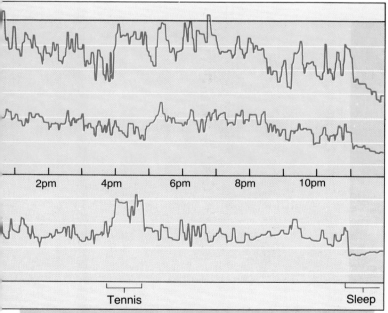

2pm   4pm   6pm   8pm   10pm

Tennis   Sleep

and systolic blood-pressure may reach 200.

■ **Interruption at 4am**. *Rousing yourself to answer the telephone at 4am can be difficult because blood pressure is so low. Not only do heart rate and systolic pressure rise but diastolic pressure must do so too, to reach minimal levels for activity.*

■ **Emotional arousal**, *such as concern about the way an 11am meeting is going, prepares the body for physical action, even if physical action is not appropriate. Thus it has a similar effect on heart rate and blood pressure to that of a game of tennis. Diastolic pressure drops slightly as blood vessels dilate.*

The impulse begins in the heart's natural pacemaker (the sinuatrial node) a tiny region of the right atrium. It has pacemaker cells, whose natural rhythm is faster than that of other heart muscle cells. When they switch on, the pacemaker cells generate an impulse that passes to other cells, stimulating them to contract.

The impulse first passes quickly through both atria, and then slows. Most of the tissues dividing the atria from the ventricles do not conduct electrical impulses. Only the specialized *atrioventricular node* can do this, and it does so at a greatly reduced speed. This allows completion time for the wave of atrial muscle contraction that has been following in the wake of the electrical impulse – only when the atria have filled the still-relaxed ventricles does the impulse reach the ventricles. Then it is carried at greatly increased speed by specialized conducting fibers, and the ventricles contract quickly and strongly (see the diagram on p43).

Why does the heart rate change?

When we take exercise our muscles require more oxygen. Since oxygen is brought to them in the blood, this means that in effect they need more blood. In order to supply it, the heart both beats more rapidly and contracts more powerfully. The amount of blood pumped per minute is called the cardiac output. Two things govern the increase in cardiac output during exercise: the severity of the exercise and how fit you are (see *Ch7*).

When we are asleep our heart rate varies in response to the changing activity levels in the brain during our dreams (see *Ch4*). Even when relaxed, heart rate varies from one moment to the next. As we breathe in, the heart rate goes up and as we breathe out it goes down. In people aged more than about 40 years the heart's natural pacemaker is less sensitive, so that this effect disappears.

The heart is richly equipped with nerve fibers and sensors – called receptors – that monitor and modify its rhythmic activity. When it is time to calm down or take a rest, the *vagus nerve* releases a nerve chemical – acetyl choline – that slows the heart rate. When the body is roused to a quicker physical or emotional pace, other nerve endings release noradrenaline, a chemical that acts on the pacemaker to increase the heart rate. The heart responds in a similar way to hormones circulating in the blood. One of these hormones is adrenaline. When we are anxious or alarmed, the level of adrenaline in our blood increases, and this too makes our heart beat faster.

Stimulants like caffeine and nicotine likewise increase our heart rate. This happens not just because they have an effect on the pacemaker cells but also because they can induce palpitations of the heart – which occur when the heart rate is *not* normal (see p45). **MH**

Four-Fifths of a Second in the Life of a Heart

If your heart is working at a rate of 75 beats per minute, it will complete a full cycle every 0.8 seconds. Here are some of the complex changes that occur in that brief moment as the chambers fill and empty.

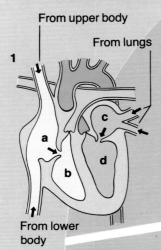

a right atrium   **c** left atrium
b right ventricle **d** left ventricle

From upper body
From lungs
1
c
a
d
b
From lower body

1 For about a quarter of a second, the muscular walls of all four chambers of the heart are relaxed and the chambers are filling with blood. Oxygen-rich blood from the lungs (red) flows into the left side of the heart; oxygen-poor blood from the rest of the body (blue) into the right. Valves between the atria (upper chambers) and ventricles (lower chambers) are open. Valves in openings leading from the heart are held closed by arterial pressure.

2 0.18 sec The pacemaker in the right atrium sends out an electrical wave – the cardiac impulse – that passes through the atrial walls in about a 50th of a second, at a rate of 60cm (2ft) per second.

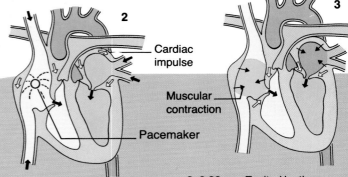

2
Cardiac impulse
Muscular contraction
Pacemaker
3

3 0.23 sec Excited by the electrical wave from the pacemaker, the atrial muscles contract from the top down, taking in this example about a 10th of a second. This corresponds to the P wave of an electrocardiograph (ECG) recording (see p44).

Oxygen-rich blood
at low pressure
at high pressure

1
16
15
14
13
ONE HEART BEAT

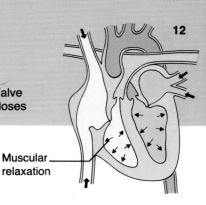
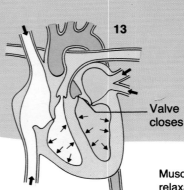

16
15

16 0.8 sec The tricuspid valve opens under the pressure from the right atrium.

15 0.78 sec The mitral valve opens under the pressure from the left atrium.

14 0.75 sec The pulmonary valve closes under back pressure from the arteries leading to the lungs.

14
Valve closes

13 0.73 sec The aortic valve closes under back pressure from the aorta. The second heart sound (see p39) can be heard. Blood pressure falls to the diastolic level (see p40).

13
Valve closes

12 0.63 sec The ventricles begin to relax. This takes about a 10th of a second and corresponds to the T-wave of an ECG recording.

12
Muscular relaxation

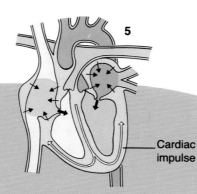

4

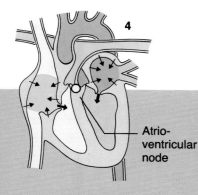

5

Atrio-
ventricular
node

Cardiac
impulse

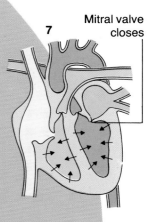

6

4 0.24 sec The cardiac impulse passes slowly (at 20cm – 8in – per second) through the atrioventricular node, the only tissue capable of conducting electricity between the atria and the ventricles. This 10th-of-a-

second delay in conduction allows the contracting atria to empty into the ventricles while the ventricles remain relaxed.

5 0.34 sec The cardiac impulse travels (at 3m –10ft – per second) by way of fast-conducting tissues networked throughout the ventricles. In a 25th of a second they excite the whole of the ventricular muscle.

6 0.38 sec The ventricles contract strongly, especially the left ventricle, reaching maximum force of contraction in a 10th of a second. This 10th of a second corresponds to the QRS complex of an ECG recording (see p44). The cardiac impulse ends.

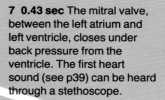

Oxygen-poor blood

☐ at low pressure

☐ at high pressure

Mitral valve
closes

7

7 0.43 sec The mitral valve, between the left atrium and left ventricle, closes under back pressure from the ventricle. The first heart sound (see p39) can be heard through a stethoscope.

8 0.45 sec The tricuspid valve between the right atrium and the right ventricle closes under back pressure.

8

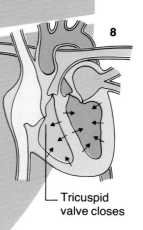

Tricuspid
valve closes

10 0.5 sec The aortic valve opens under pressure from the left ventricle to enable oxygen-rich blood to flow into the aorta, the artery leading to the rest of the body. Blood pressure rises to the systolic level (see p40).

9 0.48 sec The pulmonary valve opens under pressure from the right ventricle to enable oxygen-poor blood to flow from the right ventricle to the lungs.

11 For about an 8th of a second the ventricles empty while the atria, now relaxed, begin to fill.

Blood flows
along pulmonary
artery to lungs

To upper
body

11

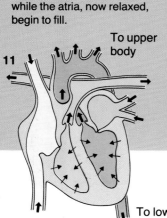

10

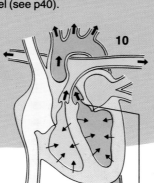

9

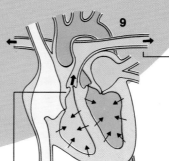

Pulmonary
valve opens

To lower body

Aortic valve opens

Irregular Heart Rhythms

An irregular heartbeat may – but need not – signal a more serious underlying disorder

UNLESS we think about it, or unless we take our own pulse, we are normally totally unaware that our heart is beating. The rhythm is completely regular and the sequence completely ordered, with each beat taking about the same time and the pause between beats being always about the same.

As soon as the pattern becomes irregular though, we notice it. There are two types of changes: either the rate speeds up or slows down, or the sequence of the heart's cycle is disturbed.

How fast can a healthy heart beat?

When you are exercising at your top level, a heart rate of 220 beats per minute less your age in years is not too high. Usually, fast heart rates, so long as the beat is regular and the ECG patterns (see BELOW) are regular, are little to worry about.

An increased heart rate occurs when you take exercise. In some people, though, it occurs inappropriately. During times of anxiety there may be an exaggerated response by the heart's natural pacemaker to the adrenaline circulating in the blood. More rarely, the pacemaker itself is in some way abnormal.

A fast heart rate is called *tachycardia*. When it has been caused by a malfunction of the pacemaker it can often be interrupted, and normal heart rate restored, by persuading the brain to increase the amount of acetyl choline it supplies to the heart through the vagus nerve (see p41).

Using an electrocardiograph (ECG), *doctors can pinpoint irregularities in the heart's electrical activity. The pattern of electrical activity generated during every heart cycle is traced through electrodes attached to the body. Some ECGs simultaneously record tracings from up to 12 standard sites but this 24-hour equipment ABOVE uses only five, allowing patients to follow a normal day's routine.*

Each tracing shows a similar pattern **1***: a "P wave," recording a mild change in the heart's voltage as the atria contract, a "QRS complex," recording a larger change in voltage as the ventricles contract and a "T wave" recording elec-trical changes as the ventricles relax. The length of time from P to R varies with heart rate. In a healthy person with a pulse rate of 75 beats per minute, it may take 0.15 sec. The QRS interval, the time that it takes the ventricles to relax, is invariably 0.1 sec. The ST interval varies with heart rate. At 75 beats per minute, the cycle is completed in 0.8 seconds.*

In a nine-site investigation of heart-attack damage **2***, some tracings (shown in blue) are normal for a reading taken from that site. Others have segments shown in red revealing abnormalities of ventricular contraction and relaxation.*
3 *These pinpoint scarred heart muscle.*

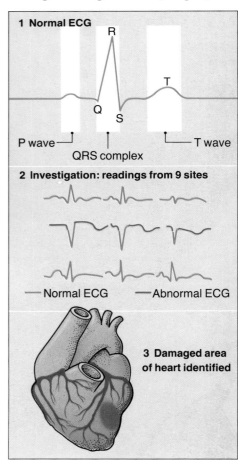

1 Normal ECG

R

Q S

T

P wave — QRS complex — T wave

2 Investigation: readings from 9 sites

— Normal ECG   — Abnormal ECG

3 Damaged area of heart identified

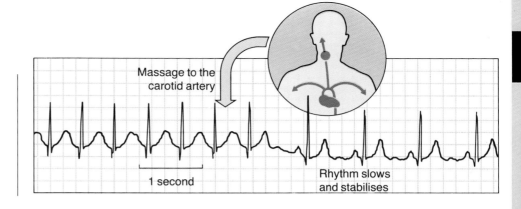

▶ **An abnormally fast heart rate** *slows down when a doctor massages the carotid artery in a patient's neck. The first six beats show a heart rate of approximately 170 beats per minute but the rate slows to 60 beats after the massage begins. Blood-pressure sensors in the artery produce changes in the nervous system that slow the heart.*

Massage to the carotid artery

1 second

Rhythm slows and stabilises

SKIPPING A BEAT

Everyone, whether they know it or not, suffers from the commonest abnormality of the heart rate – the "dropped beat." Facing an unaccustomed challenge such as a parachute jump can be a heart-stopping moment but even in everyday situations you may sometimes feel your heart "skipping a beat." Caffeine, nicotine, exercise and alcohol increase the frequency of "dropped beats."

Why do these irregularities in the heart cycle occur? The heart is normally given its instructions to pump by electrical signals from the pacemaker cells in the right atrium (see p41). On occasion, though, stray electrical signals – "ectopic" signals – can be generated from the ventricles. These can cause an extra heartbeat to be inserted into the sequence; such extra heartbeats are called "ventricular extra systoles." On an ECG the ectopic signal shows up as a beat with no P-wave (see

BELOW). This seems a long way away from an explanation of "dropped beats" but extra beats and missing beats are two facets of the same phenomenon.

If the erratic electrical signal is passed from the ventricles to the atria it activates the pacemaker cells; following this they require a little time – a compensatory

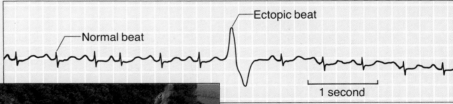

Ectopic beat

Normal beat

1 second

pause – before they can discharge again. It may be this pause that feels like a missed beat.

If, on the other hand, the impulse does not reach the atria, the pacemaker cells will discharge in the normal way, and the impulse they generate will be transmitted to the ventricles. But, if the ventricles are still refractory (have still not relaxed) after the extra beat they have produced, they cannot respond to this signal from the atria. The next beat does not occur until after the next pacemaker discharge.

Are dropped beats dangerous?

Everyone misses a beat from time to time: most often it does not matter. However, very frequent missed beats may indicate that there is an underlying heart disease. This is particularly the case when the abnormal beats come from more than one place in the heart.

Ectopic beats can, notably after a heart attack, indicate that a person is in danger. They may be followed by ventricular fibrillation (abnormal contractions of individual ventricular cells) and cardiac arrest. If you develop multiple ectopic beats after a heart attack a physician or a paramedic should give you an injection to stop them. This can, literally, save your life.

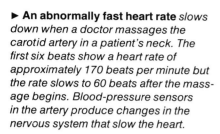

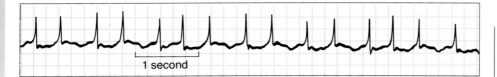

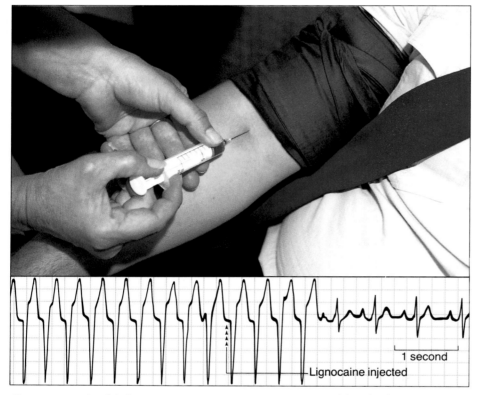

◄ **This rapid, irregular pattern** *records atrial fibrillation. There are no P waves in any of the cycles, because the atria are not contracting. Instead, individual atrial muscle cells are contracting erratically. Impulses generated by atrial muscle cells pass to the ventricles, which contract at about 100 beats per minute.*

◄ **After a heart attack** *an ECG shows an abnormally fast rate of ventricular contraction (ventricular tachycardia). No P waves are visible. Injecting the drug lignocaine prevents this fast heart rate from developing into uncontrolled ventricular fibrillation, which would lead to instant and probably fatal collapse. Within moments of the injection the heart rate slows.*

1 second

Lignocaine injected

One way to do this is to massage the blood-pressure sensor in the carotid artery at the neck. Another way is to use drugs known as *beta-blockers* – they block the action of the hormone adrenaline on the pacemaker cells. Such fast heart rates can be disturbing but are very rarely dangerous, and usually not associated with other symptoms.

When are fast rates dangerous?

Some abnormalities of the heart-beat can produce rates as fast as 380 beats per minute, and these conditions can be dangerous. The heart can be driven to contract at such a rate that the coronary arteries are unable to cope with the necessary blood flow. The victim may suffer an attack of crushing chest pain – angina – in association with the sensation of palpi-

tion; or, possibly, the heart may find itself no longer able efficiently to meet the requirements of the circulation, so that heart failure results (see p57). A person whose heart is already diseased for some other reason is particularly prone to such attacks; however, even an otherwise healthy heart can fail if it is subjected to a prolonged attack of tachycardia.

On occasion the pacemaker cells discharge earlier than they ought to, with the result that the heart's electrical system is activated too soon. There are a number of different reasons why this can happen.

In *atrial fibrillation* the atria do not contract: the individual cells discharge in a random manner, sending out impulses at a rate of 380-600 per minute. The atrioventricular node – the electrical connection between the upper and

lower chambers of the heart (see p41) – cannot normally react to impulses faster than about 200 per minute, but sometimes in atrial fibrillation, so many impulses may pass through the node that some reach the ventricles when they are not completely filled. When this happens, the ventricles do not produce the usual surge in arterial pressure, and not all the heartbeats are registered when the pulse is measured elsewhere on the body. When atrial fibrillation is uncontrolled, the heart rate measured by listening to the heart directly is faster than the rate measured by taking the pulse at the wrist.

Atrial fibrillation may cause an almost regular heartbeat – but more usually it produces a fast and irregular one. The irregularity is itself variable – and this can be felt

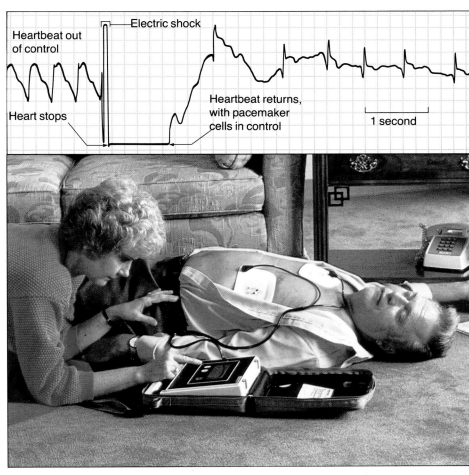

Heartbeat out of control

Electric shock

Heart stops

Heartbeat returns, with pacemaker cells in control

1 second

▶ **A shock to slow the heart.** *A woman treating her partner's heart attack uses a portable defibrillator to restore a regular heartbeat. The victim's dangerously high heart rate is stopped by a direct-current shock applied to his chest. The shock deactivates all the heart cells. The pacemaker cells recover first, taking control of the heart's beat, and reimposing a regular rhythm.*

Like atrial fibrillation, ventricular fibrillation occurs when muscle cells contract and relax without coordination, but it is a far more serious disturbance of the heart's rhythm: the ventricles twitch rapidly and uselessly, and the brain's blood supply is threatened. Striking the victim's chest (see p48) may keep them alive if electric shock treatment is unavailable. Ventricular fibrillation may occur in acute cardiac attacks or during heart surgery.

at the wrist. It can be rectified by using digitalis – a chemical commonly extracted from the foxglove plant. What digitalis does is to slow the rate of electrical conduction between the atria and the ventricles; the ventricles are therefore stimulated less frequently, and so the rate of ventricular contraction slows.

Atrial fibrillation is quite common. In rare cases infants can suffer from it because of congenital abnormalities, sometimes in the conducting fibers of the heart. In later childhood, rheumatic fever (now rare in the developed world) and other infections can cause it. In adulthood the disorder can be produced by overactivity of the thyroid gland; alcohol abuse is another possible culprit. In many cases, though, atrial fibrillation seems to be nothing more than a

natural by-product of the aging process: assuming that there are no other manifestations of heart disease, the older person with atrial fibrillation should not be too concerned.

Atrial flutter, atrial tachycardia and circus cycles

Other abnormalities can produce fast heart rates. *Atrial flutter* is much less common than atrial fibrillation, but the causes are essentially the same. The atria contract, but they do so 250-300 times per minute; most often the impulses generated by this are not conducted to the ventricles but, in the rare cases when they all are, the result can be a very fast pulse rate.

Atrial tachycardia increases the heart rate much less than atrial flutter: rates of 120-250 per minute

are the norm. Often this condition is linked with some underlying heart disease, but sometimes it can be a result of treatment with cardioactive drugs. One such is digoxin, or digitalis. In such instances a normal heart rate can often be restored by the simple expedient of reducing the dosage. Another possible treatment to reduce atrial tachycardia and atrial flutter is the use of drugs that affect the rate at which calcium can penetrate the membranes of the pacemaker cells. Verapamil is one such drug.

In a normal heart the cardiac impulse is transmitted from the atria to the ventricles solely through the conducting tissue at the atrioventricular node. About 0.15 percent of people, though, have an accessory conducting pathway between the atria and the

CARDIAC ARREST – WHAT SHOULD YOU DO?

When a person's heart fails to beat, their circulation stops and so they lose consciousness. Unless something is done at once to restore the circulation, they will die. Even if they escape death, brain cells can suffer irreversible damage within minutes, so immediate treatment is vital.

If someone's heart stops beating when you are with them, you should make sure that medical help is summoned urgently. Before it arrives, however, there are things you can do to help.

Giving heart massage

The first thing to try is hitting the person on their lefthand side, just below the nipple or breast, with your clenched fist. Do not be frightened of hitting too hard.

The blow may immediately cause the heart to start beating again.

If it does not, place the heel of one hand on the breastbone at a point about two-thirds of its length down from the neck. Put your other hand on top of the first and, your arms straight, press down hard five times in five seconds; the breastbone should go in 3-4cm (1-1.5in) each time.

Mouth-to-mouth resuscitation

Next clear the person's airway: tilt the head back so that the neck is extended, and remove from the mouth any extraneous material – eg dentures or vomit. Pinch the nostrils closed and start mouth-to-mouth resuscitation: take a deep breath, make an airtight seal between your own mouth and theirs and blow hard, so that the chest rises.

While you are giving resuscitation, stop after each two breaths and lean on the breastbone 10 times. If there is someone with you, follow this cycle: one breath of mouth-to-mouth resuscitation; five depressions of the breastbone in five seconds; one breath of mouth-to-mouth resuscitation; and so on. These techniques will maintain satisfactory circulation to the brain for up to 20 minutes. Seeing them demonstrated at first hand – for example, as part of a first aid course – will help prepare you to carry them out.

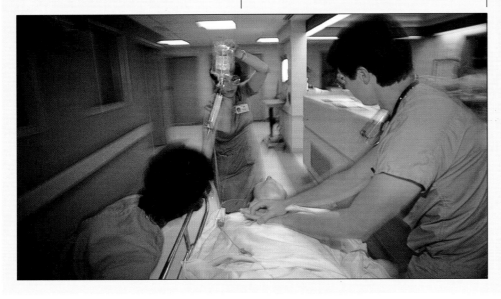

ventricles. Such people can suffer "re-entrant" or "circus" cycles of activation, in which the signals sent from the atria to the ventricles come back again.

Atrial fibrillation is a common result of this congenital abnormality; a more usual symptom of the disorder is a high rate of ventricular contraction, sometimes leading to collapse.

Lethal heart rates

Abnormalities of the atrial rhythm are uncomfortable and sometimes dangerous, but rarely lethal. Ventricular tachycardia – abnormally rapid heart rhythms originating from the ventricles – can be a much graver matter, not only because they can be dangerous in themselves but because they can lead to the development of *ventricular fibrillation*. This con-

dition occurs when the cells in the ventricles are activated in a random fashion. The person collapses immediately and, unless treated swiftly, dies. Heart attacks are the commonest cause of ventricular fibrillation.

Ventricular tachycardia can be treated using drugs that slow the rate at which sodium enters the ventricular cells at the time they are being activated. One such drug is called lignocaine.

Not all cases of abnormally fast heart rhythms respond to drug therapy. In some instances direct electric shock – *cardioversion* – may have a beneficial effect. What happens is that the electric shock, applied using electrodes placed on the chest wall, deactivates all of the cells in the heart. The first cells to recover are the pacemaker cells. These take control of the heart's

beat while the other cells are still recovering; with luck, the pacemaker cells will then be able to impose a regular rhythm.

How slow is too slow?

If fast heart rates can be dangerous, so can slow ones – known as *bradycardia*. The meaning of "too slow" varies from person to person. An extremely fit young person may have a resting heart rate of only 40-50 beats per minute. An elderly, unfit person with a rate as low as this could be in trouble: the effort of merely getting up from a chair might be enough to cause collapse.

An abnormally slow heart rate is often found when a person faints. The victim faints because the flow of blood to the brain has been reduced – partly because of the slow heart rate. Usually, recovery is fairly prompt: when the person falls over, blood reaches the brain more easily. Should someone faint in your presence, you can speed their recovery by keeping their head low and raising their legs. This will encourage the blood to move toward their head.

One cause of slow heart rates is a slow rate of discharge in the pacemaker cells. This usually occurs as a result of a heart attack or because of other damage to the heart: the chemical messenger acetyl choline slows the heart down. The effect of this can be counteracted by atropine (extracted from deadly nightshade).

Another possibility is that the impulses from the atria are failing to reach the ventricles. This is a condition known as heart block. A heart block most often occurs because the conducting tissues of the heart have degenerated. Although this can happen to people of any age, it is commonest among the elderly.

A first-degree block is not serious enough to cause noticeable symptoms. In second-degree block the pulse is irregular, because some of the cardiac impulses that originate in the pacemaker cells do not pass from the atria to the ventricles.

Third-degree heart block is the most serious type because *none* of the impulses from the pacemaker cells are transmitted to the ventricles, and the ventricles beat at their own spontaneous rate – 40 beats per minute, or even less. When the atria and ventricles get out of synchrony like this, the ventricles fail to quicken their pace to meet the needs of extra exertion or excitement, for the nervous system normally speeds up the heart by acting directly on the pacemaker cells.

In some cases, the heart might even stop completely, so that the person collapses. Usually the beat restarts and the person recovers rapidly. If this does not happen, however, they may require electric-shock treatment to get the ventricles beating normally again.

The answer to a dangerously slow heart rate may be an artificial pacemaker. Pacemaker operations are now relatively common – about 200,000 devices are implanted worldwide every year. Most stimulate both the atria and the ventricles directly. Sophisticated use of silicon chips allows pacemakers to be self-analyzing and self-programmable, responding flexibly to stimuli created by emotions or exercise. **MH**

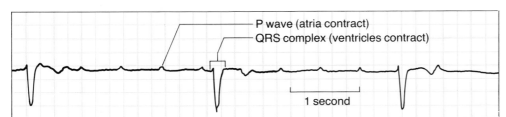

P wave (atria contract)
QRS complex (ventricles contract)

1 second

▲ **The most serious type of heart block**, *third degree (or complete) heart block, occurs when the cardiac impulse cannot get through to the ventricles. In this ECG recording, there are many P waves – the atria are contracting at a rate of 110 beats per minute, in response to the electrical impulse originating in the pacemaker cells. The infrequent QRS complex records a ventricular rate of* contraction of only 35 beats per minute. The ventricles are contracting at their own dangerously slow spontaneous rate. Complete heart block sometimes develops when coronary artery disease causes tissue near the atrioventricular node to become inflamed or to degenerate. The remedy is an artificial pacemaker.

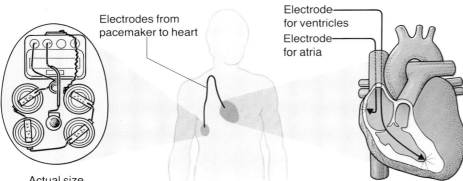

Electrodes from pacemaker to heart

Electrode for ventricles
Electrode for atria

Actual size

▲ **Linked to the heart by a wire** *along a vein close to the collar bone, a pacemaker consists of a battery-powered generating unit. This is connected to electrodes placed in contact with the heart wall. If the pacemaker is needed permanently, it is implanted under the skin in the tissue of the chest wall. A patient who needs a pacemaker for only a short period can wear the generating unit on a belt. If the heart beats irregularly on some days and normally on others the pacemaker is controlled from outside the body and varies the heart rate as necessary.*

▲ **Electrodes attached to the heart wall** *stimulate both the atria and the ventricles. At timed intervals they carry electrical impulses that trigger contractions at near the normal rate. They can speed up an abnormally slow heart or make an erratic heart beat regular. The battery of a pacemaker usually lasts for five or more years but replacing it requires only a minor operation. If you have a pacemaker you should avoid powerful radio or radar transmitters and security screens. They will interfere with its functioning.*

2 THE LIFE OF THE HEART

Age alone does not weaken the heart, and only a tiny percentage of people are born with heart defects. Yet heart disease is a major killer, and the risk rises steeply with age. A lifestyle that drives up blood pressure, and promotes a narrowing of the arteries that supply life-giving oxygen to the heart, is largely to blame.

CHANGES THAT COME WITH TIME

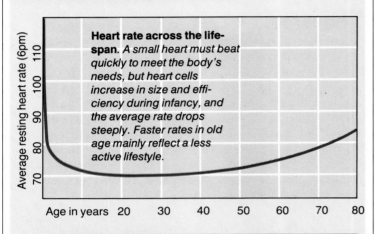

Heart rate across the life-span. *A small heart must beat quickly to meet the body's needs, but heart cells increase in size and efficiency during infancy, and the average rate drops steeply. Faster rates in old age mainly reflect a less active lifestyle.*

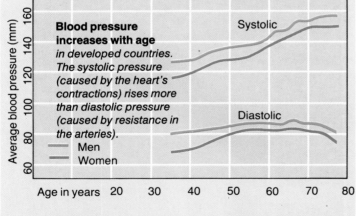

Blood pressure increases with age *in developed countries. The systolic pressure (caused by the heart's contractions) rises more than diastolic pressure (caused by resistance in the arteries).*
— Men
— Women

Systolic

Diastolic

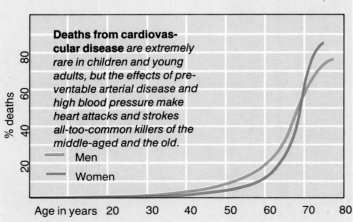

Deaths from cardiovascular disease *are extremely rare in children and young adults, but the effects of preventable arterial disease and high blood pressure make heart attacks and strokes all-too-common killers of the middle-aged and the old.*
— Men
— Women

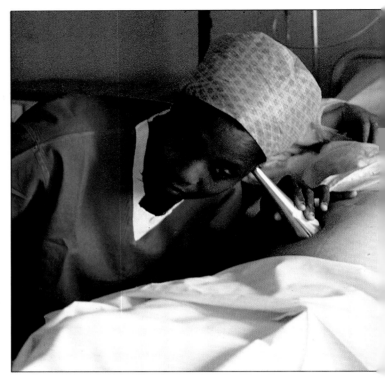

THE HEART starts to beat while we are still in the womb, usually about 20 days after conception. The rudiments of blood circulation begin even earlier, during the second week. At birth and during childhood, most people are lucky enough to suffer no serious disabilities of the heart, but in later life heart disease is the commonest single cause of death in the developed countries. The increasing risk of heart failure as we grow older is not a simple reflection of the aging process – more to blame are the effects of diet and lifestyle.

Critical times in the womb

During the second week after conception, the embryo develops a basic circulatory system. Tiny vessels lined by a layer of thin cells appear, and soon these link together to form a continuous network. Much of this network, however, exists outside the body of the developing embryo – on the surface of the cluster of cells that will become the placenta.

The heart is the first organ to develop in the embryo, forming at first a single, tubelike structure, running along the midline from the head to the trunk. Developing muscles surrounding the tube begin contracting periodically. These first heartbeats are irregular and weak but, after a day or two, they are strong enough to pump the embryo's blood around its network of blood vessels. Even though the heart's structure will change considerably during the next few weeks, it continues to

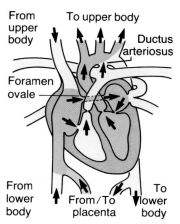

▲ **Before birth**, *oxygenated blood flows from the right heart to the left.*

◄ **Listening for the fetal heartbeat**. *The heart starts beating about 20 days after conception. By the eighth week it has developed into a four-chamber pump.*

beat without interruption for the rest of the person's life.

About four or five weeks after conception the heart begins to look more like the adult version. The tube loops and distorts to form the precursor of the four-chambered heart. Between now and the seventh week after conception development is intense, and the heart of the embryo is particularly vulnerable to outside influences. German measles (rubella) in the mother and X-rays can cause the heart to malform at this stage. **V N**

What causes heart disease in early life?

Childhood heart disease has decreased rapidly in recent years. The commonest cause is rheumatic fever: about 0.005 percent of children under 15 suffer from this in the developed countries, but elsewhere the rate can be as high as 1 percent. Rheumatic fever is most often a result of an abnormal reaction to a bacterial infection. This reaction usually affects children aged 5-14; typically it follows 1-3 weeks after a bout of tonsillitis. The symptoms of the illness start with arthritis: the larger joints, like those of the hip and the knee, show pain and swelling. Over 1-4 weeks one joint is affected for a few days and then the arthritis shifts to another.

THE MOST COMMON HEART DEFECTS

Under 1 percent of babies have heart defects at birth. Only about half of them need surgery during infancy; a further one-quarter at some stage during their first decade.

Hole in the heart

Within a few minutes of birth, the lungs take on the work of enriching used blood with oxygen. The pressure of the blood now coming into the left atrium from the lungs causes the foramen ovale (see diagram ABOVE) to close.

Sometimes this closure does not occur, and the "hole in the heart" baby may require surgery if the hole is large. There may instead be an abnormal hole linking the two ventricles. A small hole will usually close by itself during infancy.

Ductus arteriosus

The ductus arteriosus (see diagram ABOVE) is another feature of fetal circulation. It should close within two weeks of birth. If it does not, the left ventricle pumps

already-freshened blood into the lungs and surgery is necessary. **V N**

Valve faults

Operations to correct deformities of the heart valves (**1** and **2**) can usually be delayed until early adulthood, and in some cases may not be required at all.

A similar birth defect is an abnormally narrow aorta. Usually, corrective surgery can wait until after age five.

Blue babies

Transposition of the great arteries (**3**) results in a

"blue baby." It requires immediate surgery. After the lungs begin to work, the circulation on each side of the heart forms a closed loop, and this baby will die within days unless a hole is made surgically between the two atria. Later, during the first 18 months, a more extensive operation will be needed.

A commoner type of blue baby has a cluster of abnormalities known as "Fallot's tetralogy" (**4**). In some instances, the circulatory system may be able to cope without any surgical intervention. **M H**

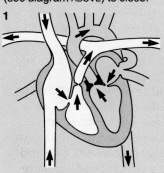

1

Narrowed aortic valve

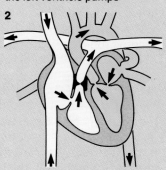

2

Narrowed pulmonary valve

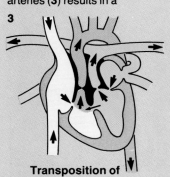

3

Transposition of the great arteries

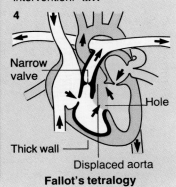

4

Narrow valve

Thick wall

Hole

Displaced aorta

Fallot's tetralogy

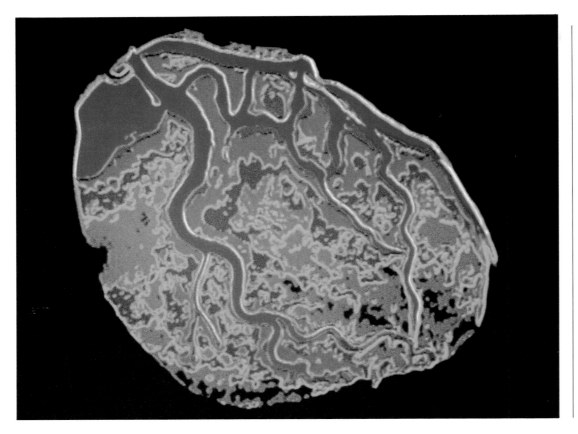

A network of arteries feeds the heart *in this computer image of the heart's outer surface. The interior walls do not absorb oxygen from the circulating blood that they pump – to feed oxygen to itself the heart must pump blood out into the aorta (the large red area in the upper left corner of the image) and through the network of coronary arteries that lie across the outer surface. The major cause of heart attacks is blockage of coronary arteries.*

The heart may be affected either early – within the first week – or later. The damage can be to the heart muscle itself or to the valves: the child can suffer heart failure, and the damage to the valves can be permanent. The best treatment when the heart has been affected by rheumatic fever is rest: in a small percentage of cases, the child should be given rest for a period of months rather than weeks. The condition can recur, so it is important that the child be put on a long-term course of antibiotics to avoid a further infection. If the child suffers another bout of tonsillitis, it is vital that you contact your doctor immediately.

A different cause of heart illness in children, and in adults, is *myocarditis* – inflammation of the cells of the heart muscle. This often follows a viral infection – influenza, for example – and can cause sudden death. The symptoms are extreme tiredness, shortness of breath, and a pulse rate far higher than the infection itself should produce.

Three-quarters of people suffering from moderate myocarditis recover within 6-8 weeks; others require up to six months, and in about 10 percent of cases there may be lasting heart damage. Because the course of myocarditis is so unpredictable it is important that, if you or your child have a flu-like illness involving fever and muscle pain, vigorous exercise should be avoided for at least 10 days; even after that, any return to exercise should be gradual. Many people have died through failure to rest when infected.

The cells lining the inside of the heart – the four chambers and the valves – are together named the endocardium. *Endocarditis* is inflammation of these cells. This inflammation is not dangerous if the heart is normal, but if there is any defect the risks can be serious. The condition commonly comes about because of bacterial infection. Our bodies are infested with bacteria, most of which are harmless. When we undergo even minor surgery – such as dental treatment – some of these bacteria can be released into the blood stream. Even then there is normally no problem: the body's defenses deal with the bacteria fairly rapidly. However, sometimes the bacteria can establish a foothold on abnormal tissue – for example, a defective heart valve. In such a case heart failure can be a fairly rapid result; otherwise you may suffer a "grumbling" illness for some weeks before the problem is suspected, diagnosed and treated.

This form of endocarditis – *infective endocarditis* – can be prevented by a course of antibiotics taken before any operation that might cause damage to infected tissues. The exact type and regime of antibiotics should be discussed not just with your normal doctor but with the surgeon who is to carry out the operation, since different approaches may be required if you have suffered from endocarditis before.

ARE YOU IN TOO GREAT A HURRY?

Time-urgency and stress can contribute to heart disease. To assess your own response to time pressure answer a frank yes or no to each of the following questions.

1 Do you bring work home from your job?
2 Does your work include frequent deadlines that are difficult to meet?
3 Do you think about your work at home?
4 Do you find it hard to fit

into the day everything you have to do?
5 Do you lack the time to prepare for contingencies – to think ahead about what you will do when a plan does not work as expected?
6 Do you find yourself hurrying and writing unclearly as you fill in checks or other routine papers?
7 Do you dislike taking the time to do jobs around the home?
8 Do you hurry when you are reading?
9 Do you feel guilty about resting?
10 Do you eat quickly?
11 Do you often feel impatient?
12 Do you find it almost unbearable to have to wait

in line or to travel behind a slow vehicle?
13 Do you find it irritating to watch people do things less quickly than you can?
14 Do you tend to evaluate performance in terms of numbers?
15 Do you gesture emphatically in conversation, eg clenching your fist, bringing it down on the table or pounding it into the palm of your other hand?
16 Do you have a tendency to

finish the sentences of others for them?
17 Do you frequently interrupt in conversation, and hurry others to finish what they are saying?
18 Do you speak more rapidly at the end of sentences?
19 Do you find yourself repeatedly bringing conversations around to yourself or subjects that interest you directly?
20 Do you pretend to listen to others while remaining preoccupied with your own thoughts?

Every yes answer scores 1 point. A person who scores 15 points or more should turn to page 59 and read about the type-A personality.

When does heart disease become a major threat?

Angina attacks, heart attacks and heart failure result from a variety of conditions commonly called "heart disease." Heart disease becomes a major threat in middle life and old age. It includes disabilities of the arteries supplying the heart, high blood pressure and defects in the valves of the heart. Irregularities in the heartbeat can also cause failure (see p44). High blood pressure and arterial disease in general are referred to as cardiovascular disease, which includes blockages and weaknesses of arteries in the brain that lead to strokes (see Ch4).

Heart attacks have become less common in recent years – largely because people have begun to realize that diet, exercise and smoking can affect the life of the heart – but they are still major killers. The risk factors for heart attacks include age: men under 30 rarely have heart attacks but they become prone over the age of 45; women do not become as susceptible until they are 60, although they begin to catch up after the menopause, 10 or so years earlier. But many other factors are involved. Death from heart disease is five times as likely for a smoker in the age range 34-45 than for a nonsmoker in this age group. Women over 35 who take the combined oral contraceptive pill (containing both estrogen and progesterone) are more at risk than others (see Ch10). A family history of heart attacks and high blood pressure is a predisposing factor that a person cannot control – the habits of eating a diet high in saturated fats and taking little exercise are ones they can (see p58).

What happens in an attack of angina?

Angina occurs when some part of the heart requires more oxygen than it can get from the blood reaching it through the coronary arteries – the arteries whose destination is the heart tissue itself. A heart weighing 300g (10oz) extracts from blood approximately 25ml (1.5 cubic inches) of oxygen every minute to satisfy its needs. The oxygen is used to produce the energy the coronary muscle cells need in order to contract. During increased activity, when the heart rate may double, the oxygen demand increases proportionally, and the blood-flow requirement in the coronary arteries may double. If the oxygen demands of the heart are greater than can be met by the supply of blood in the coronary arteries, then the cells of the heart are starved.

The commonest cause is that hardening and narrowing of the coronary arteries reduces their capacity to carry sudden increases in flow when the person is exercising or under stress.

More rarely, shortages occur when a disease of the heart valves affects the efficiency of the heart as it pumps blood into the arteries; or an anemic condition reduces the oxygen-carrying capacity of the blood.

Muscle cells short of oxygen can, if the shortage is not too severe, make up their deficiency of energy by exploiting chemical reactions that do not use oxygen. But these produce acid by-products, and this makes us feel the pain of muscle cramp. In angina it is the heart muscle that cramps – there is a pain in the center of the chest, which may spread to the neck, the jaw or the arms. The pain will go away after a rest or with the use of drugs called trinitrates that dilate the blood vessels.

What is a heart attack?

About two-fifths of heart-attack victims will have previously suffered attacks of angina, but in a heart attack, the oxygen supply to some part of the heart is restricted so severely that heart cells die. The usual cause is a coronary thrombosis, a collection of cells and blood products that completely blocks a coronary artery.

In about four-fifths of heart attacks the victim suffers pain in the chest or upper abdomen, often associated with nausea, sweating and indigestion, producing belching. The pain, more severe and longer lasting than angina, is often described as "crushing" or "squeezing" and may spread, like angina, to the neck, jaw or arms. Anxiety and palpitation often accompany it. Trinitrates – drugs that can be used to relieve or prevent angina – have no effect on this pain. Neither does an end to exertion stop it. Shortness of breath may be a further symptom, or – on rare occasions – the only symptom occurring.

There is a 50 percent chance that a heart attack will so badly interrupt the flow of oxygenated blood to the body that it ends in death. One-quarter of victims die within two hours, and a further one-quarter die within 20 days. Those who survive longer may still suffer heart failure, angina, further heart attacks or other complications. It may take a long time to recover completely, and in the period immediately following the attack the victim is especially susceptible to further attacks.

Does blood pressure increase with age?

More than 10 percent of people in Western countries are hypertensive (they have high blood pressure) and they are consequently six times more likely to suffer a heart attack than the rest of the population.

If a person is at risk of a heart attack due to the hardening and narrowing of the coronary arteries by which the heart receives its own blood supply, high blood pressure will significantly contribute to the risk – it forces the heart to work harder than it should and to be all the more likely to need more oxygen than the coronary arteries can supply.

High blood pressure also contributes to the arterial disease itself – when blood is forced through the arteries at high pressure, the arterial walls are more likely to be damaged. Narrow, inflexible arteries, in turn, raise blood pressure by creating a high resistance to the flow.

The incidence of hypertension increases with age.

TREATING HIGH BLOOD PRESSURE

Individual records show the range of blood pressure, from lowest (in sleep) to highest (in moments of excitement and exertion), in three people who wore 24-hour monitors. Both systolic and diastolic pressures (see p52) are shown.

The normal range shows much lower peaks than the moderately and dangerously hypertensive ones – their high peaks of blood pressure threaten to damage arteries.

Drug treatment is called for. From the wide range of available drugs, a doctor can usually find at least one that is free of side effects for a particular patient.

Blood pressure (mm) chart showing values 40, 80, 120, 160, 200, 240, 280, 320. Categories: Normal (Seated in doctor's office, Systolic, Diastolic), Moderately hypertensive, Dangerously hypertensive.

Drugs to lower blood pressure

Type	Some examples	Some effects	Possible side effects
Diuretics	Bendro-fluazide, hydrochlorothiazide	Increase water and salt excretion, relax blood vessels	Dizziness, impotence, diabetes
Adrenaline blockers (beta-blockers)	Propranolol, metoprolol	Slow the heart, reduce strength of contraction	Tiredness, nightmares, cold hands and feet, heart failure, impotence
Calcium channel blockers	Verapamil, nifedipine	Relax blood vessels, reduce strength of contraction	Headaches, palpitations, constipation, swollen legs
Blood vessel relaxers	Prazosin, indoramid, hydrallazine	Reduce arterial resistance	Headaches, facial flushing, dizziness

Some victims of very high blood pressure feel head-aches, palpitations and a general feeling of ill-health, but usually there are no symptoms. Thus if you are over 40, and you have a family history of hypertension or are overweight, you should have your blood pressure checked.

Not only the incidence of hypertension but its definition changes with age. A person aged 15 with a blood pressure of 160/100 (the first figure is the systolic pressure, the second figure the diastolic – see p40) has something to worry about, but this level would be perfectly acceptable in someone aged 80. At any age, if your diastolic blood pressure is below about 100, you have little cause for concern.

In the developed countries, blood pressure tends to rise until people are in their seventies and then levels off or even declines. One European study found an average of 183/101 at age 72. Rising blood pressure is probably not an integral aspect of aging – it appears not to occur in Fijians or Amazonian Indians.

The causes of high blood pressure remain obscure in the vast majority of cases. It is possible that it arises because of abnormalities in the flux of certain ions across the muscular walls of blood vessels, or in the circulation of some hormones. Whatever the cause, it is more likely to occur in people with a family history of the disease. This is a factor beyond our control. Diet and lifestyle, however, also contribute, and these are factors that we can control (see p58). MH

What is hardening of the arteries?

Atherosclerosis is commonly described as "hardening of the arteries." In fact, equally important is that this condition also *narrows* the arteries, making the heart work harder to pump blood through them. The strain exerted on the heart can be so great that it fails. Hardening and narrowing of the arteries is responsible for more deaths in developed countries than any other disease.

The arteries can be blocked in various ways, but in each case the start of the process is when platelets (cells in the blood that help clotting), cholesterol (a fat carried in the blood) and fibrous tissue accumulate in clumps on the arterial wall. The flow of blood through the artery naturally slows – possibly to the extent that a *thrombosis* occurs, in which a clump of cells blocks the artery.

A thrombosis may occur if blood leaks into a clump on the wall of the narrowed section, so that it swells up and blocks the artery; or it may occur if a body of platelets may form in one place, become detached, drift along with the blood flow, and lodge itself in an even narrower artery.

The degree of danger obviously depends on both the importance of the artery involved and the amount by

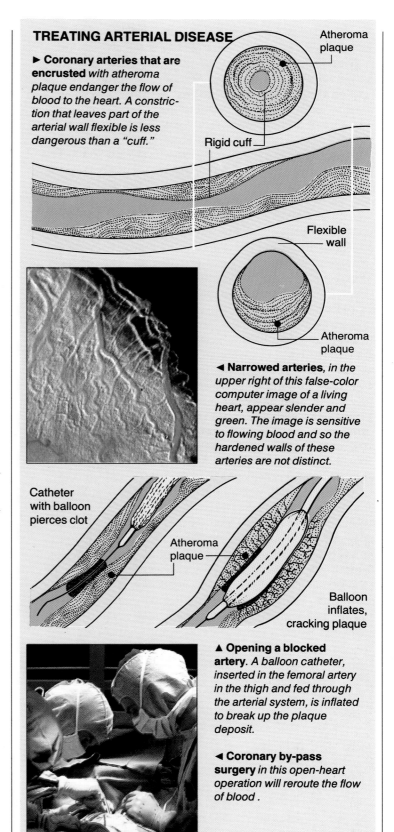

TREATING ARTERIAL DISEASE

► **Coronary arteries that are encrusted** with atheroma plaque endanger the flow of blood to the heart. A constriction that leaves part of the arterial wall flexible is less dangerous than a "cuff."

Atheroma plaque

Rigid cuff

Flexible wall

Atheroma plaque

◄ **Narrowed arteries**, in the upper right of this false-color computer image of a living heart, appear slender and green. The image is sensitive to flowing blood and so the hardened walls of these arteries are not distinct.

Catheter with balloon pierces clot

Atheroma plaque

Balloon inflates, cracking plaque

▲ **Opening a blocked artery**. A balloon catheter, inserted in the femoral artery in the thigh and fed through the arterial system, is inflated to break up the plaque deposit.

◄ **Coronary by-pass surgery** in this open-heart operation will reroute the flow of blood .

which it is narrowed. Arterial disease can affect the circulation as a whole, but in individual sufferers some parts of the body are likely to be much more severely affected than others.

Sometimes narrow and inflexible arteries are merely limited in their ability to increase the blood supply when cells are demanding additional oxygen or nutrients – a stressed heart will produce pains of angina during exercise, for example, if coronary arteries are partly blocked. But sometimes the organ or extremity, or part of it, can be completely starved of blood. In this latter case, starved cells will die. When a region of the heart dies, this creates the severe pain of a heart attack, and death may be only a short distance away. The other main parts of the body likely to be affected by arterial disease are the brain and the legs. In the arteries that supply the head it can result in strokes (see *Ch4*). Disease in the arteries of the legs can cause pain in the calves (claudication) during exercise; if this condition is not checked, it can lead to gangrene. It is much rarer for the arteries supplying the kidneys and intestine to be affected to the extent that life is threatened.

Is hardening of the arteries inevitable with age?

Hardening and narrowing of the arteries is certainly related to aging, but other factors influence its rate of progress. In Japan and other countries whose diet differs markedly from that common in the West, coronary artery disease is only rarely a cause of death among people in their late 60s. People who do not smoke are much less likely to suffer than people who do; any steps you take to reduce your blood pressure are helpful. It is probable, although not proved, that people who take regular exercise are less likely to suffer from the condition; similarly, reducing your weight and avoiding foods that are high in saturated fats (see p58) will help.

In these respects you can reduce your chances of dying young from atherosclerosis. Other factors are harder to control – your personality, for example. If you easily become angry and easily allow yourself to become anxious about wasting time – for example, in traffic jams – in other words, if you are a "type-A personality" (see p59) – your arteries may be suffering.

Some factors, such as your sex (men are more likely to suffer than women) and your heredity, are completely beyond your control.

The incidence of heart disease has declined fairly spectacularly in some of the developed countries in recent years since it has become known that changes in behavior (such as giving up smoking and reducing the amount of saturated fat in the diet) can reduce the likelihood of your having a heart attack. The reduction in deaths from heart disease has been most marked in the United States. By contrast, the rates in some of the countries of the Eastern Bloc have shot up, as have those in, for example, New Zealand and Sweden.

How does aging affect the heart?

There is still a great deal we do not know about how aging affects the human body. There are two reasons for our ignorance. The first is that it is difficult to differentiate between the effects of age-related diseases and those of aging itself. The second is that, when people retire, they tend to give up many forms of physical activity, so that the physical fitness of their muscles, heart and lungs tends to decline through lack of use.

At rest, the healthy heart works perfectly well even in very old people, although the amount of blood pumped per minute is usually less, and the heart is less able to increase its rate to compensate for the extra demands of physical exertion. Similarly, the amount of oxygen we can use in a minute declines: for the average woman of 70 or 75, merely walking at 5km per hour (3mph) may represent the upper limit of aerobic exercise that she can perform. It is believed that regular exercise maintained throughout most of adult life can delay this decline.

So far as the heart muscle itself is concerned, the process of aging appears to produce few changes. A brown pigment called lipofuscin accumulates in the cells; this seems to be a waste product and perfectly harmless. Another chemical, amyloid, is found in small deposits between the cells, but again this appears to have no harmful effects.

Some of the tissues that conduct the cardiac impulse may be replaced by fibrous tissue, bringing about a dangerously slow heart rate (see p49). Also, the valves of the heart can attract deposits of calcium, so that their effectiveness is reduced. NC

How long does it take to recover from a heart attack?

Recovery from a heart attack can take a long time, since the tissues of the heart, like those of the nervous system, cannot regenerate: healing is by a process of scar formation, not muscle-cell replacement.

Until the early 1980s there was a lot of debate about the best way of treating someone who had survived a heart attack. The main point of contention was *where* the treatment should be carried out: some studies showed that rest and pain relief at home in bed were more likely to produce recovery than the bright lights and general fuss of a hospital coronary unit. More recently, ideas have changed as methods of treatment have improved.

In particular, there are now drugs – such as streptokinase and tissue-plasminogen activator – that can be used to unblock the arteries by breaking up the throm-

▼ ECG recordings during recovery from a heart attack *show distortion and then a gradual return to normal. In this patient, the T wave, produced by changes in the electrical activity of the heart as the ventricles relax, at first appears exaggerated. After months, the T wave becomes more normal. However, in the deep Q wave, which may last for the rest of the patient's life, there is persisting evidence of heart-muscle scarring.*

◄ Hospitalization for at least 10 days *following a mild heart attack is recommended for patients of any age. The advantages of resting in familiar home surroundings are outweighed by the availability of immediate attention. After a mild attack, stairs should not be attempted for three weeks and work and normal activity should wait for 8-12 weeks.*

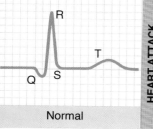
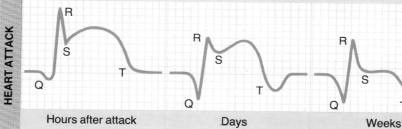
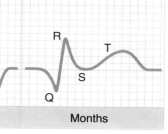

| Normal | HEART ATTACK | Hours after attack | Days | Weeks | Months |

bosis that is usually the cause of a heart attack. If irreversible damage to the heart muscle is to be prevented, these drugs have to be administered – by injection – within an hour of the onset of severe chest pain. The injections have to be done in hospital (although this may change in the future).

It is therefore now believed that even people who have suffered uncomplicated heart attacks are best treated in hospital.

Later treatment should be directed toward the prevention of further attacks. The patient is likely to be given drugs called beta-blockers, which protect the heart from further stress. Also, the blood should be thinned, initially using warfarin and then later using low doses of aspirin.

If the attack has been only a mild one, the first two or three days should be spent resting in bed, with adequate pain relief and properly administered leg exercises. After three days, assuming that there is no recurrent pain, abnormality of heart rhythm, or heart failure, the patient should be up and about for at least part of the time, and by the end of one week able to walk on the level.

After 10 days the patient may be allowed home from hospital, and should take a gradually increased amount of exercise. After three weeks it should be possible to climb a flight of stairs or have sex – perhaps some while later in the case of sex. Driving a car should be avoided for at least six weeks. Within 8-12 weeks after a mild heart attack it should be possible to return to work and normal activity.

What is heart failure?

Heart failure is the inability of the heart to pump efficiently enough – for example, due to valve faults or loss of muscle cells in heart attacks. This causes an increase of pressure in veins, the blood vessels leading to the heart. They may leak fluid into the tissues.

When the left side of the heart fails, fluid leaks from the veins into the lungs. The main symptom is breathlessness, especially after exercise or when the victim is tired. If the lungs become badly congested, there may be chest pains and blood in the phlegm. The lung fluid becomes vulnerable to infections such as pneumonia.

When the right side of the heart fails, fluid accumulates in the lower regions of the body, with swelling in the ankles, or – in someone who is bedridden – the lower back. An accompanying symptom is weariness.

When both sides of the heart fail, the condition is known as congestive heart failure. **MH**

Preventing Heart Attacks

Timely attention to diet and lifestyle can forestall or delay heart-threatening ailments

IN SPITE of the excellent available medical attention, your chances of surviving a heart attack are only one in two. By far the most effective way to take advantage of medical knowledge about heart attacks is to use it for prevention. You can save your life by reporting early symptoms to your doctor and by adopting a low-risk lifestyle.

How can medical treatment help?

A person who is at risk of heart attacks may have warning symptoms – angina, from narrowing of the coronary arteries, or headache from hypertension. If these symptoms are reported to a doctor, the risk can be calculated on the basis of blood cholesterol level, cigarette smoking, family history and blood pressure. An electrocardiogram (ECG – see p44) will indicate whether the heart is functioning normally. If you report symptoms of angina, but have a normal ECG, exercise testing may be given – by this technique, the ECG is monitored continuously while you walk on a treadmill that increases in speed and angle of incline. Changes in the ECG will indicate if there is a shortage of oxygen in parts of the heart muscle at times of increased demand.

Angina and ECG abnormalities may prompt your doctor to arrange for angiography – X-ray imaging of the coronary arteries to assess the degree of narrowing. If a serious blockage is discovered in an artery it can be removed either by blowing up a balloon in the artery (transluminal angioplasty –

see p55) or by replacing a section of the artery with vein grafts (coronary artery by-pass grafting).

There is no evidence that treatment of *mildly* elevated blood pressure is of benefit, but it is important to bring down a moderate or severe elevation (a diastolic blood pressure of 105 or over in a person younger than 65, or of 110 or over past that age). Drug treatments are available (see p54).

Foods and drinks to avoid

Medical treatment can combat the effects of high blood pressure and arterial disease, and so can a healthy lifestyle. Lifestyle, moreover, can help to prevent these conditions from developing in the first place.

Food and drink play a major

PREVENTING HEART ATTACKS WITH DIET

Arterial disease leading to strokes and heart attacks is associated with high levels of the blood-fat cholesterol, and high levels of cholesterol are associated with too much fat in the diet.

The simplest way to avoid a diet that promotes a high level of cholesterol in your blood is to stay away from high-fat foods in general. It may be useful to note, however, that only the "saturated" fats (with a simpler chemical structure than "monounsaturated" and "polyunsaturated" fats) are blamed for heart disease. Some high-fat foods, such as peanut butter and olive oil are relatively low in saturated fats.

This list RIGHT shows the saturated fat content by percentage of weight for a range of common foods.

There is some evidence that a balance of monounsaturated and polyunsaturated

SATURATED FAT CONTENT (% of total weight)	
60	Butter
58	Whipping cream
45	Palm oil
43	Lard
40-6	Most cheeses
37	Roast lamb shoulder, hard margarine
33	Salami, soft margarine
31	Pork belly
29	Luncheon meat
27	Grilled pork sausages
25	Rich pastries
24	Polyunsaturated margarine, bacon
23	Ice cream
22	Cottage cheese
21	Eggs, corned beef
19	Peanut oil, roast chicken with skin, roast leg of lamb, sponge cake
16	Corn oil, mackerel
15	Peanut butter, baked salmon, fruitcake
14	Olive oil, boiled ham
13	Sunflower seed oil, lean roast leg of pork, calf's liver, roast duck without skin
12	Tinned tuna, salmon, sardines
11	Roast chicken without skin, lean beef, avocados
10	Safflower oil, low-fat natural yogurt
6	Roast turkey without skin
4	Oysters
3	Muesli, boiled lobster, oat porridge
2	Bread, baked cod
1	Fresh skimmed milk
0-1	Macaroni, cornflakes, rice, boiled potatoes

fats helps to prevent heart disease. Olive oil (70 percent unsaturated and 11 percent polyunsaturated) may be of positive benefit in keeping levels of blood cholesterol down, because of chemical interaction between the three kinds of fat after being absorbed into the body.

There is also evidence that eating oat porridge reduces blood cholesterol. It has been argued too that beans and pulses, wholewheat foods, natural yogurt and even garlic and onions may have an anticholesterol effect.

TAKING YOUR TIME ABOUT LOSING WEIGHT

If you are more than 40 percent over-weight you run twice the risk of dying from disease of the coronary arteries, and even though the risk is smaller if you are not as obese as this, it is still bound to be one that is worth reducing. With each pound you lose, you eliminate tissue that requires oxygenated blood. Thus you reduce the number of blood vessels that need to be pumped full of blood, and thereby reduce the strain on your heart and the coronary arteries feeding it.

There are two ways in which excess weight can be lost. One is to take more physical exercise, so that your body uses more energy. The other – dieting – should be thought of as a long-term affair: "miracle" diets, which claim to be able to reduce your weight startlingly in a very short time, can place heavy demands on your body and well-being. The ideal is both to adopt a sensible diet – one that you can feel comfortable with indefini-tely – and start taking sufficient exercise – initially not too strenuous.

Most of the energy we get from food we eat is used to fuel normal body function-ing: only a small proportion is used for repair and maintenance. The amount of food you need depends on your level of physical activity and your basal metabolic rate – or BMR – which is the amount of energy your body requires just to keep ticking over at rest. The BMR differs from one person to the next. It is generally lower in women than in men, and in the elderly than in children. During periods of stress or tension it may be considerably elevated. Disorders of the thyroid gland, too, can affect the BMR.

We become overweight when we eat more food than we need to keep up with our BMR and to fuel exertion. The excess energy is stored mainly in the form of fats, most commonly in the tissues under the skin. The reason the body stores fats is so that it can draw on the energy at a later date when food is in short supply. The problem of excess weight arises because, for many people, that future moment of need never arrives.

If you eat far more than your body gen-uinely requires you will become over-weight very quickly. But, over a long period of time, even a trivial daily excess can cause significant increase; for example, if you daily consume an excess of just 250 Calories (250Kcal – equivalent to two thick slices of white bread), by the end of a year you will have contributed 10kg (22lb) to your weight. **AS**

Are you too fat? *Check your weight against your height, or see if you can pinch a fold of fat more than 25mm (1in) thick at your waist.*

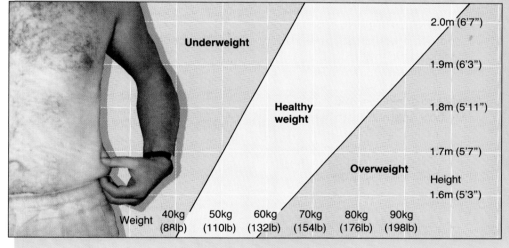

role. Caffeine, in coffee and tea, for example, increases blood pressure, both systolic and dias-tolic: 200mg of caffeine – the amount in a cup of strong tea or coffee – causes a rise of about 10mm that lasts for 2 hours. Cigarette smoking causes an increase that lasts for a shorter period unless it is combined with drinking coffee. The effect of caffeine and cigarette smoke is cumulative.

Alcohol causes an increase in blood pressure with even moder-ate levels of intake. Many studies have shown that alcohol with-drawal produces a drop of 10-15mg. The drop is reversed when alcohol consumption is resumed (this is one of the reasons why patients often achieve normal levels of blood pressure on admission to hospital and then go back to high levels when they leave).

Foods high in saturated fats contribute to a high level of choles-terol in the blood, and this is closely associated with hardening and narrowing of the arteries. To be avoided, except in moderation, are fried foods, egg yolks, high-fat dairy products (such as butter, cream and most cheese), fat meat, sausages and the skin of fowl. An additional strategy, if your doctor advises it, is to decrease the clot-ting power of your blood by taking a 300mg tablet of aspirin twice a week.

Diet can affect blood pressure through influencing the total quantity of blood that the heart needs to pump. Many studies have shown that hypertensive patients have increased concentra-tions of sodium in their tissue fluids. This has the effect of retain-ing fluid in the body (see *Ch 9*). Since sodium is one of the ele-ments in common table salt, it appears that avoiding the habit of adding extra salt to your food in the kitchen and at the table can help in preventing high blood pressure. Most people are able to excrete the great excess of salt that they commonly add to their food – but you might be one of those who cannot do this efficiently: the solution is to take no more than, or little more than, your body requires – you probably only *need* about as much as your food contains naturally, unless you are a very strict vegetarian who eats no fish and no dairy products.

Another important aspect of diet is the body weight that results. If you are overweight you are at a much higher risk of developing high blood pressure and arterial disease, and of needing your heart to pump harder than it can when you have to exert yourself or cope with emotional stress.

How does exercise help?

In the short term, exercise has an immediate lowering effect on blood pressure – about 10-12mm. The effect lasts a number of hours. Sufficient regular exercise has a long-term effect of dropping blood pressure by a further 10mm. Exercise is also an effective form of weight control, and, since training increases the efficiency and resilience of the heart muscle, it makes it possible to achieve a high cardiac output – when coping with sudden high demands – without your heart requiring as much oxygen as a less fit person's would.

Remember that if you are unfit, ill or heavily overweight, or if exercise produces dizziness or pain, you should not engage in a vigorous program of exercise, and you should probably consult your doctor. "Unfit" here means that your pulse rate is more than 120 beats per minute after sitting down following three minutes of moderate exercise (see *Ch 7*).

A *vigorous* program of exercise is not strictly necessary. If you are very unfit, swimming two or three lengths of a standard pool two or three times a week will make you feel better and gradually it will probably make you want more exercise. To maintain an adequate level of fitness, it may be enough to swim a leisurely 10 lengths three or four times a week or walk

EXERCISING YOUR HEART

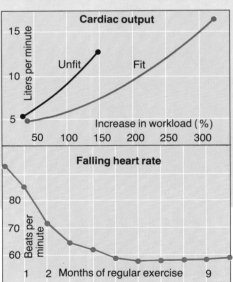

■ A fit man can make more efficient use of oxygen, and so he does not need to increase by as much the volume of blood he pumps per minute (cardiac output) as demand on the heart increases TOP LEFT. In addition, he can go on increasing his cardiac output after an unfit man has reached his limit. BOTTOM LEFT A middle-aged man's resting pulse rate drops dramatically over several months after he has introduced a moderate level of regular exercise into his lifestyle.

20 miles briskly during each week. If you do not have the time to walk, then jog. Thirty minutes a day of exercise that is challenging enough to make your heart beat faster is quite sufficient. MH

How does relaxation help?

Avoiding tension is another way to keep blood pressure down – and to prevent the moments of high stress that may trigger a heart attack.

Keeping tension down is not always easy. Your personal level of stress reflects any momentous life-changing events that you are undergoing, such as bereavement – men are particularly vulnerable to heart attacks in the six months following a wife's death. It also reflects pressure in your work and family life and all of the daily irritations that you have to put up with. Most importantly, it reflects your style of coping with these strains. Their effect is cumulative and if your response to them as they pile up is to feel desperately helpless or furiously angry, this too adds to the sum of stress experienced. People who believe that they can keep control of their life in spite of adverse circumstances and who do not anger

LEARNING TO RELAX

Heart specialists have identified a personality that is especially prone to heart attacks and high blood pressure – the "type-A personality." This personality combines an intense, hard-driving competitiveness and a persistent sense of time urgency with an easily roused hostility. The contrasting type-B personality is relaxed and easy-going.

You are not necessarily one or the other – in its most recent refinement, the idea of the type-A personality sees hostility as the crucial element – people who are hard-driving and very concerned about not wasting time, but do not rise easily to anger, are not included in the type-A category.

In a pilot project carried out over four years in San Francisco, counseling against type-A behavior, combined with training in relaxation techniques, was effective in preventing heart attacks. Rates of heart-attack recurrence fell in a group who were trained to practice patience in situations that previously had made them angry if they could not beat the clock. They learned to avoid frustration about failing to get through traffic lights before they turn red, for example, by practicing a drill of backtracking one block every time they found themselves hurrying to reach a green light. **AER**

▼ **Unwinding with a favorite piece of music** *may be enough to loosen tense muscles to the degree that blood pressure drops. Consciously tensing and relaxing muscles one by one is a more proven relaxation therapy.*

easily seem to be at a lower level of risk for stress-related illnesses.

It can be life-saving for people who are under pressure to plan for adequate rest and relaxation in the evenings and at weekends. It can also help greatly to include regular sessions of relaxation therapy in a busy life.

Maximum relaxation for a minimum investment of time

Sitting idly is not necessarily an effective way of winding down. Mastery of a relaxation technique can give you a skill that helps you to control your level of tension anywhere, at any time. Here are the instructions for a technique developed in the 1930s and widely used today – "progressive muscle relaxation."

This technique consists of first tensing then letting go each of the main muscle groups in your body and learning to associate the word "Relax" with the feeling of letting go. You should spend about 15 minutes per day practicing. Gradually, you will reach deeper levels of relaxation, and reach them more quickly. Eventually it should become possible to feel fully relaxed even in a crisis, simply by saying the word "Relax" to yourself or by taking one or two deep breaths.

1 Sit or lie comfortably with your eyes closed.
2 Breathe deeply. Hold your breath for a moment and then let it out slowly. You will feel yourself becoming more relaxed. Repeat this step two more times.
3 Breathe more naturally and allow yourself to think only of your breath going easily in and out as you feel more and more relaxed.

In steps 4-13 tense the particular muscles mentioned for 5-10 seconds, let them go and let your mind dwell for about 30 seconds

on how relaxed they are. The tensing will help you to recognize muscle tension more quickly later and know when you need to relax. The contrast between muscle tension and what you feel afterward will enhance the relaxation.

4 Clench your fists tightly, then let your hands go limp.
5 Press your hands to your shoulders with arms tense, then let your arms go limp.
6 Tense and then relax your shoulders.
7 Put your chin on your chest to make your neck tense, then let your neck go limp.
8 Close your eyes tightly, then relax and feel the relaxation in your upper face.
9 Clench your jaw, then relax it and feel the relaxation in your lower face.
10 Tense and relax your stomach and chest.
11 Tense and relax your thighs and buttocks.
12 Tense and relax your calves and legs.
13 Tense your feet, curl your toes, and then let them relax.
14 Allow a few moments of rest with calm and regular breathing. Allow yourself to feel comforted by your sense of relaxation. Let the relaxation spread deeper and deeper.
15 Allow a wave of relaxation to pass through each part of your body. If you can feel tension anywhere, let it flow away.
16 Think of the relaxation everywhere in your body.
17 Think of the easy flow of your breathing, in and out.
18 Spend about a minute thinking of the word "Relax" each time you breathe out and thinking of how relaxed you feel.
19 Count slowly from 1 to 10, feeling progressively more refreshed and awake. Open your eyes. You will feel refreshed, awake and relaxed. **AER**

3 BREATHING

The outward signs are a rhythmic rising and falling of the chest, breath moving in and breath moving out. Inwardly, the sign that the respiratory system is working well is a rich supply of oxygen reaching every cell of the body. Key cells, especially in the brain, have only minutes to live if breathing or the circulation stops.

HOW FAST CAN WE BREATHE?

A healthy adult can breathe in a lungful of air in just less than one second and breathe it out in just more than one second. We can therefore go through a complete cycle of breathing about 30 times each minute. We can keep up this rate, under exercise, for 20 minutes or even longer:

the respiratory muscles do not tire easily and healthy lungs can normally meet the greatest demands put on them. The rhythm of our breathing during heavy exercise is regulated automatically by the brain; trying to impose control over it will have no useful effect.

Breathing in

Breathing out

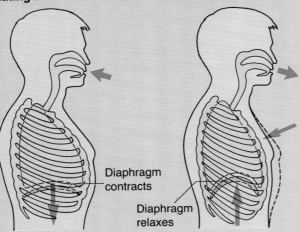

Diaphragm contracts

Diaphragm relaxes

Rib positions

When we inhale, the chest rises as the chest cavity increases in size. This happens because the diaphragm contracts and flattens, and muscles around the ribs contract, pulling them upward and outward. At the same time the lungs expand and air is dragged in.

When we exhale, the chest falls as the cavity returns to its previous size. The diaphragm and muscles around the ribs relax, and the ribs return to their rest position. The lungs empty themselves until they are half full of air. On average, at rest, we breathe out 18-20 times every minute.

BREATHING comes naturally to us; we rarely have to think about it. When we are asleep it just happens. During our waking hours we unconsciously interrupt our cycle of breathing when we cry, get water on our faces or sense something toxic in the air. When we take exercise we breathe more frequently and more deeply, but again this is an automatic response. If we are speaking or singing, however, we do deliberately alter our breathing pattern, although the reaction may be so commonplace that we do not notice what we are doing.

The act of breathing in is not quite as simple an operation as we might imagine it to be. The process starts in the depths of the brain, when sufficient quantities of the waste gas carbon dioxide have accumulated there for the brain to send out the command to inhale. This message is sent down many nerves – to the nose, mouth, pharynx, larynx, diaphragm and chest wall. The signal contains instructions to those muscles that oppose inhalation (for example, those that seal the nose and throat) that they should relax, as well as telling the muscles of the chest wall that they should make the wall expand.

Why do our chests rise and fall as we breathe?

The chest wall consists of a rigid pelvic bowl, a vertical stack of vertebrae and ribs hanging from the upper dozen vertebrae. The ribs are joined together at the front by the sternum (breastbone). The main muscle responsible for our breathing in is the diaphragm, a large dome-shaped muscle that forms the floor of the ribcage. When the diaphragm contracts it can do one of two things – or often, both of them together. First, if the abdominal wall is relaxed, the diaphragm pushes the contents of the abdomen downward and outward, so that the ribcage expands vertically. Conversely, if the abdominal wall is held tense so that the diaphragm cannot push the (incompressible) abdominal contents downward, the muscle instead acts in such a way that its edges haul the ribs upward and outward, so that the ribcage is expanded horizontally. As we might expect, if the abdominal wall is partly relaxed, the diaphragm expands the ribcage both horizontally and vertically, although in each case to a lesser extent.

The inner surface of the ribcage is lined by a moist membrane that slides over but stays tightly attached to a similar membrane covering the lungs. As the ribcage expands, this outer membrane expands along with it, and so the surfaces of the lungs are likewise dragged outwards. The net effect is that the lungs expand, and it is this that drags in the new breath of air.

Moving the ribs is not as easy an affair as it might seem. Each of them is linked by a pair of joints to the spinal column behind and by a joint to the breastbone in front. Furthermore, although each of the ribs has a different shape from each of the others, all of them must move smoothly in and out together as we take a breath. Clearly, if a joint on one rib should happen to stick, this would be likely to jam up the movements of all the others; in fact, the joints are designed to give and slide a little so that this does not happen.

When we are sleeping or at rest the process of exhalation – breathing out – is fairly simple. Healthy lungs have to be stretched quite firmly for us to be able to inhale, and when this pull is relaxed the lungs empty themselves as if they were balloons until they are about half full. As they do so they pull the ribcage inward.

This passive form of exhalation needs to be speeded up and deepened when we are taking exercise. The necessary commands come from the brain, which tells the inspiratory muscles to relax, the abdominal muscles

Controlling the way we breathe. *Particularly when singing a sustained quiet note, the urge to breathe in can be quite dramatically postponed. We can usually do this without conscious planning: when we sing or talk while sitting or exercising only lightly, the brain accepts the conflicting needs of this*

activity and of breathing and works out a program that satisfies both. However, when the level of exertion rises, the brain gives priority to the lungs, as anyone knows who has tried to hold a conversation just after running a race.

THE LUNGS

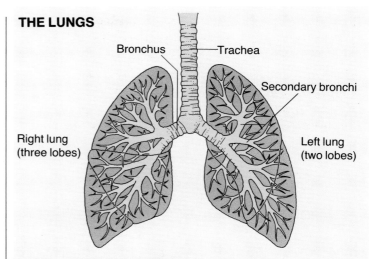

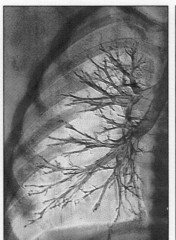

The lungs are a key meeting place *for the respiratory and circulatory systems. ABOVE The main tube (bronchus) carrying air into and out of each lung branches from the trachea and divides into smaller and smaller passages. LEFT The pulmonary artery carries blood depleted of oxygen from the heart to the lungs. Inside the lungs arteries branch out into smaller and smaller blood vessels until capillaries and air sacs lie side by side.*

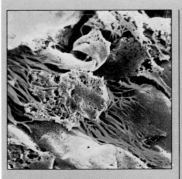

Feathery projections, *here magnified more than 3,000 times, constantly beat inside each bronchus, helping to remove dust particles by pushing them back toward the trachea. Mucus (seen in yellow in this image) also filters out dust, and removes harmful gases.*

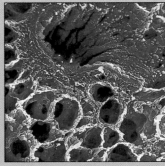

A bronchiole, *(a tiny branch of the bronchial system) carries air to a network of alveoli, minute sacs here magnified 135 times, where oxygen and carbon dioxide are exchanged. The millions of alveoli in each lung fill and empty more than 15,000 times a day.*

to tauten so that the diaphragm is driven upward, and other muscles to act in such a way that they pull the ribs downward and inward. The net effect of all these actions is to make exhalation faster and deeper than it would otherwise have been.

As the chest wall applies pressure to the outside of the lungs it tends to squash the airways. This means that we are not able to breathe out as rapidly as we can breathe in. At most the lungs can be forced down to one-quarter of their maximum gas volume before the airways shut off completely, so that no further air can escape.

Is there any danger in breathing too quickly?

The main purpose of breathing is to prevent a build-up of carbon dioxide in the body. This build-up is especially unwelcome in the head: the brain requires a fixed level of carbon dioxide so that its acidity can be properly regulated and the nerves can function correctly. If there is too much carbon dioxide the nerves slow down and become anesthetized, whereas if there is a shortage they become jumpy and excitable. It is in order to avoid these

HOW DO ANESTHETICS AFFECT BREATHING?

People can be anesthetized to depths that vary from one Martini down to the total paralysis that is required for many surgical operations. The control of breathing is one of the last automatic skills to go as people sink into deeper and deeper anesthesia.

Fortunately, anesthetists are skilled in helping your lungs breathe for you. They have many suitable techniques to choose from, but the key is the close monitoring of the level of carbon dioxide in your lungs and blood. Over short periods the anesthetist can operate manually, squeezing a balloon time and again to send the right-sized puff of fresh gas into your lungs. Changes in the volume and stiffness of your chest tell the anesthetist when it is the right time to supply each new puff. For longer periods, highly sophisticated mechanical ventilators can be used to do the same.

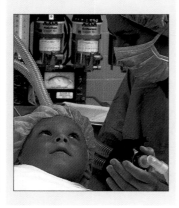

DEEP SEA BREATHING

To stay underwater for more than a minute or two you must take a supply of air with you. This air has to be breathed at the pressure of the surrounding water which, at depth, will be much greater than normal air pressure. The resulting problems depend on two times: how long you stay underwater and how long you take to return to the surface.

All the time you are underwater you are absorbing more nitrogen than you would at sea level. This nitrogen dis-

solves in all the tissues of the body but especially in the fatty insulating tissues that surround the nerves. At depths greater than about 50m (165ft) this can cause serious problems, because the poisoned tissues act on the nerves in such a way as to cause confusion and seeming drunkenness. This condition is termed nitrogen narcosis.

Even if you have dived to a shallower depth the absorption of nitrogen can cause difficulties should you ascend to the surface too quickly. The condition named the bends

(or more formally, decompression sickness) occurs because the nitrogen comes out of solution in bubbles, and these bubbles can block blood vessels and cause other tissue damage as they expand. If you do not stay down too long, and if you do not come up too quickly, you should not suffer from the bends (see graph BELOW).

Of course, we do not always have a choice in the matter: sometimes divers must make emergency ascents. One of the commonest causes of fatalities among divers is when, during an emergency ascent, they obey the instinct to hold onto the air in their lungs as long as possible, with the result that their lungs burst.

It is important, therefore, to breathe out continuously if for some reason you have to come to the surface in a hurry. Better still, try never to get into a situation where you might have to.

How long before you get the bends?

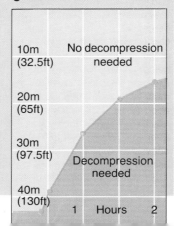

10m (32.5ft)	No decompression needed
20m (65ft)	
30m (97.5ft)	
40m (130ft)	Decompression needed

1 Hours 2

extremes that the brain automatically regulates breathing so precisely. If for some reason this system breaks down – for example, because you consciously decide to overbreathe or underbreathe – the brain adjusts its local blood flow.

If too much carbon dioxide has been lost from the brain through overbreathing, the blood flow is slowed down. One effect of this is to deprive the brain of fresh oxygen, and poor functioning or even unconsciousness can result. It is not known why the brain prefers to run the risks of oxygen deprivation rather than suffer a

shortage of carbon dioxide. The effect of underbreathing is that excessive carbon dioxide builds up in the brain. The flow in the region's blood vessels is accelerated, so that more carbon dioxide can be lost.

Most of the time our brain sorts out the pattern of our breathing without any trouble. Sometimes, though, people can overbreathe because of subconscious anxiety. We do not fully understand why this happens but it can lead to all sorts of odd sensations and twitchiness, together named the hyperventilation syndrome. The syndrome is recognized by a low level of carbon dioxide

HIGH ALTITUDE BREATHING

The higher you go, the lower the air pressure becomes, so that the brain receives less oxygen. The effects of this vary, but here is a very rough guide:

- above 3,000m (10,000ft): you feel slightly light-headed and make occasional mistakes
- above 4,500m (15,000ft): you suffer more confusion and make more frequent errors
- above 6,000m (20,000ft): you are very lethargic and very unreliable
- at 7,500m (25,000ft): you stay conscious for at best a minute or two
- at 9,000m (30,000ft): you lose consciousness within 30 seconds

These figures, of course, refer only to instances where people are abruptly exposed to low air pressure, as when an airplane loses compression. The situation is quite different when people have had a chance to acclimatize to the conditions; after all, 5 percent of the world's population lives at altitudes in excess of 3,000m (10,000ft) without being noticeably light-headed, and many communities live at much higher altitudes. So far about 25 mountaineers have reached the summit of Everest, 8,848m (29,028ft) above sea level, without the use of oxygen.

Given time your body can

deploy a series of defenses against the lack of oxygen. The first line of protection is a short-term one: the heart rate increases markedly so that the blood flow does likewise. Within a few hours, however, the body introduces a new defense which is less of a drain on its resources. This involves gradually progressive overbreathing and lasts for several days, during which time the kidneys adjust the acidity of the blood to keep the brain in equilibrium. Within a few weeks, however, the body comes up with an even better solution to the problem: in order to transport as much oxygen as possible, it produces more blood. Fetuses and infants under about two years have a yet more dramatic solution: their bodies can produce many extra capillaries, so that more

oxygen can be extracted from the blood as it passes through the tissues.

One of the problems about a sudden shortage of oxygen is that it steals up on people without warning: by the time they realize what is going on they are too confused to do anything sensible about it. For this reason aircrews rely on equipment that rapidly detects drops in pressure; modern equipment may also automatically take corrective action.

Time of emergency

The cabins of commercial airplanes are designed so that no single structural failure, such as a window blowing out, can lead to a complete drop to the air pressure outside the plane in less than about 12 seconds. This gives more time for the lungs to empty without bursting and

more time for you to slip on an oxygen mask.

Most cabins have air at a pressure equivalent to the atmosphere at about 2,500m (8,000ft) or lower, but typically fly at about 11,500m (38,000ft). At this altitude, if suddenly exposed to the reduced air pressure, a person will lose consciousness within 15 seconds. This is the minimum time for a lack of oxygen to take effect after an abrupt fall of oxygen pressure in the lung: there is a 7-8 second delay before the oxygen-poor blood reaches the brain, and then a further 7 seconds elapse while the brain uses up its own stores of dissolved oxygen. A person being strangled will lose consciousness in about half this time, because the blood flow to the brain is stopped immediately.

in the lungs or the blood, but often – by the laws of chance – this is not evident at the time when the doctor is examining the patient.

There is an easy way of curing yourself of the symptoms: simply hold your breath, time and again, for as long as you possibly can. This cannot harm you, because as soon as the level of carbon dioxide in the lungs becomes high enough the brain issues an overriding instruction to breathe again.

That statement should be taken in context, however. A normal healthy person can stop breathing for about one minute without causing any harm. For various reasons, some people try to hold their breath for very much longer than this by deliberately overbreathing for a while beforehand. This is an effective technique – the overbreathing flushes large quantities of carbon dioxide out of the body, so that the person can go without a breath for two or three minutes – but it is also an exceptionally dangerous one, being responsible for an appreciable number of deaths, especially among youthful swimmers and divers.

For example, imagine the case of a boy who wants to swim the length of his local pool underwater. He overbreathes in the knowledge that this will allow him to hold his breath longer. He starts out well, swimming vigorously in order to reach the other end as soon as possible. Because of the exertion, he is using up oxygen rapidly; however, because of the prior overbreathing, his brain is still low in carbon dioxide and so does not register that the loss of oxygen is becoming critical. At the end of the swim the boy rises to the surface. This means that the water pressure on his chest is reduced, thereby accentuating the fact that the oxygen pressure in his lungs is much lower than it should be. The result can be a loss of consciousness and, on occasion, drowning.

Is there any danger in breathing too slowly?

It is almost impossible to underbreathe deliberately: the command from the brain to take a fresh breath is irresistible. Even people with lung disease are extremely unlikely to suffer the effects of underbreathing.

However, in some rare cases excessive carbon dioxide can build up in the body. This might happen if, for example, the airways of the lungs became very severely obstructed; the circulation of the blood over the alveoli became badly disorganized or the brain lost its control of breathing.

The sensation of too much carbon dioxide is extremely unpleasant, especially if the onset is abrupt rather than gradual. As the carbon dioxide builds up it begins to poison the brain. The response of the brain is to open up its blood vessels in an attempt to flush away the carbon dioxide more swiftly. However, the dilated vessels leak,

and the fluid accumulates in the skull – which is a rigid container. There is thus pressure on the brain. Severe headaches are followed by unconsciousness.

When the carbon-dioxide build-up takes place over a longer period of time the body has some ways of compensating. For example, the kidneys can adjust the acidity of the blood so that the brain can more easily tolerate the rise in carbon-dioxide level. However, it has to be stressed that an abnormally high carbon-dioxide pressure in the lungs or in the blood is always indicative of a significant disease.

The lungs of a newborn baby have about 20 million alveoli (the tiny air-sacs where oxygen is exchanged for carbon dioxide), whereas in the adult lung there are about 300 million. Most of the 280 million difference is made up in the first few months of life and the remainder by the time the child is eight. After that the lung does not grow, as such; rather, it expands like a balloon to fill the available space.

When do the lungs first appear?

Although they are not required until the time of birth, a baby's lungs develop in the womb.

The first appearance of the lungs in the embryo is as a small bud in the floor of the mouth. Six weeks after conception this bud has developed six rudimentary branches. By the 16th week there are many more branches, so that the structure looks much more like a lung. Not until the 24th week do the alveoli begin to make their appearance.

As the capillaries of the lung region develop in the fetus, wrapping themselves around the alveoli, a certain amount of fluid leaks from the bloodstream into the alveoli. This fluid wells up in the trachea (windpipe) to be swallowed and then, eventually, released into the womb. In the last few weeks before birth the fetus makes many slight breathing movements, rehearsing for the time to come, but all these do is to shift a little fluid out of the fetal body; normally no amniotic fluid enters the lung. On occasion the fetus breathes out more vigorously in order to expel excess local fluid from the lung.

After the 24th week certain cells in the rudimentary lungs make a surfactant (wetting agent). A baby born as early as the 24th week will not survive because the lungs will be too poorly developed and, without the surfactant, too stiff for breathing to be possible. The lungs of babies born between the 24th and 35th weeks (when the production of surfactant increases markedly) often prove too stiff for the baby to be able to operate them unaided – a condition described as respiratory distress of the newborn. In such instances the lungs have to be artificially ventilated and, until they can start to manufacture enough of their own, supplied with synthetic surfactant.

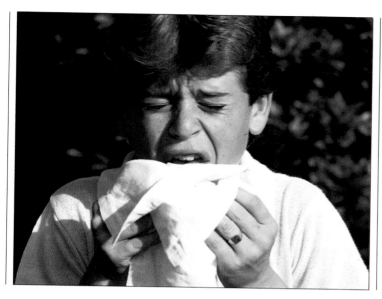

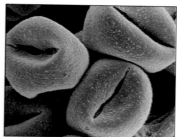

The time when hayfever strikes *depends on your allergy. People affected by oak-tree pollen, ABOVE LEFT magnified about 550 times, have attacks in the spring, when oak trees flower. People allergic to cocksfoot grass pollen, ABOVE RIGHT*

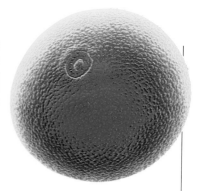

magnified almost 800 times, usually suffer later in the summer. An airborne irritant, pollen causes the sufferer's immune system to produce inflammation in the nose and eyes.

Taking the first breath

The instant of birth is the critical moment for the lungs. Within a minute or less after birth they have to start functioning with full competence. In a normal delivery the baby's springy chest is compressed as the body passes down the birth canal. This empties it of much fluid. As the infant emerges, the chest springs out again, the skin is stimulated by the unfamiliar cold, and, as the placental circulation shuts down, carbon dioxide begins to accumulate in the brain. All of these influences persuade the baby to take its first real breath.

Changes over the day, week, month and year

There is a daily cycle in the ease with which we breathe. This is barely noticeable in healthy people. During the day the airways vary in diameter and collapsibility in response both to the changing levels of certain hormones in the blood and to the accumulation of fluid in the lungs when we lie down to sleep. The airways are at their most obstructed at about 4am.

The cycle is much more obvious in people with asthma. Asthma is an allergic disease in which the airways, once triggered, overreact to an inhaled stimulus – which may be something as trivial as cool air. The disease is sometimes diagnosed by measuring the speed of an outward breath at many times during the day and night to show the 4am morning dip.

Certain asthmatics can show a cycle of breathing that extends over the week. These people suffer work-related asthma: the trigger is some substance present in the workplace but not in the open air or at home. For example, it might be the fumes from the resin of solder, which have no effect on most people but can set off asthma in some. These asthmatics are better at nights and weekends than during the working day, and better on Monday than later in the week.

Women experience a breathing cycle that corresponds to their menstrual cycle, but the effects are so small that they usually go unnoticed. These changes in lung function are mainly due to changes in the amount of water in the body. Very occasionally a woman may cough up a little blood in time with her cycle. She should consult her doctor immediately, since this may indicate that there is a ruptured blood vessel in the lung or that an unsuspected uterine tumor has spread there.

A number of annual changes affect our breathing. Cold air irritates the airway walls, causing them to narrow and to constrict a little. Chest infections and complications of bronchitis are commoner in winter. Asthma, too, often fluctuates annually in phase with whatever is acting as the trigger – for example, with the pollen count.

How does aging change the lungs?

Aging affects lung size and performance; in fact, knowledge of a person's age, sex and height (except at puberty) allows a good prediction of how the lungs should be performing. Lung function peaks at about 30 and afterward gradually declines. This drop in performance is mainly due to loss of elasticity of the tissues – the same kind of loss that makes our faces sag as we grow older. The lungs become floppier and, as we breathe out, the airways tend to collapse earlier and more completely. This slowing of our ability to breathe out eventually means that we become less able to exercise hard. **DD**

Preventing Lung Disease

Toxins such as those in tobacco are the greatest threat to healthy lungs

IF CHILDHOOD chest infections are treated promptly and well, and if you shun tobacco and you can avoid environmental hazards, the lungs will almost certainly continue to function satisfactorily until very old age.

What ailments affect breathing at different times of life?

Some babies are born with a defective breathing system, but their defects are rare, and many of them can be recognized immediately and corrected surgically. Some of these uncommon conditions, however, may take many months to become apparent.

One example is cystic fibrosis. Besides affecting enzyme produc-

tion in the pancreas in a way that severely undermines the body's ability to absorb nutrients from food, cystic fibrosis causes glands in the lining of the bronchial tubes to produce a thick mucus that clogs airways instead of a thin mucus that can trap bacteria and other foreign matter effectively. Infections and irritations lead to a gradual formation of cysts and scars in the lungs. In the past, people born with this disease usually died before they reached 20, but today treatment has improved: controlled diet, enzyme supplements, antibiotics for infec-

tions, physiotherapy that encourages mucus to drain from the lungs. The sufferer can expect to live for many years. Genetic counseling (see Part One) offers help to prospective parents who are concerned that they may be carriers of this genetic disease.

The lungs of newborn children are still damp and weakly developed, and so are vulnerable to infection. This soon improves, although there is a milder recurrence of vulnerability when children first go to school, mixing with each other and trading their germs.

About 0.5 percent of preschool children become asthmatic, and of these 80 percent will remain so for the rest of their lives. Despite much research, understanding of asthma is incomplete, and so treatment and prevention are limited. Most other once common lung diseases of youth, such as

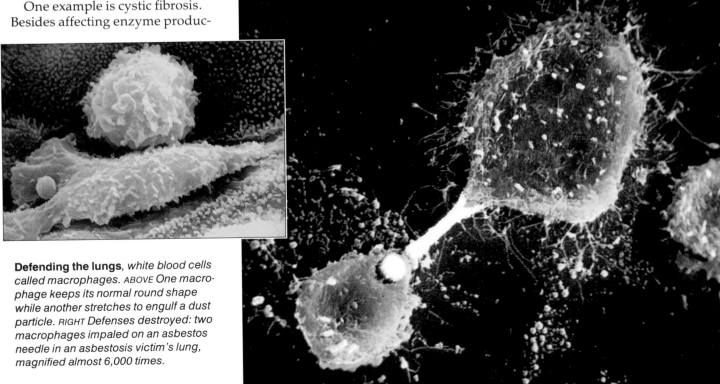

Defending the lungs, *white blood cells called macrophages.* ABOVE *One macrophage keeps its normal round shape while another stretches to engulf a dust particle.* RIGHT *Defenses destroyed: two macrophages impaled on an asbestos needle in an asbestosis victim's lung, magnified almost 6,000 times.*

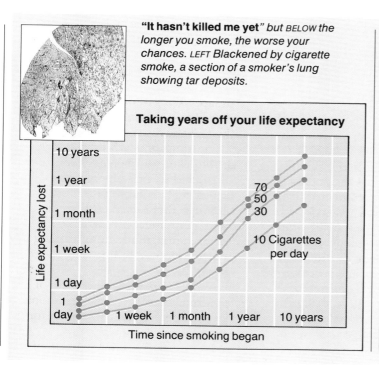

"It hasn't killed me yet" *but* BELOW *the longer you smoke, the worse your chances.* LEFT *Blackened by cigarette smoke, a section of a smoker's lung showing tar deposits.*

Clean lungs *and longer life expectancy are the rewards of giving up smoking. Your chances of avoiding lung cancer improve increasingly from the moment you quit.*

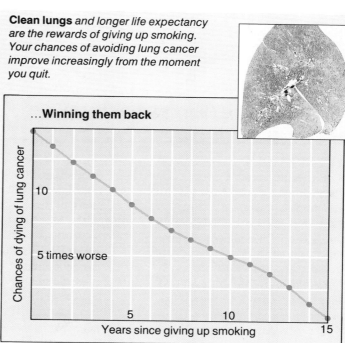

tuberculosis, no longer pose a threat because of effective screening and prevention. The tubercles that form in the lung, giving this disease its name, are fibrous capsules in which the body attempts to wall up the invading bacteria. Children born into a family in which someone has been ill with tuberculosis should be vaccinated against the disease in the first few weeks of life.

Chronic lung diseases like bronchitis, emphysema and lung cancer are generally a feature of later life. A risk of chronic bronchitis is emphysema. Like asthma, glass blowing and trumpet playing (also risk factors in emphysema) bronchitis makes you employ forceful breathing constantly, subjecting the alveoli (the air sacs in the lungs) to above normal pressure. This weakens the elastic strands in the alveoli walls – the sacs become stretched and less efficient – or they burst and blister. The main symptom is chronic shortness of breath. It can eventually lead to respiratory failure, and it makes the lungs susceptible to infection and right-sided heart failure (see *Ch 2*).

A condition to which both sufferers of bronchitis and emphysema are susceptible if they become run down, is pneumonia. This term refers to several kinds of lung inflammation in which the tissue becomes swollen, red, hot and painful. About one-third of cases of pneumonia are fatal – it is often the final cause of death when the terminal illness is heart failure, cancer, a stroke or chronic bronchitis. In people who are semiconscious or paralyzed, the normal coughing reflex is reduced, and infection reaches the lungs more easily. People over 75 are much more at risk than people in the active age ranges. Children under two are also in a high-risk age group. AIDS victims may die of pneumonia caused by bacteria that are harmless to people whose immune system is in order.

Lung cancer is almost always caused by smoking. Lung cancer typically starts in cells of the bronchi that have been damaged by smoking. A tumor spreads in the lungs and from there cancer cells spread through the bloodstream to cause secondary tumors in other parts of the body, such as the brain, the liver, the bone marrow and the skin. In the past irritation was usually due to bad working conditions – long hours in harsh environments, and prolonged exposure to dust and fumes. These are still responsible for a percentage of cases. However, the greatest culprit is smoking, and the most effective preventive measure is to avoid smoking. **DD**

COUGHING: A FIRST DEFENSE

The respiratory system's first line of defense against irritants, coughing temporarily imposes a completely new rhythm on the breathing pattern. Nerve endings in the walls of the windpipe can be stimulated – by dust particles, inhaled gases or inflammation – so that they react by demanding that the offending matter be ejected. The airways are compressed by this reaction, so that the breath is forced along them much more swiftly than usual. This rush of wind shears away unwanted material from the wall of the airway.

Using the Oxygen That We Breathe

During heavy exercise the body is using oxygen at three times the normal rate

WE BREATHE because the cells of our bodies require oxygen. The waste products of the cells include another gas, carbon dioxide, which has to be expelled from the body. The whole process of inhaling oxygen and exhaling carbon dioxide (and water) depends on the working of the lungs.
If we really want to understand what breathing is all about, however, we have to consider how the blood supplies tissues with oxygen.

The red blood cell

Blood is largely made up of a clear liquid called plasma in which move a huge number of red blood cells that transport oxygen around the body. Red cells in mammals are much the same size, whether they come from a mouse or an elephant, and the size determines how quickly the cells can pick up and discard oxygen. The process takes about one-third of a second; this is one of the fundamental time units of the human body. It determines how many capillaries are needed in each human tissue, how fast blood can travel round the body and how big human lungs must be.

Half of each red cell is made up of molecules of hemoglobin. The red hemoglobin molecule is extremely complex. Its most important aspect is that it can transport four of the very much smaller oxygen molecules to wherever they are needed in the body. Since there are about 300 million hemoglobin molecules in each red blood cell, the average red cell transports about 1,200 molecules of oxygen. The body's tissues can readily extract about 900 million of these; the remaining 300 million present a greater problem.

How quickly do we absorb oxygen?

Red blood cells are about seven microns in diameter (that is, about seven thousandths of a millimeter across). When we are at rest, they typically take about one minute to go all around the circulation. Most of this time is spent in the journey between the capillaries of the lungs and the capillaries of the tissues to which they are carrying oxygen. About one second is spent in the capillaries of the lungs. These are only 3-5 microns wide – in other words, smaller than the red blood cells – and so the cells have to crumple themselves up and roll through the capillaries as if they were operating on a caterpillar track. This distortion stirs up the suspension of hemoglobin inside the cell so that it more readily picks up oxygen in place of the carbon dioxide it has been carrying. Normally the cell has picked up its full complement of oxygen by the time it is one-third of the way along the capillary.

During heavy exercise the red cells speed through the capillaries

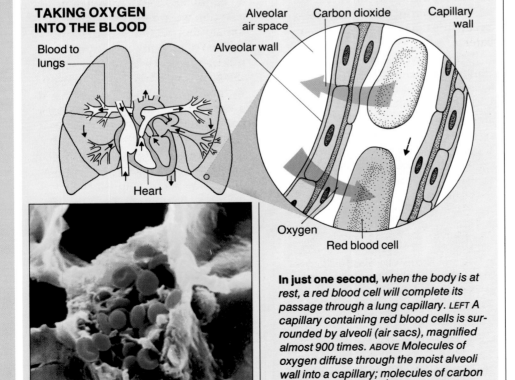

TAKING OXYGEN INTO THE BLOOD

Blood to lungs

Heart

Alveolar air space

Alveolar wall

Carbon dioxide

Capillary wall

Oxygen

Red blood cell

In just one second, *when the body is at rest, a red blood cell will complete its passage through a lung capillary.* LEFT *A capillary containing red blood cells is surrounded by alveoli (air sacs), magnified almost 900 times.* ABOVE *Molecules of oxygen diffuse through the moist alveoli wall into a capillary; molecules of carbon dioxide travel in the opposite direction.*

When we need the most air. *Very energetic activities like swimming the butterfly, playing squash or cycling hard use between 2l and 2.5l of oxygen per minute.*

Red blood cells speed through lung capillaries, collecting oxygen in one-third the usual time.

of the lungs in only one-third of a second. This gives them just enough time to take in their full quota of oxygen. The size of the lungs determines the number of capillaries available and therefore the extent to which the blood's hemoglobin can be loaded with oxygen. The body maintains a cautious balance: too many capillaries would be wasteful, but on the other hand, too few would mean that the body was not using the oxygen-absorbing capacities of the red cells to the full at peaks of exertion. The same sort of balance is established in the other body tissues, each of which normally has just sufficient capillaries to supply its peak oxygen needs.

How quickly do we use oxygen?

Most of the oxygen our body extracts from the air is used to release energy from food: in approximate terms, one liter (60 cubic inches) of oxygen releases the energy from one gram (0.04oz) of food. Four-fifths of that energy is wasted as heat, but the other one-fifth is enough, for example, to fuel an average adult male as he climbs two flights of stairs. When not exercising we need about 250ml (15 cubic inches) of oxygen per minute, just to keep our body

ticking over. During really heavy exercise the muscles need several liters of oxygen per minute but the body can supply them with only about four liters (240 cubic inches) per minute. So we run into an oxygen debt, using other limited stores of energy which have to be reconstituted with more oxygen later.

The maximum debt that can be run up is about six liters (360 cubic

inches), so we cannot keep going at top effort for very long. We always incur some oxygen debt at the start of exercise because it takes about 30 seconds to accelerate the circulation to the speed required for it to take sufficient oxygen to the muscles. At the end of any exercise the heart and lungs normally decelerate over a minute or two while the debt is repaid. The larger the debt, the longer it takes for this to happen.

How rapidly do we give off carbon dioxide?

When food is burned by oxygen, the amount of carbon dioxide produced is in strict proportion to the amount of oxygen used. The ratio of carbon dioxide to oxygen is
- 1:1 when sugars are burned
- 0.7:1 when fats are burned
- about 0.83:1 on a mixed diet

When we are not exercising we exhale about 200ml (12 cubic inches) of carbon dioxide per minute. However, the lungs must dilute this by a factor of 18 to keep the acidity of the brain correct, and some of the air that we inhale does not reach the alveoli (the tiny air-sacs where oxygen is exchanged for carbon dioxide), so in fact we breathe 4-5l (240-300 cubic inches) of fresh air each minute.

During heavy exercise our output of carbon dioxide rises more steeply than our intake of oxygen, because of the oxygen debt. As the debt is incurred the tissues make lactic acid, which could disturb the equilibrium of the brain. To neutralize this acid we have to wash away an excess of carbon dioxide and so we have to breathe very hard. On strenuous exertion, we typically breathe about 100l (3.5 cubic feet) of air each minute. The lungs take about two seconds to fill and empty, so each breath has a volume of about 3.5l (210 cubic inches). **DD**

REPLACING BLOOD CELLS

Mature, functioning red blood cells, and many kinds of white blood cells, cannot reproduce. However, these cells are constantly dying or being lost (for example, when we bleed). Red blood cells die in any event after about 120 days – some white blood cells after only a few days – and are removed from the circulation by the spleen.

The demand for new blood cells is met by specialized cells in the bone marrow. These specialized parent cells cannot perform the functions of which their daughter cells are capable: all they can do is produce a fresh supply of red or white cells. This way of replacing dead cells is particularly useful when the body is damaged by injury or infection, because the rate of production of replacement cells can very rapidly be stepped up. Mature replacement cells can appear in the blood within 24-48 hours. **AS**

4 BRAINWAVES

Whether we are awake or asleep, the brain never rests, but functions according to distinct and varying rhythms. An action as simple as opening or closing our eyes produces electrical changes in nerve cells that alter its cycle of activity.

TYPES OF BRAINWAVE

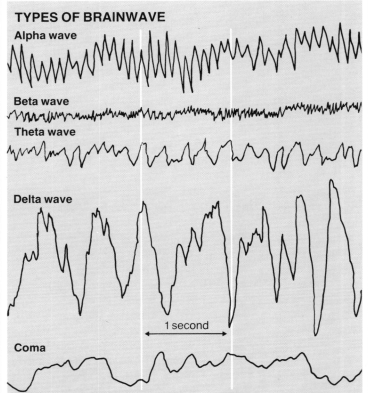

Alpha wave

Beta wave

Theta wave

Delta wave

1 second

Coma

Different brainwaves *reflect different mental states. An alpha rhythm has a frequency of 8-12 cycles per second and usually occurs when a person is awake but resting quietly with their eyes closed. Beta waves (18-25 cycles per second) arise from sensory-motor parts of the brain. Delta waves (less than 5 cycles per second) are irregular and slow, and are characteristic* *of deep sleep, although they may also occur when the brain has been damaged. Rhythmic slow waves are theta waves (3-7 cycles per second). Brainwaves during coma are very slow. Abnormal in a waking adult, slow waves are normal in young children. Adult EEG patterns do not appear until a child is 8-12 years old.*

Eyes shut   Eyes open   Eyes shut

Opening or closing the eyes *affects the pattern of electrical activity produced by the brain. While they are closed, an EEG reading shows alpha* *waves. As soon as the eyes open, the alpha pattern disappears to be replaced by random, fast waves signaling alertness.*

WHEN PEOPLE are looking for analogies of how the brain works, they often mention computers. However, this analogy is imperfect in many ways. One is that computers have no sense of time or rhythm, let alone of the complicated cross-rhythms which are the material, for example, of jazz drumming. The mere fact that people are so readily excited by rhythms makes it likely that rhythmic mechanisms are built into the ground plan of the brain.

The effect of visual rhythms on the brain can be even more dramatic than that of beating drums. In those people who are susceptible, flashing lights at a critical frequency, often about 10 per second, can cause a full-scale epileptic fit (a convulsion). Some children who are never going to be epileptic when they grow up will have a fit if they sit too close to a bright, flickering television set (television epilepsy). There is something to be said for the view that epilepsy is a disorder of the rhythmic mechanisms of the brain. If that is so, epilepsy is one of the most important links between time and health, for epilepsy of some form affects more than one person in 30 during their lifetime.

Making records of brain rhythms

The most direct clues to the rhythmic behavior of the brain come from making records of its electrical activity. Nervous activity both in nerve fibers and in the gray matter of the brain (the nerve cells that do the thinking) is accompanied by electrical currents that can be recorded by sticking contacts onto the scalp and amplifying the signal with an amplifier much like that in a hi-fi. What comes out is called the electroencephalogram, or EEG.

When a person is awake but has their eyes shut, their brain shows spontaneous rhythmic activity in the form of EEG waves with a frequency of about 10 cycles per second and an amplitude of about 0.01 volts. This is called the alpha rhythm. It appears to be due to the synchronous activity of large numbers of nerve cells in the gray matter on the surface of the brain – the cerebral cortex. If the person opens their eyes the alpha rhythm disappears and is replaced with a changing pattern of smaller, faster waves.

The alpha pattern appears when a person is responsive but is not actually paying attention to anything in particular. Higher frequencies appear when the eyes open, because activity in the cortex speeds up as signals from the eyes arouse attention. Even with the eyes shut, alpha activity may be blocked by getting the person to do mental arithmetic or to listen closely to the ticking of a watch. When the eyes are open, alpha activity may reappear if glasses with strong lenses are used to put everything out of focus and so make visual information less interesting.

Watching how the brain works. *By applying electrodes to the scalp, researchers can measure the rhythmic fluctuations of voltage that represent the electrical activity of the brain's cells. Though electroencephalograms (EEGs) usually record only spontaneous electrical activity in the brain, a more sophisticated version allows this researcher to follow the effects of a deliberate external stimulus. A shock to his right arm produces an electrical pattern that is then converted to a digital form and color-coded. On screen, the red area at the top of the image shows which part of the brain is reacting to the shock. More practically, EEGs help doctors detect epilepsy and brain tumors or monitor a patient's progress after surgery. Signals from the brain may even help in diagnosing multiple sclerosis.*

In the part of the cerebral cortex that is concerned with muscular movements of the body, it is faster rhythms, 40 cycles per second, that are linked to muscular contractions. And when the muscles are to contract harder, the frequency of the cerebral waves increases without their necessarily increasing in size.

Brainwaves cease at death, but they go on under general anesthesia and may, indeed, get bigger and either slower or faster depending on the anesthetic used. They also persist in an altered form in natural sleep (see *Ch 6*). Epileptics show abnormal EEG rhythms or may have abnormal waves provoked by flashing lights. No abnormalities in the EEG have yet been detected in psychotic patients with disordered thought processes.

Speeding up the cycle

A 10-cycle-per-second rhythm of masses of nerve cells is found widely in the animal kingdom – for example, in the human brain and in the brain of a water beetle. And the rhythm behaves similarly in the two; the rhythm disappears when humans open their eyes and when a light is shone in a water beetle's eye.

A much faster rhythm, the fastest brainwaves known, is found in the cerebellum (a part of the brain involved in controlling muscle contractions) of the higher mammals. The frequency at rest is about 250 cycles per second, the same as middle C on the piano. In animals, when a signal from a limb, for example, a touch on the paw, reaches its destination in the cerebellum, this rhythm speeds up in some parts of the cerebellum by as much as 600 cycles per second and increases in size.

This is much like what happens in the cerebral cortex, but on a much faster time scale. In the brain, greater intensity of action means faster rhythms as well as bigger voltages. That seems to be an important way in which the time factor enters into brain mechanisms. The contrast can again be made with a computer, which does not speed up its cycle of operations when it has more numbers to crunch. **MH**

WHAT IS EPILEPSY?

Epilepsy is a disorder in which a part or parts of the brain are too easily excited. It involves sudden and recurrent convulsions. They result when some brain cells send out such strong electrical signals that they drown out those from nearby regions of the brain.

Not all convulsive seizures are epileptic. About 3 percent of all children under five have febrile convulsions (ones that are brought on by a high temperature).

The convulsions of some sufferers are usually "grand mal" seizures. If the victim is standing, they will fall to the ground unconscious. Legs and arms are at first stiff; then they twitch, often violently, for about two minutes, and there may be incontinence, before consciousness begins to return gradually. Grand mal fits can be brought on in epileptic children by flickering lights – for example, a badly tuned television screen. Modern drugs can suppress these symptoms very effectively. In some cases of childhood onset the fits become less frequent as the person grows older, and may cease altogether. In the middle-aged and elderly, partial (or "focal") seizures may occur without developing into grand mal seizures. The incidence of epilepsy usually increases after 40.

"Petit mal" convulsions appear in a form of epilepsy that occurs only in children, more often girls. The child switches off from reality for a period of seconds or minutes; this can be accompanied by rapid blinking of the eyes, jerky movements, grimacing and lip-smacking. The condition is rare, but parents and teachers should be aware of it; otherwise they are likely to think that the children are simply not paying attention.

If EEG (electroencephalogram) contacts have been attached to the sufferer's scalp, then during an epileptic fit very large brainwaves can be detected all over the brain. Many epileptics show some abnormal waves between attacks, and these can help to diagnose the condition. Brainwave abnormalities also occur around brain tumors and areas of brain damage and the EEG is useful in locating these.

5 BIOLOGICAL RHYTHMS

"Biological time" – the pace of rhythmic changes in the body – is controlled by complex chains of chemical activity. They can be measured in microseconds, days, months or years. Whenever we become ill, do shiftwork or travel long distances by air, the body has to readjust the chemical timers that keep body rhythms in synchrony with each other and with the world.

HIGH OR LOW? IT DEPENDS ON TIME OF DAY

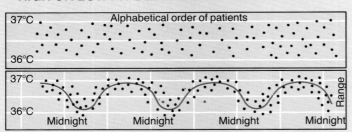

Using body rhythms to diagnose illness. TOP *If the normal limits for body temperature are plotted without reference to the time of day, no meaningful pattern emerges.* BOTTOM *When time is taken into consideration, it is clear that normal temperature has a regular pattern of variation over 24 hours. A temperature that is normal at 3am would be abnormally low at 3pm.*

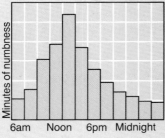

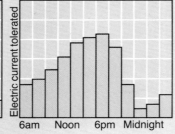

Biological clocks and the teeth. *Two good reasons for making your dental appointment for the afternoon: anesthetics are generally more effective in the early to middle afternoon, so the dentist can use a lower dose; your teeth are less sensitive to pain in the late afternoon.*

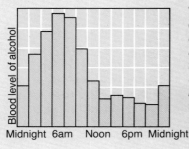

When you can least well cope with alcohol. *In the early evening, the level of alcohol in your blood is lower than the same amount of drink would produce after midnight. One for the road at the end of a late party is a very bad idea.*

OUR SENSE of time has two sources. First, we are aware of cycles in the world around us, such as the rising and setting of the sun, or the rotating hands of clocks. Our daily cycle of interactions with other people is also cyclical: the mailman comes at a usual time and members of the family look for us at the table at breakfast time, lunchtime and dinnertime. Second, we are aware of cycles in the way we feel: hunger suggests that it must be getting close to lunchtime; tiredness suggests that it must be getting late in the day.

The two ways of keeping time are usually in harmony, but they are not always. If you move suddenly to a time zone that is different by several hours, you will find it hard to sleep and eat at the appropriate times, and the discomfort of jet lag will tell you that you are not simply tired – your body, in ways that are difficult to describe, is not working in time yet with its new environment.

In fact, jet lag is a symptom of lost synchrony between numerous internal rhythms as much as it is a symptom of lost synchrony between internal rhythms and the world about you. Several chemical cycles in the jet-lagged body, responding to cues such as the changed cycle of light and dark, need to regain synchrony with the world. Some cycles catch up more quickly than others, and it takes a few days before all are back in harmony with each other.

Jet lag is one of the few experiences in which we become consciously aware of the importance to our well-being of an internal synchrony of body rhythms. Chronobiologists (specialists in biological rhythms) have found that rhythm disturbances that we are unaware of can be symptoms of much more threatening dislocations than jet travel. Disease causes subtle shifts in the daily, weekly, monthly and annual cycles of events in our body chemistry. As these cycles become better understood, opportunities for early diagnosis of illness increase. Opportunities are also being discovered to time measures against illness more effectively – for example, by giving medication to a patient at the time of day when it will do the most good.

Can we predict good and bad days?

Talk of biological rhythms brings to mind the popular cult of "biorhythms," a concept that was invented late in the 19th century and had revivals in the 1930s and the 1960s. The idea of biorhythms is that our body undergoes three very precise cycles, whatever our age or sex: we are said to be at our physical best every 23 days, at our emotional best every 28 days, and at our intellectual best every 33 days. A little work with your pocket calculator will show that, if biorhythms exist, at the age of 58 years and 67 days, you should have the best day of your life.

However, numerous scientific studies have failed to find any evidence of biorhythms. The body is affected by numerous regular cycles that are quite properly called biological rhythms, but they are not so stable that they can be used as a kind of calculus.

Losing sleep, missing exercise, eating too much or too little, worrying, smoking, drinking and taking other drugs, all have effects on body chemistry that undermine physical and intellectual ability and emotional well-being. The best way to predict when you will have a good day is to predict when you will have avoided all of these disruptions for some time before – in the case of smoking, several weeks before.

How long do body-rhythm cycles take?

Our longest biological rhythm is the life cycle. Each person who survives long enough experiences one complete cycle of birth, growth, reproduction and death. Other obvious examples are shorter: the daily recurrence of sleep and consciousness, a woman's monthly menstrual cycle, breathing in and out, and the beating of the heart. Cycles of change in our body chemistry underlie all of these – for example, the hormone changes that

occur over several years around puberty; the movements of ions across cell membranes as heart muscle tissue spontaneously contracts and relaxes in fractions of a second; the cycles of chemical change lasting millionths of a second as a signal passes along a nerve to tell the diaphragm that the time has come in the cycle of breathing for it to relax.

The level of testosterone (the principal male sex hormone) in saliva varies in a regular way. Although the numerical measures may differ between one person and another, the level generally peaks at about 7am and can reach one or more lesser peaks later in the day. This is an example of a biological rhythm that operates over a

HOW LIGHT AND DARKNESS AFFECT MOOD

The pineal gland in the brain releases a hormone called melatonin, which affects our moods. The gland secretes very little melatonin in light, production peaking during the hours of darkness – usually about 2-3am.

For reasons that are not fully understood, human beings require much more light than other mammals for the production of melatonin to be inhibited: so far as the pineal gland is concerned, the average nighttime illumination in homes or offices is indistinguishable from darkness.

One of the contributory causes of jet lag is the disruption of the rhythm of melatonin production. For most of us, jet lag is something we suffer only every year or two – if that often – but some people face much more serious problems.

For example, many people complain of a seasonal disruption of mood. They feel tired and depressed during the winter months: they tend to oversleep, move sluggishly and eat more (especially carbohydrates). The onset of spring usually lifts their spirits, but only during the summer months are they at their most energetic and active. Some susceptible people may become overactive – hypomanic – at this time. This condition – known as seasonal affective disorder (SAD) – involves the level of melatonin in the person's body. In people suffering from SAD the peak times for melatonin production change with the season. One way of alleviating SAD may be to extend the day artificially by sitting in a very bright light (equivalent to 10 100W bulbs or more) for an hour in both the morning and the evening.

The fact that light inhibits the production of melatonin also affects people who work on night shifts. Most artificial lighting is not strong enough to stop the pineal gland secreting melatonin at its usual time, and the secretion can continue into the daytime hours if the shift worker sleeps with the curtains closed. The time needed to adjust to the altered rhythm varies from one person to the next, but can take up to six days – which means that changing from day to night shifts on a weekly basis gives little time for adaptation. The result is often fatigue and sleeping problems.

DETECTING BREAST CANCER EARLY

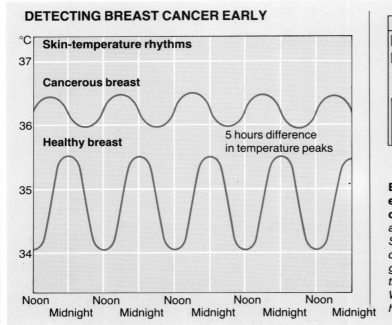

Skin-temperature rhythms

Cancerous breast

Healthy breast

5 hours difference in temperature peaks

°C — 37, 36, 35, 34

Noon / Midnight (repeated)

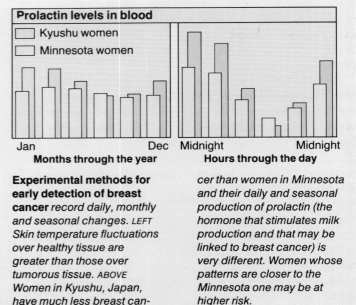

Prolactin levels in blood

Kyushu women
Minnesota women

Jan — Dec
Months through the year

Midnight — Midnight
Hours through the day

Experimental methods for early detection of breast cancer record daily, monthly and seasonal changes. LEFT Skin temperature fluctuations over healthy tissue are greater than those over tumorous tissue. ABOVE Women in Kyushu, Japan, have much less breast can-cer than women in Minnesota and their daily and seasonal production of prolactin (the hormone that stimulates milk production and that may be linked to breast cancer) is very different. Women whose patterns are closer to the Minnesota one may be at higher risk.

period of about 24 hours. Such cycles were first called circadian rhythms (*circa* in Latin means "about", *dies* means "day") by Professor Franz Halberg in 1959, and many of them, in many different areas of biology, have been discovered since then.

Women of menstruating age show monthly cycles of progesterone levels in the saliva, of skin temperature over the breasts, and of prolactin levels in the plasma of the blood.

Weekly rhythms have been detected in the changing proportion of our blood that is made up of red blood cells. In a study, the peak occurred between Sunday evenings and Monday mornings.

Some rhythms last about one year. A particularly interesting kind of circannual rhythm concerns the effectiveness of certain drugs. For example, cyclosporine – a drug used to counter the body's tendency to reject transplanted tissues – was discovered in animal experiments to be more effective at some times than at others during a period of about a year.

What governs biological rhythms?

It seems almost certain that our biological rhythms are mostly determined by genetic coding rather than by environmental influences. In other words, whenever our body follows (for example) a circadian rhythm, it is doing so mainly because of chemical patterns laid down in our genes rather than because we see the sun rise and set.

There is nevertheless an interaction between heredity and environment. Experiments with volunteers who have been isolated from the outside world (particularly

from clocks, newspapers, sunrise and sunset or anything else that helps to count the passage of time) show that the 24-hour rhythm is not built into the human body precisely. Soon after isolation the volunteers often start acting according to roughly a 25-hour cycle, suggesting that our circadian biological clock needs to be constantly set and reset in order to keep time with the world.

An advantage of the fact that we can reset our 24-hour clocks is that it makes it possible to move from one time zone to another and adjust to the change. Jet lag in modern humans shows that our inherited ability to do this without discomfort is limited to slow travel in the style of our evolving ancestors.

Not everyone has a normal internal clock. After a few weeks, some isolation volunteers drift from the 25-hour pattern. In extreme cases their sleeping and waking may follow a regular 50-hour day, although more usually the cycle becomes very irregular. The volunteers seem unaware that some of their waking periods are as much as 30 hours long while others last only four hours.

In rare cases, people have difficulty setting their internal clock to 24 hours even when all the external cues are available. Their sleeping pattern drifts – occurring later and later each day. This can cause social problems, especially when they are living with a person whose length of cycle is standard (see *Ch6*).

Can knowledge of rhythms be used to improve health?

When doctors diagnose illness, they base their judgment on a whole range of symptoms and signs. Using a single measured value such as the patient's blood pressure or heart rate on arrival at the doctor's office, is often not very useful and can sometimes be extremely misleading. Increasingly, 24-hour monitors are being used to assess heart-rate and blood-pressure problems.

An example of how this kind of monitoring could be usefully increased is suggested by the circadian cycles in the blood pressure of many newborn infants in families with a history of high blood pressure. They show much higher levels of change than those in infants from families where there is no such history. Whatever the family history, it would be an advantage to test all babies to find if they experience these wide fluctuations: once doctors had been alerted to this abnormality, they could take steps to reduce the risk that the person will suffer serious cardiovascular disease in later life.

Research is underway to develop techniques for monitoring cyclical changes in levels of hormones by testing saliva. Besides a convenient and accurate system of monitoring, this development will depend on the establishment of a larger bank of information than now exists about normal patterns of hormone change. Doctors will need to know better which deviations to regard as warning signs of illness.

Changes in the levels of many different hormones may contribute to cancers or, at least, can if detected be used as an aid to diagnosing particular cancers. A focus of research is testosterone levels in saliva, because it is believed that changes in these may be related to changes in the activity of the prostate gland. Such measurements might help in the early diagnosis of prostate cancer.

Timing medical intervention

Measurements of biological rhythms may also help doctors to make more effective use of drugs.

Cytotoxic drugs are ones that kill cancer cells by interfering with their cell division or the processes leading up to cell division. The cells of abnormal tissues often have different rhythms to those of normal cells, so better knowledge of normal and abnormal rhythms may make it possible for doctors to maximize the effect of these drugs – and reduce side-effects – by administering them at the appropriate times of day. One study found that this was the case in the use of the drugs adriamycin and cisplatin in the treatment of advanced cancer of the ovaries: the treatment was least effective if the adriamycin was given at evening and the cisplatin 12 hours later.

When a person's adrenal gland (a gland above the kidney) is not working properly, it is normal to give cortisone injections in the morning, when the gland is having its daily maximal effect; should the injections be given regularly at other times of the day the efforts of the adrenal gland can actually be further reduced. DW

WHERE HORMONES ARE RELEASED

Biological rhythms are regulated by cycles of change in our body chemistry as key organs vary the rate at which they release hormones into the bloodstream. More than *100 hormones have been identified. A major function of many is to tell specialized hormone-producing cells when it is time to release their product.*

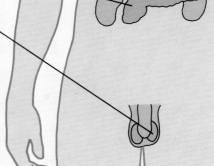

Hypothalamus Regulates body temperature, hunger and thirst, sexual function and activity of the pituitary

Pituitary gland Influences activity in other endocrine glands; controls growth and development

Thyroid gland Influences growth; controls metabolic rate

Parathyroids (behind the thyroid) Regulate the use of calcium in the body

Thymus Where infection-fighting T cells develop in children

Adrenal glands Help body adjust to stress; control balance of salt and water

Pancreas Secretes insulin; controls blood sugar level

Testes Secrete sex hormones in men; regulate sperm production

Ovaries Secrete sex hormones in women; regulate egg production

Pineal gland One of the body's clocks; regulates menstruation and maturation

WHEN HORMONES ARE RELEASED

Different hormones are released at different times. Levels of the male sex hormone testosterone, for example, peak at about 7am. The release of estrogen and *progesterone at different stages of a woman's monthly cycle control menstruation (see Ch12). Growth hormone is released in childhood and mainly at night (see Ch17).*

6 SLEEP AND DREAMING

We sleep for about a third of our lives, spending more hours awake and fewer hours dreaming as we grow older. Some insomnia can be helped by greater activity in the day – this usually means longer and deeper sleep at night.

HOW AGE AFFECTS SLEEP

▼ **During the first six months of life** *a baby gradually locks into the 24-hour cycle. The chart* BELOW *shows a typical pattern: the black horizontal lines record how long each period of sleep* lasts, and the continuous curved lines the pattern of when periods of sleep begin. Around week 15 the baby's sleep begins to synchronize with the 24-hour cycle of the world about it.

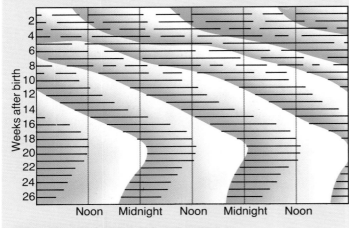

Weeks after birth: 2, 4, 6, 8, 10, 12, 14, 16, 18, 20, 22, 24, 26

Noon   Midnight   Noon   Midnight   Noon

HOW MUCH SLEEP DO WE NEED?

A newborn infant typically sleeps for 16 hours each day, about half of this time in REM sleep. As the child grows older the total amount of time spent sleeping diminishes rapidly, and REM sleep takes up a much smaller proportion of the new sleeping pattern. A young adult generally sleeps for eight hours each night, only two of them in REM sleep.

People who have coped well with a major traumatic experience seem to have shorter periods of REM sleep. This is one of the many effects associated with REM sleep for which science still has no explanation.

As people grow older they tend to sleep less each night with no ill effects: many elderly people who complain about poor sleep are in fact sleeping perfectly naturally but trying to spend the same number of hours in bed as they did when they were younger.

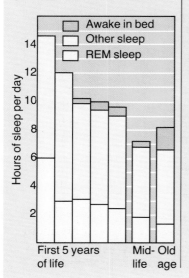

Hours of sleep per day
- Awake in bed
- Other sleep
- REM sleep

14, 12, 10, 8, 6, 4, 2

First 5 years of life   Mid-life   Old age

ALL ANIMALS with backbones sleep. In humans our sleeping pattern is one of the most obvious indications of our normal 24-hour cycle (see *Ch5*). Even animals without backbones, like insects, show what seems to be rebound catch-up sleep after periods of enforced wakefulness. Humans, like all other mammals (and like birds) have two kinds of sleep. In one kind the eyes move rapidly backward and forward behind the closed eyelids; this is called rapid-eye movement (REM) sleep, and, at least in humans, it is more often associated with dreaming. Extended periods of nonREM sleep are interspersed with shorter bursts of REM sleep.

What is sleep for?

It is astonishing that we know so little about the function of the activity in which we spend about one-third of our adult lives. All theories about what sleep is for are still only that: theories. The most plausible is that the function of sleep is to give the body time to restore itself. There is evidence to support the popular notion that people who are more active during the day sleep longer and more deeply at nights. We sleep longer during the times of life when there is maximum growth – infancy and adolescence – and people suffering diseases involving increased levels of metabolism (the chemical processes associated with the body's growth, renewal, energy production, etc) likewise sleep more deeply.

There are other theories about the function of sleep, some focusing on the function of particular stages in the cycle of sleep. Most of the latter are concerned with REM sleep and its associated dreaming. One such theory is that REM sleep has some role in the acquisition of memories and in learning.

Can disrupted or poor sleep be dangerous?

People who sleep for the average time (7-9 hours) each night are likely to live longer than those who sleep for a very short or a very long time each night. Similarly, people whose sleep patterns are markedly disrupted – for example, shiftworkers – on average suffer more illness during life and die younger.

There are other hazards associated with loss of sleep and the resulting fatigue: to choose just two examples, traffic accidents peak at times when people are likely to be at their sleepiest, and several of the major nuclear disasters that have occurred to date seem at least in part to have been caused by the poor reaction times of fatigued personnel.

Taking all of these effects together, it is certain that a normal amount of sleep, taken at the right time during the 24-hour period, is essential to the welfare of both the individual and society.

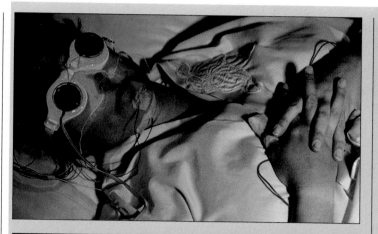

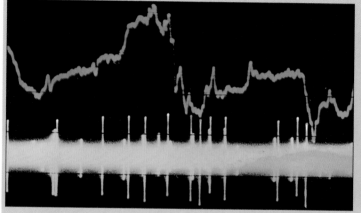

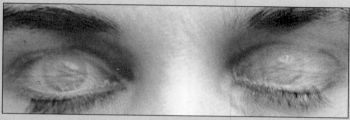

Rapid-eye-movement (REM) sleep *is so named because during this phase of sleep the eyes move rapidly backward and foreward beneath closed lids. These movements are recorded* BOTTOM LEFT *by the green trace at the bottom of this colored monitor screen. The blue trace is an EEG record of the brainwave pattern typical of both REM sleep* *and light nonREM sleep. It is mainly when awakened from REM sleep that people report they have just been dreaming. In an experiment in controlled dreaming, a volunteer* TOP LEFT *wears goggles that are sensitive to rapid eye movements – they glow red during REM sleep to raise the volunteer's unconscious awareness of the dream that is in progress.*

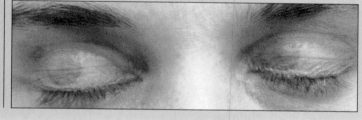

Can normal sleep be dangerous?

Even normal sleep can present dangers. Deaths from strokes, heart attacks and asthma occur disproportionately often during sleep, and the same is true for a number of other medical conditions and diseases. Certain specific medical disorders are associated with sleep: for example, some cardiac arrhythmias (periods of irregular heartbeat – see *Ch1*) occur particularly during REM sleep. In some people obstruction of the airways during REM sleep can cause apnea (cessation of breathing, usually for short periods). This may result in daytime sleepiness and headaches. Sudden infant deaths (cot deaths) are invariably associated with sleep; it is just possible that these deaths may occur during dreaming.

What is a healthy sleep pattern?

The sleep drive is strong in young adults, much less so in older people. All sorts of things can affect it, but the single most important one is the establishment and maintenance of a regular pattern of activity before sleep.

The precise activity involved varies from person to person – perhaps you prefer a bedtime snack, a warm bath or a short spell of reading – but the important point is that it should be a habit. Going to sleep at the same time each night and waking at the same time each morning (without allowing yourself to drowse on overlong) not only improves your performance during the day but also prepares you for a following good night's sleep.

Exercise during the day contributes to better sleep. Other factors are making sure that the bedroom is not too warm, limiting outside light and noise, and using a bed that is comfortable and familiar; a bed that is too hard causes more movement during sleep, more frequent awakenings, and longer periods in the lighter stages of sleep – many medical conditions could be ameliorated with attention to the sufferer's mattress.

Various drugs either interrupt or diminish sleep. Alcohol and short-acting sleeping pills can help people fall to sleep but markedly disrupt the sleeping pattern during the night (although this is less noticeable in younger adults). Long-acting sleeping pills have the disadvantage that they often cause daytime drowsiness. Smoking shortens the time spent in sleep, and caffeine, generally from coffee, makes it difficult to get to sleep.

What Is Involved In a Good Night's Sleep?

Each night we pass through repeating cycles of changing mental activity. We fall several times from lighter to deeper levels of sleep, and several times the mind moves itself to higher levels of subconscious awareness.

▼ Deep sleep declines with age. A 70-year-old spends only one-quarter of the time in stages 3 and 4 of sleep (deep sleep) that a 25-year-old does. There is also less dreaming, but almost four times as much time spent awake in bed or in stage 1 (dozing). Light sleep (stage 2) stays about the same.

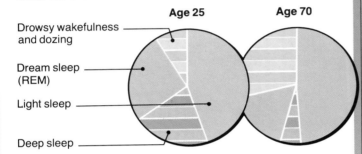

Drowsy wakefulness and dozing

Dream sleep (REM)

Light sleep

Deep sleep

Age 25   **Age 70**

▼ A typical night for a young adult. Three or four distinct cycles of sleep occur in a night. The sleeper falls into a light and then perhaps a deeper sleep in each cycle, before ending with several minutes of dreaming. A postural change often occurs after, but not during dreaming. Occasional intervals of drowsy wakefulness are usually forgotten later.

The changing pattern of brainwaves along the bottom of this diagram is not drawn to scale.

 Major change in body position

 Muscles "paralyzed"

 Vivid dreams likely

Drowsy wakefulness. In the course of a sound night's sleep, you are probably awake for three or four brief periods or more without remembering them later.

During these drowsy episodes, muscular activity and eye movement are largely voluntary, and you may turn over or move your limbs. The brain produces the regular pattern of alpha waves that are typical of relaxed, eyes-shut wakefulness (see *Ch 4*), not the rapid irregular waves that appear when the eyes are open or during periods of excitement.

Stage 2: light sleep. This is how you spend about half of your time in bed, whether you are old or young. Dreaming does occur during this stage, but is rarely remembered.

The brainwave pattern can be faster than that of stage-1 sleep. Distinctive variations in the pattern just before REM sleep are known as spindles and saw-toothed waves. Larger variations in the stage-2 pattern occur after REM sleep; they are known as K complexes.

In both cases eye movement is minimal and there is little muscular activity.

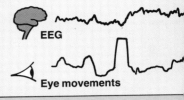

EEG

Eye movements

Drowsy wakefulness

Stage 1 sleep: dozing. In the stage, your thoughts wander and you may drift in and out sleep. Often you will experience a sensation like dreaming. As you begin to sleep, eye movements become slow and rolling, brainwaves gradually lengthen, and

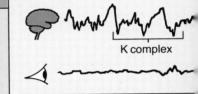

K complex

Stage 2

Stage 4: slow-wave sleep. Brainwaves in deepest sleep reach their maximum amplitude (at least 50 percent are delta waves) while heart rate and blood pressure reach their lowest points.

Sleepers usually achieve most stage-4 sleep early in

THE STAGES OF SLEEP

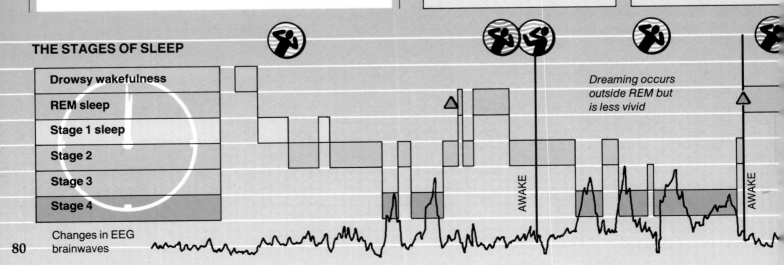

Dreaming occurs outside REM but is less vivid

Drowsy wakefulness	
REM sleep	
Stage 1 sleep	
Stage 2	
Stage 3	
Stage 4	

AWAKE

AWAKE

Changes in EEG brainwaves

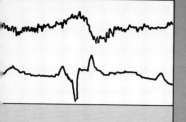

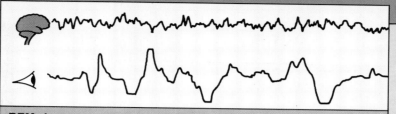

REM sleep

Rapid-eye-movement sleep (REM sleep) typically occurs when you are dreaming. The eyes dart about beneath closed lids, moving more rapidly than when you are awake. Breathing rate and heart rate become quicker, and blood pressure climbs or plummets. The brainwave pattern is similar to that of stage 1 sleep.
· Muscular relaxation effectively paralyzes you. This prevents what might otherwise be quite energetic physical activity during sleep, and stops you from acting out your dreams.

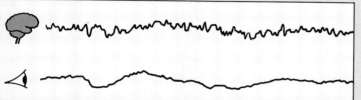

Stage 1 sleep

breathing becomes more even. Brainwaves become of higher amplitude and lower frequency than the alpha waves typical of the early stages of drowsiness. Occasionally, as sleep becomes deeper, theta waves may appear (see *Ch 4*).

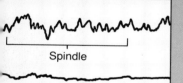

Spindle

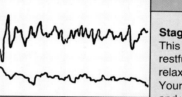

Stage 3

Stage 3: sleeping deeply. This is a period of deep and restful sleep. Your muscles relax. Your heart rate falls. Your blood pressure drops and your breathing slows. There is no eye movement but the eye-movement recorder is jogged into motion by the activity of the electro-encephalogram (EEG) which records brainwaves of a high amplitude (great height and depth) and low frequency; 20-50 percent of them are delta waves, the pattern typically produced during the soundest periods of sleep.

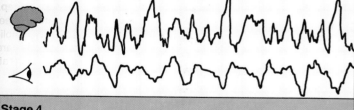

Stage 4

the night, with later periods of deep sleep tending to be shorter. Often people suffering from insomnia or other sleep disorders do not enter this stage at all.
There is no eye movement and muscular activity is at a minimum.

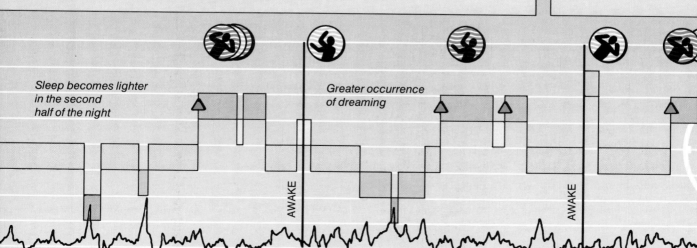

Sleep becomes lighter in the second half of the night

Greater occurrence of dreaming

AWAKE

AWAKE

4

Is there a cure for insomnia?

Each year about 10 million people in the United States alone consult their doctors about sleep problems. Until a few years ago, 50 percent of the patients would have been prescribed sleeping pills.

Today doctors are much more wary about the use of these drugs. Sleeping pills may help those who have difficulty in falling asleep, but they are at best a temporary expedient, can be addictive (see box feature) and are open to (sometimes fatal) abuse. The modern science of sleep-disorder medicine pays more attention to the specific cause of each case of insomnia and directs treatment toward that cause.

The great majority of complaints about sleep relate to either insufficient or poor-quality sleep. The loss of a habitual sleep pattern can cause great distress. Poor-quality sleep is often the result of stress or of a specific emotional trauma.

Various medical disorders – including psychiatric problems like depression – can disrupt sleep. Many middle-aged and elderly women suffer sleep problems; this may be because the disrupted sleep associated with child-rearing persists in later years.

What causes excess sleep?

The other major sleep problem is hypersomnia (excessive sleepiness). Some people simply require more sleep than others, but a number of other factors may play a part. Use and/or abuse of drugs can cause excessive sleepiness, as can a range of medical conditions, some specific sleep disorders, and some disorders that are little understood but are known to involve alterations in the brain.

WHAT ARE THE RISKS OF BECOMING ADDICTED TO SLEEPING PILLS?

Sleeping pills are still prescribed too often: while in many cases their use is justifiable, in many cases it is not, and patients are unnecessarily exposed to the risk of addiction.

The most important factor in becoming addicted is probably personality – some people are more likely to become addicted to any drug than others are. The type of drug prescribed is another factor – some are more addictive. The circumstances can also be important – you are more likely to become addicted during an episode in your life when you feel depressed and dependent. If you are prescribed sleeping pills, try to use them only when you have to, rather than rely on them each and every night – unless, that is, your doctor stresses that they must be taken as a course.

Narcolepsy is one of these disorders: patients can sleep for 18-20 hours each day and suffer from cataplexy (in response to any emotion they may suddenly lose muscular power and collapse in a crumpled heap). Also associated with narcolepsy are sleep paralysis (the person wakes during the night and cannot move) and hallucinations during the period before sleep. This rare disorder, which is almost certainly inherited, can be dramatically alleviated using drugs, particularly the amphetamines and their relatives.

Night terrors and sleep-walking

Various sleep-related problems are grouped together as "parasomnias"; they include sleepwalking and night terrors.

In night terrors, commoner in children than in adults, a person in deep slow-wave sleep appears to wake in absolute terror, often screaming, and cannot be consoled

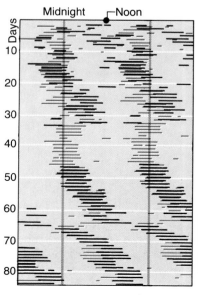

► **Unsynchronized sleep cycles** *pose problems for a couple. The woman's sleep pattern is based on a normal 24-hour cycle (shown in red) but her husband follows a 26.5-hour cycle (the black pattern). From days 1-30 attempts to sleep and wake together are unsuccessful. From days 32-45 the husband is away and the wife establishes a regular rhythm. After this they compromise with a 24.7-hour cycle, which breaks down briefly when the husband involuntarily delays half a cycle.*

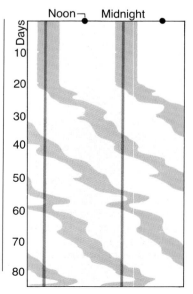

◄ **Divorced from the normal discipline of the clock,** *people in isolation experiments are surprisingly unable to gauge the length of time they have been asleep or even the length of a day. The regular pattern at the top of this record shows an isolation volunteer keeping to a 24-hour cycle while informed of the time. From day 21 help with keeping time stops, and his natural tendency to fall into a 25-hour cycle emerges, shown by the lines drifting steadily to the right one hour at a time.*

until genuinely woken; in the morning there is little or, more usually, no recollection of the event. Night terrors are not to be confused with nightmares, which may likewise cause someone to wake screaming. They usually occur early during the sleep period, while nightmares are normally experienced much later and are all too often remembered.

Night terrors can be dangerous. Sufferers can punch their fists through windows, wander around in busy streets while still effectively asleep, and so on. There have been a few reports of people who have "murdered" others, quite unconsciously, during an attack of night terrors.

Does everybody dream?

All of us dream about 4-5 times each night, but most of our dreams are forgotten: only those that are sufficiently startling to have an impact on us – perhaps to the extent that they wake us – are likely to be recalled.

Often we wake with no memory at all of the fact that we have been dreaming, let alone being able to recall what we were dreaming about. However, if people are woken up during a period of REM sleep, either by the alarm clock or deliberately in the laboratory, they will generally remember their dreams or, at least, be aware of the fact that they have been dreaming.

During REM sleep most of the muscles of the body, apart from those of the eyes and the respiratory system, are paralyzed, and this may account for many of the sensations and experiences reported from powerful dreams – like the inability to move or the feeling of being squashed by a great weight during nightmares. Not all dreaming occurs during REM sleep.

Dreams may trigger nocturnal problems – asthmatic attacks, for example, which for some sufferers only occur at night. For some, the distinction between dreams and certain kinds of hallucinations can be difficult. CS

WHEN DO WE WAKE?

Does how long you sleep depend on how tired you are? Partly, yes, but sleep also comes upon us habitually – when we have strong and well-established daily rhythms – normally, when we are getting near to the low point in our daily rhythm of changing body temperature (see *Ch5*).

Daily rhythm also tends to affect when we wake. If you go to sleep earlier than usual you will probably wake earlier but sleep longer. If you stay up late you will wake later but sleep less. When you stay up very late, however, you may run into a period of your daily cycle that your body lets you sleep right through, for as many as 16 hours, and you may wake in the early hours of the morning.

This is one of the reasons why your first night's sleep when you are heavily jet-lagged can end when neither the people at home nor those in your new time zone are waking. As your established daily rhythms are weakened in the new time zone, the ability to sleep for such long periods will be lost.

◄ **Asleep in the afternoon.** *Flying from one time-zone to another can completely disrupt our normal sleeping patterns. This couple arrived in Rome at 10am local time (3am home time) and set off sight-seeing. At 2pm Rome time (7am home time) a short nap turned into a three-hour slumber, from which they woke spontaneously at 5pm Rome time (10am home time).*

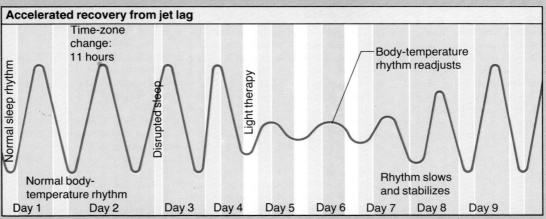

Accelerated recovery from jet lag

Normal sleep rhythm

Time-zone change: 11 hours

Disrupted sleep

Light therapy

Body-temperature rhythm readjusts

Normal body-temperature rhythm

Rhythm slows and stabilizes

Day 1 Day 2 Day 3 Day 4 Day 5 Day 6 Day 7 Day 8 Day 9

▲ **We normally go to sleep** *when body temperature is falling, and wake as it begins to rise (days 1-2). International travel across time zones (day 2) divorces sleep and* body-temperature rhythms. Days 4-6: intense light therapy before sleep can shorten the time it takes for body-temperature rhythm to adjust. The therapy is *believed to achieve its effect by inhibiting production of the hormone melatonin (see Ch5).*

7 TIME AND THE SENSES

Age is an enemy of some, but not all of our senses. Vision and hearing deteriorate in many people as they grow older; food may taste more bland as the number of taste buds on the tongue declines, but seldom do we lose our sense of smell.

RODS AND CONES – NIGHT VISION AND DAY VISION

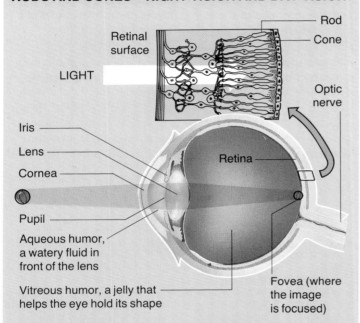

The retina of the eye is made up of about 130 million light-sensitive cells. These are of two kinds, named rods and cones for their distinctive shapes. Both rods and cones react to light, but the cones produce a different response to different wavelengths (colors) of light. The rods, on the other hand, are sensitive to very much lower intensities of light than are the cones. This is why we can still see things in very dim surroundings, but only in shades of gray.

The sensitivity of the rods is quite astounding: once the eye has fully adapted to darkness (this takes about 20 minutes) it is capable of discerning a candle flame at a distance of about 8km (5 miles). However, the rods are slower to adjust to changing levels of light, as we often find when we go to the movies.

When we come into a theater from a bright exterior we usually stumble over the dimly lit chairs (and over other moviegoers) as we try to find a seat, but we are immediately able to see the brightly lit colored images on the screen.

The rods and cones are not evenly distributed on the retina. A tiny central area directly behind the lens consists entirely of cones, and it is no coincidence that this is the region possessing the greatest power to resolve detail. Our eyes are clearly adapted so that we get the best possible view – including color – of the things that are of greatest interest to us. Conversely, there are more rods around the edge of the retina than near its center, which is why, in poor light, we see things better out of the corners of our eyes than if they are straight ahead. **EM**

THE WORKINGS of our senses require time. When we see something, for example, there is always a delay between the light reaching us and the processing by the brain of the final, recognizable image. Generally it takes 10-100 milliseconds, or more, for the light falling on the retina (the light-sensitive layer at the back of the eye) to be translated into nerve impulses that can be transmitted to the brain. It requires a further 70-200 milliseconds (longer in poor light – see box feature), for these nervous impulses to travel along the optic nerve to reach the brain. The brain then needs about 100-200 milliseconds to process the information, so that we are finally able to see the image.

It is important to remember that our sensory experiences are not a product of our sense organs – our eyes, ears, nose and so on. The sense organs receive stimuli and react by sending information to the brain for processing; they themselves do not see, hear, smell, taste or feel anything, even though it may seem that way. It is only after the processing stage that we can truly be said to have sensed something.

How does the sense of vision develop in infants?

At the time of birth the retina of the eye is still developing: the baby can see, but with only about 10 percent of adult efficiency. It takes roughly six months for the baby's eyes to achieve the same optical abilities as those of an adult: color vision, stereoscopic vision, clear focus and coordinated eye movements. Rather more time is required before the brain's contribution to the sense of vision is fully developed.

Newborn babies voluntarily turn their heads toward a diffuse light and close their eyes if a bright light is suddenly shone at them. However, it is not until they are 4-6 weeks old that they are capable of gazing intently at an object; usually this first object is the mother's face during feeding. Some young babies, especially when tired, may suffer from cross-eye (squint) from time to time. Normally this condition sorts itself out by the time they are six months old. If it persists, or if the cross-eye is present all the time, you should consult your doctor.

Human faces are especially interesting to babies. By the age of three months children are visually very alert, and will deliberately move their heads to get a better view of something that interests them. At about the same age they discover their hands, which they bring in front of their faces so that they can watch as they move them around. A toy put in the hands may, if held long enough, be brought toward the face for examination but, as soon as it is dropped, the baby shows no effort to try to see where it might have gone.

At six months babies want to see everything, watching the activities of adults or older children around them

THE BRIGHTER THE IMAGE, THE FASTER YOU SEE IT

Try the following experiment. Set up a widely swinging pendulum so that it is going from side to side directly in front of you. As you watch it you will see quite clearly that the pendulum is swinging from one side to another.

Now hold a dark filter (such as one lens of a pair of sunglasses) in front of one eye. The pendulum will seem to be traveling in a circle or ellipse, moving toward and away from you as it goes from side to side.

The explanation for this phenomenon is that the darker image is taking longer to reach the brain than the brighter one. A computer image RIGHT of a cross sec-tion through the base of the skull (with the eyeballs at the top) shows the time it normal-ly takes for light to be registered. In the covered eye, however, the dark lens delays

Optic nerve impulses

10-100 milliseconds are needed for light falling on the retina to be translated into nerve impulses

70-200 milliseconds later nerve impulses reach the vision centers at the back of the brain

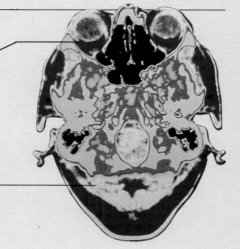

the transmission of signals from the retina to the brain. The brain is accustomed to interpreting the slightly different signals it receives from each eye to indicate the distance of an object. In this case it interprets the difference in the timing of the signals it receives from the eyes in the same way, creating the illusion of depth in the pendulum's swing.

The phenomenon is named the Pulfrich effect for the 19th-century scientist Carl Pulfrich who first explained what was happening. Oddly, because Pulfrich himself had only one good eye, he was never able personally to witness his "own" effect. **EM**

---

with considerable interest. If a small toy is placed within their reach they will stretch out their hands to grasp it, transfer it from hand to hand, and put it to the mouth for sucking and tasting. When the toy is dropped the baby will look for it briefly before forgetting about it and abandoning the search.

Year-old babies can see clearly, and their brains are well able to interpret what is seen. Children of this age pick up small objects, using their forefinger and thumb as pincers, and make a concerted effort to find a dropped toy that has rolled out of view. They can recognize people they know at a distance of 6m (20ft) or more. **PW**

The hazards of a lazy eye

All of our abilities are likely to diminish through disuse, and vision is no exception. In terms of vision, the time between shortly after birth and age 5-6 years is crucially important. Should one or both eyes be denied their normal input of light for a substantial period – for example, because of a cataract or cross-eye (squint) – vision may be permanently impaired. This is because the links between the eye and the brain break down through lack of use. The unused eye becomes "lazy" and poor eyesight or even blindness can be the result.

The earlier this condition (named "stimulus deprivation amblyopia") is discovered and treated, the quicker and more complete will be the recovery. Treatment – which involves putting a patch over the good eye for some hours each day and so making the lazy eye work – usually takes a matter of months.

Nearsightedness and farsightedness

Nearsightedness (myopia) and farsightedness (hypermetropia) commonly develop during childhood and adolescence. Nearsightedness occurs because the eyeball grows too large for the cornea and lens to be able to focus the incoming light from distant objects properly. In farsightedness, the eyeball is too short to focus on near objects properly. After the teen years, once general body growth is complete, nearsightedness is unlikely to increase much, if at all. At one time it was believed that the use of glasses could prevent nearsightedness and farsightedness but this idea is now generally discredited. Contact lenses or glasses may be used at any time after birth, although clearly it is almost impossible to keep glasses in place on a very young child. Obviously it is sensible for children – and adults – always to endeavor to have comfortable seeing conditions and good lighting and posture when reading or performing detailed tasks.

How does vision decline in age?

If you reach adulthood with good eyesight it is very likely that you will have good vision until late in life, but one problem that may bother you is presbyopia (or "old-sight"). When you look at something distant and immediately afterward at something close (as when you look out a window and then turn your attention to a book) it takes the eye a perceptible period of time to adjust its focus – about 0.25sec for the lens to contract so that you

FARSIGHTEDNESS

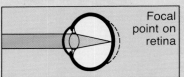

Distant objects: the eyeball is too short, but by making the lens more spherical light from distant objects can be focused on the retina.

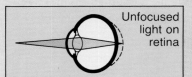

Near objects: even by making the lens very spherical near objects cannot be brought into focus.

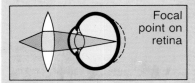

Correction: glasses with convex lenses permit the eyes to focus on near objects.

NEARSIGHTEDNESS

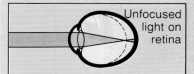

Distant objects: the eyeball is too long. Even keeping the lens as flat as it can be, it is impossible to focus light from distant objects on the retina.

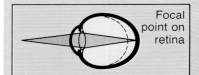

Near objects: without making the lens as spherical as would normally be necessary it is possible to focus on near objects.

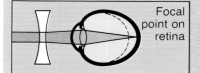

Correction: glasses with concave lenses permit the eyes to focus on distant objects.

OLDSIGHTEDNESS

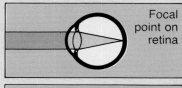

Distant objects: the eye focuses normally, with a flattened lens.

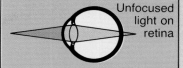

Near objects: the lens having lost its elasticity, it cannot form the spherical shape that would focus light from near objects.

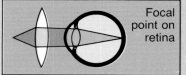

Correction: glasses with convex lenses permit the eyes to focus on near objects.

can look at something close up and a little longer for the lens to relax so that you can look at something distant. This is called "accommodation."

The time-lapse is minimal in the young, but much more noticeable after the ages of 45-50. After 50, the lens may no longer be able to change its shape to focus on near objects. Presbyopia can be countered effectively by the use of reading glasses. After the mid-sixties it is unlikely to progress very much further. One effect of the condition is that because it makes us farsighted, it cancels out nearsightedness. **EM**

What causes cataracts?

About 5 percent of older people have their vision impaired because of cataracts (where the lens becomes opaque); most people over 90 show some signs of cataracts, and often these must be removed by surgery. Many younger people – especially diabetics and those taking corticosteroid drugs – likewise may suffer from cataracts, but certainly the incidence increases with age. Overall, only 10 percent of people with cataracts suffer any obvious visual impairment. Early symptoms are a speck before the eye and being dazzled in bright light. If you then find that your vision is becoming generally blurred, you should consult your doctor at once. The customary treatment is to remove the offending lens and replace it with an artificial one. This operation is less drastic than it might sound: sometimes the patient can go home the same day.

The major cause of cataracts is almost certainly excessive exposure to ultraviolet light (a component of sunlight), although infrared light may also play a part. You can purchase sunglasses that will protect your eyes from these forms of radiation. It should be stressed, however, that no one is really sure why cataracts happen; they may often simply be a natural consequence of aging.

Diabetes, macular degeneration and glaucoma

Other age-related ailments that cause loss of vision include diabetic retinal disease, macular degeneration and glaucoma.

Diabetic retinal disease is by no means confined to older people – anyone suffering from diabetes is vulnerable – but, since diabetes is itself more likely to occur among people of middle age and upward, the associated loss of vision is commoner in age than in youth. The condition – patchy loss of the field of vision – is progressive, but laser surgery can arrest its development. Regular checks are necessary if the disease is to be caught early enough for treatment to be effective.

The cause of macular degeneration is usually unknown. The condition affects the eye's central point of focus: an initial difficulty in seeing small objects progresses to distortion of the image and then to overall blurring of vision. Often the second eye develops the same symptoms, although lagging a couple of years behind the first. It is likely that in the future laser surgery will be able to deal with this condition (it can already be used to help considerably), but for the moment most sufferers have to make do with wearing correctly designed glasses.

Glaucoma occurs when the fluid inside the eyeball fails to drain properly: the pressure inside the eyeball rises, so that the blood supply to the retina and optic nerve is impeded. Sometimes glaucoma sets in suddenly, but much more often the condition develops over a period of months or years, going unnoticed for most of this time. Glaucoma is treated either by regular eye-drops or, if necessary, by a drainage operation. If you have a family history of glaucoma, you should have your pressures checked regularly.

Why does night vision fail as we age?

As we age, the cornea (the outer layer of the eye) becomes a little more opaque, so that by the time we reach 70 we definitely require more light if we are to see an image clearly. The pupil of the eye becomes more rigid: not only does it stay smaller than that of a younger person in any specific lighting condition, its reactions to changes in illumination become slower. Both of these factors affect night driving. Older people not only have poorer night vision but also take longer to adjust to the dazzling effect of oncoming headlamps.

The cells of the retina become a little less efficient as we age. Some of the effects of this are noticeable in everyday life; others become evident only in tests. The most obvious change is that older people have greater difficulty distinguishing colors at the blue and violet end of the spectrum. There is some evidence that older people also find it harder to make out the difference between white and pale yellow.

The overall effect of these changes is that the older eye needs three times as much illumination as a younger one if it is to record the same intensity of image. NC

How long does it take to hear a sound?

When we talk about how long it takes us to *see* something, we usually ignore the time it takes for the light to reach us from the object we are looking at: light travels so fast – about 300,000kps (186,000 miles per second) – that the time it takes to reach us from any object we see on Earth is so short as to be negligible. For example, light from the horizon reaches us in 0.02 milliseconds. Sound is far slower: at sea level it travels at 332mps (1,089ft/sec or 743mph), which means that a sound would take nearly 17 seconds to reach us from the distance of the horizon. The time taken for our ear to receive the sound and transmit the information to the brain, and for the brain to process that information, pales into insignificance by comparison.

Underwater we hear things much more quickly. This is because sound travels more swiftly in mediums where the molecules are more tightly packed together. The speed of sound through fresh water is about four times its speed through air; it travels through salt water a little faster still. In space – despite the dramatic sound tracks of Hollywood science-fiction movies – sound cannot travel at all. MH

PROBLEMS OF AGING VISION

A diminished field of vision *is the result of glaucoma. Pressure in the eyeball damages the optic nerve which can transmit only a partial image to the brain.*

Tunnel vision *or retinitis pigmentosa is a hereditary condition. Peripheral sight is gradually lost as blood vessels in the retina are replaced with scars.*

A blind spot *in the center of the visual field is a symptom of macular degeneration. This develops when the blood supply to the macula (part of the retina) is reduced.*

Clarity of vision is lost *in an eye with cataract. The lens is gradually clouded, blocking light entering the eye and so reducing vision. Often, cataract affects both eyes.*

How do infants react to sound?

Babies react not only to external sounds but also to the ones they produce themselves. It is a common parental experience to see young babies produce a gurgle or squeak so fascinating that they are startled into a few moments of contemplative silence.

Newborn babies will startle if there is a sudden loud noise and will become still in response to a softer, more continuous sound – hence the use of lullabies to soothe babies to sleep. Very young babies produce sound in only one way – crying – but the cries vary in intensity and pitch, so that soon the parents learn to differentiate between signals of hunger and genuine distress calls. At about four weeks old, soon after learning to smile, babies will typically start to make soft cooing noises when spoken to gently by adults.

By the time they are three months old babies have a large repertoire of pleasant sounds when they are contented; they can also create a quite staggering amount of noise when distressed or uncomfortable. In terms of external sounds, they may begin to look around for the sources of these but as yet are unable to pinpoint their origins automatically, in the way that adults usually can. This is because their brains are not yet capable of performing the fairly subtle set of operations that is required if the direction of a sound is to be located. **PW**

WHAT ARE SOUND FREQUENCIES?

Ossicles
Cochlea
Eardrum
Eustachian tube

Sound is a wave motion. However, it is not like a wave at sea, which makes the surface of the water go up and down. Instead, a sound wave creates alternating regions of high and low pressure in the air. To understand this we can think of one of the tines of a tuning fork. If the tuning fork is designed to sound the note middle C, the tine will vibrate about 262 times each second (262Hz). When it moves toward us it will pack together the air molecules in our direction, creating a zone of high pressure. When it moves away from us, there will be a zone of low pressure moving in our direction. These alternating regions of high and low pressure cause anything in their path to vibrate.

When a sound travels into our ear it meets the eardrum, which vibrates in response to the sequence of changing air pressures. The vibrations are transmitted through a series of small bones (ossicles) in the middle ear to another membrane (the oval window), which passes them on to the inner ear. One of the two main parts of the inner ear is the "cochlea," a spiral-shaped structure filled with fluid. Inside the cochlea is the "organ of Corti," which has sensitive cells called "hair cells." Vibrations in the fluid of the cochlea stimulate the endings of the hair cells so that electrical signals are produced. These signals are then transmitted through the auditory nerve to the brain, which interprets them as a sound. **MH**

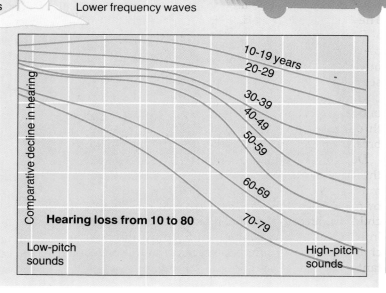

The Doppler Effect

Moving vehicle

Higher frequency waves

Lower frequency waves

▲ **The Doppler effect**. *As a police car approaches, the pitch of its blaring siren is higher than when the car speeds away from us. This is because sound waves reach us more quickly, therefore more frequently, as their source moves closer. They are delayed by the increased distance as the car moves away, and so they arrive less frequently. This effect was explained by the Austrian physicist Christian Johann Doppler in 1842.*

▶ **How hearing declines with age**. *Reaching its peak when we are about 10 years old, the sense of hearing becomes less acute as we grow older. Lost ability to hear high-pitched sounds is more marked than lost ability to hear low-pitched ones. Hearing difficulties are common among the elderly because the inner ear ceases to function properly.*

Comparative decline in hearing

10-19 years
20-29
30-39
40-49
50-59
60-69
70-79

Hearing loss from 10 to 80

Low-pitch sounds

High-pitch sounds

How do we locate sounds?

The brain relies on various clues when locating the direction a sound is coming from. First, there is the fact that the sound does not reach the two ears at the same time: the sound wave reaching one ear is out of phase with that reaching the other, and the brain is so finely aware of this that a time-difference of a mere 0.1 milliseconds is sufficient for it to make an accurate guess as to the direction from which the sound is coming. Second, the brain interprets the difference in the sound intensities reported to it by the two ears – in simple terms, a sound to our right will sound much louder in the right ear than in the left, and vice versa. Third, the brain can interpret differences in the quality of the sound: a sound from directly in front of us has a different quality than one originating behind us for the very simple reason that the outer flaps of our ears point forward. An adult brain takes these three kinds of data – and other, more complex information – and automatically processes them in such a way that it can identify the source of the sound. The brain of a very young infant has yet to learn this trick.

By the age of six months, however, the brain is becoming smarter. Babies of this age immediately turn their heads to face the direction of a parent's voice (primarily the mother's, but often the father's too). The child can immediately identify the source of a sound and, assuming the sound is for some reason interesting, will turn to look in that direction.

How can hearing be in danger during childhood?

As people grow older their hearing generally declines: they are less able to hear high-pitched sounds, and we have to speak to them more clearly and less rapidly. They may become partially or totally deaf.

Deafness is a hazard of early childhood, too – in fact, one of the "risk periods" is the time before birth, when infection of the mother with German measles (rubella – see *Chs15, 20*) or syphilis can result in her baby being born totally deaf. Another risk period is around the time of birth, when any prolonged deprivation of oxygen, through a delay in either delivery or the initiation of breathing, can result in partial or complete deafness.

During early and later childhood, hearing can be threatened by infectious diseases like meningitis and mumps. More commonly, short-term deafness is caused by middle-ear infection. Unless this is prolonged or the child is subject to repeated attacks (leading to chronic ear infection and concomitant learning difficulties), your child's doctor will simply prescribe a course of decongestants, painkillers, and possibly antibiotics. **MH**

TASTE AND SMELL

Though the number of taste buds on the tongue declines, age does not blunt our sense of smell; in fact, this sense may improve with age, as experience makes us more discerning. Most of taste is smell: if we pinch our noses and close our eyes we can eat an onion as if it were an apple. It has been estimated that we can distinguish 2-4,000 different odors.

Why should some substances produce more intense responses in terms of taste and smell than others? Saccharin tastes 5,000 times sweeter to us than sugar; we notice the smell of garlic (or, at least, its characteristic chemical, methyl mercaptan) at concentrations 3 million times lower than if it were chloroform. No one is sure why substances produce such different responses.

Taste and smell can be blunted by disease: the common cold, through its effect on the mucous membrane of the nose, can numb our senses of taste and smell for a week or two. But more commonly the blunting comes about because of adaptation: if an odor is present all the time, the brain soon stops registering it – we notice garlic on other people's breath only if we have not been eating garlic ourselves.

The nervous system responds faster to smell than to taste: it takes about one second before the taste buds transmit a relevant signal to the brain; stimuli from the cells of the nose are transmitted within 0.1 sec. **MH**

How does aging affect hearing?

As early as age 30 we start to lose our ability to hear very high-pitched sounds – those above 4,000Hz. By the time we are 60 we are likely to have difficulty hearing any sound pitched above 1,000Hz. In addition, by this age we may have problems in interpreting speech (especially when there is background noise) and in detecting the source of a sound. Another effect concerns the intensity of sounds: the difference between a sound that is too soft for us to hear properly and one that is too loud becomes less. The causes of these decreases in ability are not properly understood, but they affect 30 percent of people over 65 and 60 percent over 85.

Hearing aids can help, although often deafness can be treated much more simply: it may well be that the outer ear has become clogged up with wax, which can be easily removed. The commonest type of hearing aid is worn just behind the ear and has a separate switch so that the user can adjust it for telephone conversations. Now out of fashion but in fact very efficient for face-to-face discussions is the ear trumpet. **NC**

A Sense of Balance

Vertigo, and even travel sickness, can affect us for different reasons at different times of life.

WE OFTEN talk about the five senses, but in fact we have six. The sixth is called proprioception (or kinesthesia), and is the sense whereby the brain knows the position and state of movement of the muscles. Special nerve endings named proprioceptors report back to the brain what the muscles are doing, so that the brain constantly has a picture of the way that the parts of the body are disposed. If it were not for this sense, we would not be able to perform coordinated movements in the dark or with our eyes shut. Allied to proprioception is balance, which, although it is not really a sense, is associated with one of our major sense organs, the ear.

The ear and our state of balance

Inside the inner ear are the cochlea, which are responsible for our sense of hearing (see p88), and three hollow partial hoops, the semicircular canals, set at right angles to each other. The semi-circular canals are filled with a fluid, endolymph, and on their walls they have specialized nerve endings called hair cells. When we move the head quickly, the endolymph follows the general trend, although a little more slowly. The movement of the fluid distorts the hair cells, which transmit an appropriate electrical signal to the brain. Because of the arrangement of the semicircular canals, the brain receives information about six directions of spin – up and down, left and right, forward and back – and interprets this data to give an overall picture.

Changes in the responses of the hair cells, together with the evidence of our eyes and the information from the proprioceptors, enable the brain to get us upright and keep us that way.

Childhood vertigo

Vertigo (dizziness) is the sensation that everything else is spinning except you; it is distinct from light-headedness, where there is a momentary loss of balance. Vertigo is much longerlasting. It has a number of causes, some of which are commoner at different ages.

Childhood vertigo is most usually a result of ear infection: the pressure in the middle ear and the Eustachian tube is altered, so that the hair cells give wrong information to the brain. Older children will report the sensation; younger children may not, so be alert for signs of clumsiness or falling over. Once the underlying ear infection has been cured the clumsiness should disappear. If it does not, consult your doctor as a matter of urgency.

Vertigo in adults

In adolescence and in early adulthood the two common causes of vertigo are migraines and inflammation of the middle ear (labyrinthitis).

The vertigo of a migraine attack normally lasts for only a few hours. It usually precedes the onset of the headache; the standard measures used to ease or prevent migraines will generally have the same effect on the associated vertigo.

Labyrinthitis (also known as vestibulitis) lasts much longer – sometimes for weeks. Initially the person suffers vertigo in any position: relief can be given only by rest (preferably in the dark) and the taking of anti-nauseant drugs. After roughly a week the person can start moving about again, although cautiously. At this stage any sudden movement is likely to cause an attack of vertigo. The direction is often important; for example, an up-and-down movement may not cause the adverse reaction that a left-to-right movement does. About three weeks after the disease's initial onset the symptoms normally disappear.

Ménière's disease, which is fortunately quite rare, especially strikes people in their thirties and forties. It is thought to be associated with a disorder of the fluid contents of one of the components

Time provides one cure for travel sickness: *we adapt to the motion that has initially made us ill. Surveys have shown that, in moderately rough conditions, 30 percent of passengers on transatlantic liners are sick within the first two days of their cruise, but within two further days most of the sufferers have completely recovered. Children are particularly sus-* *ceptible to travel sickness because their brains are not yet able to cope with the differences between actual and expected sensory information that cause us to lose our sense of balance on ships or in cars or trains. By 10-12 years old, however, most have grown out of their travel sickness.*

occurs when they move their heads to look up or down. This happens because of the way that blood is supplied to the part of the brain that controls vision and balance. Most of the blood reaching this region is carried by the vertebral artery, which passes up the spinal column before joining an artery in the brain (the basilar artery).

The age-related narrowing of the artery, combined with wear and tear of the vertebrae, can mean that this part of the brain is temporarily starved of blood: light-headedness, collapse and occasionally vertigo can be the result. The attacks are short-lived, but nevertheless alarming. The best way to prevent them is to lean backward or forward from the waist, keeping the neck straight, if you want to look up or down.

How can travel sickness be eased?

Most of us are familiar with the unpleasant sensations of travel sickness. No one is precisely sure as to the exact cause, although it seems to be a result of the brain receiving apparently conflicting messages from the eye and the labyrinth of the middle ear.

Countering travel sickness is not especially difficult. Pills should be taken before, not during, the journey. There are many varieties on the market. Should you be traveling without pills there other measures you can take. You can help matters by fixing your gaze on a stable point, such as the horizon or a distant landmass; you can assist this by keeping your head completely still, perhaps by placing it in a firm head-rest. If there is no fixed point to look at you are better to close your eyes. Many people find that the symptoms are less severe if they lie down; in part this is because when we are lying down we tend to move less. **MH**

of the inner ear; it causes vertigo, nausea, vomiting and, on the affected side, tinnitus (ringing or buzzing in the ear) and deafness. Attacks vary in frequency and may last a day, a week or even longer. The symptoms can be treated as for labyrinthitis. There is no known cure for the disease, although some doctors claim that surgery can help.

There are two further causes of vertigo which particularly affect the elderly. One of these is called "benign positional vertigo." It is thought to be caused by a disorder

either of one of the semicircular canals or of the connection between the inner ear and the brain. Sufferers experience severe vertigo and vomiting whenever they turn rapidly in a particular direction. The symptoms can be treated easily enough, and the condition is likely to resolve itself after a few weeks. However, anyone who has suffered benign positional vertigo will probably be wary of making any sudden movement ever after.

The other vertiginous sensation that often afflicts older people

8 TIME AND PHYSICAL ABILITY

As time passes, our capacity for physical exertion changes. Our reactions slow down as messages between the central nervous system and muscles are transmitted less efficiently. An active lifestyle can not only retard but counteract this and other negative influences of time on our physical prowess and mobility.

RECORD TIMES FOR COMPLETING A MARATHON

10-year-olds to 80-year-olds

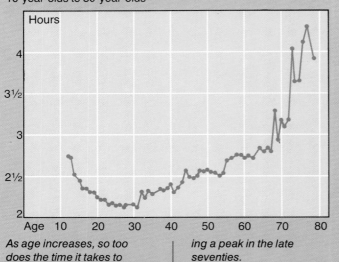

As age increases, so too does the time it takes to complete a marathon, reach-ing a peak in the late seventies.

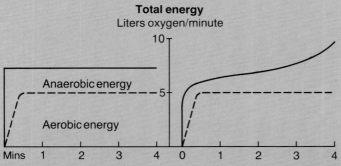

Total energy
Liters oxygen/minute

During a race that lasts 4 minutes *a well-trained athlete can take in 5 liters of oxygen per minute* ABOVE LEFT. *It is used by low-twitch muscle fibers which get their energy aerobically (that is, by using oxygen). This aerobic energy source allows for steady physical effort over long periods. Additionally, fast-twitch muscle fibers can function anaerobically,* *(without oxygen), thereby providing energy equivalent to another 9 liters of oxygen (2.25 liters per minute). This anaerobic method is best for short, highly strenuous periods of activity.* ABOVE RIGHT *Toward the end of a race, when a sudden spurt is required, is the usual time for most of the anaerobic energy to be used.*

PHYSICAL ABILITY depends not just on muscular strength or flexibility, but on the nervous system – on coordination, reaction time, and so on. All of these aspects of physical ability change during our lives, from our feeble uncoordinated movements as an infant through our skilled use of strength in youth and middle age to our (often) weak and again less coordinated abilities in age.

How do nerve fibers work so quickly?

Suppose you are playing a stroke at tennis. Your eyes signal the trajectory of the approaching ball to the brain. The signals go along the optic nerves – bundles of fine nerve fibers like wires in a telephone cable. The brain takes in the signals and, more or less subconsciously, works out the appropriate stroke to make. If it does not do it rapidly, it is too late. Then orders to the muscles, for example, to the wrist muscles of the racket hand, leave the brain in other nerve fibers (motor fibers) that run first down the spinal cord and then out in the ordinary nerves of the limbs; and that takes time too.

In situations such as this, and in many other situations in civilized life and in the more primitive life of our evolutionary ancestors, speed of reaction is crucial. One element in success is to have nerve fibers that transmit signals at a high velocity.

Each nerve in the body is a bundle of many, often thousands, of fine nerve fibers, the largest of which are about 0.02mm (0.0008in) in diameter. Signals pass down a nerve fiber in the form of electrical pulses, like the dots of Morse code in a telegraph wire, but unlike Morse code the pattern of the dots does not matter, only the number that are sent – the impulse frequency. Each dot – that is, each nerve impulse – lasts less than one one-thousandth of a second (1 millisecond).

Nerve conduction is based on electricity, which is why it is fast, but the nerve fiber is not just a simple cable, not a wire-like insulated conductor. The body has no really good electrical conductors in its makeup. Tissue fluids (mainly dilute salt solutions) conduct electricity about 50 million times worse than copper, and there is nothing better in the body. If the nerve fiber were a simple cable, the signal would fade out before it reached the other end, unless that were a very short distance.

The solution is to regenerate the impulses every milli-meter or so, at what is called a node. The nodes are analogous to the repeaters placed every few miles on undersea cables to restore the signals to strength and hand them on. These repeaters use electric power fed along the cable itself to perform this amplification. Our nerve nodes draw the currents for their amplifier from low-voltage chemical batteries based on sodium and potassium ions in the tissue fluids.

Coordination, strength, flexibility and fast reflexes *are vital aspects of physical ability. Reactions to sensory stimuli* RIGHT *are the most*

rapid. Reactions to aching pain are slower: the sensations travel along nerve fibers that take longer to transmit messages to the brain.

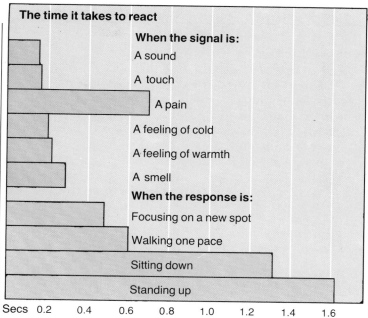

The time it takes to react

When the signal is:
A sound
A touch
A pain
A feeling of cold
A feeling of warmth
A smell

When the response is:
Focusing on a new spot
Walking one pace
Sitting down
Standing up

Secs   0.2   0.4   0.6   0.8   1.0   1.2   1.4   1.6

The nerve impulse jumps from node to node, but it does this so rapidly that it appears to move continuously. In a fiber conducting an impulse at 60m (195ft) per second, with nodes every millimeter, the impulse is passing nodes at a rate of 60,000 nodes per second.

Why are some reactions faster than others?

Human nerves transmit at speeds up to those of the fastest trains – 200km (125 miles) per hour, or 60m (almost 195ft) per second. Even so, the brain works so fast that the time spent sending signals along nerves to and from it is often a significant element in the speed of the body's reaction. For example, if someone flicks the skin of your forehead, you immediately blink; it is a reflex. And the blink muscles start contracting only about 10 milliseconds after the flick. If on the other hand the big toe is pricked with a pin, the reaction is much slower. Part of the reason for this is that it is roughly 4m (13ft) to the brain and back again. At 60m per second, that uses up at least 70 milliseconds, just in transmission time along nerves. This is about seven times the whole delay of the blink reflex, where the lengths of nerve involved are so much shorter.

Response time in the brain or spinal cord also con-tributes to reaction time. In the familiar knee jerk reflex, a tap from a rubber hammer on the tendon below the kneecap causes a jerk-like contraction of muscles in the thigh. The delay in this case is only about 20 milliseconds, and nearly all of it is transmission delay to the spinal cord and back, with only a millisecond or two for making the connection between the fibers coming in and those going out. Toward the other end of the scale, the response time of the brain in a complicated reaction, such as stamping on the brake pedal when a child steps off the curb, is of the order of 0.1sec (100 milliseconds), about 100 times longer than the delay in the spinal cord in the knee jerk.

Not everything has to be done as fast as possible. Nerve fibers responsible for pain transmit much more slowly, some at about 5m (16ft) per second, but those concerned with aching pain at only 0.5m per second or less. There are many other slower conducting types.

What happens when nerves are damaged?

Nerve transmission is slowed in many diseases, for example, in multiple sclerosis and in AIDS infection of the nerves. However, transmission delays often do not show up in practice, unless the patient is engaging in very demanding activity, such as a game of tennis. The more obvious disabilities appear to be caused by other damage to the nervous system. Measurements of nerve transmission velocity, however, can be of considerable help in diagnosis. For many years this has been done on limb nerves, but in the 1980s the scope of the technique was extended to the nerve fibers in the brain and spinal cord. The brain itself is stimulated with electrical shocks or magnetic stimuli applied through the scalp.

DIFFERENT BY FRACTIONS OF A SECOND

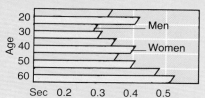

On hearing a signal, men usually react more quickly than women. In both sexes, reaction times become longer as age increases.

Age: 20, 30, 40, 50, 60

Men
Women

Sec   0.2   0.3   0.4   0.5

Speed and timing

In many things we do, rapidity of reaction is not crucial but timing is. In tennis, both speed and accurate timing are vital, but if you are playing the piano it is timing and rhythm that matter. In disease, disturbances of rhythm and timing are most obvious in cases of damage to the cerebellum, an organ of the brain at the bottom of the skull, more or less hidden by the main cerebral hemispheres. In people with cerebellar disease, limb movements and speech are irregular and jerky. MH

Will my reactions slow as I grow older?

Reactions slow as we age, but whether the effect is significant will depend on lifestyle. Elderly people who have always taken regular exercise have total reaction times that are much the same as those of younger people, but the reactions of elderly people with a sedentary lifestyle are much slower. One inescapable fact is that the speed of transmission of impulses along the nerves slows by about 15 percent between the ages of 30 and 80.

HOW MOVEMENTS ARE PRODUCED

For a movement to occur, the nervous system and muscles must work together closely. Sensory receptor nerves transmit impulses to the central nervous system in response to a sensory stimulus. Motor nerves carry impulses away from the central nervous system to the muscles. Every time we move, the central nervous system sends electrical impulses along these motor nerves to muscle fibers. The impulses cause the muscles to contract. As soon as they stop, the muscles relax.

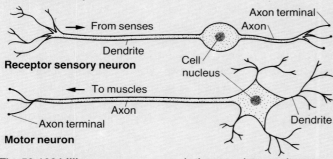

Receptor sensory neuron — From senses, Dendrite, Axon terminal, Axon, Cell nucleus

Motor neuron — To muscles, Axon, Axon terminal, Dendrite

The 50-100 billion nerve cells in the brain and spinal cord each consist of a cell body with many projections. The longest of the projections is the axon. It transmits messages to other nerve cells or to muscles, glands or organs. Shorter dendrites receive impulses from nerve cells.

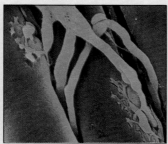

The axon of a motor nerve (magnified 95 times) ABOVE LEFT can make contact with several hundred muscle cells (the bands visible in the background). ABOVE RIGHT Each of its branches terminates in a motor end plate, which stimulates or initiates muscle movements.

How muscles contract. In a relaxed muscle, muscle fibers are organized into threads or myofibrils. Each myofibril is composed of filaments arranged lengthwise and divided by partitions of membrane (Z bands) into sections called sarcomeres. LEFT: Three sarcomeres; each has fine myofilaments – actin – and thicker ones – myosin – BELOW. The myosin has structures called crossbridges. When a muscle contracts, they attach to the actin filaments and pull them. The Z bands are drawn toward each other and the sarcomere is shortened.

Muscle Relaxed

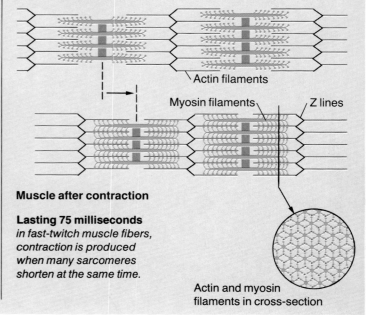

Actin filaments

Myosin filaments

Z lines

Muscle after contraction

Lasting 75 milliseconds in fast-twitch muscle fibers, contraction is produced when many sarcomeres shorten at the same time.

Actin and myosin filaments in cross-section

◄ **Carrying essential oxygen to muscle tissue**, a single blood capillary (magnified 1600 times) contains a row of red blood cells. The muscles use oxygen to release energy. In order to pump more blood to the muscles during strenuous exercise, the heart has to beat harder and faster.

In many reactions this slight slowing is not important. For example, your reaction to a child darting out in front of your car requires you to see the child, transmit the information the very short distance from your eyes to your brain, make a judgment about appropriate action, and send a signal down your spinal cord and then down the sciatic nerve of the leg to contract the muscles at the back of your calf so your foot presses down on the brake.

It is very difficult to measure all the separate components of this complex response, but it is likely that the part that takes the most time is the evaluation, integration and transmission of information in the brain rather than the conduction of the messages through the nerves.

It seems that it is the speed of this central portion of the whole reaction that can decline most severely with age. Interestingly, at all ages the reaction to a child darting out from the kerb is likely to be much swifter than that to an oncoming vehicle. N C

How muscles connect to the nervous system

The basic building block of muscle is the "motor unit": this comprises a motor nerve (a nerve bringing orders from the brain) together with the muscle fibers that contract in response to the instructions of the nerve. The greater the muscular effort needed, the larger the number of motor units that will be firing, but the body has a control system to ensure that not all of the units in a muscle fire at the same time. When sustained muscular effort is needed, the rates of contraction of the individual motor units are varied so that the muscle fibers are rested in rotation while the same overall tension is maintained.

Slow-twitch fibers and fast-twitch fibers

There are two different kinds of muscle fibers, named for the speed at which they work. Slow-twitch, or red fibers get most of their energy from chemical processes involving oxygen; they are therefore said to have a high *aerobic* capacity, and are best suited to endurance exercise. Fast-twitch, or white, fibers get their energy from processes that do not use oxygen, and, with their high *anaerobic* capacity, are best for short sharp bursts of activity. There are at least three different kinds of fast-twitch fibers; some can work either aerobically or anaerobically. Motor units are recruited into action in a

Building up the muscles. One benefit of exercise is that it causes muscle cells to increase in size and efficiency. Because women have fewer muscle fibers, their muscles cannot be developed to the same extent as men's. Weight-training routines are good for building specific muscles, though they do not improve general fitness as effectively as activities like swimming or jogging.

How athletes increase their endurance. *By training for sports that demand high endurance, athletes can increase the concentration of ATP (the body's direct energy source) in their blood. They can also expand their capacity for anaerobic exercise by speeding up the rate at which glycogen in the muscles is converted into lactic acid. Diet is as important as exercise since the body needs a greater supply of substances such as proteins and minerals. Sufficient quantities of protein, iron and other minerals, and certain vitamins, are particularly important, as are carbohydrates which influence how much glycogen is available as an energy source for the muscles during hard physical effort.*

progressive and regulated way. For low-power exercise slow-twitch fibers are used. As the effort increases, the slower of the fast-twitch fibers come into use. Finally, for maximum effort, the fastest fast-twitch fibers are brought into play.

There is a further subtlety in the way the fibers are put to work. As muscle action starts, the motor units with the smallest numbers of nerve fibers are activated before the larger ones. This means that the brain can tell the muscles to make very small movements at first, so that we have very sensitive control over our mobility and can build up smoothly to greater effort.

Our movements are affected also by the arrangement of muscle fibers. In long, strap-like muscles the fibers are end-to-end so that the muscle can shorten very considerably but has little power. In other muscles the fibers are arranged side-by-side: the ability to contract is much less, but the power is much greater. Most muscles have a combination of both arrangements. Further control is gained through muscles cooperating with each other.

How do muscles get energy?

The energy our body requires comes from the food we eat. To be able to use that energy, our bodies have to break the food down and change it chemically. Even-

tually a chemical called ATP (adenosine triphosphate) is available in the tissues. It is the body's direct source of energy.

In aerobic exercise, oxygen is used in the reactions that release energy from ATP, and an end-product is pyruvic acid. When the process occurs without oxygen – in anaerobic exercise – the end-product is lactic acid. When oxygen is in short supply – for example, when you are sprinting, and so using up oxygen faster than your body can deliver it to the muscles – your anaerobic use of energy can very rapidly convert available pyruvic acid to lactic acid.

The time during which this can continue is limited, because as lactic acid accumulates, it slows down the chemical reaction that releases energy from ATP. After the activity stops, however, more oxygen can be supplied to the muscles, and this allows the lactic acid to be converted back into pyruvic acid.

How does a muscle fiber contract?

A single muscle fiber is made up of fine strands (myofibrils), and these are in turn largely made up of the long molecules of two proteins called "actin" and "myosin." The myosin molecules are thicker than the actin molecules and also have projections called cross-

bridges that jut out at right angles along the length of the molecule.

The energy to make a fiber contract comes from ATP. The ATP attaches itself to the myosin's crossbridges in such a way that they grip onto the actin molecules. As energy is released by the ATP, the crossbridges change shape so as to pull the actin molecule along the length of the myosin molecule, rather as if the actin were on a conveyer belt. The farther along the actin is pulled, the shorter the muscle fiber becomes, and so the greater the degree of contraction of the muscle as a whole. **NR**

How do muscles grow bigger?

When the individual cells of a tissue are asked to do more work, they almost invariably get larger. This is called hypertrophy, and it is the only way that muscles can grow bigger.

The bulk of the arm muscles of weightlifters is so large because those muscles are being forced to do a great deal more work than normal. Each of the cells in the muscle fiber increases in size, length and strength so that it is able to deal with the workload imposed on it.

Other sports – for example, cycling and long-distance running – place extra demands on the muscles of the heart, which has to pump harder so that more blood circulates to the muscles to bring them the extra oxygen which they require to generate energy. In healthy adults who take regular strenuous exercise the heart is large because the muscular wall of the left ventricle (the chamber of the heart responsible for pumping oxygenated blood around the body) is thickened. The number of cells present is exactly the same as in the heart of someone who does not exercise regularly, but each cell is bigger and more efficient.

How long does it take muscles to grow?

Muscles take time to acclimatize to an increased workload. Few untrained people are able to complete a marathon, because their leg and heart muscles cannot cope with the unaccustomed demands. With training, however, the cells of the leg and heart muscles get bigger and become more efficient.

The rate at which the muscle cells grow is governed by the frequency and duration of bouts of exercise, but training must be a gradual process, allowing the tissues time to adapt to the progressively increasing demands placed on them. This is especially true as we grow older; many people have died through trying to perform sporting feats which would have caused them little difficulty when they were young.

When training stops, the size and efficiency of the muscle cells decreases rapidly. If you are an amateur athlete you should take care to ensure that you exercise regularly, even out of season. It is interesting to note that when top athletes are forced to take a break – perhaps because of injury – a return to training will very swiftly cause the return of hypertrophy, almost as if the muscles had been primed to respond quickly.

Quite a different kind of example of hypertrophy is the growth of fat cells. A fat and a thin person may have just the same numbers of these, but in the thin person they are empty of fat. When such a cell has a fat globule to store, it becomes round and full.

Hypertrophy can also be the result of disease. The cells of certain parts of the heart may grow larger so that it can pump harder to compensate for a blocked heart valve or because of high blood pressure. **AS**

How are the bones affected by training?

Exercise barely affects bone size, and therefore bone strength. Some bones, such as the femur, may increase in size slightly in the very long term, but the effect is usually minimal.

However, bones can be adversely affected by inappropriate exercise. Repetitive exercise, such as jogging can produce stress (fatigue) fractures in the long bones (commonly in the shins), especially if you suddenly increase the amount of exercise you perform. The solution is to take your time, building up gradually toward a peak of fitness. If you do suffer a stress fracture – and even international athletes can do this when training for a big event – you should stop exercise; your doctor will prescribe rest, possibly with a period in splints. Full recovery is almost certain, but you may experience further stress fractures if you attempt to return to that intensity of exercise again too quickly.

What can be done to improve fitness?

Some aspects of fitness are predetermined: your gender, your basic body shape, your flexibility, and the distribution of different kinds of fibers in your muscles are among the factors which you either cannot change or, at best, can only modify. Some people have greater capacity for work, others for endurance; some are naturally more coordinated than others.

However, even if you will never be able to run as fast as an Olympic athlete, you can still act to make yourself as fit as possible through improving your nervous system (for coordination), your muscle strength, your blood-circulation system (including the heart) and your respiratory system (the ability of the lungs to take in oxygen and release waste gases). Taking exercise is the obvious way of improving all these systems, especially when it is formalized into deliberate and specific training.

However, you should never undergo training or vigorous exercise if you have the slightest concern about your health or general physical condition. Check your fitness using the test in Part One. It is important that you are free of infection. People have died through trying to play sports while suffering no more than a minor infection. If you are in any doubt at all, consult your doctor before you start. NR

Mobility across the lifespan

Most of us are at our most mobile during youth and young adulthood. This is reflected in the ages of topclass achievers in sport. They may start their professional career as early as 14 or 16 but it is very rare that it can be extended beyond the age of 40. However, this does not mean that we need to resign ourselves to relative immobility in later years: an active life usually leads to an active old age.

At birth, infants are incapable of independent locomotion. Control of the head is poor: if they are pulled up to a sitting position, the head flops backward and, similarly, if they are held in the air by a hand underneath the abdomen, the head and limbs dangle down.

By three months babies have considerably more control over their bodies. They can lift their head and chest off the floor, supporting their weight on the forearms. They can kick their legs vigorously, and when they are held in a sitting position they can keep the head in line with the body for at least a short while.

At six months babies can roll over from front to back and, usually, from back to front. They can hold the head firmly in line with the body and, if given some support, can sit securely. If they are held upright with their feet on a firm surface, their legs can bear their weight.

When a baby learns to walk depends on the baby: there is no firm rule. As with other skills, some babies master the art sooner than others. Generally, however, by 12 months babies can sit independently with confidence, pull themselves to a standing position, and walk if they have something to hold onto (for example, the edge of a piece of furniture). Some babies will be walking independently by this age, and most achieve the skill by 18 months. If your baby delays walking much beyond 18 months, you should ask a doctor's opinion.

DEVELOPING MOBILITY
Birth to two years

Birth. Baby lies flat on its abdomen, arms and legs bent under the body, bottom in the air. There is little head control.

Three months. The baby is developing head control, able to push up on hands and forearms.

Six months. The baby has more head control, is able to sit with some support.

One year. The baby is able to stand with support. May walk around holding on to furniture or with a hand held.

When children learn to stand and walk they adopt a typical "lordotic" posture: the spine is held in a concave curve and the abdomen is pushed forward, often looking swollen. This effect disappears from about four onward. Similarly, toddlers often appear knock-kneed or bow-legged but treatment for this is rarely required, the limbs straightening in later childhood. **PW**

The physical abilities of girls and boys

In girls, physical abilities like agility, strength and control usually increase in a regular fashion up to about 14 but after this the rate of increase generally declines, mainly because at this age girls' interests frequently turn to other things. On average, girls achieve their peak of strength at 17. The physical abilities of boys show their most rapid improvement after 14, their strength doubling between 12 and 16 and reaching its maximum when they are about 21 or 22. Statistically, after puberty boys are stronger than girls (although some girls are stronger than some boys), and this difference becomes more marked until peak strength is reached.

What effect does height have on physical ability?

At all ages, height influences physical performance considerably, usually but not always to the benefit of the taller person. Tall people are stronger, heavier and better at throwing. Their potential work rate (ability to do physical work) is greater. However, their greater weight slows them when they run: they accelerate more slowly and have to work harder when going uphill. On the flat the advantage of their longer legs is canceled out by their greater weight.

Of course, these are generalizations. A short squat person can be heavier than a tall thin one, and some short people are capable of very high work rates.

Two years. The child is walking confidently and beginning to run and able to go up and down stairs.

► **A skill that is rarely lost**, *riding a bicycle can help promote a child's physical coordination, balance and strength, as well as keeping them fit and well-exercised. From 6-7 years a child's dexterity gradually increases. In the years between 8 and 12 their motor skills and coordination are refined.*

How do age and sex affect strength and flexibility?

On average, adult men are 50 percent stronger than adult women. However, women's joints tend to be more flexible than men's, an effect visible in children which becomes even more pronounced after puberty; the reason for this is not fully known. Male world athletics records are consistently faster (or higher, or longer) than the female ones. However, in events that rely more on flexibility than on strength, like gymnastics, women are usually supreme. Younger people are generally more flexible than their seniors, and respond more readily to training aimed at improving their flexibility. However, people who exercise throughout life can retain good joint mobility until an advanced age. **NR**

What is osteoarthritis?

Arthritis is a symptom rather than a disease. It is inflammation of a joint (often several joints together), so that there is pain, swelling, and possibly redness of the skin over the joint and loss of physical mobility. Of the many diseases (some infectious) that can cause it, the most common are osteoarthritis and rheumatoid arthritis.

Osteoarthritis affects 90 percent of people over the age of 40, but only to a minor extent, and often it goes unnoticed. It most commonly involves the larger weight-bearing joints, like the knees and hips, as well as the

▶ **Energetic activities** *such as dancing use a large number of muscles and joints. They improve flexibility and, by keeping the joints supple and the muscles that work them strong, they also help prevent the early onset of age-related disorders like osteoarthritis.*

joints of the fingers. People who have consistently over-used certain joints in youth through practicing a particular sport or pastime are especially likely, when older, to develop osteoarthritis in those joints.

What happens is that the coat of cartilage separating the surfaces of the two bones at the joint deteriorates; at the same time the ends of the bones may become thickened and distorted. In due course there may be pain and the function of the joint may be impaired; since the joint is now used less, the muscles that work it gradually waste away. Treatment is by painkillers, reduction of pressure across the joint (for example, a person with osteoarthritis of the hip can use a stick or walking-frame) and, if necessary, surgery, such as replacement of a hip with an artificial one. People with osteoarthritis of the knee are especially helped by weight loss.

What is rheumatoid arthritis?

Rheumatoid arthritis occurs when the membrane in a joint becomes inflamed and inflammation spreads to other parts of the joint and even other tissues of the body. The joint becomes stiff and tender, especially first thing in the morning. This disease typically attacks those in the 40-60 age-group, but people of all ages are vulnerable; about 0.5 percent of the population suffer from the ailment, often only slightly.

Any freely movable joint can be affected, the knuckles and the joints of the toes being most susceptible; the spine and hips are relatively immune. It is known to be an autoimmune disease – a result of the body's own immune defenses destroying tissues – but its causes are not fully understood. It sometimes cures itself, although often the symptoms will disappear only to recur. Anti-inflammatory painkillers can ease the symptoms; other

drugs or even surgery may be necessary.

Both osteoarthritis and rheumatoid arthritis can be extremely painful and can cause severe loss of mobility, especially among older people.

The advantages of keeping mobile

Loss of mobility is usual in later years, but the rate and degree of loss can be controlled. Some people in their eighties can complete marathons, although it takes them rather longer than younger athletes – while many people in their twenties and thirties would have difficulty finishing a marathon at all. Most of the loss of fitness among old people seems to be due to disuse: if you do not use it you lose it. In fact, even if you do use it you lose it eventually, but perhaps not so much that it matters.

In developed countries the elderly are generally fitter than those of a few decades ago because more of them continue to take part in active pastimes. A recent report by the United States National Center for Health Statistics shows 27 percent of people over 65 engage in running, calisthenics, cycling or swimming, compared with 41 percent for the population as a whole, and just as many older as younger people walk for exercise. This extension of activity has been called "youth creep."

Exercise does more than maintain physical fitness. It also helps stave off some major diseases, notably coronary heart disease, hypertension (high blood pressure), stroke, lung disease and osteoporosis (thinning of the bones), and there is even evidence that exercise provides some protection against brain deterioration. A survey carried out of Harvard alumni showed that those who had taken exercise throughout life were twice as likely to survive the years between 70 and 84 as their more sedentary contemporaries.

▼ **Keeping fit in later life** *has several health benefits. By helping to control weight, it protects against diseases like diabetes. By keeping the heart strong it helps us stay active longer. Additionally, because exercise stimulates the production of osteoid (the substance that makes bones hard), it may prevent the bones from declining in bulk and becoming fragile.*

What happens to our bones as we get older?

As we grow older we lose bone matter, a process called osteoporosis. Bone loss occurs in both sexes, starting in women when they are in their thirties and perhaps a little later in men. For up to 10 years after the menopause, women may lose bone particularly rapidly. By 70 a woman can lose 50 percent of her original bone and a man 25 percent. This sex difference is particularly significant because, on average, women start off with a 30 percent smaller bone mass than men.

Osteoporosis can be compared with high blood pressure: it often progresses quite unknown to the person who is put at risk by it. Often it is only after a fracture, usually in the spine, wrist or hip, that the condition is diagnosed. Osteoporosis causes about 1.3 million fractures a year in the United States, costing the country $6-7 billion. Most sufferers are women, partly because more women than men survive to the age when the risk becomes greatest. Most hip and wrist fractures follow falls. Those of the spine may occur simply while getting up from bed or from a chair.

The fracture of the bones of the spine, together with degeneration of the disks between them, causes the spine to hump, a major reason why we lose height in age. Of elderly women who suffer a fractured hip, about 27 percent die within a year; the death rate from this cause is greater than that from breast and womb cancer combined.

Osteoporosis cannot be completely prevented, but we can take steps to avoid accelerated osteoporosis by recognizing the risk factors, some but not all of which are within our control. People often take extra calcium, believing that this will slow the rate of bone loss, but it seems probable that the tablets have little effect if the diet is already adequate in calcium. However, taken in moderation they can do little harm unless combined with vitamin D. Women may be helped by hormone replacement therapy, although its safety has yet to be fully researched. It involves taking supplements of various ovarian hormones and has the effect of delaying the menopause, and thus also delaying the accelerated bone loss that follows it.

One great disadvantage, apart from possible health hazards, is the inconvenience of continuing to menstruate for an additional 10 years of life.

Why are accidents commoner in later life?

Each year in the United States 9,500 people over 65 die as the result of a fall, and 20 times this number sustain a hip fracture due to osteoporosis. Overall, injuries are the sixth commonest cause of death in people over 65, and the risk of accidental death increases as we grow older. Falls are the main cause for women; traffic accidents and suicide are important causes in men. The older driver may become more careful, but the older pedestrian inevitably becomes more vulnerable.

Falls are more serious in age. They are also more likely to occur. Older people can fall because of poor vision, defective balance, gait impediments, impaired righting reflexes (so that they are slow to regain lost balance), hazards around the house and careless prescription and use of tranquilizers and other drugs.

A further factor increasing the likelihood of falling is the "senile gait." By 80, many older people tend to start walking in a different way: they take small steps, stoop and bend at the hips and knees, have a reduced arm swing, walk with feet wide apart and show uncertainty when turning. A walking stick can bolster confidence as well as taking up to 50 percent off the weight-load of a damaged leg. **NC**

9 TIME FOR DIGESTION

Complex, highly regulated, elaborately timed – digestion is a major activity of the body for most of the day. When its rhythms are in harmony, nutrients are broken down and absorbed and wastes expelled with minimal inconvenience. A balanced diet is the best strategy for keeping the system in good order.

TRANSIT TIMES IN THE DIGESTIVE SYSTEM

Food →

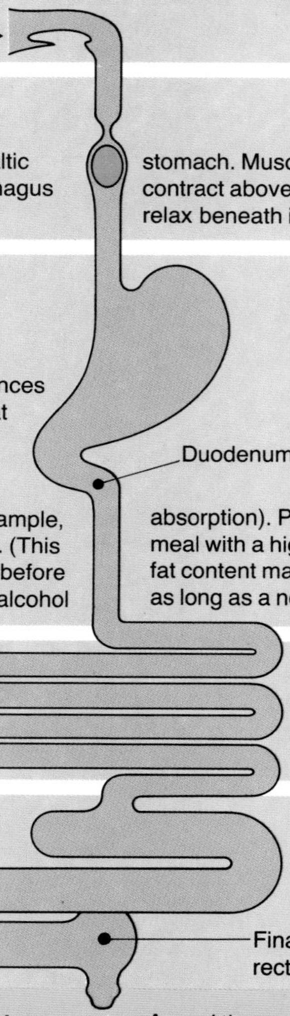

▼ **5-6 seconds**
Esophagus

After swallowing, peristaltic movements of the esophagus push food rapidly to the stomach. Muscles in the tube contract above the food and relax beneath it.

▼ **1.5-4.5 hours**
Stomach

See picture opposite

Under normal circumstances the stomach will empty at a rate determined by the kind of food being digested: the higher the fat concentration, for example, the slower the emptying. (This is why cream or olive oil before a party slows the rate of alcohol

Duodenum

absorption). Processing a meal with a high protein and fat content may take 3 times as long as a normal meal.

▼ **2-6 hours**
Small intestine

See picture opposite

▼ **12 hours +**
Large intestine

Transit through most of the large intestine in 12 hours.

Final transit to the rectum is slower.

A low-fiber Western diet *takes longer to digest. 50 percent of markers used to measure transit times in the digestive system are recovered about 48 hours after the meal in which they were taken. Recovery of all bowel markers may take more than a week. In Africa, total transit time is usually a day.*

A meal that contains a lot of fiber (such as bran, beans and other pulses, potatoes, wholemeal bread) takes only 16-24 hours to pass through the digestive system. It has been suggested that prolonged transit time may be responsible for the high incidence of cancer of the large bowel in the Western world.

A HEALTHY adult can take 12 to 48 hours to process a meal. For the vast majority of this time, we have no conscious control over digestion. In fact, the only time when we do have control is at its start: eating. We decide when to put food in our mouths, what kind of food, and how long we chew it before swallowing.

The length of time we spend chewing is important. Digestion involves breaking down food both mechanically and chemically, and both processes start in the mouth. Our teeth begin the mechanical breakdown of the food, and our saliva, secreted from glands at the back of the mouth, contains an enzyme called ptyalin that starts the conversion of some of the starches in our food into sugars; the saliva also moistens the food, making it easier to swallow.

If we chew our food well, both our teeth and our saliva have longer to act on it and, as a result, other parts of the digestive system will have less work to do. But what happens to the food after we have finished eating it?

How long does it take for food to get to the stomach?

When you swallow food it descends a muscular tube, called the esophagus or gullet, running from the back of the mouth to the stomach. The food is pushed down the esophagus by a process called peristalsis. The muscle of the tube contracts above the piece of food and relaxes beneath it. The contraction of the tube wall travels down the esophagus, pushing the food ahead of it. The whole process, from the time the food enters the esophagus until it enters the stomach, takes five or six seconds.

At each end of the esophagus is a sphincter – a ring of muscle that can contract to seal off the tube; both remain closed except when we are swallowing. Each time we swallow, these sphincters must open and close in a controlled way. The sphincter at the top opens for about one second to allow the food into the esophagus; the one at the bottom opens for about five seconds to let the food into the stomach. The whole process is governed by the nerves of the esophagus, which become active only when we swallow.

In rare cases the nerves of the esophagus become defective, the contractions become irregular and uncoordinated, or the nerves may fail entirely, so that the lower part of the esophagus becomes swollen with food. This condition is named achalasia.

Why do some foods stay longer in the stomach?

In the stomach walls are powerful muscles that pulverize the food; at the same time the food is being broken down chemically by powerful digestive juices, including hydrochloric acid, produced by the cells of the stomach walls.

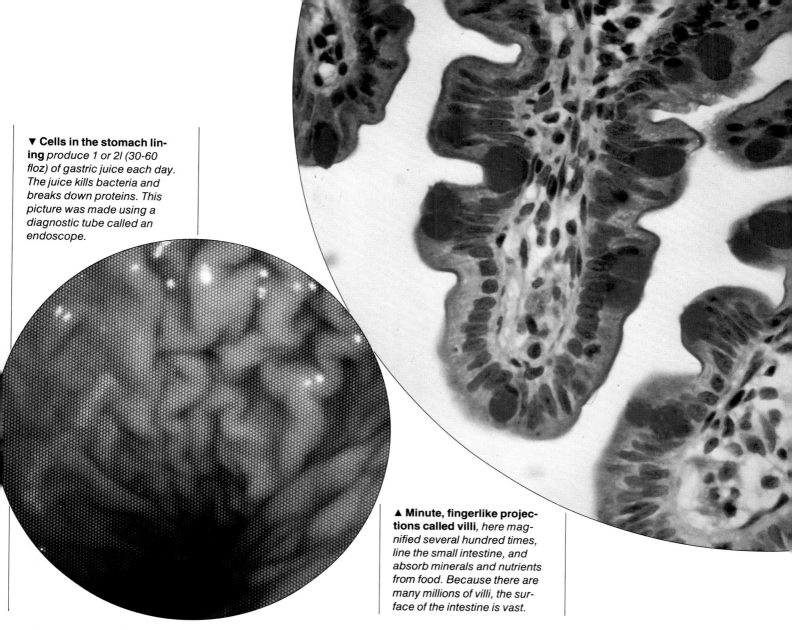

▼ **Cells in the stomach lining** *produce 1 or 2l (30-60 floz) of gastric juice each day. The juice kills bacteria and breaks down proteins. This picture was made using a diagnostic tube called an endoscope.*

▲ **Minute, fingerlike projections called villi,** *here magnified several hundred times, line the small intestine, and absorb minerals and nutrients from food. Because there are many millions of villi, the surface of the intestine is vast.*

But the stomach is not just a food-processing factory: it is also a reservoir. It holds food until the small intestine is ready to receive it, and then delivers it at a rate that suits the small intestine. The rate at which the stomach empties is controlled by nerves in the lining of the small intestine's wall. These monitor the chemical makeup of the pulverized food coming out of the stomach. If they find that it contains too much fat or acid, or is simply too concentrated for the small intestine to cope with, they send messages to the stomach muscle so the stomach empties more slowly. Fatty and acidic foods therefore take longer to digest than others.

When your stomach is full, it is a good idea to rest if you can. Any form of vigorous activity – running or jumping, for example – will cause blood to be diverted to the muscles and nervous system, so that the organs of the digestive system, notably the stomach, will be deprived of the resources they need if they are to digest your food. This explains why runners sometimes feed on pasta before they race: the pasta passes through the stomach very quickly.

So, if you eat a meal of rich foods, you feel full for a long time, but, if you have a meal of easily digestible foods, you get hungry very much sooner.

What happens in the small intestine?

When food first reaches the small intestine, certain of its nutrients stimulate the intestine's lining to release hormones into the bloodstream. These hormones reach an organ called the pancreas, which responds by secreting a digestive fluid, and the gallbladder, which contracts to expel the bile it has been building up since the last meal.

It takes a little while for these reactions to be sparked off by a meal, and they carry on for an hour or more after the meal has started. The pancreatic juice and the bile contain chemicals that further break down the food to form chemical substances. These substances can then be absorbed by the lining of the small intestine's wall and thence transported, by the bloodstream, to the parts of the body where they are needed most.

A Journey Through Your Digestion

Each part of the digestive tract has a separate role to play in processing the food you eat. At each stage food is broken up into smaller pieces than at the previous stage and propelled along by a series of rhythmic contractions. The total time taken for digestion varies according to the texture and richness of the food.

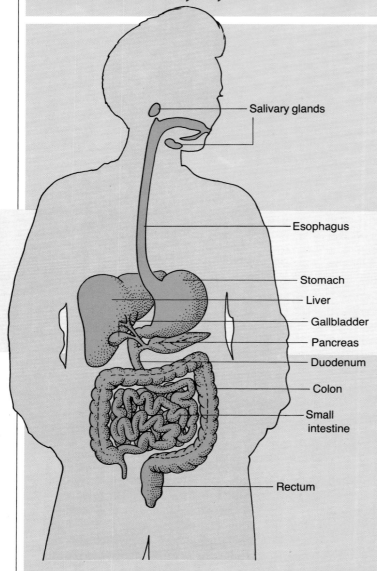

- Salivary glands
- Esophagus
- Stomach
- Liver
- Gallbladder
- Pancreas
- Duodenum
- Colon
- Small intestine
- Rectum

▲ After chewing food in the mouth the mixture of food and saliva is propelled down the esophagus into the stomach where it is churned and partly digested. Digestion is completed in the small intes-

tine, where nutrients are absorbed into the bloodstream. The residue moves into the large intestine, where its water content is reabsorbed. The residue is then expelled through the anus.

1 FROM MOUTH TO STOMACH

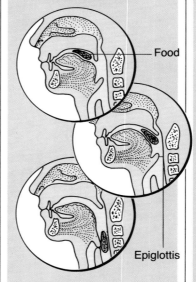

Food

Epiglottis

▲ Even before you put food into your mouth, sight and smell are enough to trigger a flow of saliva. Chewing breaks the food into smaller pieces and the tongue mixes it into a ball, or food bolus, which is pushed down the esophagus by the muscles of the pharynx. At this stage saliva lubricates the movement of the bolus as it passes down into the stomach in response to rhythmic contractions of the esophagus. During swallowing the larynx is raised and the glottis is covered by the epiglottis, preventing food from entering the trachea.

2 FROM STOMACH TO INTESTINE

▼ The graph below shows how solids and liquids move out of the stomach at different speeds, propelled by a regular pattern of contractions. The first shows the motions of two large food particles at four separate stages. Initially they are carried to the bottom of the stomach along with the liquids, then they are trapped and compressed by the contraction. If they are too big to enter the intestine they are rejected and pushed back into the stomach. This activity,

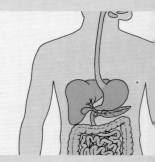

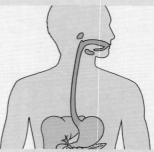

Emptying the stomach

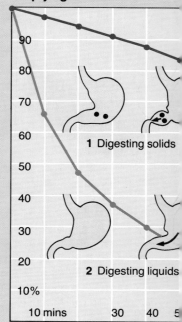

1 Digesting solids

2 Digesting liquids

90
80
70
60
50
40
30
20
10%

10 mins   30   40   5

carried out over and over again, gradually grinds down the food masses into tiny particles that can escape from the stomach into the small intestine. The time this process takes is known as the lag phase and usually lasts 30 minutes. Liquids are emptied more quickly. As the contraction starts, fluid flows along the intestine. As the tract narrows, some of the liquid is pushed back again so that only a small amount enters at any one time.

3 MOVING THROUGH THE SMALL INTESTINE

▼ The timing, speed and direction of contractions are controlled by pacesetter signals, electrical impulses that instruct the muscles when to contract. In the diagram BELOW, for example, they move from points A to H in four seconds.

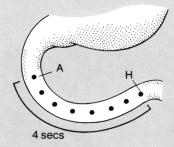

4 secs

▼ Contractions in the small intestine may be of two different kinds — stationary (mixing the contents) or moving (propelling them in front of the contraction). Stationary contractions are relatively rare, most contractions create both effects.

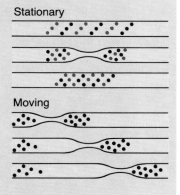

Stationary

Moving

4 SLOW PROGRESS THROUGH THE LARGE INTESTINE

▼ Contractions in the small intestine during the night do not extend to the colon, otherwise we would need to move our bowels every few hours. The three charts below show the level of contractions in three parts of the colon over a 24 hour period. The level of activity is highest after each meal, dies down during the night, and rises sharply again in the morning, usually after breakfast.

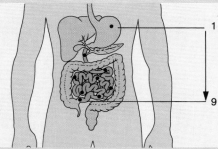

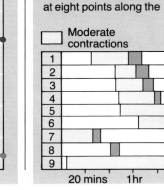

Solids

Liquids

70   80   90   100   110

▼ After a meal, regular and continuous contractions take place in the stomach and small intestine. During the night, or during periods of fasting, contractions establish themselves in a different pattern occurring in three phases. The chart below shows a typical nighttime rhythm. Contractions were measured in the stomach and at eight points along the

intestine (see ABOVE). At each point, a period of inactivity is followed by a shorter period of mild contractions and then by a brief burst of strong contractions. The periods of strong contractions are accompanied by small bursts of pancreatic juice and bile and occur in sequence along the small intestine. As soon as food is eaten moderate contractions become continuous.

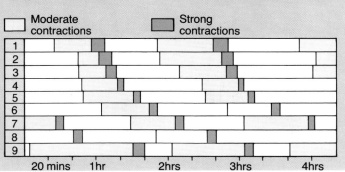

☐ Moderate contractions   ▇ Strong contractions

1 2 3 4 5 6 7 8 9

20 mins   1hr   2hrs   3hrs   4hrs

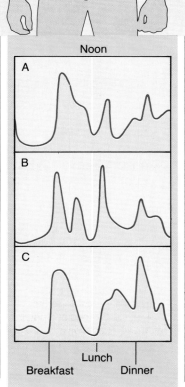

Noon

A

B

C

Breakfast   Lunch   Dinner

What happens in the large intestine?

The material delivered from the small intestine to the large bears little relation to the food as it left the plate; in fact, its appearance is more or less identical whatever meal was consumed. It contains much less fluid than it did, and little in the way of minerals or nutrients – almost all of these have been absorbed by the lining of the small intestine. All that is left for the large intestine to do is to extract more salt and water, so that the remaining mass of indigestible material can be delivered to the rectum as a solid mass of stool.

If a meal contains a food that cannot be broken down into nutrients, it will probably pass through the digestive system very swiftly. Typically, such material contains water that the small and large intestines are unable to extract because they cannot break down the material holding the water. Eating such foods may give you the urge to move your bowels soon after a meal: the material

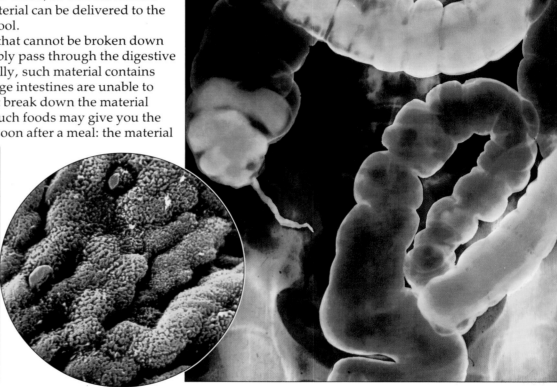

■ **The final stages of digestion** *take place in the large intestine.* MAIN PICTURE *The waste from three separate meals moves slowly toward the rectum. Muscle movements that push the food toward the rectum occur only three or four times a day.* DETAIL *Cells in the lining of the intestine absorb water. If bowel movements are infrequent, more water is absorbed and stools are dryer and harder.*

arrives in the rectum swiftly and pushes out any stool already stored there. Many commonly used laxatives work on this principle, as do some low-calorie diet foods.

Another reason why you sometimes feel the need to move your bowels soon after a meal concerns the way that, when food first arrives in the small intestine, the intestine's lining produces hormones that stimulate the pancreas and the gallbladder. These hormones – and possibly others released by the lining of the small intestine – induce peristaltic contractions in both the small and large intestines. If there happens to be a mass of stool in the rectum at the time of eating, these hormones can make it necessary for you to move your bowels.

In general, the more fiber (roughage) you eat, the more likely it is that you will have a mass of stool stored in your rectum at mealtime, and so the more likely that you will feel the urge to move your bowels soon after.

Why do we get hungry when we do?

Hunger is little understood. The sensation of feeling hungry is probably caused by nerves in the intestine sending messages to part of the brain, the hypothalamus, telling it that the stomach and intestine are empty.

However, things are not that simple: at nights we can go for 12 hours or more without feeling hungry, whereas in daytime we feel hungry more frequently. This is because at nights the digestive system moves into a different mode, named the "fasting pattern." It does this also during the day if we deliberately fast for a long enough period. The glands that secrete the digestive fluids (saliva, stomach acid, pancreatic fluid and bile) slow down their production for most of the time.

The fasting pattern has three phases. The first lasts 10-50 minutes; during this phase there are no contractions of the muscles of the digestive system. The second phase lasts 30-110 minutes; during this phase there are sporadic contractions of the muscles. The third phase is much shorter, lasting 4-8 minutes; during it the contractions occur at maximum strength and frequency. The muscles then go back into the first phase.

This cycle repeats every 90-130 minutes until we eat again, but its timing differs in different places along the digestive tract, starting at the sphincter between the esophagus and stomach and moving on progressively. The colon – the major part of the large intestine – does not follow the cycle; if it did we would find that we had to shift our bowels every hour or so during the night. Instead, during the fasting pattern contractions in the colon fall to a very low level and stay that way until we next eat.

The third phase of the cycle may be short but it is also the most important and the one we notice most when mealtime is approaching. The vigorous contractions of the digestive system's muscles push anything ahead of them, clearing the system of the debris and bacteria that accumulate there during the inaction of the first phase.

No one knows what makes hunger go away. Possibly hormones which the small intestine releases when it is processing food are responsible. The small intestine releases these hormones even when processing only small amounts of digestible food, which may be why a low-energy, high-bulk meal can satisfy our immediate hunger just as well as a high-energy one.

What causes infrequent bowel movements?

Some people need to move their bowels more often than others. One person might pass two or three soft stools each day, another just three stools per week. If you have always needed to shift your bowels often, there is little cause for concern. However, if you have always needed to move your bowels only rarely, it is worth taking action to change this: apart from the fact that passing hard stools can be uncomfortable, it seems possible that infrequency of bowel movements can increase the risk of cancer in the large intestine and of diverticular disease (see p109). The best ways of increasing the frequency with which you move your bowels are simple: take more exercise and increase the amount of fiber in your diet.

Anal fissures can be caused by constipation. These are long splits that extend up from the anus into the anal canal. When you defecate you feel severe pain, and there may be bleeding. Women are more likely to suffer. Increasing the amount of fiber in the diet can help, as can taking laxatives. A minor operation may be needed.

Hemorrhoids – piles – are a common consequence of repeated bouts of constipation. The veins around the anus, because of the frequent pressure put on them as you strain to defecate, swell up, and the blood in them may clot. Hard stools, as they pass through the anus, may temporarily rupture the veins, so that blood appears with the stools. Whenever you experience anal bleeding you should consult your doctor.

Constipation is common during pregnancy. It can be countered by eating plenty of fruit and vegetables and drinking a lot of liquid; it is a good idea also to move your bowels whenever you feel the urge, rather than putting it off. You should take laxatives only when they have been prescribed by your doctor.

One cause of constipation can be *hypothyroidism* – underactivity of the thyroid gland at the base of the neck. This gland produces a hormone named *thyroxine*. The treatment of the condition is straightforward: as soon as you are diagnosed as suffering from hypothyroidism you are put on a course of daily thyroxine tablets which lasts for the rest of your life. There are various symptoms of hypothyroidism which you can easily detect yourself: feeling the cold more than you used to, constipation, dry skin or hair, frequent tiredness, and weight gain.

What are the causes of diarrhea?

When you suffer from diarrhea it is usually a sign that your bowels are trying to expel some irritant or poison. Because the matter is being pushed through the bowels so swiftly, there is little time for water to be removed from it, which is why diarrhetic stools are so fluid.

A number of health problems can cause diarrhea. Gastroenteritis – any form of irritation and inflammation of the intestine, usually produced by a viral infection – is a common cause.

Food poisoning is another: if you shared a meal with other people and they, too, are suffering from diarrhea, then food poisoning is obviously the most likely culprit. There are various ways in which food poisoning can come about. Sometimes food can contain poisonous chemicals produced by the food itself; other times bacteria can be responsible for producing the offending chemicals. Chemical pollutants, like mercury, can cause food poisoning. Salmonella, a type of bacteria, can cause very serious illness, especially in the very young or very old. Cooking food thoroughly kills salmonella bacteria and many other organisms which can affect your health – for example, the eggs of tapeworms and other parasites.

Dysentery – severe diarrhea – can be caused by either bacteria or amebas. Your physician will probably prescribe drugs to deal with it. If you have dysentery you should make a point of washing your hands thoroughly

Early digestive problems
*occur because nervous co-
ordination of the system has
not yet been fully established.
Colic occurs when trapped
air or gas bubbles cause
severe abdominal pains. The
baby will lie on its back
screaming, fists clenched
and legs drawn up. The most
usual time for colic is in the
evening between 5 and 10. It
is often called "three-month-
colic" because babies are
most prone in their first three
months. Wrapping the baby
up tightly or simply cuddling it
can give relief. If your baby
swallows air when it is feeding, it may show colicky
symptoms. Sitting it up for a
minute while gently rubbing
its back or abdomen will help.*

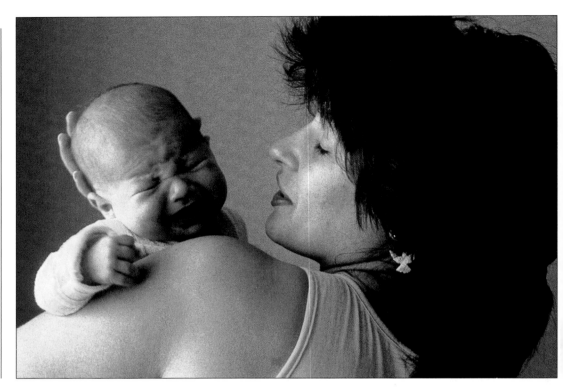

after every bowel movement in order to ensure that you
do not pass on the infection to others.

Why do infants have delicate digestion?

Different problems of digestion are associated with
different ages. If we vomited as frequently in adulthood
as we did in babyhood we would have cause for concern,
yet some digestive ailments which are at worst irritating
in the adult can threaten the life of a baby. Mild diarrhea
and vomiting in an adult usually cures itself. In an infant
this may be lethal.

At birth our nervous system has not fully developed:
small children are only able to control their movements
in a haphazard fashion. As the nervous system matures,
the control of the body improves. The immaturity of a
baby's nervous system is probably the reason why digestive behavior is so different in infancy.

Young babies often bring up some of their food. This
is no cause for concern as long as their bodyweight is
continuing to increase normally. True vomiting is a
much more violent process, and may be caused by
gastroenteritis, or some other condition.

Celiac disease (sometimes called sprue) is often first
discovered during infancy. This disease occurs when the
lining of the small intestine is sensitive to a protein,
gliadin, found in the gluten of wheat, oats, barley and
rye.

The protein damages the lining of the small intestine
so that it fails to digest and absorb enough food. Many

people with celiac disease have a relative with the same
disorder. The only treatment is a gluten-free diet for the
rest of the person's life.

Digestive problems in youth and middle age

All digestive problems that are typical of older people
can occur earlier in life, (for example, hiatus hernia – see
p109 – is frequent in pregnancy) but some conditions
more commonly appear earlier than later.

Ulcerative colitis occurs most usually in young and
middle-aged adults. Inflammation develops all along the
wall of the large intestine, usually starting in the rectum
and working up.

Early symptoms include a pain in the left side of the
abdomen and bouts of diarrhea, with blood being passed
with the stools; there may also be nausea, sweating, loss
of appetite and a high fever. Treatment is by use of anti-
inflammatory agents, with or without steroid drugs.

People with continuing disease, or a particular family
history, may require an operation to remove their colon:
this is often necessary in the inherited condition known
as familial polyposis coli (see p175). Ulcerative colitis can
be exaccerbated by stress, and is sometimes associated
with diseases of the spine.

Duodenal ulcers are four times more common in men
than in women. These are raw areas in the duodenum –
the tube that leads from the stomach to the rest of the
digestive tract. The pain comes because the stomach
acids attack the raw tissues. Your doctor may prescribe a

drug to reduce the production of stomach acid. Otherwise you can best help yourself by stopping smoking, by reducing your coffee and alcohol intake and by eating more slowly, taking more frequent and smaller meals. Ulcers in the wall of the stomach seem to be brought on by much the same causes as duodenal ulcers, although they are more likely to strike manual workers than office workers. Most often they can be cured by rest, in conjunction with the steps advised for duodenal ulcers.

The aging of the digestive system

Older people are more susceptible to digestive problems. This probably reflects mainly the cumulative effects of poor diet and incidental illnesses. However, it is likely that during a person's life some of the nerve cells in the intestinal walls die and are not replaced, adding to the digestive problems of the elderly.

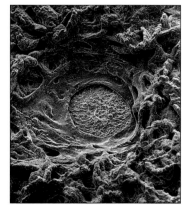

Indigestion can be an occupational hazard *if your job involves frequent business lunches* ABOVE, *but any erratic eating habits encourage digestive disorders. Stomach ache, heartburn and nausea are often symptoms of an ulcer in the stomach wall* RIGHT. *Though some people are more prone because they naturally produce large amounts of stomach acid, you increase your chances of developing an ulcer if you smoke heavily or drink too much coffee or alcohol. Rest and improved eating habits are the answer.*

Indigestion is a catch-all term to describe any form of discomfort that occurs, particularly among the elderly, during or soon after eating. Younger people who regularly suffer constipation, are overweight, smoke heavily or are pregnant, are also especially likely to experience indigestion. The condition may be caused by an underlying disease, such as a hiatus hernia.

The hole through which the esophagus penetrates the diaphragm to reach the stomach is called a hiatus. Sometimes the lower part of the esophagus as well as a section of the stomach can be pushed back up through this hole. The result is called a hiatus hernia. Most such hernias cause no symptoms, but they may produce heartburn, which on occasion can extend to the neck and shoulders. The best ways of dealing with hiatus hernia are to lose weight, raise your pillows by about 10cm (4in), avoid alcohol and smoking, take antacids and eat frequent light meals in preference to fewer, larger ones. Rarely, if the problem persists, surgery may be required.

Cancers of the esophagus, stomach and intestines

Cancer of the esophagus is rare. It causes pain and/or difficulty in swallowing; people aged 50-60 who smoke and drink heavily are the most likely sufferers. The earlier the condition is detected, the more likely it is that it can be successfully treated.

Cancer of the stomach was once common, but its incidence is diminishing in the developed nations; men are more susceptible than women. The early symptoms (occasional vomiting, vague indigestion and loss of appetite) are minor, and tend to be ignored. Later symptoms are more significant: weight loss, pain in the upper abdomen, blood in the stools or in the vomit, and so on. There is no cure when the condition is diagnosed late, but the symptoms can be ameliorated with drugs. If the condition is discovered early, there is a good chance that it can be cured.

Cancer of the large intestine is much more likely to be cured if diagnosed early. The symptoms include blood in the stools and a change in the nature of your bowel movements – diarrhea or constipation.

What is diverticular disease?

Diverticular disease is the presence of small sacs which develop in the walls of the colon. These sacs form most often in people whose diet is low in fiber; they are found in nearly one-third of people over the age of 60, and a small percentage – mostly women – suffer diverticulitis (inflammation of the sacs). Untreated, it can have serious consequences – for example, an abscess in the colon. To avoid the formation of the sacs in the first place, increase the amount of fiber in your diet. JC

The Life of the Teeth

Usually in place by the time we reach 18, with good care our teeth can last a lifetime

THE TEETH are a key part of the digestive system – without them we would be unable to chew our food properly. At birth, many of the teeth have already formed, but they only start to appear in the mouth at about six months (although it can be as late as 14 months) when the first of our 20 milk teeth (deciduous teeth) come through. As a child grows, the teeth develop within the jaws. Between the ages of 6 and 14, the milk teeth are gradually lost and replaced by up to 32 permanent teeth.

We can lose teeth through accident or disease; sometimes teeth have to be removed if a dentist has concluded that there is no way of treating them. The gaps left by lost teeth can be filled with bridgework or dentures.

Does teething hurt?

In the past teething has been blamed for anything from sleeplessness to pneumonia – or even convulsions or death. Some doctors today, however, maintain that the only thing produced by teething is teeth. The truth probably lies somewhere between these two attitudes.

During teething, babies often become irritable and dribble excessively; sometimes the gums are sore, so that the infant refuses hard food – and, occasionally, all food. However, the process of teething in itself never produces any serious symptom; if a baby is ill it is simply a coincidence: Teething is a natural process, and the worst any infant is likely to suffer is minor discomfort. It is very rare for medical intervention to be needed. **PW**

When do children start to acquire their permanent teeth?

The first permanent teeth to appear are usually the first molars, large grinding teeth that appear behind the last milk teeth when a child is about six years old.

Between seven and eight years, the lower first incisors (the cutting teeth at the front of the mouth) are lost. The milk teeth then fall out in roughly the order in which they came through. This replacement process goes on until a child is 12 to 14 years old, when the second molars erupt. As late as 18 to 24 the third molars or wisdom teeth begin to appear. Very often there is not enough space for these, and they only partly erupt. If this is the case and the gum around them becomes infected, the teeth have to be removed.

How should children take care of their teeth?

Tooth decay (caries) occurs when bacteria in the mouth interact with the sugar present in all types of food to produce acids which break down the enamel surface of the tooth. It can be minimized by cleaning the teeth properly after meals and by avoiding prolonged contact between the teeth and sugary substances. You can help keep your child's teeth in good condition by encouraging them to eat savory snacks rather than candies and by reducing the amount of snacks they eat.

Regular toothbrushing should start as soon as the child has its first tooth, and should be supervised by you until the child is six or seven years old since young children, although usually eager to brush their own teeth, may not be brushing them effectively. There are toothbrushes designed specially for infants, but it is usually fine for a child to use the same toothpaste as its parents. Those that contain fluorides significantly reduce decay, though no single fluoride-containing toothpaste has been shown to be more effective than any other.

Babies and infants often swallow some toothpaste, and there has been some concern that this might harm them – especially if the toothpaste contains fluorides. All the evidence suggests that there is nothing to worry about, however, even if the child is taking fluoride drops or tablets at the same time.

When should children take fluoride drops or tablets?

In areas where there is little fluoride in the drinking water – either added or occurring naturally – it may be a good idea to give a child fluoride drops or tablets from birth. These supplements are unnecessary if the fluoride content of the water is greater than 0.7 parts per million.

The enamel (the hard outer part) of both the milk teeth and, under the gums, the permanent teeth (apart from the wisdom teeth) forms during the period between birth and 5-6 years, and it is at this time that fluoride supplements will be particularly helpful in the prevention of tooth decay.

How do problems vary as we age?

The amount of tooth decay in Western countries is falling, but still about 14 percent of adults in the United States and 30 percent

TEETHING TIME

In what order do an infant's first teeth appear? The lower incisors (biting teeth) at the center of the mouth appear first. Shortly afterward, the upper central incisors come through, followed a month or two later by the incisors at each side (generally the upper ones appear before the lower). The first molars (the grinding teeth toward the rear of the jaw) usually appear when the child is about one, by which time there will probably be 6-8 incisors. The full set of 20 milk teeth is made up by the four canines (eyeteeth). During the discomfort of teething, babies often become irritable and produce large amounts of dribble, but it is extremely rare for illness to arise or for medical intervention to be necessary.

6-7 months — Upper central incisors erupt

8-9 months — Upper lateral incisors

6 months — Lower central incisors

12 months — Lower lateral incisors

◀ **As soon as children have a tooth** *it is important to teach them to care for it. Parental supervision should continue, throughout the preschool and early school years, to ensure that children are brushing effectively.*

Permanent teeth: **1** Incisors **2** Canines **3** Premolars **4** First molars **5** Second molars
Milk teeth

▲ **Behind the scenes,** *permanent teeth are developing and moving into place in the jaws of a six-year-old. This is usually when first molars appear behind the back milk teeth. Then incisors, premolars and canines follow, until the second molars come through at 12-14 years. Straightening teeth that arrive crowded and crooked makes it easier to keep gums and teeth healthy.*

in Britain have none of their own teeth left.

Tooth loss is usually a result of poor tooth care during childhood. Moreover, 50 percent of people in the Western world never visit a dentist. The use of fluoride, together with an increasing awareness of health, however, is gradually improving the situation. It is particularly important to establish good tooth care in children, as they are more prone to decay than adults: most primary decay occurs before 20.

Crowded and badly occluding teeth (where the upper and lower teeth do not meet properly) can be a major problem. The best time for treatment is as early as possible, preferably during childhood and adolescence. At least 30 percent of teenagers would benefit from orthodontics (the treatment of crowded teeth): they would be able to keep their teeth and gums clean more easily, and chew their food more efficiently, and their teeth would look much better.

Some children lack one or more of their permanent teeth. There are three main reasons for this. Firstly, the tooth may not have developed; this occurs most commonly with the upper incisors and premolars. Secondly, the tooth may be impacted; that is, the teeth on either side do not provide enough space for it to erupt, and it has to be extracted. This problem usually affects the upper canines (the slightly pointed teeth between the incisors and premolars), the premolars and, most often, the wisdom teeth.

Thirdly, teeth are lost through accident or decay. Gum diseases – gingivitis and periodontitis – affect about 90 percent of adults (children are less susceptible). If gum disease is not treated, bone supporting the teeth can be lost so that they become loose. Young adults who do not clean their teeth properly can be prone to acute gum disease, with swollen, bleeding gums, a bad taste, ulcer-

ation and a great deal of pain. This type of condition can be treated easily by a dentist and hygienist, and advice should be sought quickly. Older adults are susceptible to chronic gum disease, with slow loss of tissues surrounding the teeth, and bouts of acute swelling. This can be treated effectively by your dentist.

Although less decay is now seen in the Western world, wear and sensitivity of the teeth is a common problem. Wear of the teeth results from brushing with too hard a brush, drinking acidic drinks, and grinding the teeth. All tooth problems are usually treatable if they are caught at an early stage, and it is advisable that you have a dental checkup at regular intervals so that problems can be nipped in the bud. Children should be seen by the dentist every 4-6 months, as development of the teeth must be checked. The time between visits for adults can vary according to the condition of their teeth but should not be more than six months to a year. **IMM**

10 KEEPING FLUIDS IN BALANCE

The body cannot respond instantly to every demand that we put on our fluid control systems. A sudden increase in salt consumption can lead to bloating. A body used to taking in and routinely excreting excess salt can become dehydrated during unaccustomed exertion in hot conditions.

A RAPID FILTRATION SYSTEM

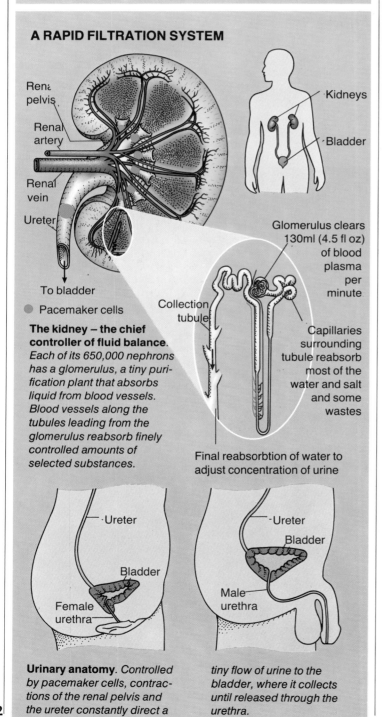

Renal pelvis

Renal artery

Renal vein

Ureter

To bladder

Kidneys

Bladder

Pacemaker cells

The kidney – the chief controller of fluid balance. *Each of its 650,000 nephrons has a glomerulus, a tiny purification plant that absorbs liquid from blood vessels. Blood vessels along the tubules leading from the glomerulus reabsorb finely controlled amounts of selected substances.*

Collection tubule

Glomerulus clears 130ml (4.5 fl oz) of blood plasma per minute

Capillaries surrounding tubule reabsorb most of the water and salt and some wastes

Final reabsorbtion of water to adjust concentration of urine

Ureter

Bladder

Female urethra

Ureter

Bladder

Male urethra

Urinary anatomy. *Controlled by pacemaker cells, contractions of the renal pelvis and the ureter constantly direct a tiny flow of urine to the bladder, where it collects until released through the urethra.*

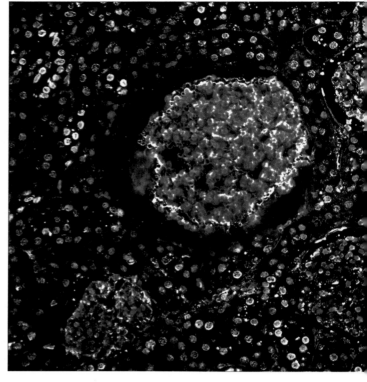

THE KIDNEYS can be thought of as extremely efficient filtration and purification plants. They are also fine-tuning devices, being the organs chiefly responsible for the precise balance the body maintains between the quantities of liquid and salt that we take in and the quantities we lose.

Nearly a quarter of the blood that the heart pumps each minute is directed to the kidneys. A liter (34fl oz) or more of blood flows through them each minute, and from this the kidneys eventually produce about 1ml (0.03fl oz) of urine. The remaining 999ml (3.5fl oz) pass back into the circulation.

Why do we need to produce urine? Blood arriving at the kidneys is rich in urea, a waste product produced when cells burn energy. The body needs to dispose of it. Urea is picked up by the blood as it circulates through the tissues, and about half of the urea arriving at the kidneys is removed from the blood into the urine. Also removed may be drugs and other impurities that the body needs to expel.

The body also needs to balance water intake with water loss. And it needs to balance salt intake and loss: in order to keep constant the concentrations of sodium and chloride in the body fluids a fraction of these elements (they make up common table salt) are removed in the urine. Traces of the elements of other salts that we consume, and which have to be kept in balance, are removed as well – for example, potassium chloride, a constituent of most cereals and vegetables.

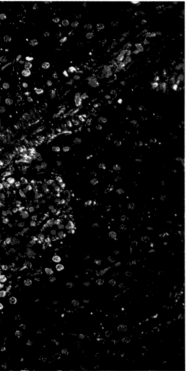

◄ **Purification centers in the kidney**. *The large round shapes in this cross section of a kidney (magnified 625 times) are glomeruli. The small circles are capillaries. The glomeruli absorb about a tenth of the fluid in the capillaries, which rapidly reabsorb almost all of this, leaving wastes and a controlled fraction of water and salts behind as urine.*

► **The body's main fluid input** *is the liquids that we drink. If we drink too much the brain signals to the kidneys that the blood is becoming too dilute.*

How is the body's fluid balance controlled?

We have three sources of fluid input: the liquids we drink, the liquids contained in the foods that we eat, and the fluids produced by our metabolism. The average daily intake of liquid for a young adult not working hard is about 2.5l (85fl oz) of water, of which 1.5l (51fl oz) comes from drinks and 800ml (27fl oz) from the fluids in solid food. About 200ml (6.8fl oz) is a product of the body's metabolism.

There are three ways in which we lose fluid: urination, evaporation from the skin and in our breathing, and in the liquid portion of the feces. In general, in a young adult not taking too much exercise, urinary output is about 1.5l (51fl oz) per day, a small amount of fluid is lost in the feces, and about 800ml (27fl oz) is lost through evaporation. Exercise and other factors can increase the rate of loss through evaporation, and the body has to compensate. The first thing that happens is that the

circulating fluid becomes a more strongly concentrated solution of the many materials that it is carrying. Changes in concentration are monitored by the area of the brain called the hypothalamus and any increase causes the hypothalamus to instruct the pituitary gland to produce more of a hormone called antidiuretic hormone (ADH). ADH acts on the collecting ducts of the kidneys, so that they channel more water back into the blood: the urine becomes more concentrated and the blood plasma becomes more dilute.

If instead you drink a lot of fluid, so that the blood becomes diluted, the pituitary's production of ADH is suppressed and the collecting ducts channel less water back into the blood; the urine becomes less concentrated and the blood less dilute.

How quickly do the kidneys respond to fluid loss?

When our bodies lose a lot of water – perhaps through vomiting or diarrhea – the kidneys respond immediately to reduce water loss. Urination does not stop altogether – about 500ml (17fl oz) per day is necessary if the body is to excrete all its waste products. At such times, urine is very concentrated.

We can lose a lot of fluid through evaporation from the skin. The 800ml (27fl oz) or so that we normally lose in this way each day can increase to about 3l (101fl oz) during manual work or heavy exercise, and in hot climates this may double or even quadruple. The kidneys respond by increasing the amount of water that they return to the bloodstream; at the same time, we experience the sensation of thirst, and so our fluid intake increases.

The kidneys respond equally quickly to excess liquid intake. If you drink one liter of plain water, within 15 minutes the normal secretion of ADH will be suppressed. The kidneys start to produce a dilute urine soon after, the maximum effect occurring about 40 minutes after you take the drink. Return of water to the bloodstream is suppressed until the blood has come back to normal, usually about an hour later. When they are working at peak demand, the kidneys can produce urine at about 16 times their normal rate.

Many drugs – called diuretics – are used to increase urine flow; they are particularly useful for people suffering from heart failure or raised blood pressure. Other substances that affect the kidneys include alcohol. This interferes with both the production and the action of ADH – one of the reasons for hangovers is dehydration, because for every liter of beer you drink you excrete at least a liter of fluid and usually more. A way of taking the edge off tomorrow's hangover is to drink one or two large glasses of fluid, preferably two-thirds water and one-third fresh orange juice, before going to bed.

How is salt balance controlled?

Human blood contains solutions of salts – chiefly sodium chloride (common table salt) – which may be a relic of the oceans as they were when our earliest land-living ancestors first left the sea. Human cells have adapted to function in a precisely composed solution of these salts. As a consequence, salt solutions affect fluid retention, and the body has to keep salt composition in balance in order to keep its fluid inputs and outputs in balance. If too much salt is retained, too much fluid will be retained to keep the salt solution from becoming too concentrated. The tissues may become bloated, and an increase in blood volume may contribute to high blood pressure. If too little salt is retained, too much fluid will be excreted as the kidneys work to stop the blood from being too dilute.

In response to concentrations of sodium in the body fluids, hormones regulate how much salt leaves the body in the urine and perspiration.

Within the kidney, cells close to the arterial blood supply monitor changes in blood pressure. The same cells can monitor the amount of sodium in the urine. The cells respond to falling pressure by stepping up their secretions of a hormone called renin. This acts on circulating substances to produce angiotensin I, an inactive hormone converted by an enzyme – angiotensin converting enzyme – to angiotensin II. This is highly active, both directly on blood vessels, which it causes to constrict, thereby increasing blood pressure and by stimulating the adrenal gland to produce a hormone – aldosterone – which increases sodium retention by the kidney.

Conversely, when a person consumes more salt than the body needs to maintain the correct concentration of salt in the body fluids, aldosterone production declines. It is possible that abnormal overproduction of aldosterone is a contributing cause of chronic high blood pressure.

The production of hormones, the activation of enzymes and the retention or excretion of sodium and fluid take time, and this means that the kidney is involved in day-to-day, rather than minute-by-minute control of blood pressure.

Many of the available drug treatments for high blood pressure exert their effects through the kidneys, either by increasing the amount of fluid the kidneys excrete (diuretics) or by dampening the angiotensin system.

Diet can also be important. Adding salt at the table should be unnecessary. Most of our food, especially processed foods, contains more than enough salt to meet human needs – shaking extra salt onto a meal simply gives our excretory systems extra work.

Acclimatizing to changes in salt intake

Because changes in salt-balance regulation do not occur quickly in the body, it may take a few days to acclimatize to a lower salt intake than the one you are used to. At first you will continue to excrete salt at your old level and may feel hunger for salt as a consequence of not replacing what you lose.

Taking the trouble to acclimatize, however, is an important precaution for people moving to hotter climates or heavier work than they are used to. It was once a common practice to encourage workers in hot factories – such as steel mills – to take salt tablets while they sweated at their work. However, this stimulates the body to excrete salt at a high rate. It is better to train the body to make do with a low salt intake – gearing its excretions of salt to a very low level – so that massive quantities are not lost when there is sudden heavy sweating. Such losses can accelerate the loss of liquid as the body tries to keep its fluids from becoming too dilute. Dehydration and heat stroke can result.

Salt replacement during heavy sweating, however, is the proper strategy when your body has not had the chance to acclimatize, and it is the right strategy when a dysentery victim loses a dangerous volume of fluids to diarrhea and vomiting. The victim's thirst should be slaked not just with water but with a thin, lightly salted, slightly starchy gruel.

There are conceivable situations in which it would be an advantage to acclimatize your body to a high salt intake. If you are adrift at sea, you can dehydrate yourself by trying to use salty seawater to solve your thirst problem: if you take in more salt than you can excrete,

Fluid loss by evaporation. *Holding a jar of fluid collected from the specially designed plastic shoes he wore during a body-temperature control experiment, a research volunteer models the headgear that will help science to understand more about evaporation from the scalp. In normal conditions we lose about 800ml of fluid through skin pores every day, much of it by direct evaporation, not as sweat. In hot conditions, the need to regulate internal body temperature can greatly accelerate this loss.*

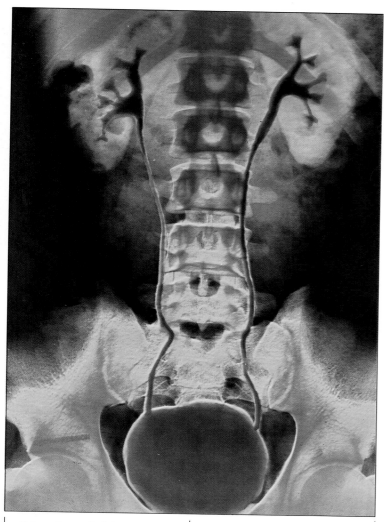

Urine channeled from the kidneys to the bladder *appears in red in this color X-ray image. The kidneys* *appear in green. Every minute of the day contractions of the ureters force urine toward the bladder.*

water. This can occur at any time, but most people find that they need to urinate on waking, at lunchtime, in the evening, and last thing before going to bed.

Urine is the liquid extracted from the blood by the kidneys. This liquid passes to a part of the kidney called the renal pelvis which, driven by pacemaker cells, contracts at regular intervals to squeeze urine into a tube – the ureter – that runs down the side of the spine. Every minute each ureter contracts 1-5 times to push a small amount of urine on toward the bladder, a balloon-like structure made up of muscle cells. The two ureters are kept closed except when delivering urine to the bladder; during urination the bladder contracts and the ureters are squeezed shut, so that urine cannot be pushed back up toward the kidneys.

Once there is about 100-200ml (3.5-7fl oz) of urine in the bladder, you feel the urge to pass water; this urge is stimulated by a reflex action that causes the bladder to start contracting periodically. Like most reflexes, this one can be overridden by conscious effort. As the bladder continues to fill, its size increases, so that the pressure is kept at the same level. However, when the volume of urine approaches 300ml (10fl oz) the bladder can expand no further and you experience the almost overwhelming urge to urinate.

You can continue to restrain the urge for much longer, but after a while you are likely to urinate spontaneously. Of course, you can consciously empty a bladder that contains far less urine than this; and fear, anxiety and so on can induce a powerful urge to urinate even when there is little liquid in the bladder.

What stops us from urinating while asleep?

After we have learned, as children, the art of continence, it is rare for us to need to urinate during sleep until late middle age; if the urge is strong enough, it almost always wakes us. Generally, though, the body automatically inhibits the reflex emptying of the bladder. Also, of course, we do not drink while asleep.

Another factor is that one of the body's daily rhythms (see *Ch5*) governs the production of antidiuretic hormone, ADH. Although the release of ADH by the pituitary gland is largely controlled by the concentration of the plasma (liquid portion) of the blood, more of it is secreted while we sleep, so that the body retains more water, and less urine is produced. Drinking a lot of liquid before going to bed, however, suppresses this secretion of ADH.

The first urine you pass after you wake is usually the most concentrated you pass all day. This is why tests involving urine samples – like hormonal pregnancy tests – demand a specimen produced first thing in the morning.

salt concentrations in the body fluids become too high for proper cell functioning. However, if you have some fresh water on board, mix in a little seawater each day. As the water supply gradually becomes saltier, you become acclimatized to excreting salt at higher and higher levels of concentration. By the time you reach the maximum that your body can tolerate, you will have stretched your water supply, you will have maximized your potential to cope with excess salt, and perhaps you will have reached shore.

Where does urine come from?

The kidneys produce urine continuously, but most of the time we are not aware of the fact. Instead, we notice it only when our body tells us that we need to pass

How are urinary disorders affected by age?

Most of us learn the trick of nocturnal continence during early childhood, but the minority of children who fail to do so is surprisingly large: it is estimated that 10 percent of children of five are not reliably continent at night, many children still suffer from the problem of bedwetting at 10, and an unfortunate few experience difficulties right through adolescence. Generally, throughout our adult lives we run little or no risk of bedwetting, although incontinence becomes a problem once more in old age (about 20 percent of people over 65 may develop at least a small degree of incontinence).

However, various urinary disorders can cause difficulties during youth and middle age. These disorders are gender-oriented, because the male and female urinary tracts are very different. In particular, the urethra – the tube which runs from the bladder to the outside world – is only about 1-2cm (0.4-0.8in) long in a woman but about 10cm (4in) long in a man.

This means that women are much more susceptible than men to infections of the bladder (called cystitis): because the distance is short, bacteria normally present around the opening of the vagina can easily work their way to the bladder. The bacteria irritate the lining of the bladder, so that much smaller volumes of urine stimulate the urge to urinate.

Moreover, since the reflex is triggered so much earlier, the need is considerably more urgent: the woman feels that her bladder is bursting and, particularly if she has had children, must urinate soon or suffer an embarrassing bout of incontinence. The infected urine is very acidic, so that passing it hurts; the inflammation, frequency and urgency may disturb sleep.

What to do about cystitis

Urinary infections can occur in children. If your normally continent child experiences a sudden episode of bedwetting, it is possible that the child has a urinary infection. During school years, girls are about 25 times more likely than boys to suffer from such infections. All urinary-tract infections require medical treatment. Frequent infections in a girl, and any infection in a boy, may require investigation.

Recurrent cystitis affects many women, and can cause a lot of distress. Infection needs prompt treatment with antibiotics, and the affected woman should increase her fluid intake considerably. The pain caused by the urine's acidity can be relieved by taking alkalis, such as sodium bicarbonate. A better approach, though, is to try to reduce the chances of infection. Women should make a practice of urinating after sex, and should avoid gar-

Kidney stones *such as this can reach a diameter of 25mm (1in). It is the smaller ones capable of passing from the kidney that cause pain. Rare before the age of 30, they are more common in hot climates, where high rates of evaporation from the skin lead to a higher concentration of calcium in the urine.*

ments like tight-fitting underwear or jeans which generate the warm environment in which bacteria thrive. Drinking a lot of fluid reduces the risks of cystitis. Traces of "biological" washing-powders on clothing can irritate the delicate urethral opening, and so increase the chances of bacteria lodging there. From earliest days, little girls should be instructed to wipe themselves, after defecation, from front to back.

Another difference between women and men concerns the mechanism of the sphincter controlling the outflow of urine from the bladder. In a woman the effectiveness of this is determined by the angle of the bladder neck. After childbirth – particularly if the birth has been difficult, or if the woman has had several children – the muscular lining of the vagina can become lax. Since the front wall of the vagina supports the bladder, this laxness interferes with the function of the sphincter, so that control can be lost. Whenever the pressure on the bladder is increased – for example, during coughing, sneezing, laughing or exercising – the bladder may leak urine. Surgery can counter this. Many of these problems can be prevented, however, if, during and after pregnancy, the woman practices exercises that tense and relax the vaginal muscles.

Problems with the prostate

In men, the urethra passes through the prostate gland. In many after 40, this gland increases in size, and about 10 percent of these men will go on to experience a partial obstruction of urine flow. This means that the bladder has to exert more pressure to empty itself, and so its muscular wall thickens.

The symptoms of this are initially subtle. The man finds that he has to urinate more frequently, has difficulty starting, and does not produce the same torrent as before. As the gland gradually grows bigger the obstruction becomes more serious: more and more urine

TIME FOR DIALYSIS

People whose kidneys fail temporarily or are damaged through longstanding inflammation need to have their blood purified artificially by a process called dialysis.

There are two types of dialysis. In haemodialysis the patient is connected to a kidney machine through which their blood passes many times.

Inside the machine blood flows into a tube made of semipermeable cellophane that is submerged in dialysate – a solution similar to normal body fluid. Waste substances pass through the cellophane into the solution and the clean blood is returned to the patient's body.

Dialysis takes place 2-3 times a week and each session can last up to eight hours. It is usually carried out in hospital, though long-term

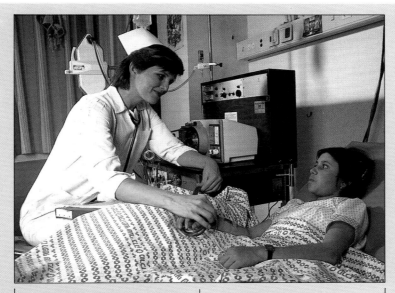

patients may have a machine at home. In the late evening they connect them selves up to the machine, disconnecting themselves the next morning.

In peritoneal dialysis the patient's blood is cleaned inside their own body using

▲ **Coping without the use of her kidneys.** *When the kidneys do not work, the body can tolerate for only two or three days the poisons that build up in the bloodstream.*

the peritoneal membrane which lines the abdominal cavity. This is usually carried out in hospital and takes several hours.

Patients with permanent kidney damage, however, may be trained to use "continuous ambulatory peritoneal dialysis" (CAPD) at home. They have a catheter fitted permanently through their abdominal wall and four times a day 2l (68fl oz) of dialysate fluid is run into their abdominal cavity from a plastic bag.

Toxins from the blood filter across the peritoneal membrane into the fluid. After 4-6 hours the fluid, now full of waste products, is drained back into the bag. The process of emptying and filling again takes about half an hour. In some cases, peritoneal dialysis has kept patients in good health for as long as 10 years.

may be left in the bladder. The man has to get up more frequently during the night, produces a weak stream of urine, and is likely to leak urine every time he coughs or sneezes. By the time such a man is in his late sixties it is likely that his bladder is no longer a muscular organ but just a big floppy bag. Men who find they need to urinate far too frequently, who have difficulty starting to urinate or whose urinary stream is feeble should see their doctors.

How does kidney performance vary with age?

Each minute the kidney of a fit young adult clears about 130ml (4.5fl oz) of plasma, removing waste products. Children's kidneys cannot match this rate, while those of the elderly often clear a mere 60ml (2fl oz) of plasma per minute. Kidney damage – perhaps as a result of a relatively common disease, such as diabetes or hypertension – can reduce this figure very much further and perhaps result in complete kidney failure, with only 1-2ml (0.03-0.06fl oz) of fluid being processed per minute. In the Western world, about 30 out of every million people under age 50 die from kidney failure, and this figure is matched by those in the age-range 70-80. Dialysis and kidney transplantation have saved hundreds of thousands of lives worldwide.

Two kidneys disorders affect children especially. These

are nephritis and nephrotic syndrome; both are special cases of a more general ailment called glomerulonephritis which, as one might expect from the name, concerns the glomeruli (see p112). The cause of nephrotic syndrome, most commonly encountered in children aged 2-4, is not fully understood. The glomeruli are damaged, so that proteins are able to leak from the blood into the urine; at the same time, the production of urine is inhibited, so that fluid that ought to have been excreted from the body instead accumulates in the tissues just beneath the skin. Nephritis is rather less common. It is normally preceded by a bacterial infection of the throat. The body manufactures antibodies to kill the invading bacteria, but then continues to produce these antibodies, which start to attack the kidneys.

Cancer of the kidney – Wilm's tumor – is fortunately very rare. It is largely confined to children under five. About 5 percent of children aged 2-12 who die of cancer die as a result of Wilm's tumor.

In later life, a different type of kidney tumor – a hypernephroma – can kill; again these tumors are for–tunately rare, accounting for only 3 percent of all deaths from cancer. They occur most often in men over 40. The formation of renal calculi – kidney stones – is likewise more often seen in men than in women, and usually in people over 30; usually the problem sorts itself out naturally, most often the process may be painful. MH

11 TIMES OF FERTILITY

Beginning even before we are born, the process of becoming fertile is one of the body's most complex and carefully timed achievements. Every month, under the influence of hormones, a woman's body prepares itself for possible pregnancy. Male fertility has no "times of the month" but is based on a regular cycle of sperm production.

WHEN IN THE MONTH IS A WOMAN MOST FERTILE?

◄ **Maturing in the ovary** for about 14 days, a human egg follicle prepares to burst and release its ripe egg. Because it does not always occur exactly half way through the menstrual cycle, this moment of ovulation is difficult to predict accurately.

1	— Menstruation	17– Day of ovulation	31
1		14	14 days	28
1		13		27

First day of cycle   Unsafe days

A woman whose menstrual cycle is only 27 days probably ovulates (that is, is at her most fertile) about 13 days after the preceding period. If her cycle is normally 31 days long, her time of greatest fertility is around day 17. However, sperm cells can survive for several days in the female genital tract, and even the most regular of cycles can be irregular sometimes, so a woman may be fertile for at least two days either side of the most likely day.

Some women feel a sharp pain in the abdomen just before or after ovulation starts. This is known as mittle-schmertz (see *Ch 12*). Other ways of determining the time of ovulation include carefully recorded temperature charts and the use of urinary dip-sticks to measure the surge of LH (luteinizing hormone) associated with ovulation.

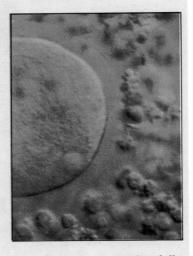

▲ **Only one egg reaches full maturity** in each ovarian cycle, though up to 20 may start to develop. The mature egg is surrounded by a ring of follicle cells. When the pituitary gland releases a surge of LH (luteinizing hormone) the egg is expelled from its follicle.

IT IS more obvious in women than in men that fertility is related to time. A woman is extremely unlikely to conceive before her first period, and then is fertile only during the middle of the menstrual cycle, between periods. She cannot conceive at all after the menopause. However, a man's fertility likewise changes in various ways connected with the passage of time, even though, after puberty, he may remain fertile for the rest of his life.

How does a woman first become fertile?

For a woman to be able to conceive, her ovaries must have released a fertile egg (ovum, plural ova). This process does not start until after puberty has begun. It is often assumed that its onset is signaled by menarche, the first period, but in fact all that menarche shows is that the ovary has started to produce sufficient quantities of two hormones – estrogen and progesterone – to affect the lining of the uterus. During the first few cycles it is possible that no eggs are produced, and the periods may be irregular. In time, the pattern settles down to a monthly bleeding, with ovulation (the production of eggs) occurring about 14 days before the start of each new period.

However, the story of egg production starts long before this. Development of the female reproductive system begins in the uterus, when the female fetus is about three months old. Germ cells, those cells which are capable of developing into eggs, appear in one part of the fetal body and migrate around it to an area near where the kidneys will develop. Here they are surrounded by other cells, so that a primitive ovary forms. At this time the fetus has about 600,000 germ cells, and these will multiply rapidly until, when the fetus is aged about six months, there are almost seven million germ cells. From this time on the numbers decrease so that, by the time the ovaries are fully developed, about 10 weeks before birth, each contains about 1-2 million germ cells. The body will produce no further germ cells, and the numbers will continue to decline steadily until the woman's menopause.

The production of eggs, and hence the menstrual cycle, is controlled by the hypothalamus, a region at the front of the brain. Before puberty the hypothalamus is immature, so that no eggs are produced. However, for reasons which are not fully understood, when a growing girl – of whatever age – attains a weight of about 45kg (100lb), the hypothalamus starts to release a hormone called LHRH (luteinizing hormone-releasing hormone), which triggers and encourages the development of new eggs. At first the system does not function smoothly, so that it may be two years or more before girls settle down to a regular monthly cycle. Very irregular periods can be confusing and inconvenient to an adolescent girl, so sometimes doctors may recommend the use of contraceptive pills to regulate the cycle until the body's natural rhythms can take over.

How are eggs produced?

Once the hormones associated with puberty are received by the ovaries, some of the germ cells (which are now more correctly termed primary oocytes) set off on the journey toward ovulation. They increase in size and their chromosomes begin to divide. This process of division – meiosis – is different from the type of cell division that occurs in all the rest of the body's cells (mitosis – see p184).

Before birth the oocytes begin to divide meiotically as soon as the chromosomes have duplicated themselves; then the chromosomes go into a sort of "suspended animation" until puberty. After puberty, for reasons which are not wholly understood, in each menstrual cycle (see *Ch12*) some of the oocytes, stimulated by FSH (follicle-stimulating hormone, produced by the pituitary gland), continue developing. The nutrient cells surrounding the oocytes begin to multiply and produce hormones that prepare the lining of the uterus (the womb) for the arrival of a fully developed egg.

As the nutrient (granulosa) cells grow and multiply, fluid accumulates between them. A cavity (follicle) is formed, and the egg is pushed toward one side of this

WHEN IN HER LIFE IS A WOMAN MOST FERTILE?

At the time of puberty each of a woman's ovaries contains about 300,000 oocytes – the germ cells that can develop into eggs. Most of these germ cells, however, never become eggs: they simply die off in the ovary – a process called astresia. As the number of germ cells in her ovaries decreases with age, the chances of a woman conceiving decrease. This effect is hardly noticeable even when a woman is in her later thirties, but by the time she has entered her forties she is significantly less likely to ovulate normally.

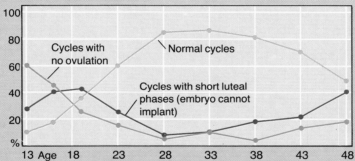

The watershed is the climacteric, when egg production decreases and finally stops altogether. This typically occurs between the ages of 45 and 55, and is signaled by the cessation of regular

menstruation – the menopause. It is not a sudden event: often it occurs over a timescale of months or years. Conception is unlikely during the climacteric, but it is still quite possible; women who do

not wish to have a "late" baby should use some form of contraception.

In the simplest terms, the menopause (the cessation of menstruation) occurs because the ovaries have run out of eggs. The hypothalamus and the pituitary dramatically increase their output of hormones in an attempt to keep the ovaries working, but to no avail. Most women experience some or all of the symptoms associated with the "change": hot flushes, night sweats, vaginal dryness, depression, irritability, anxiety and many others. Some women experience profound psychological changes.

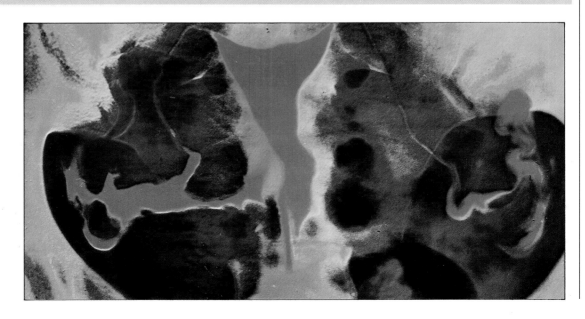

Linking the uterus with the ovaries, *the two fallopian tubes show up as red areas to the left and right of the uterus, the central red triangle, in this X-ray of a woman's pelvic region. Each tube is about 10 cm (4in) long. A ripe egg is released into one of these and contractions carry it downward to the uterus where it arrives 4 days after ovulation. Fertilization may occur in the tube if sperm cells arrive in time.*

cavity. Around the middle of the menstrual cycle the follicle, by now about 2.5cm (1in) across, bursts, expelling the egg. The egg is picked up by tiny fronds at the end of the fallopian tube, and from here passes toward the uterus. Once the egg has been released the nutrient cells remaining in the ovary change in nature to form the corpus luteum (see *Ch12*)and start to produce the hormone progesterone; this is named the luteal phase of the menstrual cycle. The progesterone further prepares the lining of the uterus for the implantation of the egg.

Why are women infertile during pregnancy?

The production of eggs ceases temporarily during pregnancy. This is because the hormonal communications between the hypothalamus and the ovaries are disrupted by other hormones produced by the developing placenta. If the egg fails to be fertilized and grow in the lining of the womb, the parcel of nutrient cells (the corpus luteum) in the follicle normally dissipates about two weeks after the egg has been released. However, if the egg is fertilized, a placenta forms and soon releases a hormone called human chorionic gonadotrophin, or hCG. In response to this, the corpus luteum is maintained and, during the first eight weeks of pregnancy, produces high levels of the sex hormones estrogen and progesterone; after this time, the placenta takes over the production of these hormones.

The estrogen acts on the hypothalamus, which in turn stops the pituitary gland from producing any more FSH; the result is that ovulation is suppressed. No further menstruation occurs until after the baby has been born.

After the birth, the pituitary gland produces another hormone, prolactin, in response to regular breast-feeding. This hormone acts to prevent ovulation, and so breastfeeding women will for at least a while experience no periods. Regular and frequent breast-feeding is a useful method of contraception during this time. Women who do not breast-feed can expect ovulation to start again within about six weeks of their giving birth.

However, a mother who is breast-feeding is not necessarily infertile. If there is a long gap between one session of breast-feeding and the next, the pituitary may temporarily fail to produce enough prolactin to forestall ovulation. Another point to remember in this context is that ovulation precedes menstruation: the first period after a woman has given birth is a sign that, 14 days earlier, she was fertile. **PB**

When in his life is a man fertile?

Unlike women, men do not have a regular cycle of fertility. Before puberty a male is infertile; around puberty he is infertile most of the time but can be fertile

on occasion; after puberty, once the testicles have begun to function in the adult mode, men are fertile until a very advanced age: cases of men in their seventies, eighties or nineties fathering children are well known.

All the eggs a female will ever produce are present, in rudimentary form, at the time of her birth. When a boy is born, however, there are no sperm-generating cells (spermatocytes) present in his body. Instead there are germ cells (spermatogonia) capable of producing sperm cells plus other cells which can provide support for the germ cells when they become active.

Girls' first ovulatory cycles after puberty are likely to be infertile, and much the same is true of boys' first sperm cells. However, as the size of the testicles increases during puberty the production rate of viable sperm cells increases.

There is evidence that, in later years, the size of the testicles and production of sperm cells decrease markedly, but this has yet to be proved.

Each of the testicles is largely made up of a vast number of tubes – the seminiferous tubules. Each of these tubes is tightly packed and highly coiled – if stretched out, one would be about 70cm (27.5in) long – and both ends of each of them join onto one of about 30 straight tubules. These latter converge toward the head of a tube called the epididymis – which would be about 6-7m (20-23ft) long if straightened out – that leads from the testicles to the vas deferens. The vas deferens, which would be about 40cm (15.75in) long if stretched out, transports the sperm to the penis, at whose tip the sperm are eventually ejaculated.

The testicles become activated at puberty. In each of the seminiferous tubules the spermatogonia begin to divide; some produce further spermatocytes while others divide in such a way that, about 64 days later, they will each have generated 512 sperm cells; these are delivered to the nearest tubule.

How long does a sperm cell survive?

The production of sperm cells occurs constantly; each batch of sperm cells produced by a single germ cell, however, represents a regular cycle. First a spermatogonium divides to produce a set of primary spermatocytes; about 20 days later these begin the process of duplicating their genetic material, a process which ends about 20 days later. These cells then in turn divide to produce secondary spermatocytes. About eight hours later these new cells, too, divide to produce yet another generation of cells, the early spermatids. The cluster of early spermatids owing their origin to the same germ cell are linked by bridges of a jelly-like substance called cytoplasm. Gradually they mature to become late spermatids and the bridges disappear.

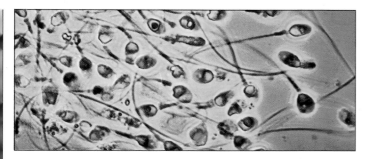

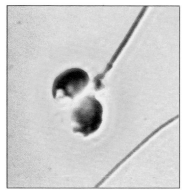

Normal and abnormal sperm. *Propelled by whip-like movements of their tails, sperm ABOVE have oval-shaped heads that are full of chromosomes. In each ejaculation there is a small percentage of deformed sperm which may, for example, have two heads LEFT or two tails BELOW. Too many of these can reduce fertility.*

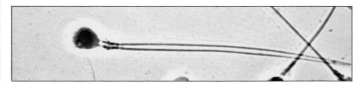

Spermatids are fairly simple cells. They develop to become mature sperm cells, or spermatozoa, the highly refined cells that can negotiate first the male and then the female genital tracts to fuse with and fertilize an egg.

While spermatids are still developing they spend some weeks lodged in and nurtured by other cells of the seminiferous tubule, the Sertoli cells. Fully developed sperm cells contain very little by way of material that they can draw on for energy, and so they depend on nutrients in the surrounding medium as they make their way through the male genital tract. In the early stages, while the sperm cells are journeying toward the epididymis, the fluid produced by the Sertoli cells is responsible for providing the immature sperm cells with such nutrients.

Each day the Sertoli cells release into the seminiferous tubules about two billion sperm cells. It takes about two weeks for the sperm cells to travel from here to the beginning of the vas deferens. Traveling through the vas deferens takes a further two weeks. By the time of their rapid ejaculation, only a small proportion of the daily production of two billion sperm cells survives, the rest having been lost mainly through spillage into the urine.

We can see that the total lifespan of a sperm cell from its origin to its loss through elimination or ejaculation is about 2.5-3 months. It is for this reason that men who have had a vasectomy (a sealing-off of the vas deferens) are advised to behave as if they were still fertile for some while after the operation has been carried out. Three months or so after the vasectomy, to ensure that the operation has been a success, a semen sample is taken and examined to ascertain that it contains no residual sperm. Were the test carried out before this time, it might reveal sperm cells that had already reached the vas deferens before the operation was carried out.

What causes impotence?

There are various reasons why a man may become infertile. The two basic ones are impotence and inadequate (or abnormal) sperm formation. The former can have far more devastating psychological effects.

In the vast majority of cases impotence is a direct result of psychological factors such as anxiety about sexual performance. If the man's partner can discuss the situation sympathetically and can downplay the "performance-oriented" aspects of sex, it is likely that the episode will be short-lived. The psychological aspect of impotence does mean that episodes are likely to become more frequent with age – family stresses, increased demands at work and so on can adversely affect sexual potency.

Illness, too, can cause impotence. Any infection that causes a fever – influenza, for example – is likely to affect sexual libido. Diseases like diabetes may produce impotence through their damaging effects on the nerves that initiate and maintain the male erection; however, such cases can now often be cured medically.

Prescribed drugs are another cause of impotence. Among them are many of those used to treat high blood pressure and a few of those used in the treatment of mental illnesses. These side-effects certainly exist, but unfortunately not much is known about them: doctors and patients alike are reluctant to discuss them. However, any time that you enter a new regime of tablets and discover that your sexual potency seems to be affected, you should consult your doctor. Coping with illness exerts a considerable psychological stress: you should not be expected to add to that the stress of coping with impotence.

Most men, when they wake up, have an erection. This is not due to sexual excitation; rather it is because there has been a cross-over between the nerves responsible for controlling the bladder's release of its contents and those responsible for dilating the blood vessels in the penis. A man who suffers from impotence yet regularly experiences an early-morning erection is unlikely to be impotent for any physiological reason, such as disease. The cause of the impotence is much more likely to be something psychological – or alcohol or some other drug.

121

How does deficient sperm production affect fertility?

Of all cases of infertility, 40 percent are due to inadequate sperm-cell production. This means that, whenever a couple are experiencing difficulty in conceiving a child, the first thing that should be medically tested is the fertility of the male. The test is fairly simple to perform. Men are required to abstain from sex for 2-3 days and then to ejaculate into a wide-mouthed, sterile plastic container; this container should be sealed immediately and, still kept at room temperature, delivered to an appropriate laboratory within two hours. The staff of the laboratory examine the sample in four different respects. First there is the volume of the ejaculate, which is normally 2-5ml (0.5-1.5 teaspoonsful). Then a sample of the

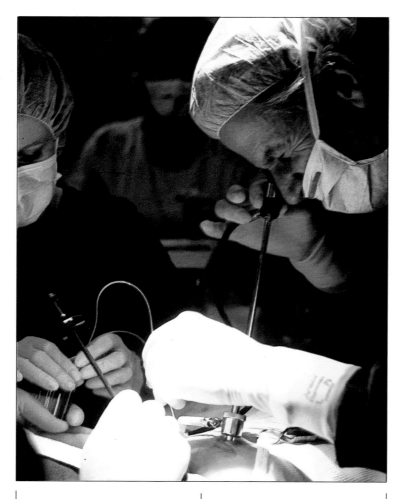

When the reproductive cycle needs assistance *doctors may use GIFT (gamete intrafallopian transfer). By surgical intervention, an egg and sperm are enabled to meet at the top of the fallopian tube. An optical instrument inserted into the abdomen enables surgeons to perform the operation.*

ejaculate is viewed microscopically to evaluate sperm-cell density (which ought to be greater than 20 million sperm per milliliter of ejaculate – usually 40-60 million). Third, the motility of the sperm cells are assessed: at least 40 percent of them should be "swimming." Finally, the laboratory staff look at the appearance of the sperm cells: on average more than 50 percent will be abnormal (this is hardly surprising, since the production of sperm is a very complex process). These are all optimum figures. They can vary widely. If there is a deficiency, there may be a number of causes.

One possibility is that there is some abnormality in the cells of the testicles – perhaps because the man has been infected by mumps or has been exposed to radiation or toxic chemicals; in such cases the pituitary tries to drive the testicles by producing higher levels of hormones.

A second possibility is that there is a physical blockage – possibly following infection in, for example, the prostate gland or the seminal vesicle – so that the testicles fail to deliver the sperm adequately to the penis.

A third possibility is again a simple one: sperm cells fail to be produced because the environment is unfavorable. The testicles function at their best when they are at a temperature of about 32°C (90°F); any prolonged increase in temperature – for example, a daily hot bath that lasts about a half-hour – will cause them to produce fewer sperm cells. The ancient Romans assumed that hot baths were a reliable method of contraception; however, it should not be regarded as an infallible way of temporarily sterilizing the male.

Recreational drugs and excess alcohol commonly reduce the number of viable sperm cells in the male ejaculate. **MH**

What causes infertility in women?

One common reason for impaired fertility in women is the scarring of the fallopian tubes that sometimes follows infections such as sexually transmitted diseases like gonorrhea and chlamydia. Other reasons for difficulty in conceiving include blockage of the fallopian tubes for some different reason, such as infection following childbirth, and failure to ovulate (because of hormonal irregularities). Although blame has been ascribed to certain forms of contraception, therapeutic abortions, and deliberately delayed pregnancy, (for as she grows older a woman has less chance of conceiving), in many cases the cause is never found (unexplained infertility).

Can cycles be manipulated to enhance fertility?

The most obvious way to enhance the likelihood of conceiving a child is to make love at a time when the female partner is producing eggs. For most couples it is eggs. Two possible solutions are GIFT (gamete intrafallopian transfer) and IVF (in vitro fertilization).

In IVF, injections of FSH and LH are used to stimulate the woman's body into producing many more eggs than usual. An injection of hCG is given so that the eggs mature in advance of ovulation. About 36 hours after the hCG injection has been given, the eggs are retrieved by puncturing the follicles; the surgery can be viewed directly, using a kind of telescope inserted into the abdomen (a laparoscope), or indirectly, using an ultrasound scanner. Either way, the egg is extracted and placed with some of the man's sperm in a dish in an incubator, and hopefully fertilization takes place. The fertilized egg is left in the incubator for two days, by which time it should have divided twice. It is then implanted in the uterus using a fine plastic catheter.

In GIFT, hormones are used to stimulate simultaneous production of a number of eggs, and the eggs are retrieved in the same way as for in vitro fertilization. However, the eggs are not removed for fertilization and culture outside the woman's body. Instead, they and a small sample of the father's sperm are immediately placed in the mother's fallopian tubes. If all goes well, fertilization will be brought about in the usual place.

The easiest way to assist sperm-cell production in men with low fertility is to avoid the factors which hinder production. These include wearing tight pants (which increases the temperature of the testicles), obesity, smoking and excessive use of alcohol.

If, even after all these factors have been countered, the man still has difficulty in fathering, it may be worth resorting to sex therapy. Sex therapists help couples to find the best methods of having intercourse, and the best times to have it. The pioneers in the field were William H Masters and Virginia E Johnson, who claimed a success rate of 20 percent. In fact, in about 5 percent of cases infertility rights itself without the need to turn to medical or any other treatment. **PB**

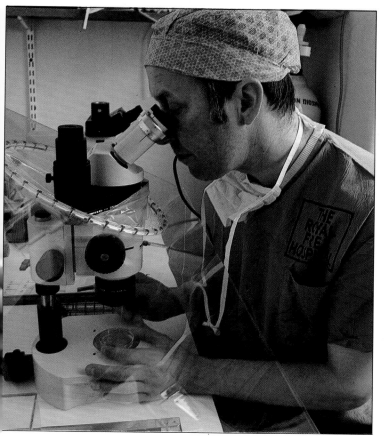

Fertilization outside the body. *In in vitro fertilization, after surgeons have removed an egg, it is separated from its follicle using a mouth pipette. The sperm is added six hours later and the fertilized egg implanted in the womb after 40 hours. Ten days afterward doctors test to see whether the egg has been successfully implanted.*

sufficient to make love frequently around the middle of the menstrual cycle, but couples who find that they are still unsuccessful should seek medical advice. Monitoring changes in cervical mucus, basal body temperature and levels of LH (luteinizing hormone – see *Ch12*) can indicate more precisely the time of ovulation.

Where a woman ovulates irregularly or not at all, it may be worth calling on various drugs – popularly known as "fertility drugs"; one example is clomiphene. Naturally occurring hormone combinations, such as FSH (follicle stimulating hormone) with LH, can be used to stimulate the development of eggs. If a woman's body creates eggs but does not release them at the appropriate time, doses of a hormone called hCG (human chorionic gonadotrophin) can simulate the surge of LH that should occur around the middle of the menstrual cycle.

It may be that a couple's difficulties in achieving conception are due to the poor quality of the man's sperm cells or a problem in the transport of the sperm to the

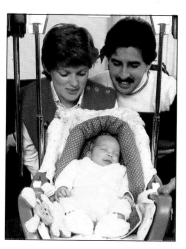

Inaccurately named "test-tube" babies, *children produced through in vitro fertilization are in fact conceived in a petri dish. Since the first test-tube baby was born in 1978, many others have been born. Because surgeons may implant two fertilized eggs for a better chance of success, and both sometimes survive, a slightly higher proportion of twins develop from in vitro fertilizations.*

Countering the Cycle of Fertility

Different contraceptive methods are suited to different times in your life

MANY contraceptive methods work in a way that does not rely on a knowledge of the body's rhythms. Barrier methods such as the condom and the diaphragm mechanically prevent the sperm meeting the egg. Spermicides kill sperm. It is not known precisely how intrauterine devices – the "loop" or "coil" – work, but those that contain copper may have a toxic effect both on sperm and, before implantation, on the fertilized egg. They also cause a mild inflammation of the lining of the uterus, so that the egg fails to implant.

Some contraceptive methods, however, exploit the fact that women have a monthly cycle of fertility.

The rhythm method

The most obvious is the rhythm method. The theory is simple enough. The most fertile time of the woman's cycle is established, and intercourse is avoided at that time.

However, given the variability of the exact time of ovulation in any particular woman's monthly cycle and variations in the length of the cycle, coupled with the fact that sperm cells can survive in the female genital tract for several days, the so-called "safe period" is in fact far from safe.

However strictly she may follow it, a woman who relies on the rhythm method throughout her active sexual life has about a 10 percent chance of an unwanted pregnancy. Even assuming this risk is acceptable, the method brings with it another major disadvantage – the psychological one. For the rhythm method to have any chance of success at all, the period of abstinence from intercourse during each cycle should be about 10 days or more.

Breast-feeding as contraception

One natural method of contraception is frequent breast-feeding. During the time that she is breast-feeding on demand a woman does not ovulate, and so cannot conceive. This is nature's way of ensuring that children are reasonably spaced – benefiting the health of both the children and the mother. Long gaps between breast-feeding sessions, however, can prompt ovulation to restart (see p120), so it may be advisable to use an additional form of contraception while breast-feeding.

The introduction of the indiscriminate use of bottled feeds to the Third World has had an unfortunate dual impact: babies are being born closer together, so that the infant mortality rate rises and the mothers' health deteriorates due to over-frequent pregnancies.

Contraceptive pills

Certain kinds of contraceptive pills depend for their effectiveness

---

CONTRACEPTION AT DIFFERENT TIMES OF LIFE

Which forms of contraception are most suitable at different times of life?

Before marriage the most important aspects of contraception are reliability, reversibility and protection from sexually transmitted disease. The oral contraceptive pill is the easiest and most reliable, and the health risks to young women are minimal, but it gives no protection from disease. The best plan is to use the pill in conjunction with condoms.

Newly married couples who are not at risk from sexually transmitted diseases can choose from the pill, condoms or the diaphragm. Intrauterine devices are not recommended because of the slight risk of infection and hence of difficulty in later conception.

During breast-feeding a woman is infertile; however, it is difficult to predict when she may start to become fertile again. Contraception may therefore be an advisable safety precaution. Condoms and the diaphragm are appropriate, as is the progesterone-only oral contraceptive pill (the estrogen in the combined pill can have an adverse effect on lactation).

For family spacing, the degree of reliability desired depends on the impact the arrival of an unexpected child would have. Intrauterine devices are probably the best option, since they are well tolerated in women who have already had children and the method is easily reversible. Older women – especially those who smoke, have high blood pressure or are over-

THE PILL: ADVANTAGES AND RISKS

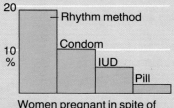

Start 1 ▶ 2 ▶ 3 ▶ 4 ▶ 5 ▶ 6
7 ▶ 8 ▶ 9 ▶ 10 ▶ 11
12 ▶ 13 ▶ 14 ▶ 15 ▶ 16 ▶ 17 ▶ 18 ▶ 19 ▶ 20 ▶ 21

The most reliable contraceptive, *the pill is at least 96 percent effective when taken according to instructions. Its pro-*

20 — Rhythm method
Condom
10% IUD
Pill

Women pregnant in spite of contraception

tection is reduced by an attack of vomiting or diarrhea lasting for more than one day, by some antibiotics, or if you forget a pill. ABOVE *21-day "combination pills" are taken, one a day, for 21 days, followed by seven pill-free days when a period or "withdrawal bleed" occurs. The triphasic contraceptive pill varies the amount of estrogen and progesterone taken in each third of the menstrual cycle. The dispenser is marked with numbers to reduce the chances of forgetting a pill.*

Change in life expectancy (months)
+1
0
−1
−2
−3
Age
22 27 32 37 42

Life expectancy *declines slightly in women over 30 who have used the pill for five years. By this age the advantage gained in a reduced risk of death during childbirth is reversed by a slightly higher risk of clots in veins, small strokes, gallstones, heart attacks and liver tumors.*

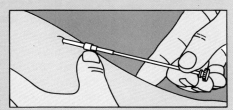

Giving protection for five years or more, *a timed-release contraceptive capsule developed in Sweden and Finland is implanted beneath the skin. Steadily feeding a steroid drug into the bloodstream, it prevents ovulation. Irregular periods may be a side-effect.*

weight – are advised not to use oral contraceptive pills. If sex has become less frequent between the couple, barrier methods may well be perfectly adequate.

When the family is complete, reliability is the prime concern. Intrauterine devices are a good option; oral contraceptive pills probably are not. Sterilization is an easily available choice, but both partners should realize that the operation will be difficult to reverse and should be regarded as permanent.

As the menopause approaches, the risks of conception grow less. Nevertheless, pregnancy at this time of life can be potentially hazardous. Barrier contraception should be sufficient, although some women opt for an intrauterine device or sterilization. After the menopause, contraception is not necessary.

on a chemical manipulation of the woman's cycle of fertility.

Basically there are two different kinds of contraceptive pill.

The combined oral contraceptive pill contains low doses of the hormones estrogen and progesterone; these are either in a constant ratio or in proportions that mimic the hormone changes of the natural cycle of the ovaries. The estrogen acts on the pituitary gland and the hypothalamus, and prevents the release of follicle-stimulating hormone (see *Ch12*). The ovaries remain relatively inactive: follicles do not form and eggs are not released. Furthermore, the

lining of the uterus is maintained in a state that is unlikely to allow the implantation of eggs.

The progesterone, on the other hand, keeps the cervical mucus in a state that is unsuitable for sperm penetration. This kind of oral contraceptive pill is taken daily for three weeks out of each menstrual cycle's four; sometimes, inactive pills are supplied for the fourth week, to reduce the risks of losing track of when to stop and restart. During the fourth week the estrogen and progesterone levels fall. This induces shedding of the uterus's lining to produce an effect similar to a menstrual period.

The combined oral contraceptive pill is the most effective reversible means of contraception to be widely available. Very rarely it can bring the hazard of serious side-effects – for example, clots in veins, small strokes, gallstones, heart attacks and liver tumors. The percentage risk is extremely small, particularly in young women.

Moreover, the pill can have various health benefits: menstrual periods tend to be lighter and less painful and the risks of ovarian cysts and of cancer of the ovaries and uterus are reduced.

The other kind of oral contraceptive pill is the progesterone-only pill, or "mini-pill." This contains progesterone but not estrogen. It is taken daily, and has little effect on the ovarian cycle. It seems to work primarily through the effect the progesterone has on the mucus of the cervix, barring the progress of sperm. The progesterone may also hamper the transport of eggs down the fallopian tubes.

The progesterone-only pill is safer in terms of health – since the potentially harmful side-effects of the combined pill are connected with estrogen but its failure rate is slightly higher than that of the combined pill. **PB**

12 THE MENSTRUAL CYCLE

The average woman will probably experience about 400 menstrual periods in her reproductive lifetime. Controlled by a "menstrual clock" located in the brain, each normal period follows an intricately timed – but unused – opportunity for a fertilized egg to implant in the lining of the womb and develop into a new life.

THE BASIC ANATOMY

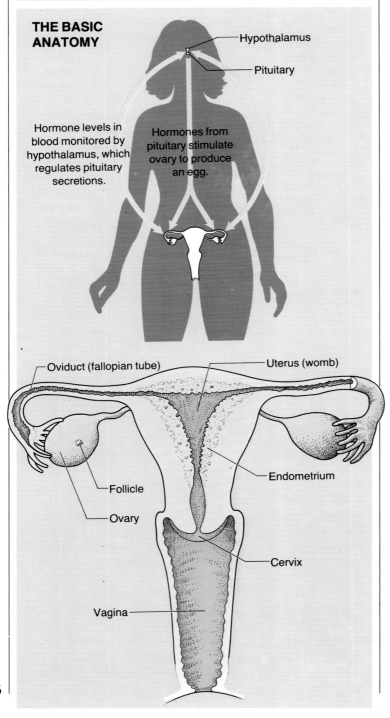

Hormone levels in blood monitored by hypothalamus, which regulates pituitary secretions.

Hormones from pituitary stimulate ovary to produce an egg.

Hypothalamus

Pituitary

Oviduct (fallopian tube)

Uterus (womb)

Follicle

Endometrium

Ovary

Cervix

Vagina

MOST WOMEN recognize that they go through cycles of how they feel about themselves, their bodies and other people. The clearest sign of an underlying rhythm is menstruation, or monthly bleeding. Until this century, menstruation was thought to be governed by the phases of the moon, as it occurs every month. The myth of the regular 28-day cycle grew out of similar observations; and although all women know that a cycle rarely takes exactly 28 days, for convenience doctors still use this length of time as a standard.

What is happening when a woman menstruates?

There are two major events in the menstrual cycle: one invisible – ovulation (monthly release of the egg); and one highly visible – menstruation (the monthly bleeding, or menses, or period).

Ovulation occurs about half way between one period and the next. The two-week build-up to ovulation is called the "follicular phase," named after the follicle, the little sac of fluid in the ovary that grows up to 2cm (nearly an inch) in diameter and bursts at ovulation, releasing the egg. During the following two weeks, called the "luteal phase," the burst sac is called the corpus luteum. It continues to have a central role – producing progesterone, the hormone that readies a woman for the pregnancy she will have if the egg is fertilized.

Throughout the cycle the ovary produces hormones – natural chemical substances that act as messengers when released into the bloodstream by body organs (see *Ch5*). When they reach a target cell, hormones trigger a command in that cell – to grow for example, or to produce another substance. The ovary is itself both a hormone-producing organ and one of the many organs controlled by hormones from glands in the brain.

During the follicular phase, the ovary produces increasing amounts of estrogen, the female hormone, which is necessary for puberty in women and lack of which is the cause of dry hair and skin, dry vagina and thin bones at the menopause. Estrogen levels increase to a peak 48 hours before ovulation, after which production drops. It rises again the following week, but falls just before menstruation. After ovulation, the burst follicle (now the corpus luteum) turns a deep yellow color and develops more blood vessels on its surface. It starts pumping out the hormone progesterone, the hormone of the luteal phase. However, as the menstrual cycle draws to a close, the corpus luteum shrivels up and progesterone production almost ceases.

Describing the menstrual cycle in terms of follicular and luteal phases is useful when trying to understand how the ovary works, but most women think in terms of premenstrual, menstrual and postmenstrual phases of the cycle. The premenstrual phase is at most the entire 14

CHANGES IN THE UTERUS

▼ *How the endometrium – the inner lining of the uterus – sloughed off during the period, develops and thickens during the menstrual cycle.*

▶ *Projections from the fully developed endometrium line the interior of the uterus like a thick, soft, spongy carpet.*

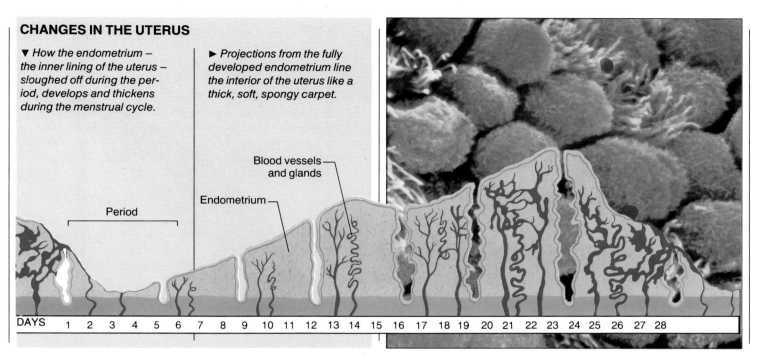

Blood vessels and glands

Endometrium

Period

DAYS 1 2 3 4 5 6 7 8 9 10 11 12 13 14 15 16 17 18 19 20 21 22 23 24 25 26 27 28

days of the luteal phase, and at least the latter part of it. The menstrual phase is the first 5-7 days of the follicular phase. The postmenstrual phase is the rest of the follicular and usually the early part of the luteal phase (see page 130).

Does a normal cycle take exactly 28 days?

Although the standard menstrual period is taken as 28 days, it can vary in normal women from 24 to 35 days, and even then it can sometimes differ from period to period by several days on either side. This is usually because of the variable lifespan of the follicle. The time taken for the corpus luteum to run its course and collapse is fairly uniform, taking roughly 14 days, whereas the follicle can last from 9 to 17 days.

Many factors can affect the length of the cycle and its phases. The ovaries are regulated by hormones from glands in the brain, and one of them, the hypothalamus, at the top of the chain of command, is influenced by emotions and a woman's reaction to her environment. Emotional stresses, such as anxiety, worry and chronic fatigue, can disrupt the menstrual cycle. Under-nourishment and excessive exercise can stop periods altogether, as it sometimes does in ballet dancers and long-distance runners who train all day while remaining underweight (see p134). Women living together, for example in a college hall of residence, can also influence each other by unconsciously detecting almost imperceptible changes in body odor. Several studies have shown that the periods of such groups of women may become synchronized by this means.

What are the phases of the premenstrual cycle?

Menstruation occurs when the inner lining of the uterus (or womb) is shed along with some blood and fluid. This inner lining is a blanket of cells called the endometrium. Spiraling their way up between these cells are little arteries that supply the cells with oxygen and nutrients. Under the influence of estrogen and progesterone the cells multiply, so that by the end of the luteal phase the endometrium is thickened and ready to accept the early embryo should conception occur. With the drop in estrogen and progesterone at the end of the luteal phase, the endometrium stops growing. At the same time the arteries close off, cutting the lifeline of oxygen and nutrients to the endometrial cells and to the cells of the arteries themselves. These cells therefore start dying and breaking up. When the arteries relax again, they start bleeding and this blood appears along with the sloughed-off cells as the period discharge.

Most women bleed for between 5 and 7 days, with some brownish discharge for a few days on either side. This represents a blood loss in all of some 20-60ml (almost 4-12 teaspoonfuls) per cycle. Excessive bleeding can sometimes be a problem (see p134). Some women simply lose more fluids than others, however, and they may feel that they have very heavy periods when in fact their blood loss is normal and they are in no danger of becoming anemic. Menstrual blood does not clot, as it contains special anti-clotting substances released by the uterus, but many women see large clot-like collections of red blood cells.

How do hormones control the menstrual cycle?

The regular rhythm of menstruation depends on the harmonious interplay of four main chemical messengers, or hormones: follicle-stimulating hormone, estrogen, luteinizing hormone and progesterone.

1 The pituitary gland, located at the base of the brain and chemically controlled by an adjacent part of the brain called the hypothalamus, releases the hormone FSH (follicle-stimulating hormone) into the bloodstream.

8 If the ovum on its journey to the uterus is not fertilized and so fails to embed in the uterine lining within a few days, the corpus luteum shrinks away: progesterone production ceases and the level of estrogen in the blood drops. Menstruation is triggered.

7 Besides estrogen, the corpus luteum produces yet another hormone: progesterone (the "pro-pregnancy" hormone). Progesterone stimulates the lining of the uterus to bring itself into a state of final readiness to receive the ovum. And while progesterone is in the blood, the hypothalamus prevents the pituitary from secreting either LH or FSH.

6 The sudden surge of LH in the bloodstream causes the now fully mature follicle to burst and release its ovum – which passes into a duct that leads ultimately to the uterus. Meanwhile, LH stimulates the empty follicle on the surface of the ovary to develop into a structure called the corpus luteum ("yellow body").

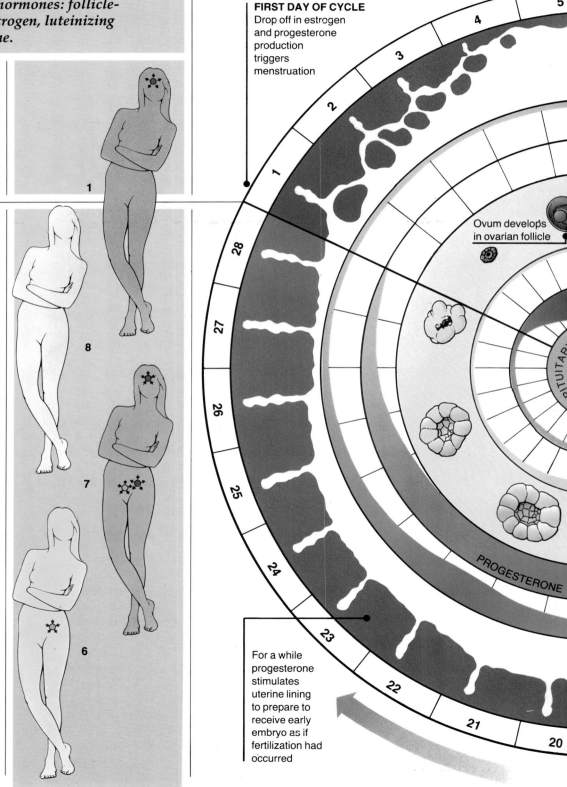

FIRST DAY OF CYCLE
Drop off in estrogen and progesterone production triggers menstruation

Ovum develops in ovarian follicle

PITUITARY

PROGESTERONE

For a while progesterone stimulates uterine lining to prepare to receive early embryo as if fertilization had occurred

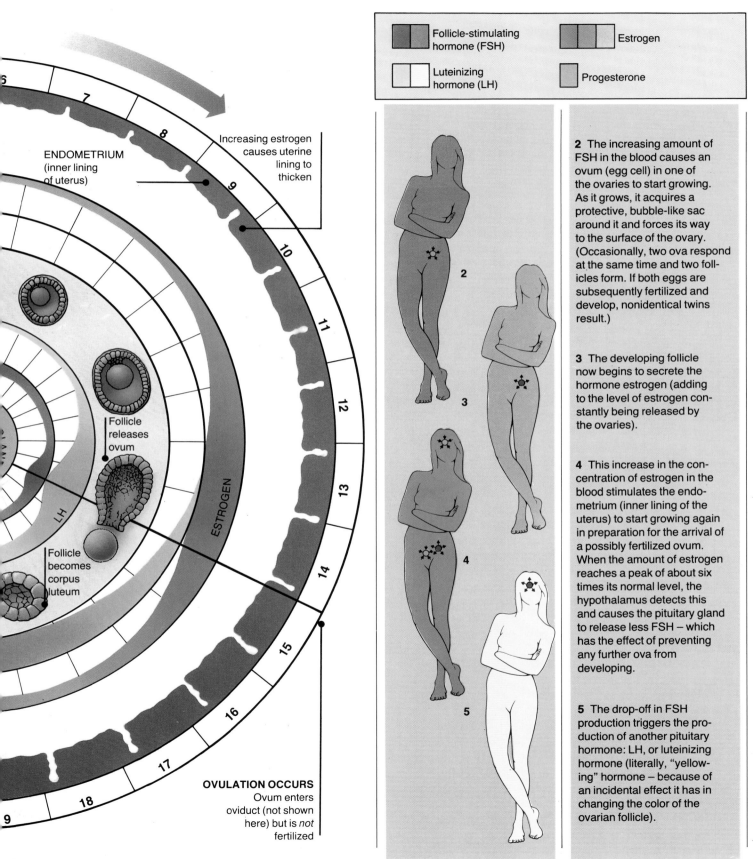

Follicle-stimulating hormone (FSH)

Estrogen

Luteinizing hormone (LH)

Progesterone

ENDOMETRIUM (inner lining of uterus)

Increasing estrogen causes uterine lining to thicken

Follicle releases ovum

Follicle becomes corpus luteum

LH

ESTROGEN

OVULATION OCCURS
Ovum enters oviduct (not shown here) but is *not* fertilized

2 The increasing amount of FSH in the blood causes an ovum (egg cell) in one of the ovaries to start growing. As it grows, it acquires a protective, bubble-like sac around it and forces its way to the surface of the ovary. (Occasionally, two ova respond at the same time and two follicles form. If both eggs are subsequently fertilized and develop, nonidentical twins result.)

3 The developing follicle now begins to secrete the hormone estrogen (adding to the level of estrogen constantly being released by the ovaries).

4 This increase in the concentration of estrogen in the blood stimulates the endometrium (inner lining of the uterus) to start growing again in preparation for the arrival of a possibly fertilized ovum. When the amount of estrogen reaches a peak of about six times its normal level, the hypothalamus detects this and causes the pituitary gland to release less FSH – which has the effect of preventing any further ova from developing.

5 The drop-off in FSH production triggers the production of another pituitary hormone: LH, or luteinizing hormone (literally, "yellowing" hormone – because of an incidental effect it has in changing the color of the ovarian follicle).

129

What do changes in the cervical mucus mean?

The endometrium is not the only uterine tissue to be affected by the menstrual cycle. The cervix, or neck of the womb, also responds to the cyclical influence of the ovarian hormones. The cells on the surface of the cervix become plumper under the influence of estrogen in the first half of the cycle. The condition of the cells affects the interpretation of cervical smears, and so it is important that only smears taken at the same stage in the cycle should be compared.

Also on the surface of the cervix are many little glands which produce and discharge mucus – a clear, sticky liquid. The consistency and quantity of this mucus changes with the cycle, and knowledge of these changes can be used to track the stage the cycle has reached. As ovulation approaches and levels of estrogen rise, the cervix starts to produce copious amounts of thin, watery mucus. This thinner mucus is saltier and more alkaline than at other times in the cycle. At ovulation it develops a characteristic tackiness or stretchiness, so that if a little is scooped up between two fingers, the strand of mucus will continue stretching to a surprising length without snapping. The high salt content of the mucus at this stage can be shown by a test known as "ferning." If the mucus is smeared on a slide and allowed to dry, under a microscope the extreme saltiness will give it a frond-like pattern that resembles fern leaves.

During the luteal phase, under the influence of progesterone, the mucus becomes much thicker and stickier, and there is much less of it. This thicker, more tenacious mucus is impenetrable to sperm trying to find their way through the cervix and into the uterus. It is only the thinner mucus produced at ovulation that allows the sperm to swim through and onward. This property is used by doctors to assess factors contributing to infertility. If the wrong type of mucus is being produced around the time of ovulation, the sperm will not reach the egg and conception will not occur.

How does the cycle affect body temperature?

The temperature of the body when it is resting is known as the basal body temperature, or BBT. It is best checked first thing in the morning before exercise or food, both of which raise the temperature. (Ailments due to infection such as colds and sore throats also affect the thermometer reading.) Normal body temperature is about 37°C (98.4°F). Before ovulation, the BBT is one-tenth of a centigrade degree lower than this. After ovulation, the temperature rises by 0.2-0.3°C (0.36-0.54°F). This is caused by progesterone acting directly on the temperature-regulating center in the brain. But this pat-

tern becomes apparent only with hindsight, after several cycles have been observed, and many women show no regular pattern of temperature change. As a method of family planning, therefore, it can be somewhat unreliable (see *Ch10*).

Why do the breasts become tender before a period?

The most common premenstrual symptom in women is breast tenderness. Around 70 percent of women complain of their breasts feeling tender and sensitive to the touch. This is possibly due to an increase in sensitivity in nerve endings, but is also partly due to the increased fluid retention that occurs during menstruation. This causes the breasts to increase in volume and become quite tense – an effect of progesterone at the end of the luteal phase. Similar feelings are experienced in early pregnancy when there are also high levels of progesterone. Numerous other premenstrual symptoms are reported, including swings of mood.

Are period pain and abdominal discomfort normal?

Most women experience some degree of lower abdominal discomfort associated with their period. This can range from a few hours' dull ache on the first day of the period to severe pain that calls for a rest in bed. It is usually of a crampy nature and may be accompanied by loose bowel motions. Period pains (dysmenorrhea – p135) may be present from the beginning of a woman's menstrual history, or they may crop up halfway through her life, in which case the pain is more likely to be due to some gynecological problem. Dysmenorrhea has this crampy character because it is caused by spasms in the muscle of the uterus. During these spasms, the pain felt is rather like the pain in an overworked leg after prolonged running.

During a period there is sometimes also pain or a dull ache in the lower back. This is because some of the nerve fibers that supply the uterus have their origin in the lower spine.

Some women also have a short-lived acute, lower abdominal pain in mid-cycle, at the time of the ovulation. Doctors call it "mittelschmertz." It is caused by the follicle rupturing to release the egg. The fluid in the follicle, which trickles out along with the egg, contains substances which irritate the lining of the abdomen and give rise to abdominal discomfort.

Pain can occur in the week before a period if the corpus luteum bursts rather than collapses. This rupture, too, releases fluid, and in addition a small amount of blood that likewise gives rise to irritation and abdominal discomfort. Severe pain at this time is not normal – if it occurs, a doctor should be consulted.

CHANGES IN THE FLOW OF MUCUS

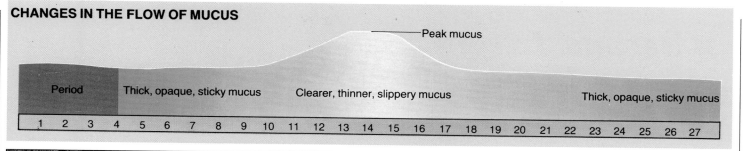

Peak mucus

| Period | Thick, opaque, sticky mucus | Clearer, thinner, slippery mucus | Thick, opaque, sticky mucus |

| 1 | 2 | 3 | 4 | 5 | 6 | 7 | 8 | 9 | 10 | 11 | 12 | 13 | 14 | 15 | 16 | 17 | 18 | 19 | 20 | 21 | 22 | 23 | 24 | 25 | 26 | 27 |

CHANGING BODY TEMPERATURE

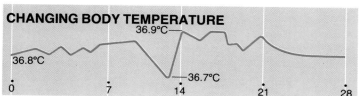

36.9°C

36.8°C

36.7°C

0   7   14   21   28

◄ *The strikingly beautiful frond-like structure of the cervical mucus at the time of ovulation, greatly magnified. If tested by stretching a little between the fingertips, it forms a clear, shimmering strand – in contrast to the thin, watery mucus leading up to ovulation and the thick, pasty mucus found before and after the period.*

▲ *Although the basal body temperature varies by only a fraction of a degree during the monthly cycle, it is a useful indicator of the successive phases of the menstrual cycle – if interpreted in conjunction with variations in the consistency of the cervical mucus.*

Can the cycle affect a woman's appearance?

In the premenstrual phase the skin can become greasier, giving rise to spots and blackheads. Acne sufferers will notice at this time a deterioration in their skin condition, with a flare-up in numbers of inflamed pustules. The glands in the scalp that produce natural oily substances may likewise become more active.

These changes are due to the influence of androgens – the male hormones that the ovary produces before converting them into estrogens or other female hormones. Androgen-based hormones also are ingredients in certain contraceptive pills: women with acne should take a brand without this type of hormone.

The hormonal fluctuations can also cause regular but subtle changes in the distribution of body fat. Usually this passes unnoticed, but sometimes it is detectable in a face which, at a certain time of the month, seems very slightly longer or squarer than usual.

Can the cycle influence a woman's sex drive?

In other mammals there is a clear relationship between sexual intercourse and the menstrual cycle (called "the estrous cycle" in animals). The female of most species is receptive only during estrus, the time when external signs of readiness coincide with ovulation, and conception is most likely. The human female is unique in showing no obvious signs of ovulation and also in the degree to which she is receptive when not ovulating. It has not, in fact, been established that her receptivity varies at all in response to monthly patterns of change in hormone levels, although some studies report a higher rate of sexual frequency during ovulation, and a heightened tendency to be influenced by sexually arousing pheromones. Women's sexual arousal is probably much more dependent on other factors, such as mood and environment (see *Ch12*).

Sex drive may be increased during the time of menstruation because of a release from the inhibition of the fear of pregnancy, but equally there may be a negative effect because of the unpleasantness of the menstrual discharge.

During menstruation and the immediate postmenstrual week, the skin of the vagina becomes a little thinner and more delicate due to a lack of estrogen. Intercourse may therefore be uncomfortable or painful. Because of this more fragile vaginal skin, the woman may also be more prone to infections such as thrush (a common yeast infection) and more liable to itch.   **SS**

Why Do Periods Become Irregular?

When periods are missing, infrequent or heavy, there is usually nothing wrong

IF YOUR periods begin any time between 24 to 35 days after the start of your cycle, you are perfectly normal. If they are more erratic than this, or absent, it may be an important signal about your physical condition, but seldom reflects a serious medical problem. It is common for periods to be irregular near the beginning and the end of the reproductive years, and to stop altogether at times during the years between.

When periods do not occur

Absence of periods is called amenorrhea. It is the natural condition up until menarche (first menstruation) which may occur any time from 11 to 20 years of age. In a very small number of cases, genetic abnormalities mean that the ovaries do not produce hormones, or there is no uterus, and menstruation will never occur (see Ch16). These are cases of primary amenorrhea.

Secondary amenorrhea occurs when established periods stop. The commonest reasons are pregnancy and the menopause. These must always be excluded before seeking other causes.

Because the menstrual cycle is controlled by the hypothalamus, the changes in brain chemistry that come with emotional and physical stress may affect periods. It is not known precisely how this occurs, but athletic training or even an emotional upset, or the stress of an accident, injury or operation, can lower levels of the hormone from the hypothalamus that releases luteinizing hormone

WHAT CAUSES EXTRA BLEEDING?

Many women have heavy periods simply because of the natural variability between women. Some will have to change pads or tampons frequently and they may see what look like large clots, even like pieces of liver, in the menstrual flow. They may need iron tablets to make up the iron carried away in lost blood. There is no evidence that women can reduce a high volume of menstrual flow through self-help.

The desire to be free of heavy periods is often a motivation for having a hysterectomy (removal of the uterus). However, the volume of loss is usually not measured accurately — doctors often rely on the woman's own impression. The woman herself is then in the position of having to contribute to an informed decision about surgery (which carries a low but potential risk to life). In fact, it is menstruation itself, with all of its negative associations, that many find distressing — not an objectively heavy flow.

An irregular change from lighter to heavier periods can have several causes, the most common of which are not reasons for concern:

- approaching menopause
- stress
- recent insertion of an intra-uterine device

For a year or more before the menopause, when the periods become less regular, they may become longer and heavier. For some women, stress has the opposite effect to those described most commonly — rather than delayed or missed periods, they have ones that are longer, heavier or both. Similarly, stopping the pill can sometimes have this effect. Intrauterine contraceptive devices (the coil or loop) can at first make periods heavier. This is normal, but the device should be checked to make sure that it has not dislodged.

More serious causes of heavy bleeding include:

- fibroid tumors in the uterus
- pelvic infection
- cervical erosion
- cervical cancer
- unnatural growth of uterine lining tissue

Fibroids are small, noncancerous tumors inside the uterus. They can be removed surgically, sometimes by a hysterectomy. Cervical erosion and cervical cancer can cause bleeding between periods (see p137). Endometriosis is an uncommon condition in which tissue of the kind that is shed from the lining of the uterus during your period starts to grow on the ovaries or inside the abdomen. These tissues bleed during the period. Hormones, and sometimes surgery, are used to treat the condition. Pelvic infection (Pelvic Inflammatory Disease) can cause heavy and painful periods. Treatment is with antibiotics.

from the pituitary. Periods may disappear. They return when training is relaxed or emotional life returns to normal. For some women who lead very demanding lives, however, it may become the norm to miss periods.

Does weight affect periods?

Periods tend to stop when women lose about 15 percent of their normal weight. The proportion of body fat seems to be a factor. The extra layer of fat under a woman's skin that gives her a

smoother, less muscular appearance than a man seems to be needed for her fertility. Losing body fat is a second reason why a hard-training athlete may stop having periods. Regaining weight will restore them. This disruption of menstruation is not harmful.

Women who are overweight may have disturbances of their cycle because they produce too much male sex hormone. Losing weight may be all that is required to restore the periods to normal. Periods may not return

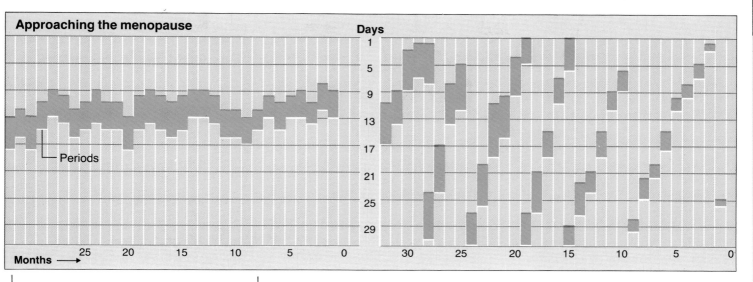

Approaching the menopause

Days

Months →

As the menopause comes closer, *two very different but normal patterns: LEFT periods gradually become shorter and then stop abruptly; RIGHT the time between periods becomes irregular. The length of the periods varies. Gradually they become shorter and stop forever.*

immediately after a pregnancy. They may be delayed, too, after a miscarriage or an abortion.

Breastfeeding commonly stops periods, and it may take two or three months for your normal cycle to reappear after weaning a baby.

About 5 percent of women who use oral contraceptives fail to have a period when they stop their pills at the end of each month. In itself this is not a problem, but it makes it more difficult to be sure that you are not pregnant. On giving up oral contraception, some women will take a short time before they have regular periods again, but this is not a serious long-term problem. Women who stop the pill to have a baby have the same chance of becoming pregnant in the two years that follow as women who have not used this contraceptive.

Sometimes, periods may stop because the pituitary produces too much of the hormone prolactin, one of the hormones responsible for milk production in the breast. Some women may find a milky discharge from the nipple. This overproduction is due to a small benign tumor in the pituitary which can be diagnosed by X-rays and blood tests.

It is important to check whether recent menstrual changes are associated with increased body hair. In the majority of cases this reflects slight shifts in the types of hormones produced by the ovary and the adrenal glands but, rarely, it may reflect serious underlying changes in the control of the hormonal system.

Infrequent periods

After menarche, the complicated interaction between the hypothalamus, pituitary and ovaries does not work smoothly. It is not known why this should occur in the early reproductive years, but by the age of 20 the pattern is usually normal. Toward the menopause, periods become irregular not because of problems with the hypothalamus but because the ovary begins to fail and cannot feed back the correct information to the brain.

As in the early years, during the middle of your reproductive span irregular hormone release from the hypothalamus is the most common reason for periods that are hard to predict. The situation is usually similar to one that stops periods altogether in another woman. For example, when life becomes particularly stressed, you may not miss a period completely, but experience a delay. Some women's periods are always fairly unpredictable, but this should be a matter for medical attention only if the woman wants to have a baby and finds it difficult to become pregnant. SS

WHAT CAUSES BLEEDING BETWEEN PERIODS?

Sometimes a woman has bleeding between periods that does not result from hormonal changes. This bleeding is usually lighter than the normal period. It is usually aggravated by intercourse, with bleeding during or after sex. The cause is most often an "erosion" on the cervix (a slight opening out of the cervix which exposes part of its surface). Very occasionally the cause is cancer of the cervix. It is most important to have regular cervical smears to check for cancer in any case, but bleeding between the periods will also prompt your doctor to arrange one, as well as more detailed examination of the cervix. If cancer is found, laser therapy, surgery, radiation treatment and (rarely) chemotherapy may be employed.

The Menstrual Cycle: Self-Help

Self-help diets, exercise and mood-management can ease period pains and premenstrual stress

DURING the premenstrual and menstrual stages of their monthly cycle, women may suffer from both emotional and physical complaints. Many of these can be helped by good diet and moderate exercise. Taking a positive attitude to menstruation is also part of the antidote to its problems.

Premenstrual symptoms

For about 50 percent of women the premenstrual phase may involve depression, anxiety, aggression, loss of concentration, irritability or anger. Unwelcome physical effects include bloating, leg cramps and breast tenderness. Before blaming PMS (the premenstrual syndrome), it is important to establish that the trouble is pre-menstrual and does not occur throughout the cycle.

About 10 percent of women seek treatment, but no consistent remedy for PMS has established itself and almost any of the standard medications, hormone treatments, recommended diets, psychotherapies and homeopathic therapies that have arisen will help 30 percent of sufferers at least in the short term. Diet and exercise are the main self-help strategies, with high-fiber foods to be recommended and salty ones to be avoided.

How can I avoid feeling bloated?

An important factor in premenstrual stress is the retention of fluids in the body tissues. Salt in the diet contributes to this. As menstruation approaches, hormone changes may in some women upset the the system that regulates salt – and hence fluid – balance (see *Ch 9*). Tissues may become uncomfortably bloated, and this may cause the breasts to feel tender. The heart has to pump an excess of blood around the body, working against a higher-than-normal blood pressure that contributes to feelings of tension.

By giving up the habit of adding salt at the table, or in cooking meat, fish and other foods that are naturally salty, you will probably keep your intake down to a level that your body can manage more easily.

KEEPING A PMS DIARY

To see whether your PMS-type symptoms are really related to your menstrual cycle, you should keep a diary. Select the five symptoms from this list that most affect you:

◆ feeling swollen, bloated
◆ loss of efficiency
◆ irritability
◆ gain in weight
◆ difficulty in concentrating
◆ tiredness
◆ mood swings
◆ tension
◆ restlessness
◆ depression

At the end of each day, over a period of several weeks, rate each of the symptoms on a scale, from 0 to 3: 0 means that you have not experienced the symptom that day, 1 that you have been bothered by it slightly, 2 moderately and 3 very much. Also note whether you are having a period and whether you are taking medication.

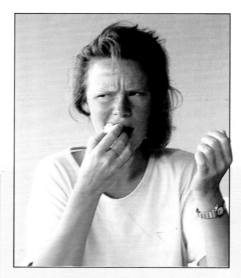

Adding tensions to tensions *is something to avoid if you suffer from premenstrual stress. This is a time to ease off on small extra pressures such as the severe weight-loss diet that you started earlier in the month. A good general diet, high in fiber and moderate in salt, helps to combat the tendency to become bloated with extra tissue fluids.*

When you have recorded at least one complete menstrual cycle during which you took no medication, add up the total of all your symptom scores for the 14 days before your period. Add up the total for the rest of the cycle separately.

If the difference between the two totals is more than 10, and if the score for the 14 premenstrual days is at least twice the score for the other days, then you are probably suffering from a genuine case of the premenstrual syndrome, reflecting a high sensitivity to the changes that result from ovulation.

Mood swings

A number of physical and emotional fluctuations are related to stages of the menstrual cycle. The physical changes are well understood but none of them has been shown to cause the changes in emotional states which many women experience. Research suggests that the degree of mood change depends partly on whether a woman expects to experience them. Public discussion of premenstrual tension and the unpleasant aspects of the menstrual cycle may actually cause some of them.

Feelings of physical and emotional well-being typically characterize the

Premenstrual bloating may also be eased by fiber in the diet: whole grains such as brown rice and wholemeal bread, fresh fruit (particularly bananas and oranges), dried fruits and beans help the body to remove salts and fluids. Some herbal teas act as diuretics – substances that stimulate a greater volume of urine – and this can ease fluid retention.

High levels of caffeine and sugar aggravate tension.

Can exercise help?

Lack of physical fitness affects all the body's systems, including those that are stressed by premenstrual tension: the digestive system becomes sluggish and the heart does not pump the blood around the body efficiently. Regular walking, swimming or cycling, however, can improve tolerance to the physical strain of premenstruation.

Some nonsufferers report that they feel particularly productive and fit during the premenstrual phase. This reflects the fact that

people benefit – up to a point – from increased stress. If you suffer from PMS, however, you should avoid putting yourself under pressure, if possible, as your period approaches. Avoid trying to get too many things done.

What can I do about period pains?

Painful periods (dysmenorrhea) are better understood than premenstrual tension. Pains arise because the uterus produces too much of the hormone prostaglandin, which has the function of stimulating contractions of the uterus to help it shed its lining. If contractions are too strong, the muscles cramp.

Levels of this hormone can be reduced by taking aspirin at the time of the bleeding, and at least 70 percent of women will have significant relief.

"Pelvic tilt" exercises can also help. They stimulate the flow of blood to the pelvis and the uterus. In a standing position, hold one hand on your lower stomach and the other against the small of your back. First push down on your back while tightening your buttocks and lifting up your abdomen with the pelvic muscles. Then push down on your abdomen from the front and lift the buttocks to tilt your pelvis. Rock up and down in a slow rhythm for one or two minutes.

Regular general exercise might also help simply by generating higher levels of natural painkillers – beta endorphins – in the body.

Many women complain of vague lower abdominal pains which may begin before the period and seem to be aggravated by the flow. The pains may also be aggravated by intercourse. Very often, this pain is in fact in the bowel and is due to irritable bowel syndrome (see *Ch 8*), rather than any problem with the reproductive tract. **ss**

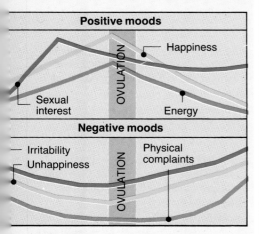

Positive moods

Happiness

Sexual interest

OVULATION

Energy

Negative moods

Irritability

Unhappiness

OVULATION

Physical complaints

middle of the cycle and tend to decline after ovulation.

During several days preceding menstruation many women report that they often feel irritable, unhappy and sometimes aggressive.

13 TIME AND SEXUAL AROUSAL

Bringing about a similar cycle of physical changes in men and women, sexual arousal can occur whenever we feel attracted to someone. How long it takes to become aroused varies from person to person, though women generally need longer than men. Provided our health remains good, there is little evidence that our capacity for arousal declines with age.

THE SEXUAL RESPONSE

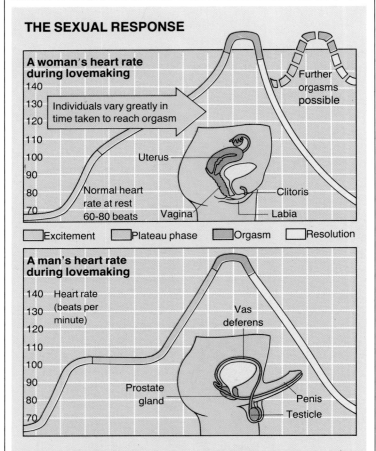

A woman's heart rate during lovemaking

Individuals vary greatly in time taken to reach orgasm

Further orgasms possible

Uterus
Clitoris
Normal heart rate at rest 60-80 beats
Vagina
Labia

☐ Excitement ☐ Plateau phase ☐ Orgasm ☐ Resolution

A man's heart rate during lovemaking

Heart rate (beats per minute)

Vas deferens
Prostate gland
Penis
Testicle

1 Blood flows into the pelvic region. The penis and the clitoris become erect. The vagina becomes lubricated and expands. The labia swell and become erect. Nipple erection occurs in women and some men.

2 Muscle tension increases. Both the clitoris and the penis become more fully erect. The labia and the head of the penis increase in size and may deepen in color. Lubricating fluid is released through the penis.

3 Rapid involuntary spasms of the pelvic region, including contractions of the womb. The prostate gland contracts, releasing fluids that mix with sperm. Ejaculation occurs as rapid muscle contractions force semen out of the penis.

4 The body returns to normal.

MOST MAMMALS have regular sexual cycles – the females are on heat at predictable intervals and it is only at these times that they are sexually interesting to males. Human beings are very unusual and possibly unique in that, throughout their reproductive lives, they are capable of entering a cycle of sexual arousal at almost any time. A number of theories have been put forward to explain why this should be; for example, the high wastage of human embryos and fertilized eggs (see *Ch15*) may have made frequent sex necessary for the survival of the species.

Whatever the reason, humans have no specific time for sex. It occurs as a result of a relationship – however fleeting – between the two people involved. On occasion it may occur because they wish to have a baby, but the vast majority of sexual encounters are concerned with the creation and maintenance of a bond between a man and a woman.

How long does sexual arousal take?

The phases of sexual arousal are much the same in men and women: the key feature is the engorgement with blood of many organs in the pelvic region, most notably the genitals. The female breasts enlarge with blood, and the nipples in both sexes may also distend.

The time it takes to become sexually aroused varies according to how you feel about yourself and your partner, the circumstances, how you are being stimulated, your previous sexual experience, your age and countless other factors. There are also differences in arousal times between one person and the next. Many couples learn the most successful ways of arousing each other after some experience together, but even they can be thwarted by outside influences.

On average, at all ages, women take longer to become sexually aroused than men. The reasons are not known. Age plays a more important part in male arousal than in female: a young man may become aroused in seconds whereas an older man may require many minutes.

Some couples say that they get most pleasure out of sex if they can synchronize their orgasms, but for most of us this process is fraught with problems: the woman desperately tries to speed up her time to orgasm while the man equally desperately tries to slow down. This discrepancy in timing between the sexes can be overcome if foreplay is concentrated on the woman, so that she is already highly aroused before the man enters her.

Are there times when we are more easily aroused?

Science has shown little evidence for cycles of human sexual receptivity, but many people say that they experience them. Often women report a relationship between their interest in sex and their menstrual cycle: just before and just after a period and in the middle of the cycle are the most frequently reported times of increased sexual interest. A link between heightened sexual interest and the time of greatest fertility would seem logical, but it is not easy to explain the peaks before and after a period. In men there are no obvious cycles.

The most common time for sex is late on a Friday evening, but this almost certainly has a purely social origin. Many men say they prefer sex in the morning, but this seems to be simply because men commonly wake with an erection. After the man has emptied his bladder, he often loses much of his interest in sex.

What part do hormones play in arousal?

The link between sex hormones and sexual arousal is not fully understood. The male sex hormone testosterone increases sexual activity in both sexes, and it is thought that its natural level in women is what produces their sexual libido. There is also strong evidence that a woman's degree of sexual interest can be affected by her partner's testosterone level; this probably comes about through the action of pheromones, chemicals that are given off by the body in extremely tiny quantities and can affect the behavior of other people. ATS

Sex and aging

Many people worry that as they grow older their sex life will deteriorate, but there is no reason why most of us should not continue to be sexually active into old age. The key is physical and emotional health.

One interesting fact concerning sex and aging is psychological. As we grow older, most of us find that – apart from occasional fleeting whims – we are sexually attracted by people of our own age-group. Moreover, we become more selective in our tastes, with affection and regard becoming more important than simple sexual stimuli.

As a general rule, those who abandon their sex lives in later life are often unconsciously using age as an excuse. The effects of age itself are usually minimal. Poor physical health can certainly affect performance. Other factors may include medications, alcohol, psychological influences and simple disuse; in men a prostate operation may impair performance.

Aging itself causes changes, but these are not necessarily debilitating. Men are likely to be slower to develop an erection, and it may be smaller and less firm; they may also take longer to recover sexual potency after a climax. On the plus side, they can maintain their erection for longer and, because of sheer experience, are likely to be more skilled sexual partners. Older women, too, may take longer to arouse; vaginal lubrication may be less effective and orgasms may be less intense. None of these factors need rule out an excellent sex life; in fact, they can encourage a better sex life, with partners becoming more affectionate and less inclined to have a performance-oriented approach to sex.

What effect does the menopause have on sex?

The idea that women lose sexual interest after the menopause is a myth; indeed, many women find that the menopause heralds the most exciting time of their sexual lives.

A main feature of the menopause is change occurring in the vagina. The lining usually becomes much thinner and drier, and sometimes its ability to produce lubricating secretions may be lost. This can make intercourse difficult or painful for the woman, which in turn can lead to loss of sexual interest. However, these menopausal symptoms respond very well to hormone replacement therapy.

The "male menopause" is a much more elusive event. Many men become less responsive in their fifties and this can sometimes lead to impotence. In rare cases the cause may be that the body's production of the sex hormone testosterone has decreased, but most often the reasons are more connected with factors such as boredom, fatigue, drinking, anxiety or depression. Often the male menopause is merely a hiccup in a man's sexual life, and full potency is soon recovered. However, impotence caused by poor physical health can and does occur in later life, and is much harder to treat.

Sexual frequency in old age

Sex for older people has now become "respectable." Only a decade or two ago it was regarded with distaste by much of society, especially by the young; now it is being eagerly encouraged from all quarters. The pendulum may have swung too far, so that some older couples feel guilty, abnormal or inadequate about the fact that they do not have sex frequently.

Sex is not an essential ingredient of a healthy life or a loving relationship. Celibacy and marital bliss are not incompatible, despite popular surveys which seem to suggest that old age is a time of sexual athleticism. Such surveys are based on questionnaires, and so must be treated with skepticism. People who fill in questionnaires about sex may be overly eager to discuss their sex lives for all sorts of reasons, and some may be responding with an empty boast.

Ultimately, people find from experience what suits them best. You and your partner should have sex as often or as rarely as you wish. NC

14 THE MOMENT OF CONCEPTION

The first moment in the development of a new human life occurs about 30 hours after a sperm meets an egg. By this time, sperm and egg have fused to form a single cell. Its microscopic gene package will determine when and in what variety trillions of further cells will follow.

HOW GENES ARE COMBINED

In mitosis (see Ch 21), the 46 chromosomes in a cell first duplicate and then split to give rise to two daughter cells. In meiosis, seen here, the cells divide again to produce germ cells with 23 chromosomes.

Primary oocyte containing mother's genes. (One chromosome only is shown.)

Genes replicate in primary oocyte

Primary oocyte is ejected from ovary and divides. A secondary oocyte and a tiny "polar body" result.

Sperm cell pierces secondary oocyte's membrane,

Secondary oocyte divides. A second polar body results, and an egg containing mother's and father's genes.

Mother's and father's genetic materials fuse.

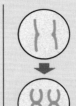

Primary spermatocyte, containing father's genes. (One chromosome only is shown.)

Genes replicate in primary spermatocyte

Primary spermatocyte divides

Secondary spermatocytes divide to form sperm cells

Sperm cells pack genes into a head and develop tails.

Cell fusion is under way *in the center of this electron-microscope image of a fertilized egg. The surrounding layer is the "zona pellucida." Inside it, on the lower left edge of the egg are the discarded polar bodies.*

FERTILIZATION is the process by which the genetic material in a woman's egg fuses with the genetic material from a man's sperm cell. From the time that the egg and sperm cell meet to the time that their genetic material has fused takes about 30 hours. But first they must meet.

How does the egg change after ovulation?

The cell released from the woman's ovary (see *Chs 11, 12*) is not yet a fully developed egg. More properly called an oocyte, it divides twice by a process called meiosis to form the egg. The first of these divisions begins during fetal life and is only completed at the time the oocyte is released. A small secondary cell – the polar body – is discarded, while in the main cell the chromosomes (carriers of genetic information) are aligned in readiness for the second and final division, which happens when sperm and egg meet. The oocyte is surrounded by a sticky mass of nutrient cells (granulosa cells) which help it to be captured by the fallopian tube and then transported down it toward the uterus (the womb). **PB**

How does the sperm reach the egg?

In the process that men experience as the sexual climax there are two significant events. First there is emission, when muscles of the vas deferens (the tubes carrying sperm from the testicles to the prostate gland) contract rhythmically. These contractions propel sperm cells – and seminal fluid from the prostate – into the rear of the urethra, some distance behind the base of the penis. One of the muscles in the penis then produces rhythmic contractions to force the mixture of sperm and seminal fluid up the urethra to the tip of the penis. Then there is ejaculation, when the mixture is ejected from the tip of the erect penis. The distance traveled by the fluid between emission and ejaculation is typically about 20cm (8in), yet the time between the two events is under 10 seconds; the sperm cells are traveling at about 60 times the speed they could manage under their own power.

However, this contributes nothing to the velocity with which the sperm cells travel through the female genital tract. Once in the vagina, they move under their own power. If ovulation has just occurred, then the vaginal mucus will be thin, offering much less resistance than at other times of the month (see *Ch 12*). The sperm cells are helped on their way, in the next stages of the journey, by muscular contractions of the uterus and fallopian tubes, but, even with this help, progress is much slower than during the interval between emission and ejaculation; the fastest-moving sperm cells take 30 minutes (perhaps less) to travel the 15cm (6in) or so from the site of their

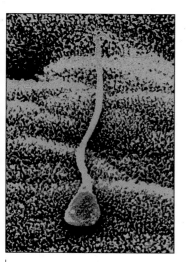

Making its way to the site of fertilization, *a sperm cell is helped through the uterus (the womb) by contractions of the uterine wall. Fertilization can take place only in the fallopian tubes – by the time an unfertilized egg cell enters the uterus, it has begun to disintegrate.*

A meeting between sperm and egg-to-be. *The first sperm to penetrate its outer membrane will stimulate this secondary oocyte (the large sphere) to perform its final stage of meiotic division and become an egg.*

ated into the body of the oocyte. This bonding of the two membranes stimulates the oocyte into its second meiotic division, another polar body being shed. The main cell is finally an egg, and fusion, the last step in fertilization, now occurs.

Most cells divide by a process called mitosis (see *Ch21*). In mitosis, the 46 paired chromosomes in the parent cell are reproduced exactly in each of the two daughter cells. In the process of meiosis, however, the egg is left with 23 unpaired chromosomes; these fuse with 23 unpaired chromosomes from the sperm cell, so that a cell with a new genetic composition is created, from which a child showing characteristics of both parents can develop. Fusion is complete about 30 hours after oocyte and sperm cell have met; within a few hours after this, the new cell divides by the process of mitosis, producing identical daughter cells. From this time onward, development (see *Ch15*) occurs because of repeated mitotic cell divisions.

What happens to eggs that are not fertilized?

An oocyte that is not fertilized within about two days of ovulation fragments and dies. Since the oocyte measures less than 0.1mm (0.004in) across, its loss goes unnoticed. Women who have been sterilized by having their fallopian tubes sealed up need have no worry about there being a build-up of unused oocytes in their tubes: they are easily absorbed by the body.

Can more than one sperm cell fuse with the egg?

It rarely happens that more than one sperm cell fuses with a single egg. Part of the function of the protective layer surrounding the oocyte is to prevent more than a single sperm cell entering. Also, when the membranes of the sperm cell and the oocyte fuse, enzymes are released to bar further sperm cells from penetrating the zona pellucida.

However, sometimes the system breaks down and two sperm cells penetrate the oocyte. There are three possible outcomes of this.

First, there could be fusion of all three sets of genetic information to produce a cell nucleus containing 69 chromosomes. This condition is called triploidy. The developing embryo almost always dies in the early stages. Second, the set of female chromosomes may combine with the set of chromosomes from only one of the sperm cells: the other set is rejected, and the development of the embryo proceeds normally. Third, the chromosomes of the two male cells can fuse. This is extremely rare, and the result is not a developing embryo but instead a placental tumor (called a hydatidiform mole). This must be removed as it can become cancerous. **PB**

arrival in the vagina to a fallopian tube, where they may fertilize an egg; that is, on their journey they average 5mm (0.2in) per minute.

Only a tiny fraction of the sperm cells survive the journey to the fallopian tubes, and about half of these reach the tube which, that month, will not receive an egg. Once there, however, they may remain fertile for a few days. So, when intercourse takes place regularly, it is likely that there will be small numbers of functional sperm cells in the receiving fallopian tube whenever an egg is released. **MH**

How do sperm and egg fuse?

The sperm cell has a number of barriers to pass through before it can fuse with the oocyte.

First there is the layer of granulosa cells. The sperm literally dissolves its way through this layer when a tiny sac in its head portion (the acrosome), releases enzymes that disrupt the structure of the layer.

The next obstacle is a membrane called the zona pellucida: the sperm penetrates this using both straightforward physical thrashing and the chemical effects of another enzyme released by the acrosomal cap.

Once the sperm cell has drilled through the zona pellucida, the membrane surrounding it bonds with the oocyte's inner membrane, so that the sperm cell's head, containing the man's genetic information, is incorpor-

15 NINE MONTHS OF PREGNANCY

The time before birth is a period of constant and complex growth and development. Stage by stage, the fetus becomes recognizably human, and the mother too experiences a sequence of physical changes as her body adjusts to the baby's needs.

HOW ONE PREGNANCY DEVELOPS

At 2 weeks *after the start of her last period, Jane conceived. Records showed she weighed 60kg (137 lb) and her blood pressure was 120/80.*

At 13 weeks *she had gained 1kg (2.2lb). Her blood pressure had fallen to 110/75. At 16 weeks, tests showed that the baby was developing normally.*

At 20 weeks *(the halfway mark) Jane's weight was 64kg (141lb) and her blood pressure was at its lowest (100/70). She could feel the baby moving.*

At 26 weeks *Jane weighed 65kg (143lb). From this time on she began to gain about 500g (18oz) per week. Her blood pressure was 110/75.*

At 37 weeks *the baby was fully mature. Jane's weight – 71kg (156lb) – began to increase more slowly. Her blood pressure regained its original level.*

At 40 weeks *the expected delivery date went by. Jane's weight was now static at 72kg (158lb) and her blood pressure had risen to 125/85.*

At 42 weeks *Jane's weight fell to 71kg (156lb). Her blood pressure was 130/90. Tests (see Ch16) showed there was no cause for concern.*

One woman's experience of pregnancy gives an indication of some of the changes that occur in the mother's body and when they take place. Each pregnancy is unique, however, and the rate at which events proceed varies. Regular routine tests reassure the mother that everything is under control, and she can choose to have additional tests. If she is worried about the baby having a genetic disorder, for example, chorionic sampling at 8-10 weeks into the pregnancy can determine if any is present (see Part One).

DURING the rest of our lives we never experience a more important nine months than the time we spend in the womb. In a remarkably short time we are transformed from a single fertilized cell into an incredibly complex organism: a human being. Every step must follow a strict timetable or the entire process will dissolve into confusion and failure. This means that anything which affects a pregnancy is important in terms not just of what it is but of when it happens.

Three phases mark development between conception and birth. During the first, important changes take place in the fertilized egg. During the second, the embryonic phase, rudimentary versions appear of the many organs that make up the completed human being. This process is largely complete after about 10 weeks of pregnancy. During the third, or fetal, phase the further changes are mainly a matter of growth and maturation of the various organs, each at its own rate. The exception is the nervous system, which even by the time of birth is still not complete structurally.

Growth before birth: the pre-embryonic phase

The pre-embryonic phase starts when a sperm cell fuses with an egg and lasts until, about 14-18 days later, the cells of the fertilized egg differentiate themselves into those that form the embryo and those that will form its life-support system, the embryo's contribution to the placenta.

The process of fertilization of the egg takes about 30 hours. At the end of this time the egg divides to give two equal-sized cells. This is a very slow development rate compared with that in nonmammals; for example, within 24 hours of fertilization a frog egg becomes a free-swimming tadpole. The reason is that nonmammals have large, yolky eggs. The yolk is a source of nutrients which are transformed quite rapidly to become the tissues of the new young. A mammal's egg has no yolk, and so must derive its nutrients from its mother.

Setting up this system takes time. The human egg attaches itself to the lining of the mother's womb about 5-6 days after conception. It then invades the tissues of the lining in a process called implantation. This invasion is performed by the outer cells of the fertilized egg, which digest the mother's cells as a source of nutrients. From this time onward, growth becomes much faster.

About 11 days after implantation, the contact between womb wall and egg begins developing into the highly specialized structure called the placenta. This has two components, one from the mother and one from the pre-embryo. The maternal component has countless blood vessels that can bring nutrients to the developing egg. The other component is derived from the pre-embryo's outer cells and the underlying blood vessels that will eventually carry blood to and from its heart. The two blood systems at no stage actually mix: they are always separated by a thin layer of cells across which nutrients are passed. The placenta also acts as an anchor, preventing the embryo, and later the fetus, from being dislodged as the mother moves about.

A 90 percent loss rate

About 90 percent of all fertilized eggs fail to survive the pre-embryonic phase. Most are lost in the very early stages, so that only about 20 percent reach the lining of the womb. The reason for much of this massive wastage may involve genetics. Each egg should have 46 chromosomes (thread-like structures that carry the genes), 23 supplied by the egg and 23 by the sperm cell. Quite often one or other of the packages is missing some chromosomes or has a few too many. As the pre-embryo begins to develop, division of cells goes awry. Soon the pre-embryo is so abnormal that it dies. Only on very rare occasions – when one particular chromosome (such as number 21) is the only extra one – is it possible that a few babies with an extra chromosome will survive until birth. Such children suffer from Down's syndrome, and will be both physically and mentally handicapped.

The fact that humans produce so many abnormal pre-embryos – far more than other mammals do – may in part reflect the use of alcohol and other drugs. More important, though, seems to be the fact that, the sooner conception occurs after ovulation (the production of an egg by the ovary), the less likely there is to be an abnormality. In most mammals the female will mate only at the time of ovulation, but the human female acts under no such constraint. The egg may therefore be several days old by the time conception occurs.

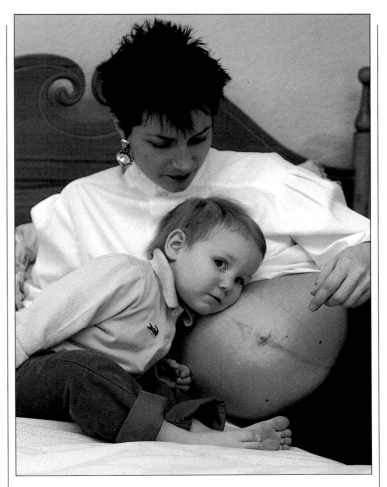

The first signs of life. As a pregnancy progresses vibrations from the baby's kicking can be felt. The mother can usually feel this at about four months, though the baby starts moving around as early as 7-8 weeks.

HOW DOES AGE AFFECT PREGNANCY?

The youngest successful mother ever recorded was aged five years old when she delivered a child weighing 2.7kg (5.9lb). The oldest mother on record was aged 57 years 129 days, although it is claimed in Genesis that Sarah bore Isaac at 91.

The problems of childbearing are greatest at the extremes of reproductive life, but very young mothers are naturally less at risk than very mature ones, since their constitution is normally more robust. With proper care, even quite young girls can deliver perfectly healthy children. The drawbacks are more likely to be psychological or social than physical.

Pregnancy in older women is a more complicated issue. First, it is less likely: at 40 a woman is less than 50 percent as likely to conceive as she was at 20. The risks of genetic abnormalities in the baby are very much higher: in the case of Down's syndrome, the chances increase by a factor of 25 between the ages of 20 and 40 (see Part One). The probability of miscarriage increases gradually over the years until 40, when the risk goes up quite sharply. Older women are more likely to suffer from diabetes and hypertension, both of which can cause complications in pregnancy. Finally, a woman aged 40 is four times more likely to die during childbirth than a woman of 20, although this should be seen in proportion: the mortality rate is still less than 1 in 10,000.

These statistics may seem gloomy, but in fact older women have less reason for concern than it might appear. If you are planning a late pregnancy – perhaps for reasons connected with your career – you should consult your doctor in advance so that, if you have a medical problem, it can be identified and treated.

Whenever pregnancy occurs in later life, the development of the fetus can be carefully monitored. This means that any abnormalities can be diagnosed early on in the pregnancy and, if desired, an abortion can be carried out. With modern medical assistance there are few reasons why a woman's age should present an insurmountable obstacle to a healthy and successful pregnancy. **PM**

From Single Cell to Embryo

Each day after an egg is fertilized marks a major step in the embryo's development. Before it is much larger than a pea, body systems are in place, a primitive heart has started to beat and most other internal organs have appeared.

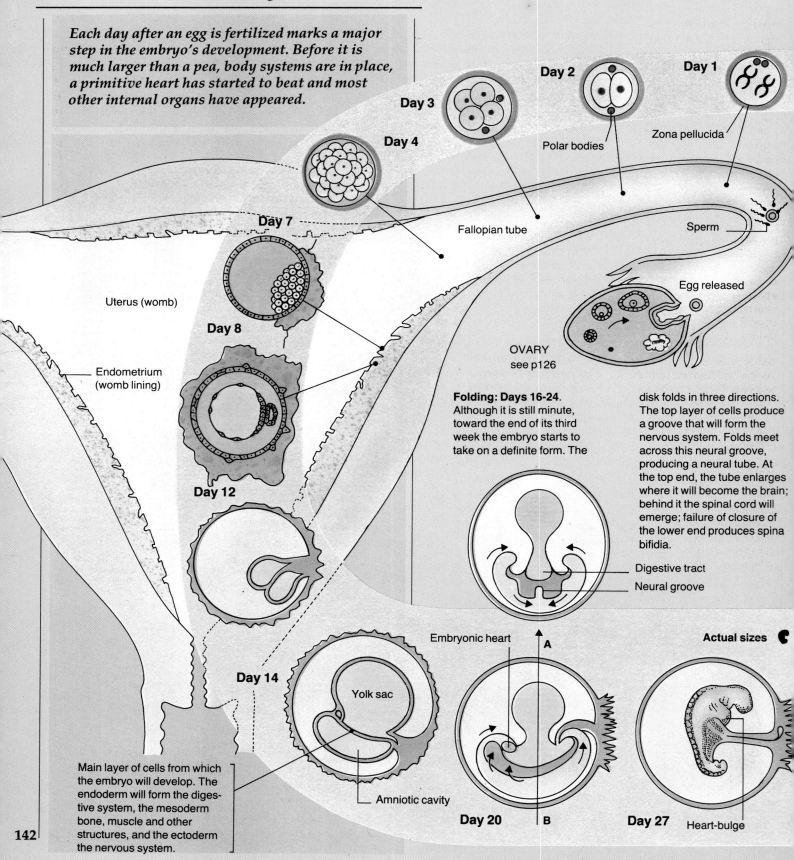

Day 1

Zona pellucida

Day 2

Polar bodies

Day 3

Day 4

Sperm

Egg released

Fallopian tube

OVARY
see p126

Day 7

Uterus (womb)

Day 8

Endometrium (womb lining)

Day 12

Folding: Days 16-24. Although it is still minute, toward the end of its third week the embryo starts to take on a definite form. The disk folds in three directions. The top layer of cells produce a groove that will form the nervous system. Folds meet across this neural groove, producing a neural tube. At the top end, the tube enlarges where it will become the brain; behind it the spinal cord will emerge; failure of closure of the lower end produces spina bifidia.

Digestive tract

Neural groove

Embryonic heart

Actual sizes

A

Day 14

Yolk sac

Amniotic cavity

Main layer of cells from which the embryo will develop. The endoderm will form the digestive system, the mesoderm bone, muscle and other structures, and the ectoderm the nervous system.

Day 20

B

Day 27

Heart-bulge

Day 1. After fertilization the egg contains two separate gene packages called the pronuclei. One of these contains the male chromosomes, the other the female chromosomes. The pronuclei move toward each other to meet and fuse in the center of the egg (see *Ch14*). The transparent layer surrounding the egg is known as the zona pellucida.

Day 2. About 30 hours after fertilization the egg divides into two new cells, each containing a full complement of chromosomes. The polar bodies have not yet disappeared. These are extra structures formed when the oocyte, or immature egg, divides (see *Ch14*).

Day 3. About 20 hours later another cell division produces four cells. From now on the cells divide rapidly, doubling in number each time. This first stage in development is known as "cleavage."

Day 4. Repeated cell division produces a ball of cells called the morula which continues to pass down the fallopian tube. At about the 12-cell stage the ball of cells enters the uterus (this happens about 72 hours after fertilization).

Day 7. Inside the ball of cells, spaces between the cells enlarge and join up so that a single fluid-filled cavity develops. Within the cavity a group of cells begins to form that includes those which will form the embryo. The zona pellucida disappears. The morula has now become a blastocyst. It begins to implant in the lining of the uterus, cells of its outer layer penetrating the lining and making contact with the mother's blood vessels.

Day 8. The embryonic stage begins as the inner layers (the endoderm and ectoderm) differentiate to become different types of tissue.

Day 12. By this time the embryo is fully implanted. The amniotic cavity begins to expand. It will eventually contain the fluid-filled amnion that encloses the embryo completely.

Day 16-20. By day 20 the embryo is a curved, three-layered disk. Its outer layer (the ectoderm) is continuous with cells which produce a separate membrane (the chorion). A stalk (which will become the umbilical cord) now connects the embryo to the chorion.

Why do some fertilized eggs fail to implant?

Of the 20 percent of fertilized eggs that survive to reach the womb lining, about half fail to implant properly and are lost in the flow when next the mother menstruates. Why does this not happen every time?

The fertilized egg produces a hormone called human chorionic gonadotrophin (more usually, hCG). Monthly bleeding occurs because the corpus luteum (part of the ovary) ceases to produce the hormone progesterone. The hCG from the fertilized egg enters the mother's bloodstream and eventually reaches the corpus luteum, which it stimulates to continue producing progesterone. Unfertilized eggs do not produce hCG, and so do not have this effect. Also, if a fertilized egg does not produce enough hCG in time to affect the corpus luteum, it will be shed in the monthly flow.

Another feature of the pre-embryonic phase is the formation of genetically identical twins (or triplets, etc). Once the embryo has established itself, this duplication cannot take place. An example of how it can come about occurs very early after conception. When the first two cells divide they should produce a single mass of four cells, but sometimes they can instead split into two halves, each having two cells. Each of the halves then behaves like a separate fertilized egg and develops independently all through the embryonic and fetal phases.

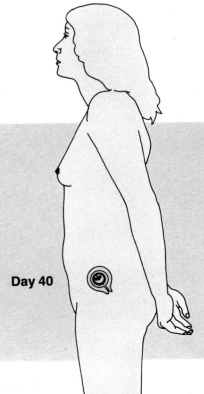

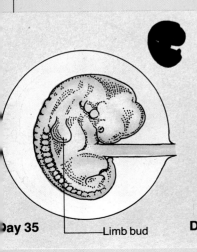

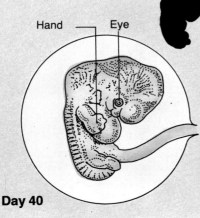

Hand   Eye

Day 27 to day 40. In this period the embryo's body organs begin to develop. At 28 days the heart is developing as a tube. It starts to beat about four days later. Arm and leg buds appear at 34 days, and by now primitive blood vessels are functioning. By 40 days the stomach has formed and the primitive eyes are visible.

Day 40

Day 35   Limb bud   **Day 40**

Rapid development: the embryonic phase

The embryonic phase lasts about six weeks, until just over two months after fertilization. Its start, at about two weeks after conception, is signaled by the formation of what is called the "primitive streak." This is about the time when the mother will notice that she is missing a period and so counting from the last period, it is the end of the fourth week of pregnancy. By this stage the pre-embryo has divided into an outer layer of cells, which will all become part of its life-support system, and an inner cell mass, of which some cells will contribute to the placenta and some to the developing embryo. Two kinds of tissues that form in the inner cell mass are called the "epiblast" and the "hypoblast"; together they form a double layer in the shape of an oval disk. The primitive streak starts when a group of epiblast cells at one end of the disk begin to multiply very rapidly. The epiblast disk becomes larger, and some of the divided cells migrate to lie between it and the hypoblast – rather as if they were becoming the filling in a sandwich (see p 142). Other cells from the epiblast insert themselves among the hypoblast cells, so that eventually all the hypoblast cells are pushed away into the egg's outer layer.

The result is a disk with three layers. This disk is the embryo, and from its cells the fetus will form. In general terms, the top layer of the disk will give rise to the fetus's skin and nervous system, the bottom layer will give rise to the digestive tract and the lungs, and the center layer will give rise to the rest.

Another important transition occurs at the primitive-streak stage. The place on the epiblast where the rapid division of cells occurs represents the rear end of the embryo. From now on, the embryo has a left and a right, a front and a back, and a top and a bottom.

The transformation of the three-layered disk into a miniature primitive fetus is extremely complicated. One of the earliest and most obvious events is when an area of the top layer of cells pulls in on itself to form first a groove and then a tube that runs down into the center layer. This "neural tube" will eventually develop into the brain and spinal cord, as well as all the nerves linking them with other parts of the body.

Another early development is that the center layer of the disk becomes divided up into segments (called "somites"). This is the first stage in the development of discrete blocks of bone, cartilage and muscle. The middle layer is also the place where the rudimentary heart and blood vessels, as well as the blood itself, are formed, so that – during the sixth week of pregnancy – a primitive circulatory system is set up. This circulation is important not just because it can carry blood around the developing embryo but also because it can take the embryo's blood to the site where nutrients can be brought in from the mother's bloodstream.

When does the embryo begin to look human?

In the sixth week of pregnancy, the embryo looks nothing like a fetus, let alone a baby. The first change toward that appearance is when the disk rolls up to form an elongated bag. The neck of the bag becomes narrower

HOW DOES RADIATION AFFECT THE BABY?

We are all bathed daily in a variety of radiations, from cosmic rays to visible light. Two kinds – together described as ionizing radiation – can damage living tissue: these are gamma rays, which are given off by radioactive materials, and X-rays, which are used for diagnostic purposes and to treat some cancers. The effects of ionizing radiation on the embryo or fetus depend on the quantity of radiation and the age of the pregnancy.

The embryo is much more vulnerable to higher doses of radiation than the fetus, because during the embryonic stage the major organs are still in the process of being formed; severe abnormalities or miscarriage may result. In the fetus, growth may be slowed or arrested, and the poor rate of growth will continue after birth.

The doses of X-rays used by doctors and dentists are too low to have such effects but it is remotely possible that even these low doses might make it more likely that the person will suffer malignant diseases, such as leukemia, later in life. The balance of opinion is that pregnant women have little to fear should it be desirable for medical reasons that they be X-rayed, but that, where there are alternative methods of achieving the same result, these should be used instead.

The effects, if any, of exposure to other forms of radiation are not known. It is believed that leakage from domestic microwave ovens is harmless, but research is continuing. There is a possibility that leakage from VDUs (visual display units, used for computer or wordprocessor monitors) might increase the chances of early miscarriage, but there may be other factors involved (such as sitting still for long periods).

There have been some worries concerning ultrasound (which is, strictly speaking, not a form of radiation), but recent research has failed to confirm these: the current opinion is that, while unnecessary ultrasound scans should be avoided, routine scans are highly unlikely to be in any way harmful to the unborn baby. **PM**

WHEN IS ABORTION POSSIBLE?

From the medical point of view, an abortion can be done at any stage during the pregnancy, but in practice, unless there is serious fetal abnormality, few doctors will agree to perform an abortion after the fetus is about 18 weeks old. The reasons are: the risks to the woman's health and to her ability to have children in future; the chance that the fetus may be born alive; the fact that fetuses by this stage are able to feel pain and distress. **PM**

and narrower until it is sealed off at the primitive navel. The top layer of the disk is left on the outside of the bag and the bottom layer forms the inside lining; the cells of what was once the center layer are sandwiched between the other two except in two small areas at the front and back of the rolled-up embryo. These areas of opposition of the two upper and lower layers eventually break down to form openings that are the primitive mouth and anus connecting the inside and outside of the embryo.

From here on development proceeds rapidly. Small outgrowths appear in the seventh week of pregnancy: these will become the limbs. The central tube develops a series of out-pockets: these will become the bladder, the windpipe and lungs, and the liver and pancreas. The tube itself starts to show distinct regions corresponding to the mouth, nose, esophagus, stomach, duodenum and small and large intestines. The kidneys and (depending on sex) the ovaries or testes develop, and the bones and muscles start to take shape. The eyes, ears and facial features become apparent. In the ninth week of pregnancy, the sex of the embryo becomes visible, and by the 10th week it has become a fetus: a tiny, human-like form – only about 30mm (1.2in) long – with its rudimentary system of organs in place.

The embryonic phase: what can go wrong?

During the embryonic phase there is a massive reorganization of the original cells, and so it is hardly surprising that the risk of things going wrong is high. It is during this time that most congenital abnormalities develop. Among these abnormalities are defects in the formation of the heart, cleft palate, hare lip and spina bifida (where the neural tube fails to close up fully and sink down into the embryonic disk's center layer, so that nerve tissue is left exposed on the outside of the body). Many of these abnormalities will not be detected until much later, in the fetal phase – by, for example, ultrasound examination.

Why do these abnormalities occur? In most cases we are not certain. There is good evidence that exposure of the mother to various factors – drugs, chemicals, certain foods, infections – plays a part, but it is very hard to establish a definite link. It is likely that it is not just individual factors that are to blame but specific combinations of certain of them. Clearly it is a good idea to play safe during pregnancy by avoiding smoking, alcohol and drugs. In a few cases a direct link has been established between cause and effect; one example is the (now proscribed) drug thalidomide, which caused many babies to be born with severe limb deformities.

Of the 10 percent of pre-embryos that survive, about 15-25 percent are lost later, almost all during the embryonic phase. The age of the mother and the number of pregnancies she has experienced in the past have an effect on this loss rate. As in the pre-embryonic phase, many embryos fail to survive because of genetic defects in the original fertilized egg, but congenital abnormalities are also likely to lead to an early spontaneous termination of pregnancy, or miscarriage.

Most miscarriages go unnoticed: they happen so early in the pregnancy that the mother is unaware that she has been pregnant. Either there is very little bleeding from

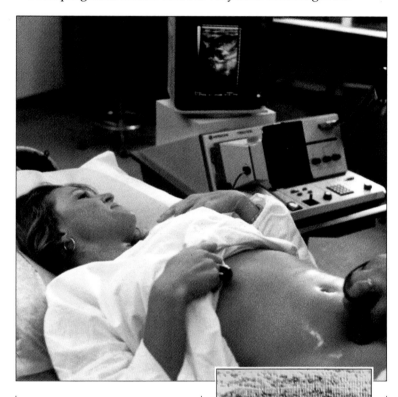

A picture of the baby in the womb is provided through ultrasound scanning ABOVE. A sound transmitter is moved over the mother's abdomen, and images of the baby appear on a television screen. RIGHT An image produced by an 8-week-old fetus. Though they are difficult for nonexperts to interpret, ultrasound images can give information about the size and position of the placenta, the size of the baby's head and abdomen, and even the inside of its heart. The first scan, at 8-12 weeks, confirms the expected delivery date and there may be further scans at 16-17 weeks and 34 weeks to make sure that the baby is developing normally. Research suggests that ultrasound scans can reduce a mother's anxiety during pregnancy and may thereby make the baby itself more healthy and alert.

the miscarriage or, if the bleeding is appreciable, the mother simply assumes that she is having a later or heavier menstrual period than usual. The causes of miscarriage are rarely discovered; even after a mother and father have experienced a series of miscarriages there is only a one-third chance that doctors will be able to identify a reason.

As a general rule, the longer a pregnancy continues, the less the likelihood of a miscarriage, although the risks are slightly higher at five and 10 weeks of pregnancy. After 16 weeks a miscarriage is very unlikely.

Growth and development: the fetal stage

The remainder of pregnancy, after the embryonic phase, is taken up with the growth and development of the fetus. This stage therefore typically lasts about 28 weeks.

At first, although the fetus has a recognizably human shape and a set of organs that can be related to those of a baby, it is minute. The fetal phase is characterized not only by growth but by the development of the organs toward the ability to function independently. Changes in the nervous system are a good example of the way this happens.

The tiny fetus has a rudimentary nervous system in which the primitive brain and spinal cord can be distinguished clearly. During about the first eight weeks of the fetal period the number of cells in the brain region greatly increases, so that by about 18 weeks of pregnancy the fetal brain has acquired most of its cells. However, this is not the whole story: for a brain to function effectively it is essential not only that all the cells are present but that they are linked together in the right way.

Evidence that this is happening can be seen from the fetus's movements. From the time the fetus first appears it makes some minor uncoordinated motions, but the first signs that the fetus is able to respond to the events going on around it do not appear until the period between 18 and 22 weeks of pregnancy. The next stage is when the fetus produces occasional patterns of movements, occurring in bursts. Then, from about 34-6 weeks onward, these behavioral patterns become coherent, producing coordinated movements: this is the time when the fetus kicks most enthusiastically.

The detection of organized electrical activity in the brain is done using an electroencephalograph (EEG). Such activity is not seen in the fetus until about 24 weeks, but by 34-8 weeks the patterns of EEG activity are similar to those seen in a newborn baby. Even by birth, however, the EEG pattern is not fully matured, and the anatomical structures of many individual nerves in the brain are still primitive.

The maturing of the nervous system during the fetal phase is therefore a prolonged, continuous process, and the same is true of the development of all the other systems of organs in the body.

The fetal phase: what can go wrong?

The fetus is hardy, but there can still be problems during this stage of pregnancy. Congenital abnormalities that arose earlier are likely now to make their presence felt for the first time. However, most of the fetus's difficulties are concerned with nutrition.

For a fetus to grow properly it needs adequate nutrition, as provided by the mother through the placenta. There are a number of ways by which this nourishment can become insufficient. The mother may herself be incapable of supplying the necessary nutrients, but in fact, mothers suffering from malnutrition can produce perfectly healthy, full-size babies – when it comes to a

MAKING ROOM FOR THE BABY

Normally slightly smaller than a clenched fist, during pregnancy the uterus needs to expand to accommodate the growing fetus. If its walls simply stretched, they would lose the muscular ability needed to expel the fetus at birth, so instead their cells enlarge. After the birth, they return to their normal size within a few weeks. Because the uterus increases its volume about 1,000 times, however, it pushes aside other organs including the bladder, the stomach and the

intestines. These changes may cause digestive problems such as constipation and heartburn, as well as breathlessness and a need to urinate frequently. Another change in the mother's body takes place as the pelvis "loosens" – that is, the gaps between its bones open slightly. This is to allow it to accommodate the baby, and to make it wide enough for the delivery.

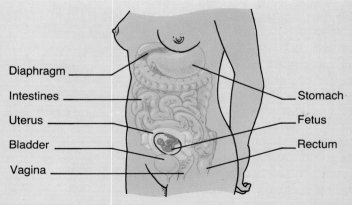

Diaphragm
Intestines
Uterus
Bladder
Vagina
Stomach
Fetus
Rectum

Until about the 12th week of pregnancy, the uterus enlarges slowly. Pregnancy has not yet begun to show,

though the uterus is emerging from the pelvic cavity and can be felt through the abdominal wall.

DOES SEX DURING PREGNANCY CARRY RISKS?

There seems to be no reason why couples cannot continue to enjoy sex throughout pregnancy, although it makes sense to give a little thought to the positions employed during intercourse.

At one time couples were advised to use condoms while the woman was pregnant. The reason for this was that semen contains a group of hormone-like substances, "prostaglandins," which, in sufficient quantities, can be used to induce labor. However, it is now known that the amount of prostaglandins present in a normal ejaculation is not nearly enough to precipitate premature labor. Similarly, although in at least some pregnancies the fetal heartbeat slows down during intercourse, there is no proof that this does the fetus any harm. **PM**

contest for nutrients between fetus and mother, the fetus inevitably wins. Both the fetus and placenta produce certain hormones that act on the mother's body so as to make sure that the needs of the fetus are preferred to those of the mother.

There may, however, be a fault in the workings of the placenta. The effectiveness with which the placenta transports the mother's nutrients to the fetus and removes the fetal waste products is to a great extent determined by the mother's blood supply to the placenta. Drinking alcohol and smoking can greatly reduce this supply as well as interfere with the efficiency with which materials are exchanged between her bloodstream and the fetus's. The result is the birth of an underweight baby, who may be both physically and mentally disadvantaged in later life. Abnormal blood pressure in the mother can have similar effects.

It is possible for the mother's body to supply too much of certain nutrients. In such cases the fetus is perfectly willing to overindulge itself. For example, diabetic mothers can provide excessive amounts of glucose, so that the baby is overweight at birth. Another effect of excess glucose is to retard the development of the baby's stress-response system: it cannot release adequate quantities of adrenaline into its bloodstream when it needs to become aroused.

If the mother takes drugs – either prescribed or illicit – these may be able to cross the placenta and so affect the growth and maturation of the fetus. They may also have other effects. For example, the fetuses of mothers addicted to drugs like barbiturates and opiates may themselves become addicted, and so suffer withdrawal symptoms after birth.

Infections of the mother are in general far less likely to cause problems during the fetal than the earlier phases, but the risks are not nonexistent. The example of German measles (rubella) demonstrates the way in which the same external influence can have different effects at different times during the pregnancy. This viral disease disrupts whatever developmental processes are active at the time. If it strikes during the embryonic phase the mother may miscarry, or the result may be major deformities of the eye, heart, mouth, lips and other organs. The effects on the fetus are less drastic, but they can still be serious: they may include hearing problems, mental retardation and general failure to thrive.

Toward the end of pregnancy the fetus is especially susceptible. Should the mother suffer a physical blow to the abdomen, labor is a likely result. However, by this stage the fetus is so well developed that it will probably survive, and so the event is usually regarded as a premature birth rather than a miscarriage.

When all the figures are counted together we find that only about 8 percent of fertilized eggs survive the three phases of pregnancy to result in a living baby. This is a startling example of nature's profligacy. **MJ**

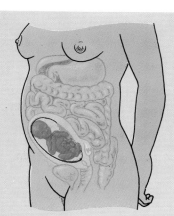

By week 16 a woman is noticeably pregnant. The uterus is now enlarging quickly.

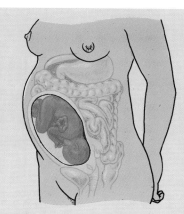

Indigestion is common at 28 weeks. Skin on the abdomen becomes very stretched and thin.

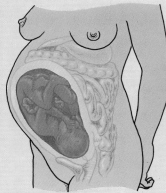

At 36 weeks the uterus is pressing against the rib cage. Pain in the pelvic region may occur.

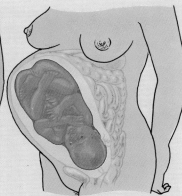

At 40 weeks the baby's head engages and the uterus drops, putting pressure on the pelvis and groin.

16 TIME OF BIRTH

Timed to occur when a baby's body becomes capable of functioning independently, the moment of birth is difficult to predict accurately. If the timing fails, the baby's life may be at risk. How long the birth takes can be equally unpredictable, though labor proceeds in recognizable stages. Careful monitoring of each stage alerts doctors to possible complications.

HOW DOES a fetus in its mother's womb know when it is time to be born? Does its own biological clock begin to tick during early development, or does it read information from its mother? Experts do not know the answers to these questions; they cannot tell if the fetus is aware of normal clocktime, or if it could, for example, share its mother's feelings of jet lag. However, they do know that the whole process of pregnancy and childbirth is carefully controlled by a natural timing mechanism. There even seems to be a marked preference in the time of day that babies are born – the characteristic pattern is a nocturnal labor and a morning birth. Babies born around dawn or in the morning usually arrive healthy and strong, whereas babies born in the afternoon have a slightly increased chance of developing complications, and the incidence of stillbirth is slightly greater in the afternoon than at other times of the day or night. Modern medicine offers several ways of controlling late, early or difficult births, but what is the normal pattern of timing when nature takes its course?

THE STAGES OF LABOR

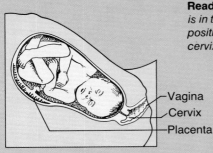

Ready to be born, the baby is in the normal upside-down position, its head against the cervix.

— Vagina
— Cervix
— Placenta

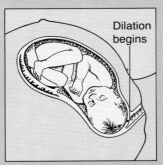

Once labor begins the uterus contracts and the baby's head presses on the cervix.

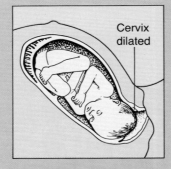

Dilation begins

Cervix dilated

The first stage ends when the cervix completely opens and the baby's head passes through.

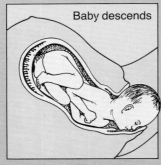

Baby descends

The second stage is the actual birth. The baby rapidly descends the birth canal and its head appears.

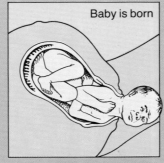

Baby is born

Once the head appears the baby usually emerges quickly. Delivery of the placenta is the final stage.

Delivery at home is an option the second or third time a woman gives birth, though first-time mothers, those expecting twins and those with health problems are advised to go into hospital. The familiarity of home surroundings and the presence of family and friends are the chief attractions of home birth. Prompt attention in an emergency is the chief advantage of hospital birth.

When will the baby be born?

Pregnancy begins the moment that the mother's egg (ovum) is fertilized by a sperm cell from the father. From this moment 38 weeks normally elapse until the birth of the baby – just less than nine calendar months. However, for practical reasons, it makes more sense to estimate the time of birth by basing calculations on the beginning of the last period before conception. Doctors always talk about the age of the fetus – the fetal maturity – in terms of the number of weeks that have elapsed since this time. The first day of this last period must have occurred about two weeks before conception, so that on this basis the average pregnancy lasts roughly 40 weeks.

Predicting the precise day that the birth will occur is an approximate science. Only 4 percent of babies arrive exactly on time, and only a few mothers can remember exactly when their last period was. Moreover, many women have irregular periods, while others may have a certain amount of vaginal bleeding early in pregnancy and quite reasonably assume that this is merely a slightly unusual period.

Much better estimates of fetal maturity can now be obtained by doctors using high-frequency soundwaves – ultrasound – to build up a picture of the fetus. Until about 24 weeks into the pregnancy, the time since conception can be estimated quite accurately by measuring the diameter of the fetus's skull. PM

What are the stages of labor?

Labor is triggered when certain chemicals are passed between the mother and the fetus, but the exact nature of these interactions is not known. First there are irregular, painless contractions within the womb; these intensify over a period of weeks until they are regular, last longer and can be overwhelmingly painful. The muscles of the walls of the womb are contracting so that the cavity is reduced in length from the rear forward.

Often it is soon after contractions have become regular that the amniotic fluid (the fluid that surrounds the fetus, protecting it from outside pressure) is released, as the membranes that have been containing it burst. This allows the fetus's head to descend toward the cervix, and the body reacts by increasing the intensity of labor.

The process of labor is a continuous one, but it is often thought of as occurring in stages – a *latent phase* (or pre-labor phase) followed by the three stages of labor itself. In practice it can be difficult to tell when one stage ends and the next begins.

The latent phase may last only a few minutes or it may extend over weeks. The contractions gradually build up and the cervix prepares itself for the forthcoming events.

HOW LONG DOES LABOR LAST?

Normal stage-one labor with a first baby: about 9 hours	Very fast stage-one labor causing distress to baby: 2¾ hours	Delayed stage-one labor; forceps delivery: 12½ hours

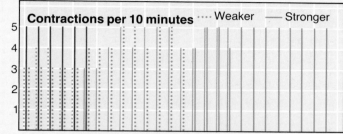

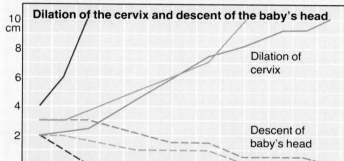

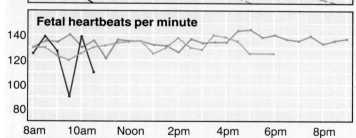

Three hospital records *of stage 1 of labor (the dilation of the cervix), including a normal delivery, a delayed one and a very fast one.* TOP *Strength and frequency of contractions help to determine how long a labor lasts, for it is partly the baby's head pressing against it that stimulates the cervix to dilate. In both the normal delivery (9 hours) and the delayed delivery (more than 12 hours) contractions are weak and infrequent at first, occurring 3 to 4 times in 10 minutes. Gradually they become stronger and faster, eventually reaching a rate of 5 per 10 minutes. In the fast labor (less than 3 hours), contractions are immediately strong and fast, coming at a constant rate of 5 per 10 minutes.* CENTER *In the normal labor the cervix dilates 7cm and the baby's head descends 2cm in 9 hours. By 5pm, stage 2, birth of the baby, is ready to begin. It may take seconds or an hour. In the slow labor, dilation takes longer and the baby's head descends 3cm. These events occur too rapidly in the fast labor and the baby's heart rate* BOTTOM *is very erratic, showing that it is distressed.*

During the latent phase the mother at first experiences some minor discomfort, followed by backache and intermittent pains in the lower abdomen; once the contractions have regularized, the pain is experienced higher in the abdomen.

The first stage of labor starts when the contractions become regular and the cervix begins to get wider (dilate): typically the cervix is 1-3cm (0.4-1.2in) wide at the end of the latent phase and increases to 10cm (4in) wide by the time of full dilation, which signifies the end of the first stage of labor. Until the cervix is completely dilated the baby cannot be expelled from the birth canal. The time taken for this first stage varies from one woman to the next. On average the first stage lasts 12 hours if this is the woman's first baby and 7 hours if the woman has given birth before.

The second stage of labor starts when the cervix is fully dilated and ends with the delivery of the baby. The mother's voluntary pushing to help expel the baby from the birth canal is unique to human beings. The time taken for the second stage, like that taken for the first, depends on whether this is a first birth or not: on average it lasts about one hour for a first baby and half an hour if the mother has had children before.

The third stage of labor ends when the placenta is delivered; this stage typically lasts 5-60 minutes if left to nature. Today, hormone injections are often given at the end of the second stage in order to reduce the length of the third. The motive for doing this is to minimize the chances of the mother suffering a dangerous hemorrhage as the placenta is inefficiently torn away from the wall of the womb.

Monitoring the baby's heart rate

When it is in the womb the healthy fetus has a heart rate of 120-160 beats per minute. However, this rate is not regular, as it is in adults: the fetal heart can become much faster during periods of consciousness and activity.

When the womb contracts during labor the supply of blood to the fetus is temporarily decreased. The reaction of the fetus may be to increase or decrease its heart rate; or the heart rate may not change at all. If the heart rate decreases there may be some cause for concern, and the attending doctors may set up a constant monitoring system.

When the heart rate decreases it means that the effect of the womb contraction has been to alter the balance of the oxygen and carbon dioxide levels and the acidity of the blood supplied to the fetus. This effect does not last long, and the fetus quickly recovers – although if it happens often or for prolonged periods the fetus may eventually be affected. There is a small chance that

reduced blood supply to the fetus's brain can cause damage, because the brain may be starved of oxygen. The same is true if, even at rest, the fetus's heart rate slows from time to time, showing that it is under stress.

These slowings of the heart rate fall into two different categories, depending on when they occur. Some occur at the time of the contraction, and soon return to normal. Others occur toward the end of a contraction, and the return to the usual rate is slow. In the second case especially, the attending doctor will immediately take action to find out what is happening.

Birth signals the time for milk production *but a woman's body prepares for breast-feeding before this. In the eighth week of pregnancy, levels of the hormone prolactin, which controls milk production, rise. During pregnancy estrogen, secreted by the placenta, prevents prolactin from causing too much milk to be produced. When the baby is born this control ends and prolactin levels peak. The breasts produce a clear, high-protein liquid called colostrum that nourishes the baby for a few days before the milk flow starts.*

How soon should the baby take its first breath?

Within a minute of birth, 95 percent of babies take their first breath. Others can take a little longer, especially if pain-killing drugs such as pethidine have been taken by the mother during labor.

Areas of a healthy baby's brain tell it to take a breath when the acidity or the carbon dioxide level in its body rises to a specific amount. This occurs very soon after birth, and stimulates the baby's first breath.

If there is a delay, the process can be helped by flicking the baby's foot or by drying its skin with a towel, or even by puffing oxygen into its face. If these simple techniques fail, the heart rate falls and more dramatic methods may be necessary to help the baby to breathe normally.

The first breath heralds dramatic changes in the baby's respiratory and circulatory systems. The lungs begin to function (see *Ch 3*) and the direction of blood-flow through the heart (see *Ch 2*) changes from the fetal to the adult pattern. **SM**

PREMATURE BIRTH

Since only 4 percent of babies arrive exactly when they were expected, clearly the other 96 percent arrive either early or late. Usually the time difference is a matter of about a week, and there is no cause for concern.

The extent to which a premature birth might affect the baby depends on how prematurely it has arrived. Babies born up to six weeks early will almost certainly survive and run little risk of being handicapped. On rare occasions, babies born as much as 15 weeks early have survived, but many have suffered handicap.

A premature baby's chances of survival do not depend solely on the length of the pregnancy. Other factors that play a part include gender (girls are more likely to survive than boys) and birth weight (the heavier the baby the better the chances of survival); and on the negative side, infection, illness in the mother (such as diabetes) and a difficult labor. **PM**

POSTMATURE BIRTH

Babies born after the full term of 40 weeks are known as postmature. Medical opinion is divided as to what, if anything, should be done about them. There is a very slightly higher chance that a baby of over 42 weeks will die around the time of birth, but when doctors intervene and labor is induced there is a greater chance that the doctor will have to resort to a Caesarean delivery, which increases the risks to the mother's life.

Babies do mature at different times, therefore some will only reach their maturity after 40 weeks, and consequently will retain a fully functioning placenta for longer. If the baby is fully mature and labor fails to begin, the placenta may be unable to continue functioning beyond its allotted lifespan, and the baby is at risk.

If a fetus is more than a week or two overdue, modern medical practice is to check on its health by monitoring its heartbeat; ultrasound may also be used. If there are any warning signs, labor is induced and the fetus continues to be closely monitored until birth. Otherwise, there seems little reason for any form of medical intervention. Few pregnancies extend beyond 44 weeks, and often the "delay" is only apparent – that is, there has been some confusion over the date of conception. **PM**

Born too early, *a baby is rushed to hospital for special care. Because it has missed the last weeks of pregnancy, its body has not developed an insulating layer of fat or learnt to regulate its own temperature. An incubator provides crucial warmth.*

17 HOW CHILDREN GROW

Growth and physical development are far from being rigidly timed, but they have three easily recognized major phases – infancy, childhood and adolescence. At each phase parents can become concerned about progress, but only if a child appears to be seriously out of harmony with normal development is it likely that there is a growth disorder.

HOW LONG BONES GET LONGER

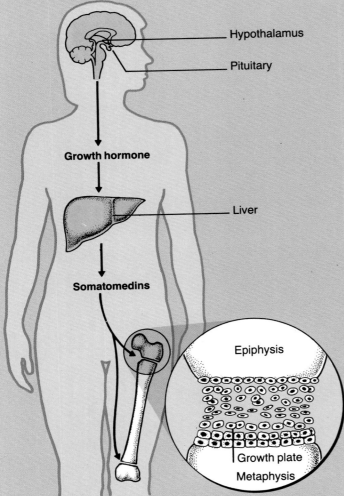

- Hypothalamus
- Pituitary
- **Growth hormone**
- Liver
- **Somatomedins**
- Epiphysis
- Growth plate
- Metaphysis

Tissue development *is regulated by chains of body chemicals. Hormones from the hypothalamus in the brain regulate the production of growth hormone in the pituitary. Growth hormone prompts the liver to manufacture chemicals called somatomedins that stimulate* growth plates in the long bones. New cells produced at the epiphysis, the end of a bone, pass to the metaphysis, a region between the bone shaft and epiphysis. When growth is complete, hormone changes prompt the epiphysis and bone shaft to fuse.

CHILDREN grow in three distinctive phases. First comes infancy. In the first year of life, a baby triples its weight and increases in complexity from a helpless bundle to a toddler showing the early signs of independence, but by 18 months the rate of increase in height drops off – the monthly height gain may be only half what it was in infancy. The 18-month-old is already in the second phase, a time of gradual change. Height continues to increase, usually at a rate of 5-6cm (2-2.5in) per year, but the rate slowly decreases until suddenly, in the third phase, the adolescent growth spurt reverses the trend. In girls this usually occurs at about 12 and in boys at about 14.

These three phases of a child's growth are timed by the body in different ways. The rapid growth of infancy is really just an extension of the growth in the womb: the major influence is adequate nutrition, and this is a time when parents are especially concerned about how to feed their offspring and how often. During childhood the main controller of growth is growth hormone, produced by the pituitary gland in the brain. To parental concern about nutrition there may now be added worries about hormone levels. These are usually allayed when the adolescent growth spurt comes about spurred both by an increased production of growth hormone and by an increase in the production of sex hormones.

How much should the baby weigh?

The average newborn baby weighs 3.4kg (7.5lb). On average boys weigh about 140gm (5oz) more than girls. Babies often lose a little weight – rarely more than 10 percent – during the first few days after birth.

The birth weight is usually regained during the second

THREE STAGES OF GROWTH

FAR LEFT In the first year of life, infants grow more quickly than at any other time – with a good diet, a baby's weight may treble. CENTER Through most of the childhood years, growth is slow but steady, with height increasing more than breadth. LEFT In puberty a growth spurt is synchronized with the process of becoming sexually mature.

week, and then the baby grows very rapidly. During the first three months the weight gain is likely to be 190-200g (6-7oz) per week. Weight gain during the second three months is less rapid, but still about 140g (5oz) per week. During the first six months, then, a healthy baby's birth weight is likely to double, and by the end of the first year it may well have tripled. Never again does a person gain weight so rapidly.

The weight gain is rarely regular, and sometimes there may be brief periods of weight loss. Short-term irregularities – perhaps caused by minor illnesses – are unimportant: what is significant is the longer-term trend. During the first few weeks babies should be weighed weekly, but afterward, if the baby is healthy and feeding well, it need be weighed only every month or two.

Of course, there can be enormous variation between babies. If the figures given above are not attained, it does not necessarily mean that the baby is ill or receiving insufficient food. However, if your baby's weight gain is a long way short of these figures you should consult your doctor, just in case there is a problem.

What about the baby's other dimensions?

The average newborn baby is 50cm (20in) from the top of the head to the base of the heel. Measuring a baby's length is difficult, even for experts, because newborn children naturally lie with their legs bent at the hips and knees, and are reluctant to straighten them. As with weight, the length of the body increases very rapidly during infancy – by about 25-30cm (10-12in) between birth and the first birthday. Even during the growth spurt at puberty this rate of increase in length will never again be attained.

At birth, the average baby's head measures 35cm (13.8in) around the widest part. During the first few days the measurement may decrease a little as the head regains its normal shape after the distortion produced by the process of birth. Afterward the head grows rapidly, reflecting the growth of the brain. During the first few months the circumference may increase by as much as 5-8mm (0.2-0.3in) per week. On average, the circumference increases from 35cm (13.8in) at birth to 44cm (17.3in) at six months and 47cm (18.5in) at one year. If a healthy baby has an unusually large or small head this is commonly because one or both of its parents have a similar head-size. However, if a baby's head consistently grows faster or slower than normal you should consult your doctor.

When should the soft spots close?

Most newborn babies have two soft spots (fontanelles), a larger one toward the front of the head and a smaller one toward the rear; a few babies have a third, lying between these two. The fontanelles are not holes: they are areas of skull made of a tough membrane. In due course the membrane is replaced by bone; this is the "closing" of the fontanelle.

The rear fontanelle, if present, usually closes early in life – within the first few months. The fontanelle at the front of the head is small at birth and usually enlarges during the first few months; it then shrinks again, normally disappearing when the child is 9-18 months old. However, the closure can occur any time between four months to four years after birth. The time of closure is rarely important if the baby is well and the head is otherwise growing normally.

How often should babies be fed?

Breast-fed babies should be fed on demand – ie, when they cry and seem to be hungry. Some babies, especially very young ones, will need to be fed frequently, perhaps even every hour or so during their first few weeks of life. Fortunately for the mother, this rate is less during the night. Sooner or later a baby settles down to a more predictable pattern, usually demanding to be fed every three or four hours.

Bottle-fed babies are less able to regulate their own intake, and depend much more on the parent knowing how much the baby should have. Most young babies require, each day, about 150ml of milk per kilogram of bodyweight (about 2-2.5 fl oz per pound). The requirements of different babies vary, so these figures should be regarded as only general guides.

It is counterproductive to force a regular pattern of feeding on a breast-fed baby. Frequent feeding is important because it ensures that the mother's breasts will continue to produce adequate supplies of milk, and if she tries to impose a regular feeding pattern on the baby, with relatively long periods between each feed, her milk supply could become inadequate for the baby's needs. The baby will naturally become unhappy about this, and the maternal anxiety this causes may have the effect of further reducing the milk supply.

The volume of milk taken at any one feed can vary considerably. It depends on such factors as the time of day, the baby's appetite, and the mother's mood. The only way you can tell if your baby is getting enough to drink is to check its longer-term weight gain. Measuring short-term weight gains – for example, after each feed – is not reliable, and when weight falls in the short term as it often seems to do this can make the mother anxious, and then the milk-supply may diminish.

When should weaning start?

Until babies are about four months old, breast or artificial milk, in progressively increasing quantities, is perfectly capable of meeting the child's nutritional needs; there is no particular advantage in introducing solid foods before this. In fact, there may be disadvantages. For example, the bodies of small babies have little control over the amount of salt and water in them. Solid foods tend to contain more salt than milk does, and so too-early weaning can cause a salt and water overload, particularly if the baby is suffering from some other ailment.

By the time a baby is three months old, thoroughly pulverized food placed on the back of the tongue will be moved to the back of the mouth and swallowed. A month later, most babies can perform this trick with ease. This may represent an important phase in the child's development, and so most doctors recommend that the introduction of solid foods as part of the diet should start before the child is six months old; otherwise, it is believed, it may be more difficult to accustom the child to solid foods later on.

The child's first solid foods should be sieved or blended until they are smooth and lump-free. There is no reason why you should not simply pulverize a small portion of the meal cooked for the rest of the family, assuming it is bland and does not contain too much salt. Proprietary foods are equally satisfactory. The type of food is unimportant, although many parents start with fruit and vegetables and then progress to meat and cereals. Initially you should give the baby just a tiny amount before each feed, increasing the quantity as the baby becomes more used to solid foods and grows.

By the time the baby is six months old it will probably be able to cope with lumpier food and also to hold a rusk or biscuit, bring it to the mouth, and suck at it. By seven

SHOULD BABIES BE BOTTLE-FED?

Ideas about the feeding of infants change from time to time. Current medical opinion is that babies should be breast-fed, with weaning starting when the child is aged 4-6 months. One reason for this is that it is believed that the physical bond between child and mother is psychologically good for both; another is that obviously human breast milk has naturally evolved to be the ideal food for human infants.

However, modern artificial feeds – usually made using cows' milk that has been modified so that it is as much as possible like human milk – are nutritionally satisfactory in every way. The details of one formula may differ from that of another, but they are all essentially the same: there is usually little point in shifting to a different brand if your baby seems unsettled. Manufacturers' instructions should always be followed to the letter.

You should never feed babies using milks – including soya milks – which have not been specially prepared for use by infants. Soya-based baby milks are available, but should be used only with professional advice and supervision. If your reason for bottle-feeding is convenience – for example so that father and mother can share the duties of feeding – it is possible for the mother to express breast milk into a bottle for use as and when required. Bottles should always be properly sterilized.

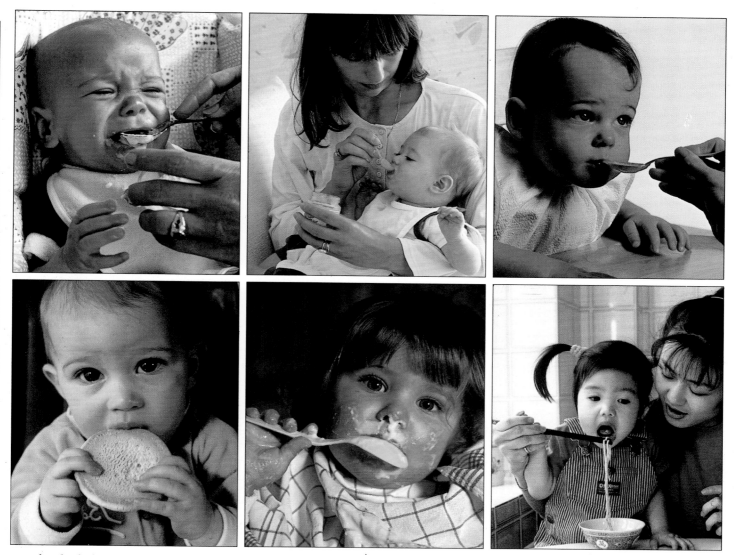

months the baby may be able to drink from a cup or training beaker, and at age nine months the child may experiment with the use of a spoon. However, it is likely that the first successful attempts at self-feeding will not occur until the age of about 15 months. Those attempts, almost certainly, will be very messy.

When should children be given vitamin supplements?

During the first few months of life, the mother's breast milk supplies the baby with all the required vitamins, unless she is for some reason vitamin-deficient. Proprietary infant formulas are fortified with iron and vitamins so, as long as the baby is being given enough to eat, there should be no question of vitamin deficiency. Once babies begin weaning – particularly when unmodified cows' milk is substituted for breast milk or infant formula – vitamin supplements should start; they should be continued for at least two years and preferably five.

LEARNING TO EAT

1 *At three months old, attempts at eating solid food may be unsuccessful, but babies of four months* **2** *are likely to cope much better with spoonfeeding.* **3** *As a baby's body control begins to improve, the next challenge is to eat in a sitting position without the support of its mother.* **4** *The progression from being fed to self-feeding begins at about six months when babies can manipulate objects skillfully enough to hold a rusk and put it in their mouths.* **5** *Usually able to hold a spoon at nine months,*

babies may start to be frustrated at being fed and want to try feeding themselves. At 15 months, however, efforts at self-feeding from a spoon are still likely to be messy because the baby has only weak control over its movements. **6** *As coordination improves, self-feeding becomes more sophisticated, even using implements that require considerable skill.*

HOW DO NUTRITIONAL NEEDS CHANGE DURING CHILDHOOD?

A child's nutrition must fuel not just the repair and maintenance of the body, as in an adult, but also normal growth and development. About 5 Calories (5 Kcal) of energy is needed to fuel each 1g increase in body weight (about 14 Calories per ounce). During the first year of life children need 80-120 Calories gram of bodyweight (36-55 Calories per lb). The requirement, in terms of bodyweight, decreases after the first year by about 10 Calories per kilogram of bodyweight (5 Calories per lb) in each three years.

However, energy requirements vary with growth rate. Extra energy is needed during periods of rapid growth, especially in infancy and adolescence, and also when the child is ill, because additional energy is needed to combat infection and to repair damaged body tissues.

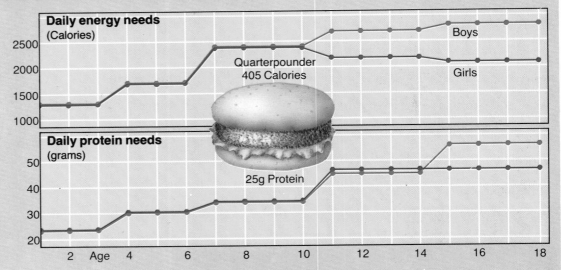

On average, of the calorie intake of a three-year-old, 60 percent is used to maintain normal body functions, 16 percent for growth, and 15 percent for physical activity. For a nine-year-old the relevant figures are about 50 percent, 12 percent and 25 percent. In early adulthood, when growth has ceased, about 75 percent of calories are used to keep the body functioning and about 20 percent for exercise. At all ages a few calories are used for other purposes – for example, the digestion of food – and a few are lost in the feces.

Tables of recommended daily allowances of various nutrients are available from many sources. The figures they give are averages, so your child may need up to 15 percent more or less of any nutrient. If weight gain and growth are normal, the child's dietary intake is almost certainly satisfactory.

How do children grow taller?

Children get taller because their long bones grow and their spinal column gets longer. Growth of the long bones of the legs occurs throughout childhood and is largely under the control of growth hormone. The rate of elongation of the spine is influenced by the sex hormones and it is therefore considerably affected during puberty.

The major bones of the legs get longer because of the formation of new bone at their ends. These bones consist of main shafts at each end of which are growth centers comprised of cartilage. As the child gets older, this cartilage progressively becomes bone. Once the band of cartilage has completely turned into bone, the growth plate is fused to the shaft of the long bone; the long bone's length can increase no further.

It is often said that children do much of their growing during sleep. This is not in fact true. Nevertheless, there is a little truth in the old idea. The pituitary gland releases most of its growth hormone at night, when the child is asleep. This occurs mostly during "slow-wave" sleep (see Ch 6).

The growth clock: fast or slow?

Many different factors contribute to a child's height. The most important is the height of the parents: tall parents usually have tall children and short parents usually have short children; when one parent is tall and the other short, the child is usually of medium height.

Hereditary factors aside, a child's height is likely to be affected by the environment in which it grows up. There are direct relationships between short stature and, for example, social disadvantage, poor education, overcrowding, poverty and malnutrition. Children reared at high altitudes tend to be shorter than those raised at sea level. Chronic illness and/or its treatment can interfere with growth – for example, the prolonged use of oral steroids to treat severe asthma can affect growth.

Some variation in human height is probably due to the different total amounts of growth hormone released by the pituitary glands of different people. Blood tests taken three or four times per hour for 24 hours show that, during this period, tall children secrete more growth hormone than short children.

Some children grow faster than others. At the end of

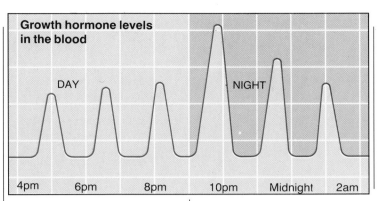

Growth hormone levels in the blood

DAY

NIGHT

4pm   6pm   8pm   10pm   Midnight   2am

◄ **Do children grow more in their sleep?** *The pituitary releases most of its growth hormone at night. Because the hormone stimulates growth only by activating other chemicals, however, its effects are not immediate and a child's growth is more evenly spaced over the day.*

◄ **Faced with a world made for taller people,** *a six-year-old considers how to reach an upper shelf. Predicting a child's height is particularly difficult in the first two years of life, before growth hormone begins to influence size. Factors that determine how tall children grow include environment – poor nutrition can restrict growth – and, most importantly, the height of parents.*

the first year the difference in height between the tallest and shortest healthy children is about 10cm (4in), while at the end of the 19th year it is about 25cm (10in). It is possible that faster-growing children, destined to be taller adults than average, produce more growth hormone than those children whose adult stature will be shorter than average.

Some children have delayed growth: their "growth clock" runs slow. When most people of their age-group have reached their adult stature, these children are still growing, and may finally become as tall as, or even taller than, those who have towered over them all through childhood and adolescence. Often a slow growth clock is a family trait, so if you were a late developer yourself it is possible that your child will be as well.

The key to discovering whether or not a child has a slow growth clock is *bone age*. The development of the bones follows a predictable sequence of changes, and these can be observed using X-rays. Usually the bones of the wrist and hand are studied. If, for example, a child at age seven shows the bone development of a typical five-year-old, that child has extra growing time to come. Conversely, if the bone age is greater than the chronological age, the child is ahead of the normal growth

sequence, and will stop growing earlier. On its own, bone age cannot accurately reveal whether a child is a fast or a slow developer, but it can be reassuring to find that a short child is likely to continue to grow for longer than usual, or that an abnormally tall child will probably cease growing sooner than usual.

Can short children be made to grow taller?

Only rarely is it necessary for short children to be given treatment to help them grow more quickly. If they have short parents, it is probable that they will become short adults. If their growth clock is running slow, there is usually nothing that need be done about it. The vast majority of slow-growing children fall into these two categories.

Some late developers, usually boys, feel very self-conscious in late childhood and adolescence about the fact that they are so much smaller than their peers. For psychological reasons, it may be useful to boost their growth using anabolic steroids or testosterone.

A very small number of children suffer from growth hormone deficiency. They usually look young for their age, and are frequently rather fat, especially around the abdomen. Sometimes the growth hormone deficiency is because the child has an abnormally small pituitary gland – or the gland may even be totally absent (in which case the child's development will be suffering also from the lack of other hormones produced by this gland). Children who have received radiotherapy to the head for the treatment of cancer sometimes develop growth hormone deficiency. However, in many cases it is impossible to establish the precise reason for the lack.

Growth hormone deficiency can be treated by injections of synthetic growth hormone. There are two major disadvantages of such a course. First, it is extremely expensive. Second, the regular daily injections may have to be carried out over a period of many years, from the time the condition is first diagnosed to the time when the bones assume their adult form. Growth hormone treatment is therefore suitable only for children who really need it.

Monitoring a Child's Development

Physical growth and changes in body chemistry develop at different rates and against separate timescales. The charts below show how normal patterns of development relate to age from birth until just after puberty.

IS YOUR CHILD THE NORMAL HEIGHT?

These charts show the normal range of height and the rates of growth for boys and girls growing up in the United States.

The heights are expressed in centiles. If you imagine 100 children lined up in order of height and numbered 1-100 then the height of the 25th child is said to be on the 25th centile, the height of the 90th child is said to be on the 90th centile, and so on.

The average height in the range is on the 50th centile. Figures for the United States are likely to be higher than

those for other countries. If you keep a record of your child's growth each year, you will probably find that, after the age of three or four years, height increases at a fairly constant rate, normally by about 5-7.5cm (2-3in) every year.

Plot your child's changing height on the appropriate chart below. A line drawn through the points ought not to cross any centile lines until puberty, which is the time of the growth spurt. In a year an adolescent may grow by as much as 15.5cm (6in).

HOW DO BODY PROPORTIONS CHANGE?

Each part of the body goes through its own sequence of changes, at its own speed, as the child develops. This means that the proportions of the body change while the child grows.

The head of a baby is large in proportion to the body. As the baby grows through childhood, the size of the body increases relatively more than that of the head. The rate of growth of the head is governed by the growth of the brain, most of which occurs during the first few years of life: normally by the first birthday it is two-thirds of its adult size and by the second birthday four-fifths. The head reaches its final size by the time the child is about 12 years.

In infancy and early childhood the vault of the skull grows more than the face; this

is why the heads of small children have their "baby-faced" appearance. After the pre-school years the face grows more rapidly, and the head attains a more adult appearance. At the same time the jaws grow to accommodate the permanent teeth; further enlargement of the lower jaw occurs during puberty.

A child's lymphatic system comprises the lymph glands, tonsils, adenoids, thymus and spleen. These glands are involved in protecting the body from infection, and they increase in size throughout childhood, reaching a maximum at 10-12 years, after which they decline. Children's tonsils often look very large, but it is rare that their size alone requires that they be removed by surgery. The adenoids, however, may be

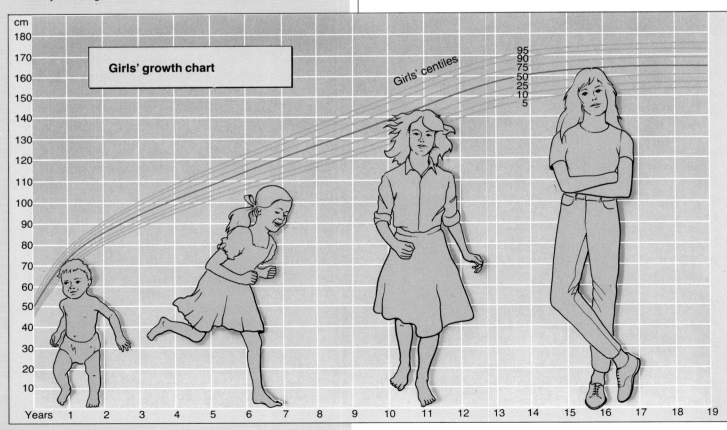

cm
180
170
160   **Girls' growth chart**
150
140
130
120
110
100
90
80
70
60
50
40
30
20
10

Girls' centiles

95
90
75
50
25
10
5

Years 1 2 3 4 5 6 7 8 9 10 11 12 13 14 15 16 17 18 19

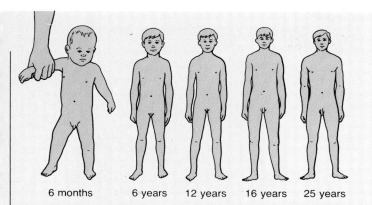

6 months   6 years   12 years   16 years   25 years

so large in proportion to the rest of the head that they block the tube leading from the middle ear to the throat (so that hearing is impaired) or obstruct breathing through the nose. Surgery to remove the adenoids is reasonably simple.

The fatty tissue under the skin decreases during the first few years of life. At about seven years it is at its minimum, and many parents become concerned that their children may be underweight. Afterward the fatty tissues reaccumulate, the nature of the distribution differing between girls and boys.

During later childhood the limbs lengthen relative to the trunk with the result that the child may look awkward and gangly. Much of the growth of the trunk occurs during adolescence.

GROWTH OF THE BODY'S SYSTEMS

Rates of growth and change vary from one of the body's systems to another in the period from birth to puberty. The curves on this graph have been drawn to a common scale by calculating growth figures at successive ages. Neural and skeletal development progress steadily through childhood, but genital development is almost completely dormant until the onset of puberty. The rate of lymphatic development, accelerating rapidly at first, peaks just before puberty, then slows in the adolescent years.

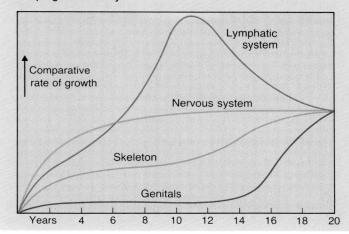

Comparative rate of growth

Lymphatic system

Nervous system

Skeleton

Genitals

Years   4   6   8   10   12   14   16   18   20

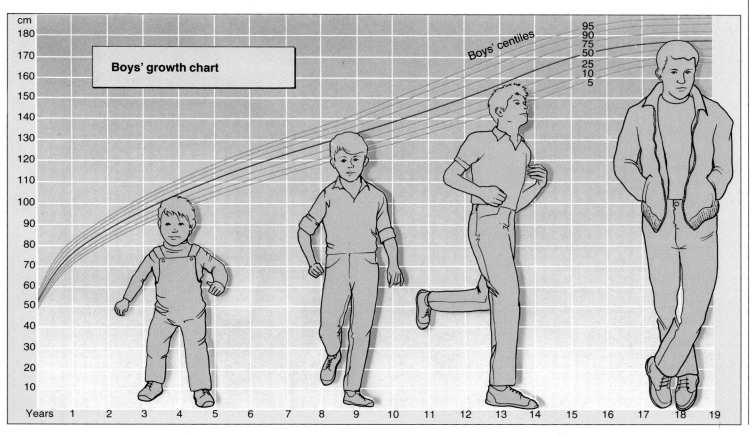

Boys' growth chart

Boys' centiles

95
90
75
50
25
10
5

When should puberty start?

Adolescence is a time of great change, the most obvious being puberty: the development of the physical features – the secondary sexual characteristics, such as breasts and face hair – that immediately distinguish adult men from adult women. It also includes changes in the size, shape and composition of the body. Puberty is usually a time of emotional and psychological turmoil, when children benefit from parental attention that is both emotionally supportive and sensitive to their need to feel recognized as emerging adults, with a capacity for independence.

It usually starts at age 10-12. On average, girls enter puberty a few months earlier than boys. People often believe that the time difference is far greater than this. The reason is that the first sign of female puberty, the beginnings of breast development, is much more obvious than the enlargement of the testicles, which is the first sign of male puberty. A normal, healthy child may enter puberty at any age between 9 and 13, for a girl, and 9 and 14, for a boy.

The duration of puberty varies greatly from one person to the next. The development of the female breast usually takes four years but may take five or more, or as little as 18 months. The development to the adult form of the penis and testicles normally takes four years but may take only two.

How much of a worry is late or early puberty?

Abnormally early puberty is termed precocious puberty. It is hard to say what is "abnormal" in this context, but when puberty occurs in girls aged less than eight years or boys less than nine years it is usually considered precocious. The hormones of the body which trigger the changes of puberty start to be produced much earlier than is the norm. There are many possible reasons for this.

Precocious puberty in girls is rarely a cause for concern: most often it is simply that their biological clocks are running fast, and frequently other members of their family have likewise undergone early puberty. In boys, though, there is more cause for concern, since in most cases there is some underlying disorder – possibly a brain tumor or a malformation of the brain. You should consult your doctor.

The abnormally early development of the secondary sexual characteristics may not indicate the onset of puberty as a whole. Sometimes these changes may occur because a tumor in the ovaries or testicles is secreting hormones. Early breast development is quite common in girls and usually signifies no health problem; it may

Three stages of puberty. TOP *In early adolescence, a girl's face becomes fuller, her pelvis begins to grow and her breasts bud.* CENTER *By midadolescence, between 13 and 15, the first period has usually occurred. Girls' hips* broaden, *their breasts develop and body hair appears.* BOTTOM *In late adolescence, between 16 and 18, all the physical characteristics of adulthood have been established.*

occur if the child has been eating contraceptive pills.

It is even more difficult to decide when puberty is occurring too late, but most girls should show some signs of breast development by 13 and most boys of testicular enlargement by 14. If puberty has yet to start by those ages there may be a health problem, although it may still be that the child is a late developer. Rarely it may be that the brain is failing to produce the hormones that initiate puberty. In one condition – Kallman's syndrome – the failure is linked with a lack of the sense of smell. In another condition, found among girls, one of the two X chromosomes normally found in the human female is missing, so that the ovaries are present at birth but wither away during childhood. Since the onset of puberty depends on the ovaries being present and functioning, such girls will be incapable of bearing children and will never menstruate. They will also have stunted growth and occasionally are mentally retarded. For all of these reasons, you should seek medical advice if your child's puberty is significantly delayed.

How should girls develop during puberty?

The timing of events during puberty is very variable, but the sequence of events is much more predictable.

Usually breast development begins at age 10-11. The focus of breast development is the areola, the ring surrounding the nipple. Typically it is of diameter 12.5mm (0.5in) before puberty and 38mm (1.5in) afterward. The first signs of breast development are usually more easily felt than seen: there is a small nubbin of tissue beneath the areola. The breasts gradually enlarge while maintaining a smooth convex surface. A secondary mound arises beneath and around the areola. Finally the secondary

mound is reabsorbed into the general contour of the breast and the adult shape is attained.

The appearance of pubic hair is quite unrelated to breast development, although in most girls it becomes evident after the breasts have started to form. The average age at which pubic hair starts to appear is about $11\frac{1}{2}$ years. In up to one-third of normally developing girls pubic hair may appear before the breasts start to develop, and in about 3 percent of cases it does not appear until the child is at age 15.

All through puberty the internal female sex organs – the ovaries, uterus, and vagina – grow progressively larger. One striking sex-related development is the first period: menarche. In the United States this usually happens at $12\frac{1}{2}$-13 years of age, but the range is wide, with some girls not starting to menstruate until they are 16. The time of onset of menstruation is related more to bone age than to chronological age.

During the first few years of menstruation, periods may be irregular, so that sometimes months can pass between one and the next. The girl may not be capable of conception, even though she is menstruating, but it is quite possible that she is indeed fertile, and sexual experimentation can result in pregnancy.

How can you predict when a child's first period might occur? A clue is given by the state of breast development: the first period rarely occurs before the breasts are well developed. Similarly, it does not normally occur before a critical weight of about 50kg (110lb) is reached, usually after the adolescent growth spurt has started to slow down. The onset of menstruation can come as something of a shock to the pubertal girl, so it is a good idea for parents to talk about the subject with their children well in advance.

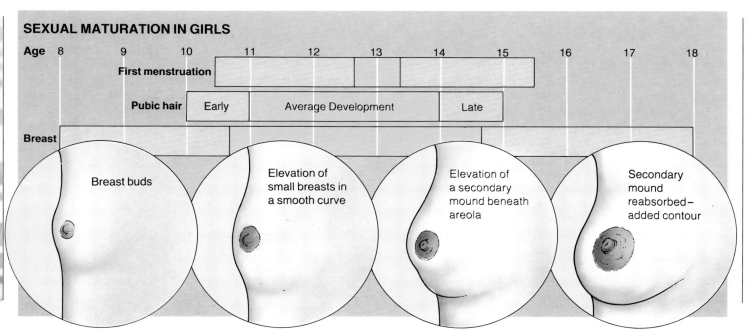

SEXUAL MATURATION IN GIRLS

Age	8	9	10	11	12	13	14	15	16	17	18
First menstruation											
Pubic hair			Early	Average Development				Late			
Breast	Breast buds			Elevation of small breasts in a smooth curve			Elevation of a secondary mound beneath areola			Secondary mound reabsorbed – added contour	

161

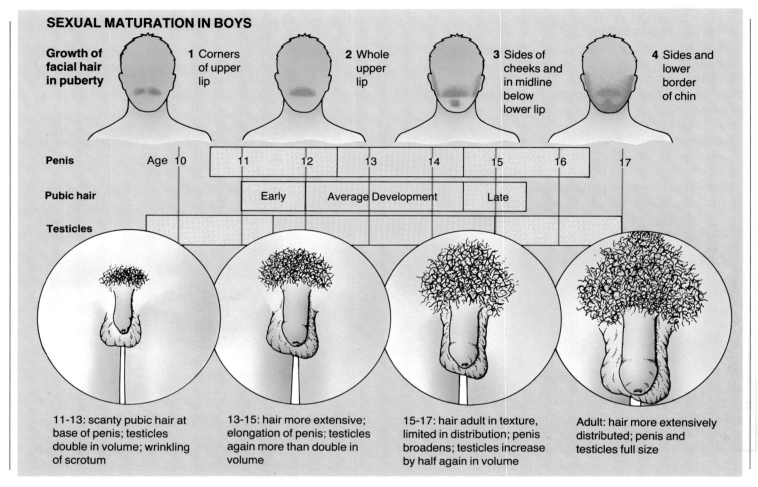

SEXUAL MATURATION IN BOYS

Growth of facial hair in puberty

1 Corners of upper lip

2 Whole upper lip

3 Sides of cheeks and in midline below lower lip

4 Sides and lower border of chin

| Penis | Age | 10 | 11 | 12 | 13 | 14 | 15 | 16 | 17 |

Pubic hair — Early · Average Development · Late

Testicles

11-13: scanty pubic hair at base of penis; testicles double in volume; wrinkling of scrotum

13-15: hair more extensive; elongation of penis; testicles again more than double in volume

15-17: hair adult in texture, limited in distribution; penis broadens; testicles increase by half again in volume

Adult: hair more extensively distributed; penis and testicles full size

How should boys develop during puberty?

The first sign of male puberty is enlargement of the testicles. At the onset of puberty the size of the testicles may double or quadruple. The most rapid growth occurs around 14, although the testicles typically double in size between then and adulthood. The size of the adult testicles may vary considerably from one man to the next, but in a normal male this has no effect on sexual efficiency.

At the same time as the testicles are growing, the skin of the scrotum is changing. Its texture becomes more wrinkled and its color deepens, so that it becomes darker than the surrounding skin.

About a year after the testicles begin to enlarge, the penis does likewise, becoming first longer and then broader. The final size is usually attained at 14-15, but this may occur some while earlier or later. The size of the penis frequently worries adolescents. It varies considerably but, as with the testicles, this does not affect sexual efficiency. The enlargement of the penis is accompanied by growth of various glands associated with it. The first ejaculations usually occur during sleep about a year after

the penis has started to enlarge. During the first few years after this it is likely that the sperm count will be fairly low, so that the boy is unlikely to be capable of fathering a child. However, as with girls, you cannot depend on this infertility.

The development of pubic hair normally starts later than development of the penis and testicles. Unlike the case in girls, the hair often extends in a narrow line up towards the navel. As the hair increases in quantity and spreads further around the groin, the hairs become curlier and coarser.

The development of body and face hair lags about two years behind that of pubic hair, although the timing varies considerably. At some stage during late puberty the voice changes ("breaks") as the vocal cords become longer.

The areola surrounding the nipples generally doubles in size during puberty, from about 12.5mm (0.5in) to 25mm (1in) in diameter. The breasts bud in 20-35 percent of boys during puberty, sometimes on one side only. This is usually only a temporary effect, and should cause no concern. On extremely rare occasions the condition may merit surgery to remove some of the breast tissue.

When should the adolescent growth spurt occur?

In girls the growth spurt usually starts fairly early in puberty – indeed, it may be the first sign that puberty has begun. The peak of the growth spurt normally occurs around age 12. A girl normally has her first period soon after the peak of her growth spurt; after this she is likely to grow only about another 4cm (1.5in) in height.

By contrast, the growth spurt in boys generally occurs quite late, reaching its peak 2-3 years after puberty has started; unlike the case with girls, it is never the first sign of the onset of puberty. By this time the penis and

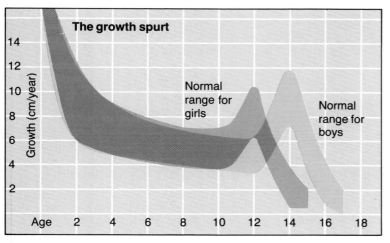

The growth spurt

Growth (cm/year)

Normal range for girls

Normal range for boys

Age

testicles are well developed and there is a fair amount of pubic hair, although the latter has yet to attain its adult distribution.

Delayed growth in puberty can be very distressing for boys, and the psychological scars may be with them for the rest of their lives. While others of their age-group are shooting up in height, these boys seem hardly to be growing at all. However, if their testicles are growing, they can be reassured that rapid growth should occur at some time during the next two years.

Growth during the spurt starts with the extremities and works inwards. Typically the hands and feet are the first to show a surge in growth; then there is rapid growth of the legs, followed 6-9 months later by rapid growth in length of the spine.

Adult men are, on average, taller than adult women. This has a great deal to do with the adolescent growth spurt. Before puberty the difference in average height between boys and girls is insignificant. However, boys commonly have two years' more growth before the start of the growth spurt, and during the spurt itself grow rather more rapidly. After the spurt, the growth of girls ceases more rapidly than does that of boys, who may add a further 5cm (2in) to their height in the fourth and fifth years after the start of the spurt.

How does the shape of the body change?

The changes in body shape and composition during puberty are different in boys than in girls. These changes are controlled by the sex hormones – androgens in boys and estrogen in girls. The changes are more pronounced in girls than in boys.

The most obvious change in boys is the increase in their muscle mass, accompanied by an increase in strength. They develop bigger hearts and lungs than girls, and in their circulation have more red blood cells and higher concentrations of hemoglobin (the chemical which enables the red blood cells to transport oxygen around the body). The effect of these changes is that boys are better adapted than girls for hard physical work and athletic performance. The shoulders widen and, because the average boy's growth spurt occurs later than the average girl's, the legs are likely to be longer.

In girls the hips widen. There are also differences between the sexes in terms of the fatty tissues under the skin. In girls these increase throughout puberty, although the rate at which they do so declines, whereas boys actually lose fat, becoming leaner.

In both sexes the important area of height gain is the spine, whereas before puberty the center of growth was the legs. Children who enter puberty later than usual seem for a while to have abnormally long legs and an abnormally short trunk. **PW**

Same birthday, different growth rates. *A family of sextuplets dramatically illustrates how individual the timing of the growth spurt can be. Though brought up in the same environment and given the same nutrition and care, each child is at a different stage of development. The* effects of early or late maturation may level off eventually, so late-developers catch up with, and sometimes overtake, faster-developing contemporaries.

163

18 HOW ADULTS AGE

As we age the body's enormous capacity for renewal helps to compensate for the increasing rates at which we lose body cells. By keeping fit and controlling weight we can greatly assist the body's efforts to last us a lifetime.

CELLS WE REPLACE AND THE ONES WE DO NOT

You are born with almost all the muscle and nerve cells you will ever have. There are billions of these cells, and if you escape catastrophic losses due to accident or disease, the numbers of them that you lose in everyday wear and tear are not significant enough to undermine health – even though, like brain cells, they may be counted in terms of thousands lost per day.

However, some types of cells, such as skin, are lost at such a rate that they must be constantly regenerated. The cycle in which cells are created, mature, function and then divide to create new cells is called the "cell cycle."

It has four phases: in the first, the cell divides to produce two smaller daughter cells; in the second, the daughter cells grow and then perform the function that their parent did; in the third, the genetic material in the cell replicates – it doubles in preparation for a new cell division; the fourth phase is a 2-4 hour pause before cell division.

Until recently it was thought that the cell cycle could carry on indefinitely. In some cancer cells (see *Ch19*) it does, but it is now known that in normally functioning cells it cannot. To a great extent this does not matter: long before these cells have split their maximum possible number of times, you are already dead.

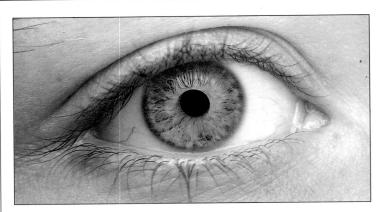

WE ARE made up entirely of cells and their products, and all through our lives our bodies attempt to achieve and maintain the numbers and the quality of cells that we need. The kinds we make, and how often, and the quality of the product they provide, depends in part on age. Between conception and birth, for example, cell multiplication is rapid. Throughout infancy, childhood and adolescence, there is a high demand for new tissue: the bones and organs have to increase in size as the child grows. The skin needs to increase in bulk to cover the larger surface area; the digestive organs need to expand to accommodate the greater demands of growth and increasing activity (see *Ch17*).

When growth stops, we routinely maintain most of these tissues, replacing lost skin cells, for example, or lost osteoid, the cell product that gives bones their strength and hardness. At key stages in early development, however, certain kinds of cells stop multiplying, and as their numbers gradually decline, they are replac-

Cells that regenerate

Cell division (1-2 hours)

Ready for cell division (2-4 hours)

Daughter cells mature and take on the same function as parent cells. This working phase may last only a few hours before more new cells are needed. On average, skin cells in a child stay in this phase for 100 days, in a 70-year-old only for 45 days.

Replication (10-20 hours)

Those that do not

Fetal cell division

After birth some cells – eg nerve cells and the cells that do purification work in the kidneys – never divide again. Cells grow bigger or smaller according to the body's needs. Red blood cells do not divide, but special parent cells in the bone marrow replace them frequently (see *Ch3*).

Eventual cell death

Accelerating the aging process. *Maximize your vitamin D production is the message of a suntanning aid, but adults need only tiny amounts of this vitamin, and excessive exposure to sunlight can cause skin cancer and causes the skin to appear* *prematurely old. The sun breaks down elastic tissues in the skin, which becomes thinner and wrinkled. Fair-skinned people are most affected. Extreme cold has the same effect on exposed skin, so faces, necks and hands age the fastest.*

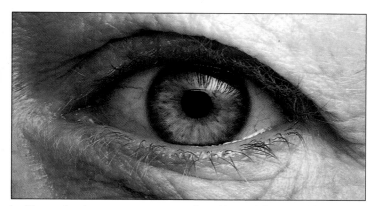

Signs of aging. *ABOVE LEFT Skin around a 23-year-old woman's eye is smooth and free from wrinkles, but by the age of 50 ABOVE bags and lines often appear. This happens because the skin loses its elasticity and cannot* | *withstand the stretching that laughing, frowning and other facial expressions involve. After the menopause a woman becomes more susceptible to wrinkles because her skin produces much less oil.*

ed. As we age, some cells that replace themselves, do so with an altered rhythm and cells that produce important products may do so less efficiently.

Does this mean that old age is a grim prospect? In fact, the losses that are a natural part of aging normally leave us ample scope to pursue a high quality of life throughout our later years. Debilitating losses of irreplaceable cells are due to diseases that are by no means inevitable. Even coming to terms with changes in our appearance is not entirely a matter of simply accepting the inevitable. A spreading waistline, for example, can be controlled.

Day-to-day replacement of skin and hair

We often lose cells from the surfaces of organs, and these provide good examples of the way the body keeps up our tissues once growth is complete. The surface cells of the mouth, stomach and bowel linings are among the most frequently replaced, because cells are often scraped off by the passage of food and feces.

The outer layers of the skin, too, need to be constantly renewed throughout our lives. As they rise from the deeper layers of skin, where cell division takes place, skin cells are gradually transformed into keratin, a cell product that makes skin tough and waterproof. Linked groups of keratinized skin cells are constantly shed because of the wear and tear of daily life, especially in exposed areas and those that are most often washed.

The modified skin cells that produce hair are another case of surface shedding. A hair grows from a living root where cells proliferate. Like skin cells, they produce keratin, but the keratin is organized to form a rather different structure than the one that forms the surface

scale of skin. Fine hairs, such as those that cover most of the body and aid our sense of touch, grow at a rate of about 1.5mm (0.05in) per week. Coarse hair grows more quickly: 2.2mm (0.08in) per week. Eyelashes and underarm hairs last only about four months before they are shed – scalp hairs last about four years.

A fingernail or toenail grows in a similar way, from a region of dividing cells under the skin that lies over the base of the nail. Daughter cells keratinize and link together to form fresh nail. The average growth rate is 0.5mm (0.02in) per week, with toe nails being the slowest. Fingernail growth is slowest in the little finger, fastest in the middle finger. AS

Why does the skin wrinkle in old age?

The most obvious changes caused by aging are those of the skin. The skin of the face, neck and hands is usually the first to become wrinkled, weatherbeaten and blotchy because these are the areas most exposed to the sun, atmospheric pollution, cosmetics and frequent washing. A preventive measure against looking old too early is to avoid excessive suntanning.

The skin of the trunk, buttocks and thighs may remain smooth and unblemished into your fifties and sixties, and perhaps even your seventies. However, even in these regions the skin is affected by aging. In a child, the cells in the outer layer of the skin have a lifespan of about 100 days, but by the time a person is in their seventies this lifespan has probably dropped to about 45 days. At the same time, the amount of fat in the layers immediately below the skin has decreased (although it has probably increased in the trunk region). Because of both these effects, the outermost layer of the skin becomes both thinner and less securely connected to the underlying layer of connective tissues.

The connective tissues, too, are affected by aging. Not all of the material of our tissues consists of cells. Some of it comprises products made by the cells (fibroblasts) of the connective tissues. Among these are the collagen fibers and elastic fibers, which act as a sort of skeleton for our connective tissues. These tissues are fleshed out by a soft material called mucopolysaccharide, which is likewise made by the fibroblasts.

As we age, chemical reactions occur to link up adjacent molecules in the collagen fibers, so that their physical properties change. The easiest way of appreciating these changes is to think of the physical differences between a piece of veal and a piece of beef. The network of collagen fibers under the skin shrinks, and its structure deteriorates. Because the outer layer of the skin is now thinner and less elastic, it wrinkles. It is also likely to be dry (sometimes itchy) as the glands which exude natural skin oils become less active.

Why does hair turn gray and become thin?

Another familiar sign of aging is that the hair turns gray. At 50, it is likely that half of the hairs on a person's head will be gray. This happens for two reasons: first, cells in the roots of an affected hair may produce less pigment; second, minute air bubbles tend to form in the outer layer of the hair's shaft, and this reduces the effect of pigmentation.

Baldness is another matter: the likelihood of your going bald is determined by a sensitivity of the hair root bulbs to androgens – male sex hormones. Nobody as yet knows the details of the process, but sooner or later, in almost all men, an increasing number of hair follicles in the scalp start to produce fine, barely visible body hairs rather than long thick scalp hairs. There is usually a progression; hair first recedes at the temples, then thins at the crown before receding backward from the forehead.

In women, balding is less noticeable. Hair thins out everywhere on the scalp, usually without exposing any area completely. When this happens to a woman, it is usually an effect of the menopause, after which higher levels of androgens are produced by her body.

Other tissues that change as we age include the nails, especially the toenails: they thicken, become ridged and grow less quickly. The lens of the eye becomes less flexible, so that there may be difficulty focusing on nearby objects (see *Ch 7*). The flexible fibers in the walls of the arteries deteriorate, so that these blood vessels are more rigid, but this is not usually the chief cause of arterial disease in older people – preventable atherosclerosis is much more significant (see *Ch 2*). The ligaments grow

A recipe for excess weight. *By failing to review your diet and your pattern of exercise as you grow older, you may risk becoming overweight. As your lifestyle becomes less active, the amount of energy you use declines, and the body starts to replace muscle with fat. This change is accelerated by a tendency in middle-aged and older people to drink more alcohol*

| 20 | Age | 30 | 35 | 40 | 45 | 50 | 55 |

Falling energy use

Food intake not reduced

Increasing alcohol intake

(which has a high calorie content), than they did when they were young.

less resilient and elastic so that, even if not affected by arthritis (see *Ch 8*), joints become slightly stiffer. Exercise helps to keep them supple.

The changing composition of the body

Starting about the age of 25, there is a decline in the total amount of protein in the average person's body – a decline in their "lean body mass."

Partly this is accounted for by the fact that the bones have now stopped growing and have begun a long and gradual decline in bulk (see *Ch 8*). Organs like the brain and kidney too have begun to shrink.

The main loss of bulk, however, is in the size of muscle cells. Just as muscle cells get bigger in response to increased demand (see *Ch 8*), so they get smaller when the demand decreases. As we get older and physically less active, especially the muscles of the legs atrophy. Meanwhile fat tissue is on the increase.

On average, a 25-year-old man weighing 75kg (165lb)

GOING BALD

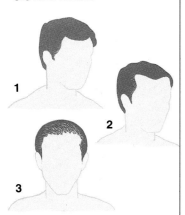

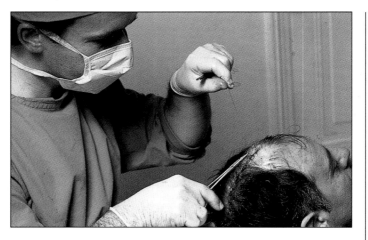

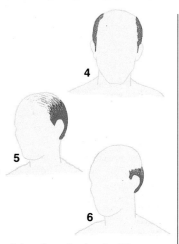

Starting with a full head of hair 1, a typical pattern of male baldness begins with hair receding at the temples 2. Next, the hair thins out gradually on the crown of the head

3, until there is a clear bald spot 4. Hair loss may slow down after this stage, but if it progresses the back of the head becomes bald 5. In the last stage, hair is left in fringes

at the sides and back 6, though for many men baldness never develops this far. ABOVE No cure for baldness exists, but one solution is to replace hair surgically. Hair

taken from the back of the scalp is transplanted to the bald area where it grows normally.

Taking positive action *to reduce his weight, a middle-aged jogger resists the aging process. Though some effects of aging lie beyond our control, adapting your lifestyle to health needs can stop the build-up of excess fat that often occurs in the fifties and sixties (see graph opposite). Combining regular exercise with a reduced calorie intake is the best solution.*

has a lean body mass of 61kg (135lb) and he has 3kg (7lb) of fat. At 65 his lean body mass is 49kg (108lb) and he has 28kg (62lb) of fat.

The amount of water washing around inside us also tends to decline. The water content of an embryo is about 90 percent. This dwindles to 80 percent at birth, 70 percent at maturity and 60 percent or less in old age. Some of the water may be lost from the tissue spaces, but most is probably lost from within the cells.

Why it is important to control weight

Since we tend to replace muscle and other components of the lean body mass with fat as we age, then even if we keep weight constant (which too few of us do), we are building up excess fat tissues. Our calorie requirements are actually diminishing as we become more sedentary, and a reduced intake will suffice. It is also important to introduce regular exercise to compensate for the fact that, as adults, we walk when children run, or – more likely – drive in a car. Not only does exercise burn up unwanted calories, it keeps the heart strong (see *Ch 2*) and it may stimulate bone cells to produce osteoid, and so help to maintain bone mass.

Obesity is a form of malnutrition because it encourages the development of arthritis, hypertension and arterial disease. In addition, it will add considerably to any physical disability acquired in later life.

It also contributes to diabetes. Diabetes has an insulin-dependent and an insulin-independent form. Insulin-dependent diabetes occurs mainly in young people. The pancreas produces very little or no insulin, which the body needs in order to use glucose, the sugar into which we convert most of our food. To control the disease, insulin must be taken into the body by injection. Insulin-independent diabetes mainly affects people over 40. Over the age of 70, about 10 percent of people are diabetic in this way. About a third of sufferers have a family history of diabetes. They are usually overweight and the pancreas may be producing less insulin as it ages. More food is being consumed and converted to glucose than the pancreas can deal with. To control the disease diet is effective together with tablets that lower the level of glucose in the blood. If diabetes is not controlled, a number of problems in aging can be badly complicated. Especially, decline in kidney function is likely to be accelerated; blood vessels become blocked; retinal disease may produce blindness.

Do nutritional needs and habits change as we age?

The basic rules for a healthy diet do not vary significantly for elderly people – they just become even more important. Recommended intakes of protein, vitamins and minerals do not differ significantly as we age. Most surveys indicate that the diet of healthy older people is similar to that in earlier life, although it is a little reduced in quantity in accordance with their lower energy requirements.

Poor nutrition in unhealthy older people is common, but starvation seems to be more often a consequence of illness rather than a cause. Malnutrition in the broader sense – including faulty dietary habits – is more widespread.

Constipation (see *Ch 9*) is more common among the old than the young, because physical inactivity tends to encourage inactivity of the intestine so that the transit time taken for indigestible material may increase from 40 hours or so in a fit, active adult to 72 hours in a retired and rather inactive person to 4 days or more in a dependent nursing-home patient. During this delayed passage through the large intestine, so much water is absorbed that the stool becomes hard and difficult to pass. The same occurs when the call to pass a stool is neglected, or when medicines (many analgesics, for instance) delay the passage, or not enough water is drunk.

Constipation may need to be treated with laxatives, but can usually be prevented by ensuring a sufficient intake of dietary fiber. A major proportion of fiber itself appears in due course in the stool – 20 percent in the case of most fibrous foods, up to 50 percent in the case of wheat bran. This helps the stool to retain water in the intestine. The remainder is broken down by bacteria which then multiply and contribute significantly themselves to the bulk of the stool.

Problem drinking is prevalent in people past retirement age. Some are people who have maintained their habit over decades and others take it up through boredom or grief. Alcohol kills brain cells, and since the aging brain has less spare capacity than that of a young person, older people have more reason to moderate their intake.

Aging and the menopause

The most obvious sex difference in aging is the fact that there is a definite point in a woman's life when she ceases to be fertile – the menopause, when the menstrual cycle (see *Ch12*) stops. After the menopause, female organs become somewhat smaller, for example, the number of cells in the breast tissue falls, and the size of the muscle cells in the uterus diminishes. Linked to these changes are some not so obviously related to finishing with reproduction. This is when many women become susceptible to baldness. After the menopause, there is an accelerated loss of bone tissue (see *Ch8*). Women begin to catch up with men in the rate that they suffer heart disease. Women who receive hormone replacement therapy in order to combat bone-tissue loss appear to be at a lower risk of heart disease. This suggests that female reproductive hormones may have been preventing heart attacks in younger life.

Cells that are not replaced

From soon after birth we make do with a gradually diminishing number of brain cells, for lost nerve cells are not replaced. We lose on average about 50,000 of them each day of our lives, and our brain grows correspondingly lighter as we age. This is not as worrying as it might seem: the rate of loss is highest during the period the nervous system is developing toward maturity, at which time it has about 10 billion cells – enough to last for several hundred years. Moreover, the rate of loss varies from one part of the nervous system and the brain to another. The point is that the nervous system, like all other systems, has a considerable reserve capacity, so that large numbers of its cells can die or be destroyed before its function is seriously impaired.

Similarly, although the most frequently damaged kidney cells – tubular lining cells – are replaceable, certain others (glomerular cells – see *Ch10*) are not. An 80-year-old has two-thirds to one-half as many glomeruli as a 40-year-old; in effect, the equivalent of only one kidney. The surviving glomeruli can cope perfectly well in normal circumstances; only when the demands are great, do problems occur. Muscle cells too, although they may be trained to increase in size, do not increase in number. We are supplied from birth, however, with all the muscle cells we need.

Does our intellect decline as we age?

When groups of people of different ages are tested for intelligence, learning ability, short-term memory and reaction time, the older groups do progressively less well

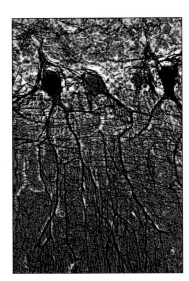

Losing about 50,000 cells per day, *the brain becomes lighter as we age, but the loss does not cause a decline in brainpower – there are enough brain cells to last for several hundred years. These Purkinje brain cells (the three dark cells at the top of the image – magnified 625 times) are among the largest nerve cells in the body.*

(and their individual results show a wider range of performance). This might seem to suggest that intellect inexorably declines with age. However, many of these differences are a result of history: younger people have had different educational opportunities; they have usually taken in more from the media and have had different experiences than their elders. Another important factor is that people who have suffered from strokes and from Alzheimer's disease are included in the comparisons.

Not until the age of 70 is there a statistical decline in average intellectual abilities, and some people retain their full mental acuity until very much greater ages than this. These people are generally those who both started off with a higher IQ and have remained socially active, continued their education and so on. However, they share with everyone else the phenomenon sometimes called "benign senescent forgetfulness" – that is, they

Keeping mental powers alive. *If no diseases or accidents impair the brain's function, creativity and mental coordination need not decline with age. People who continue to learn and develop talents are likely to retain their intellectual abilities into their seventies and beyond.*

sometimes have difficulty remembering things. Studies have found that younger people who lead a busy life are much more likely to complain of being hampered by poor memory than older retired people. The reason seems to be that busy people have more appointments and lists of jobs to remember and are under more stress.

Usually age-related mental decline gives no outward sign. However, when the brain is put under stress – when people are tested to the limits of their mental ability – the effects of aging may become evident.

Why do older people have strokes?

A stroke is the result of a sudden disturbance of the blood supply to a part of the brain: this region may then be severely damaged or, more commonly, die. The less common cause of a stroke is that one of the arteries of the brain has burst, so that blood seeps into the brain tissues and clots there or spreads over the surface of the brain, putting pressure on brain cells. The more common cause is oxygen starvation: an artery supplying the brain has become blocked, usually because of atherosclerosis.

The way that people are affected by a stroke varies considerably. About one-third die, either immediately or after a few days spent in a coma or in a state of clouded consciousness. People who sustain a series of very minor strokes may be affected in their intellect. On occasion a stroke affects one or two limbs in a fairly minor way and recovery is rapid. In general, one side of the body is paralyzed and sensation, vision and speech are affected.

A stroke attacks suddenly. By contrast, recovery is a slow process, and cannot be guaranteed; it involves physiotherapy carried out over a period of, typically, three months, as other cells in the brain learn to take over some of the functions of cell complexes that have been lost. About 40 percent of people who survive a stroke will never again be able to walk outdoors, and 10-20 percent will spend many years – perhaps the rest of their lives – in institutional care.

In the age-group 35-44 an almost negligible 0.025 percent of people (one in 4,000) or less have strokes, and those affected will almost certainly have extremely high blood pressure, a heart condition or one of various rare blood or arterial disorders; using oral contraceptives can increase the risk of a stroke in middle age, but only very slightly. People in their mid-seventies to mid-eighties run a very much higher risk: their chance of suffering a stroke is 2 percent (one in 50). One reason why this is a disease of old age is that smoking, poor diet and lack of exercise in young and middle adulthood are contributory causes, and they take time to have their effect. High blood pressure usually lies behind burst blood vessels in the brain. Arterial disease is the reason for blocked blood vessels. In many countries, especially the United States,

fewer people are having strokes as a result of a healthier lifestyle that is aimed at reducing the risk of high blood pressure and arterial disease (see Ch 2). Stroke accounts for more demand on hospital services than any other disease; in Western countries it is the third leading cause of death after heart disease and cancer.

What is Alzheimer's disease?

Alzheimer's disease used to be called "presenile dementia," because it was suspected of being a disease with different causes than those of dementia in very elderly people. By "dementia" is meant an all-embracing impairment of the intellect, memory and personality. Alzheimer's disease is the commonest cause, and it may strike before old age. The disease is rare in youth and less rare in middle age. It affects older people to the extent that about 20 percent over 80 suffer from it.

The cortex (outer part) of the brain becomes thin and in certain areas substantial numbers of brain cells die. Among these are cells responsible for producing key neurotransmitters – chemicals that carry messages from one brain cell to the next. There is a drastic reduction in the quantities of these neurotransmitters, and abstract thought, learning ability, initiative, concentration and interest are impaired. The short-term memory fails, and later the long-term memory does as well. The course of the disease may extend over several years.

The causes of Alzheimer's disease are not understood: theories include the existence of a slow virus (one that needs decades to cause an illness), chronic aluminum intoxication, head injury in youth, and genetic defects.

What is Parkinson's disease?

Parkinson's disease is rare in people aged under 50 but affects about 1.5 percent of people over 60. It is due to a gradual deterioration in nerve centers in the brain that affect movement. In particular the neurotransmitters dopamine and acetylcholine are made available to this part of the nervous system in the wrong proportions.

Parkinson's disease causes trembling of the hands (sometimes of the legs and trunk as well), stiffness and slowness of movement. The disease progresses over a period of years, and may result in falls, fractures and immobility. Usually there is no detectable cause for the brain deterioration, although in a few cases there is a link with certain infections of the nervous system or with drugs. A very minor degree of protection is offered when tobacco smoking stimulates dopamine production.

Treatment can be by physiotherapy. If the condition is severe, considerable relief can be provided by the use of levodopa (also called L-dopa) medication, although this can have unpleasant side-effects. NC

19 ABNORMAL REGENERATION

Cancer cells are out of rhythm with the rest of the body. They may multiply at abnormally fast rates, and spread uncontrolled through the tissues. Some begin to spread after as long as 10 years, others in less than a year, but in all cases early treatment is vital. Regular health checks can help by identifying symptoms in time.

HOW FAST DOES CANCER SPREAD?

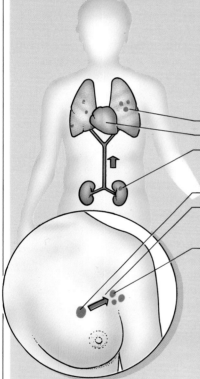

◄ Spreading through the bloodstream, *cancer of the kidney invades small veins in the kidney. Clumps of tumor cells are carried in the main vein of the body to the lungs, where secondary tumors grow.*

— Secondary tumors in lung
— Heart
— Primary cancer in kidney

— Primary cancer in breast
— Small clumps of cancer cells spreading along the lymph system
— Secondary cancer growing in lymph nodes

◄ Spreading through the lymph system, *breast cancer invades lymph channels, which carry clumps of cancer cells to lymph nodes in the armpit. Here secondary tumors grow.*

Some cancers spread rapidly, some at a slower rate, invading and destroying tissue in other parts of the body. Some – such as breast cancer – are extremely variable; in older women it can spread very slowly. Here are some other examples:
Very very slow Small superficial tumors of the skin, such as rodent ulcers, almost never invade other tissues.
Slow Cancer of the cervix: up to 10 years before invading other tissues. Regular cervical smear tests ensure that cervical cancer is treated before it spreads.
Quite slow Cancer of the

large intestine: 5-10 years before invading; often detected early and removed.
Faster Cancer of the stomach, cancer of the kidney, cancer of the lung, melanoma (skin cancer containing dark pigment): 1-5 years before invading. Because melanomas are visible in the skin, they are more often detected and removed than other fast cancers.
Very fast Leukemia, testicular cancers: less than 1 year before invading. Both leukemia and testicular cancers can be treated with drugs after they spread.

MOST body cells that reproduce themselves do so in a well controlled manner to match the body's needs at the time. However, sometimes a new line becomes established in which the daughter cells, while identical to the parent in appearance and function, do not respond to the controls governing their rate of duplication. They multiply even when there is no need for them to do so. The expanding mass of daughter cells is a tumor.

Most tumors grow slowly and regularly, gradually compressing the normal tissues around them. These are called benign tumors because they are relatively harmless; they rarely cause death. However, the cells of some tumors fail to respond to controls that inhibit cells from destroying those around them. These malignant tumors grow not just because the cells are reproducing more rapidly but also because they are invading and destroying the cells of surrounding tissues. Malignant tumors – cancers – are a major cause of illness and death.

How do tumors affect health?

The symptoms of a benign tumor are usually produced because of their size. Some benign tumors of the breast and fatty tumors under the skin can be felt as lumps. Other benign tumors produce bleeding. For example, tumors protruding from the lining of the bowel wall can be damaged by the passage of feces, so that they bleed.

Occasionally, however, benign tumors can have serious effects because they happen to be located in a vital spot. For example, a benign tumor in the membranes covering the brain can cause serious illness just through pressing down on a vital region of the brain's tissues. Benign tumors growing into any of the body's narrow tubes can obstruct the movement of material along it; one instance is where benign tumors obtrude into the lower branches of the windpipe, blocking the passage of air to the lungs. A third way in which benign tumors can cause serious effects is if they occur among cells that normally secrete one of the body's controlling hormones. Far too much of the hormone is produced, and the body suffers accordingly.

Malignant tumors can produce any of the effects of benign tumors, but are far more dangerous because of their ability to invade and destroy surrounding healthy tissues. They are also far more difficult to treat, because unlike benign tumors they cannot simply be extracted surgically. Moreover, they frequently spread to other parts of the body to produce secondary cancers.

How quickly do cancers develop and progress?

Each kind of cancer is unique, and even a single kind of cancer can behave quite differently in different people. It is therefore impossible to predict when a cancer will arise and how it will behave. One problem is that the abnormal cells must duplicate many times before they produce a lump big enough to produce any detectable symptom. By then it may be too late. Although some cancers develop and grow slowly, and take a long time before they start to spread to different parts of the body, others probably arise quickly, grow rapidly and spread early.

What are the warning signs?

Although we can never pinpoint a tumor when it first develops, in certain instances there are some clues that a change is occurring in the nature of the cells. One example is in the cervix, which connects the womb with

Attacking a cancer cell.
White, "killer" blood cells (the small cells on the left) can detect and destroy abnormal cells, such as this large tumor cell. It may survive and multiply if the barrier of small blisters on its surface inter- *feres with the white cells' attack. Though we may produce several cancer cells every day, the immune system usually prevents them from growing into malignant tumors.*

the vagina. The surface cells may undergo a change in appearance which can be seen by direct examination; samples of these "dysplastic cells" can be taken in a cervical smear and looked at through a microscope. They show many of the features of the cells from cancers, and certainly have the potential to develop into a cancerous growth. It may be many years before they do so, so laser treatment or surgery to remove areas of abnormal cell growth from the surface of the cervix may remove the risk of cancer. All women should receive regular cervical smear tests, even after laser treatment or surgery.

The surface lining of the stomach may likewise have dysplastic cells. Patients who have had gastritis for a long while run a high risk of stomach cancer. Likewise people who for 20-30 years have suffered ulcerative colitis (see p108) may have areas of dysplastic cells in the walls of the colon. In both cases the doctor will arrange for an endoscopic biopsy in which an instrument with a light is passed into the body on a tube and a small portion of the potentially affected organ is removed for examination. Invasive breast cancer is probably preceded by dysplastic change in cells lining the ducts deep within the breast, but invasion occurs early so the detection of dysplastic cells does not usually give enough warning for the disease to be headed off.

In some instances it is possible to tell quite accurately how long a particular type of cancer takes to develop because it can be triggered off by a short-duration event that can be pinpointed. For example, exposure to a short burst of high-intensity radiation can give rise to a number of cancers, notably leukemia (cancer of the white blood cells). In 1945 the citizens of Hiroshima and Nagasaki were exposed to just such a high-intensity burst of radiation. Leukemia developed in the survivors, on average, seven years later. Likewise, quite short exposures to certain types of asbestos fiber can lead to the development of a form of cancer that affects the surface of the lungs and the internal lining of the chest wall. The delay between the exposure and the appearance of the cancer is frequently as great as 20-40 years.

DETECTING CANCER EARLY

Even if your general health is good, regular screening for cancer is important. For women, screening for breast cancer should be a priority. One way of doing this is by carrying out an examination of the breasts every month after a period (the technique is explained in Part One). After the menopause, 3-yearly screening by X-ray (mammo- graphy) is advisable (see Part One). Experimental methods of screening for breast cancer include testing levels of the hormone prolactin and monitoring the skin temperature of the breasts (see Ch 5).

Additionally, any woman who is sexually active should have a regular cervical smear test (see Part One). By showing up any precancer cells, this can predict up to 20 years in advance the possibility that cancer will develop.

Both men and women can be screened for cancer of the bowel. Samples of the feces are analyzed for microscopic specks of blood.

Certain early warning signs may – but do not always – indicate cancer. These include lumps in the neck; sores that will not heal; blood in the urine or feces; prolonged constipation or diarrhea; unexplained vaginal bleeding; or changes in any moles on your skin. General symptoms that occur when the cancer is more advanced are constant tiredness, loss of weight or a persistent cough.

If cancer is suspected, a doctor can arrange examinations by X-ray, or by biopsy, which involves some tissue being removed and analyzed for malignant cells.

The History of a Cancer Tumor

Genetic material is disrupted every day in some body cells. Only a fraction of them are affected in such a way that they could multiply into cancer tumors, and only a fraction of those with the potential ever do.

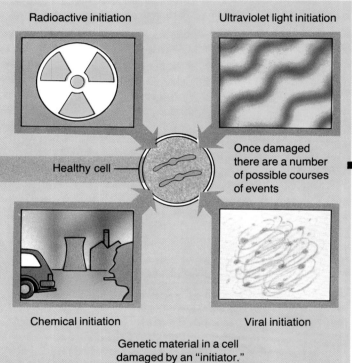

Radioactive initiation

Ultraviolet light initiation

Healthy cell

Once damaged there are a number of possible courses of events

Chemical initiation

Viral initiation

Genetic material in a cell damaged by an "initiator."

1 CELL DAMAGED BY "INITIATOR"	2 REPAIR	3 CELL DEATH

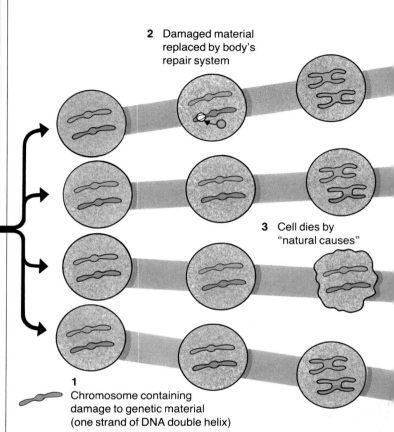

2 Damaged material replaced by body's repair system

3 Cell dies by "natural causes"

1 Chromosome containing damage to genetic material (one strand of DNA double helix)

1 INITIATION

Cancers can be triggered by excessive exposure to X-rays, radioactivity and ultraviolet radiation. Cells are particularly vulnerable when they are in the cell-division phase of their life cycle. So, the more frequently a particular kind of cell divides in the normal, healthy condition, the more likely it is to develop a cancer: cells such as those of the bone marrow, skin and the linings of the stomach and intestine replace themselves frequently and so can be seriously damaged by doses of radiation that have little effect on cells which divide less often. This is why the early symptoms of radiation sickness are diarrhea and vomiting, reddening and blistering of the skin, and severe anemia and loss of white blood cells (derived from special cells in the bone marrow).

Many chemical factors are known to increase the risks of cancer; such chemicals are called carcinogens. Some of the polycyclic hydrocarbons, for example, which are widespread in car exhaust fumes, factory smoke and cigarette smoke, are capable of inducing cancer. The polycyclic hydrocarbons in cigarette smoke may play a part in the development of lung cancer; but tobacco smoke contains other possible carcinogens, as well as some radioactive substances. In the animal kingdom there are many examples of cancers produced by viruses that convert a normal cell into one which has the potential to become malignant. This comes about because some of the genetic material of the virus is incorporated into that of the affected cell. Virus-induced cancers are rare in human beings – there is only circumstantial evidence of links between viruses and cancer in humans.

2 Repair of damage.

Genetic material is damaged frequently, but only rarely are the resulting abnormal cells able to survive long enough to generate a tumor. The body has various means of carrying out repairs at cell level. An important repair agent is endonuclease, an enzyme (chemical capable of speeding up reactions involving other chemicals). Very rarely people are born with a lack of endonuclease. They are more susceptible than others to skin cancer during childhood.

3 Cell death.

Often the damage done is so severe that the cells are incapable of functioning properly. Because they cannot reproduce, the

4 LATENT CANCER   5 IMMUNE RESPONSE   6 PROMOTION   7 INVASIVE CANCER

Once repaired cell continues to divide into healthy "daughter" cells

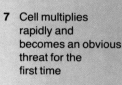

The time between initiation of cancer in a single cell and the development of disease may vary substantially. Some usually take from 5-10 years and are often detected and treated. Others, particularly leukemia, spread rapidly and may have taken hold in less than a year.

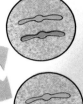

4 Abnormal, damaged cells can remain unchanged and latent for long periods

7 Cell multiplies rapidly and becomes an obvious threat for the first time

Cell raw material reabsorbed

6 Promoter agent stimulates the cell's abnormal genetic material

Killer cell

5 Damaged cell can be destroyed by killer cells which are able to recognize abnormalities

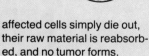

affected cells simply die out, their raw material is reabsorbed, and no tumor forms.

4 Latent cancer. A few damaged cells survive, so that defective genes are passed on to new generations of cells. In the early stages the cells containing the malfunctioning genetic material look and behave like ordinary cells. This latent state in the development of a tumor can last for many years; the genetic weakness is present but it has no obvious effect until other factors intervene.

5 Immune response. The body's immune-defense systems are able to identify and destroy foreign materials. Abnormally developing cells are often recognized and swiftly destroyed. A specialized part of the immune system known as killer cells single out diseased cells for individual destruction.

6 Promotion. The abnormal cells are influenced by a new agent, a "promoter," which stimulates or allows the genetic defect to start making its effects felt. The damaged cells look different from normal healthy cells, and they divide too rapidly, uncontrolled by the actual needs of the body. The result is either a benign tumor or, if the cells are capable of invading and destroying surrounding tissues, a cancer. It is not known exactly what substances are promoters of human cancers, but experiments on animals suggest that very large doses of saccharin and the cyclamates may act as promoters of cancer of the bladder.

7 Invasive cancer. It is the ability to invade and destroy adjacent tissues that distinguishes a malignant tumor from a benign one. The effects of this can extend far beyond the part of the body in which the tumor has appeared, because clusters of abnormal cells can be transported by the circulatory systems. Secondary cancers can become widespread throughout the body as the abnormal cells continue to develop rapidly. In addition, the primary causes and the promoter agent may not be identified and may continue to cause malignant tumors.

How do cancers spread?

The most disturbing feature of some cancers is that they can spread to other parts of the body, often quite remote from the original sites. This occurs because of the ability of cancerous cells to invade nearby tissues. Should those tissues belong to either the lymphatic system or the blood-circulation system, the cancer can be carried to other parts of the body.

In lymphatic spread the original tumor invades the walls of one or more lymphatic vessels, and the malignant cells continue to multiply on the inside of the vessel. Clumps of tumor cells break off and are carried by the liquid to the nearest lymph nodes (areas which act as filters of the lymph fluid). Many of these clumps of cancerous cells die, but a few survive and continue to multiply to create secondary cancers which eventually destroy and replace the tissues of the lymph nodes.

In bloodstream spread the malignant cells invade the walls of blood vessels, usually thin-walled veins, and are spread in the same way as in the lymphatic system. The drifting clumps of tumor cells are trapped in quite specific sites, usually the small blood vessels of the lung or liver. Primary tumors in the stomach and bowel frequently send clumps of cancerous cells to the liver; primary tumors in other sites (for example, the kidney) often cause secondary cancers to form in the lungs or bones.

Knowing where a malignant tumor has originally formed can help greatly in any attempt to remove the cancer from the body by use of surgery. For example, most of the lymphatic channels in the breast drain into lymph nodes in the armpit, so if a person has breast cancer enlargement of these nodes should be looked for immediately; if it is decided to remove or irradiate them at the same time as the tumor in the breast, the chances of the cancer being locally cleared may be improved.

With some kinds of cancer the relevant lymph nodes cannot be removed by surgery, in which case they may be treated by radiotherapy. A difficulty is that in some instances there may be countless different parts of the body where secondary tumors might have formed, so that neither surgery nor radiotherapy of all the potential sites would be practicable. There are now many drugs, called cytotoxic drugs, that act as cancer poisons, and so help patients no matter how many secondary cancers may have formed (see Ch 5). The availability of increasing numbers of these drugs means that many malignant tumors can be treated with some hope of success.

At what ages do people develop cancer?

No one is immune from cancer: even newborn babies may possess a cancerous tumor. However, this is very rare, and only a few kinds of cancer are likely to affect young children, the most common being a form of leukemia and some kinds of brain tumors. There are also two special cancers which are particularly associated with this age-group: nephroblastoma, which affects the kidney, and neuroblastoma, which affects the adrenal gland.

With some kinds of cancer, the chance of a person being affected depends on whether or not their parents

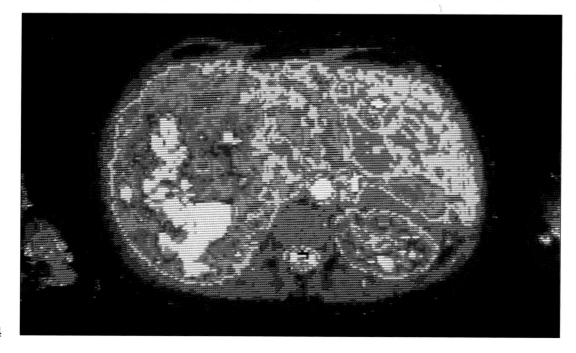

◄ **A cancer that has spread to the liver**. *The original tumor, a primary cancer of the large intestine, is not visible in this computer-aided image: a horizontal cross section of the abdomen. The white patches represent secondary growths that have invaded the liver. Symptoms of this cancer include blood in the stools, abdominal pain and weight loss. Evidence suggests it may be linked to low-fiber diet (see p102).*

▲ **A cancer affecting the white blood cells,** *leukemia develops when parent cells in the bone marrow are defective or when white cells in the blood become out of control. Very fast-developing leukemias occur more often in children.*

▼ **Unless it is diagnosed early,** *a malignant tumor in the ovary will squeeze and destroy surrounding tissue that contains the developing eggs. Regular medical examination allows your doctor to notice early any unusual enlargement of an ovary.*

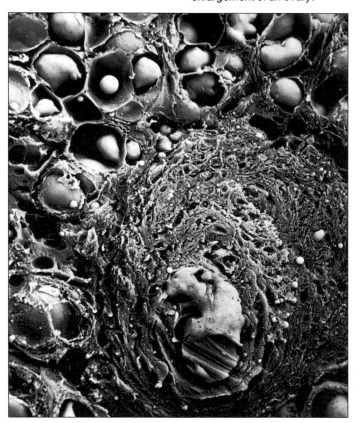

have a genetic predisposition. Xeroderma pigmentosum is one such, and commonly makes its presence felt in childhood. It comes about because the person lacks a particular enzyme called endonuclease, which acts to repair defects in the chromosomes. Sufferers are extremely sensitive to the ultraviolet rays in sunlight; skin exposed to the sun develops patchily pigmented scaly areas in which numerous skin cancers develop in due course. Probably all of us suffer genetic damage to the cells of our skin when it is exposed to ultraviolet rays; but in most people the endonuclease swiftly puts the matter to rights.

With or without an inherited weakness, everybody runs the risk of skin cancer if they expose themselves to too much ultraviolet radiation; the tumors are most common in the elderly. Skin cancer is especially prevalent in white-skinned people who are enthusiastic sunbathers, and it is becoming more frequent; it is thought that this may be due to the depletion of the ozone layer, which acts as a shield, protecting us from the bulk of the sun's ultraviolet radiation.

Another example of an inherited susceptibility to a cancer is familial polyposis coli, which affects the bowel and rectum. The children of parents who carry the genes for this cancer have a 50 percent chance of being afflicted by it during youth or middle age, usually between 30 and 40 (otherwise it is more commonly a feature of later life). It normally starts in adolescence, when the person begins to develop benign tumors in the internal lining of the large intestine and rectum. Such tumors are fairly common in older people (over 60), but occur in at most twos and threes; in familial polyposis coli the sufferer develops them in such large numbers that surgical removal of them all is impossible without removing the entire colon. As time goes on, one or more will develop malignant characteristics.

Cancers are unusual in older children and adolescents. Most frequently seen are brain tumors, primary tumors of the lymph nodes (lymphomas) and highly malignant bone cancer (osteosarcoma). Young adults, too, are unlikely to suffer from cancer, although men may suffer tumors of the testicles and women cancer of the cervix or breast, while malignant lymphomas (tumors of the lymph system) occur in both sexes. In middle age, cancers are much more frequent in women than in men, mainly because of the high incidence of breast and cervical cancer.

After 55, the older you become, the greater the chance that you may suffer from common cancers like those of the lung, bowel, stomach and skin. Almost all men over 85 suffer from cancer of the prostate gland; luckily, in most cases, however, the cancer does not spread outside the gland, and so the condition can be controlled by drug treatment. **A S**

20 TIMES OF INFECTION

When infection takes root in the body, the outcome depends on a race. The invading organism must reproduce quickly and achieve large numbers if it is to have its best chance of infecting a new host. The immune system must respond quickly to prevent these numbers if it is to minimize damage.

TIMES OF EXPOSURE

Breathing moisture that another person has sneezed out is one of the common ways of being exposed to infection. Sneezing creates violent currents in the air, seen BELOW through special photographic techniques. Moisture carried in these currents provides transport for virus particles and bacteria that need to be breathed in by new hosts if the infecting species are to survive. Food and water contaminated by sewage can also expose us to infection, as can direct contact with infected blood.

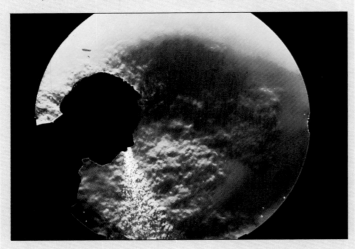

TIMES OF INCUBATION

If you know you have been exposed to a particular infection, you will not know whether you have caught it until is has had time to incubate. Here are some well-known infections and their periods of incubation.

ILLNESS	INCUBATION TIME	INFECTING AGENT
Bacillary dysentery	1-2 days	Bacteria in sewage
Viral gastroenteritis	1-2 days	Virus in sewage
Influenza	1-3 days	Airborne virus
Polio	5-10 days	Virus in sewage
Whooping cough	7-16 days then 1-14 days to whooping	Airborne bacteria
Typhoid	7-21 days	Bacteria in sewage
Measles	9-15 days	Airborne virus
Chickenpox	10-20 days	Airborne virus
Mumps	14-21 days	Airborne virus
Rubella (German measles)	14-21 days	Airborne virus
Rabies	20-90 days	Virus in saliva
Hepatitis A	21-35 days	Virus in sewage
Mononucleosis	30 days or more	Airborne virus
Hepatitis B	60-180 days	Virus in blood

WHETHER YOU become ill with an infection and how ill you become depend first on whether a sufficient dose of the infecting organism enters your body; this can depend on where you are, what you eat, who you come into contact with and when. Second, it depends on the interaction of two biological cycles: on the one hand, the cycle of multiplication and spread of the organism; on the other, the cycle of the body's defensive reaction. Our understanding of how all of these events happen has provided powerful tools for preventing infection and for minimizing the damage that it does.

By "infection" we usually mean a disease caused by a microscopic organism. Not all microscopic organisms cause disease – those that do are called "pathogens." Pathogens include certain bacteria, viruses and microscopic fungi, and some single-celled animals.

Are we more susceptible at different times of the year?

New cases of malaria occur in the rainy season, when the mosquitoes that carry the disease are abundant. Rocky Mountain spotted fever is a threat to people who go hiking in the springtime, because this is when the ticks that carry the disease drop from low branches onto passing mammals, to lay their eggs in mammalian skin.

Many other illnesses also reflect seasonal change. Diseases affecting the stomach are commoner in summer and chest infections are commoner in winter. In winter, people tend to gather in groups in heated rooms with the windows closed; the atmosphere allows rapid transfer from one person to another, in droplets of exhaled moisture, of the viruses and bacteria responsible for chest infections. In summer, people consume more unheated foods – cold cuts, salads and cold drinks – so that bacteria affecting the stomach are more easily spread.

Seasonal changes can also affect how people feel, and this in part explains our impression that we get fewer colds at some times of the year. People in temperate climates feel good in summer when the weather is warm and they are not as likely to regard a cold as a bad one at that time of year. Suffers of osteoarthritis are much more likely to complain that their joints hurt when the weather is cold and damp. During a warm spell, even though they are still suffering from the condition, there are very few complaints.

In addition to these seasonal variations there are epidemics that recur in a regular pattern, when large numbers of susceptible people are brought into close contact. For example, meningitis outbreaks normally happen at the start of a school term, when a carrier who shows no symptoms of this disease is brought into contact with a number of vulnerable schoolmates. Every four years there is a peak in the number of children suffering whooping cough, because during this period a sufficient number of unvaccinated children has built up to spread the disease.

Why is there an incubation period?

The time from first exposure to a virus or a bacterium to the time when symptoms develop is called the incubation period of the illness caused. This period varies, but what happens is roughly the same.

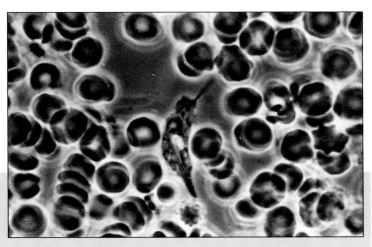

HOW DO BACTERIA CAUSE DISEASE?

Bacteria are single-celled organisms belonging to the plant kingdom. They are found everywhere, and it is impossible to avoid them completely. Millions live in mutually advantageous harmony with us – some help us to break down the food in our digestive tract and give bulk to our feces.

Some bacteria, however, produce chemical toxins that destroy or interfere with vital tissues. They provoke the body to a defensive reaction, and this reaction is part of what makes us feel ill. When the body's response is not effective, poisoning can result – for example, in fatal cases of diphtheria, poisons paralyze the heart muscle.

Examples of bacterial infection include many of the ill-defined stomach upsets that we seldom take to the doctor, but also some very serious illnesses – whooping cough; tuberculosis and leprosy, for example: these three all spread in droplets produced by the sneezes of people who harbor the bacteria.

Cholera and typhoid fever are examples of diseases caused by bacteria passed in feces from a host's body and taken in by a new host in contaminated food or water.

Food poisoning is due to bacteria: salmonella bacteria multiply in meat and dairy products, are consumed in food that has not been kept or prepared properly and then infect the digestive system; staphylococci and botulinus bacteria produce toxins in food.

Tetanus bacteria are common in the soil of all but the very coldest countries; they enter the body through open cuts and sores and produce toxins that lock the muscles.

Syphilis and gonorrhea are both bacterial infections spread by sexual contact.

Rickettsias are a family of tiny rod-shaped bacteria that

About to be engulfed *by attacking white blood cells, an unwelcome bacterium falls prey to the body's immune system.*

usually cannot live outside a host. They are carried by lice, fleas, ticks and mites. In humans bitten by lice in the tropics rickettsias cause typhus. Ticks burrowing beneath the skin of hikers help rickettsias to produce Rocky Mountain spotted fever in western North America.

HOW DO VIRUSES CAUSE DISEASE?

A virus is not a living cell like a bacterium, but an inanimate particle. It has genes, however, and can produce copies of itself when it enters a cell of another organism. It subverts the host cell's metabolism to make it possible for its own genes to replicate. The new virus particles may leave the cell gradually or burst out, often killing the host cell in the process.

We often feel ill, even with simple virus infections, because of the body's defensive response. This response is essential, for if it is not effective there can be serious damage – for example, severe cases of polio lead to paralysis through the permanent destruction by the polio virus of nerve cells in the brain and spinal cord.

Viruses cause minor colds or flu, cold sores and other herpes infections, and gastrointestinal upsets.

The influenza virus, *budding from the surface of a host cell in the lining of the nose, magnified almost 40,000 times. Viruses are unable to reproduce without invading the cells of other organisms.*

Most of the common childhood illnesses – chickenpox, measles, mumps – are caught by breathing in virus particles from other children, particularly when they cough or sneeze. The virulent forms of influenza that emerge from time to time are all viral infections.

AIDS (acquired immune deficiency syndrome) is caused by a virus that spreads through sexual contact and by blood contact. It reproduces in and destroys a key type of immune cell, thereby damaging the victim's ability to resist infection: it turns otherwise harmless infections, some never noticed by healthy people, into fatal diseases.

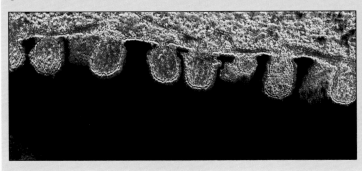

First, the invading organism must escape the body's initial defenses. The polio virus, for example, is swallowed with food, drink or perhaps water from a swimming pool that has been contaminated by fecal material from a contaminated person. The virus is resistant to the acids of the stomach (which destroy many other pathogens). It travels through the digestive system to lodge itself in the wall of the intestine, where it multiplies, gradually spreading throughout the body. The place where it first lodges is called the primary focus of the infection.

The rate at which a disease-causing organism multiplies at the primary focus depends on a number of factors. The first and most important is its ability to bind in place, so that it is not simply cleared by mechanisms such as coughing, urination, etc. Viruses, in particular, need to encounter and penetrate appropriate host cells.

A second important factor is the amount of the disease-causing organism present, because if there are too few individual organisms they will be unable to establish a primary focus. The number required varies widely from one type of pathogen to another: fewer than 500 shigella bacteria can produce dysentery, but several million polio viruses, which are much smaller, are needed to ensure that at least one of them comes into contact with a suitable cell surface.

Once the virus has succeeded in entering a cell it starts to reproduce. The outcome of the infection then depends on the result of a race between the rate at which the virus reproduces and the rate at which the body can generate a protective response. If you have already had polio, or you have been immunized, the race is easily won. Your immune system will promptly recognize polio as an old foe. During the previous encounter a line of immune cells will have been established that is specialized in producing polio antibodies – chemicals that attack and destroy polio viruses. A few of these cells will still exist, releasing antibodies into the circulatory system at a low rate. They will now proliferate and release antibodies at a high rate until the virus is cleared from the body.

In bacterial infections too, the immune system responds to known enemies with a ready-made system for producing specific antibodies. You may need to endure several attacks of malaria, however, before you become resistant to the sudden and frequent mass incursions into the bloodstream launched by the parasite that has taken up residence in your liver. If you later move to an area where malaria does not occur, this partial immunity rapidly wanes.

Why are early symptoms indistinct?

Typically, the second stage of an infection that survives the incubation period is the "prodome," a time when symptoms appear but do not identify a specific illness – raised temperature, malaise and rashes may indicate that the patient is unwell but they do not assist the doctor to make any accurate diagnosis.

These symptoms appear because no pre-existing immune mechanism is at hand, and the invading organism has started to spread through the body. Small fragments of the organism are being passed to immune cells in the lymph nodes for identification, and these cells are beginning to manufacture antibodies, but the antibody production system takes time to become established.

Meanwhile the body releases chemicals into the bloodstream that inhibit the invader. These chemicals produce a fever and a general feeling of malaise.

As a bacterial infection develops, a form of medical intervention that may help the body to resist is to give the patient antibiotics. These chemicals (eg penicillin) are effective only against certain strains of bacteria.

Infections that produce distinctive symptoms

The vast majority of people who are infected with polio virus have only a mild fever and a faint rash. In their case either the body has produced an immune response promptly or the particular strain of the virus

HOW DO FUNGAL INFECTIONS OCCUR?

Most microscopic fungi that enter the body are attacked and killed. RIGHT This smooth fungal cell is being swallowed from below by a macrophage, one of the specialized cells of the immune system.

Fungi that invade human tissues – for example, athlete's foot entering broken skin between the toes – usually need to take advantage of damage that has already occurred. When aspergillosis spores are inhaled by someone who has already had a respiratory disease, they may germinate in old scars in the lungs and bronchial passages. Colonies growing here may cause the sufferer to cough up blood.

A common fungus is the yeast candida albicans. It is often present in the body, but only grows and invades in special circumstances – for example, when the body's hormone balance is upset or when antibiotics have killed off beneficial bacteria that normally keep it in check. Large colonies of candida can cause sore patches in the mouth or throat (oral thrush) or the vagina (vaginal thrush) until balance is restored.

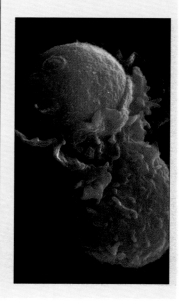

that has infected them is unable to spread or infect the nervous system.

Sometimes the virus may win the race. Polio infection spreads to involve the nervous system, where reproduction of the virus kills nerve cells, leaving muscles paralyzed.

This is the phase in which the symptoms of the disease clearly identify it: the varicella virus, for example, produces chickenpox blisters: the toxins of the tetanus bacterium begin to lock the jaw muscles of its victim.

SINGLE-CELLED ANIMALS THAT CAUSE DISEASE

Bacteria and microscopic fungi are single-celled plant life. Single-celled animals can also cause disease, especially those spread by tropical insects.

Protozoans are a subkingdom of single-celled animals. Some are parasites and among the worst are plasmodia, infesting mosquitoes and humans, in whom they cause malaria. Trypanosomes infest tsetse flies, cattle and humans, in whom they cause sleeping sickness.

Recurrent attacks of malaria are a consequence of the parasite's complex life cycle. Most species of plasmodium reproduce in the liver, from which large numbers of the parasites are released at regular intervals. These pass through the circu-latory sytem multiplying within red blood cells, which they destroy. This provokes a reaction from the body, experienced as a malarial fever. Feeding mosquitos draw in plasmodia with a meal of human blood, and the stomachs of the female mosquitos provide a site for the next stage in the parasite's reproductive cycle.

Another protozoan, an amoeba causing dysentery, may also settle in the liver.

▼ **Toxoplasma**, *seen parasitizing a host cell magnified almost 5,000 times. Toxoplasma is a protozoan parasite, common worldwide and dangerous to the fetuses of pregnant women not already immune to it.*

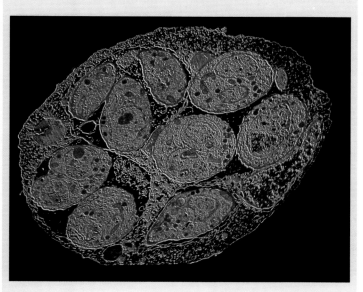

The final stage of an infection is a period either of convalescence or of complication. If the patient is badly weakened, secondary infections such as pneumonia can set in, or cell losses or toxins can so badly affect us that death results.

Infections that take hold before birth

We are susceptible to infection even in the womb. Normally the mother's immune system protects the fetus adequately, but this may not be the case if the mother herself is, during or even before pregnancy, infected by a pathogen to which she has not previously been exposed. The pathogen reproduces in or passes through the placenta, so that the unborn baby is infected.

The consequences of the infection may be greater or lesser, depending on the stage of pregnancy. This is particularly well understood in the case of rubella (German measles).

In about 90 percent of the cases where a fetus is seriously damaged by rubella, the infection occurs during the first four months of the pregnancy. Usually the result is a spontaneous abortion, but sometimes the fetus can survive, although the child will often be born with severe deformities (see *Ch15*).

Infections of the mother late in pregnancy may initially seem to have had little effect on the newborn child but, sadly, there may have been damage caused that is not immediately obvious. Sometimes there may be a significant localized abnormality.

The mother may not even have noticed an illness. The symptoms of the cytomegalovirus infection, for example, are generally rather milder than those of the common cold. But the child may be born severely mentally retarded. Babies born with a congenital infection are themselves likely to be very infectious.

It is fortunate that congenital infections are rare. They are rare because the organisms responsible are so common that most mothers are infected by them long before pregnancy, and so develop an immunity that they can share with the fetus.

Other examples of disease-causing organisms that affect unborn babies include toxoplasma (a protozoan – a kind of single-celled animal), common in the intestines of dogs and cats. It can cause enlargement of the fetal liver, abnormalities of development of the nervous system, and fever and convulsions in the newborn, while producing negligible symptoms in the mother. Listeria is a bacterium causing death to the fetus, but only a digestive disorder in the mother. A baby infected with the varicella virus can be born with a more widespread and severe infection than the chickenpox this virus usually causes. If a mother passes the AIDS virus on to her child, its ability to develop immunity to common diseases will be impaired. A mother who is a chronic carrier of the hepatitis virus can pass on the virus to her child, who may develop the disease after birth. Infection with this virus at an early age is a particularly important risk factor for developing liver cancer later. A mother who suffers from syphilis can infect her unborn child with the bacterium that causes this disease.

In many countries it is now the practice to inject pre-adolescent girls with live rubella vaccine so that they are immune to the disease by the time they are of child-bearing age. It is important to check, before any such injection, that the girl is not already pregnant, since the vaccine virus can itself infect the fetus. Prevention of other congenital infections is much more difficult.

The common childhood illnesses

Just after birth, an infant is protected from most common infections by the antibodies it has acquired as a fetus from the placenta of the mother. It is susceptible to infections to which its mother has not been exposed. After 6-12 weeks, the inherited antibodies lose their effectiveness, and the infant must develop immunity by undergoing infection.

Many of the infectious diseases that killed children early in this century, although now much less likely to be lethal, seem just as prevalent today; for example, over 90 percent of children still suffer chickenpox. The fact that far fewer children die of infectious diseases is in part due to improved therapy – especially the availability of anti-biotics – but that is not the whole story.

In developing countries children are less well nourish-ed and they are less resistant to measles. Many die as a direct consequence of this infection. Those who survive are more likely than survivors in developed countries to succumb to other infections.

This may be because the body's immune system is infected with the measles virus, and it is less able to tackle some other infections. In the developed countries, by contrast, general health measures make it a lot less likely that the person will be infected by these infections, so that the numbers of people dying as a result of mea-sles are negligible.

Another factor is that the organisms responsible for infections can change, so that their effect is reduced. A prime example is the streptococcus bacterium respons-ible for scarlet fever.

Since 1900 the incidence of scarlet fever has declined markedly, and the only likely explanation is that the res-ponsible streptococcus strain has evolved in such a way that it is no longer as harmful to human beings. It has been suggested that the decline in cases of cholera and bubonic plague may likewise be the result of evolutionary changes in the bacteria concerned.

Why some people cope better with influenza

The symptoms and severity of infectious illnesses vary with age: most are more serious among the very young and very old. To see why this is so we can take the influenza virus as an example. A first infection can make a person extremely ill, but once we have suffered a first bout of influenza we are relatively resistant to reinfection by the virus for many years. There are many different strains of the virus, and the antibodies we created to cope with the first virus do not defend us completely from a different strain, but they can reduce the severity of its attack. The longer it has been since a related infec-tion, however, the less effective this transferred immunity will be. In part, older people may be more susceptible to influenza because of this: an immunity they established long ago is fading.

However, during major influenza epidemics older people also suffer more severely than their juniors. Epi-demics of severe influenza occur because the virus has undergone some major genetic change, so that the anti-bodies developed by our bodies in response to previous infections are incapable of dealing with the new strain. This means that younger people and older people are on an equal footing with regard to established immunity, and the difference in the impact of the epidemic on the two age groups suggests that older people are less capable of mounting an immune response.

Many older people are also less resistant, and less capable of recovery, because they are less fit and often suffering already from other illnesses, particularly chest diseases like emphysema, chronic bronchitis and asthma. In weakened lungs, a secondary bacterial infec-tion may prove fatal – bacterial pneumonia is a major cause of death among elderly influenza sufferers. Even relatively minor persistent illnesses in the background can make of influenza a major health complication.

Infections that stay with us for life

After recovery from measles or mumps, you are immune to the disease for life, and no one can catch it from you. The same is true of many other infections, but some can remain in the body for life; even though we feel no ill-effects ourselves, we may be able to pass the infec-tion on to others - we continue to be carriers long after recovering.

In the case of some diseases, infection during infancy can produce no symptoms at all, yet the person can still infect others later in life. The best example of this is the Epstein-Barr virus, which causes mononucleosis (glandular fever). In the developing countries this virus infects virtually every child before the age of two, with little effect except to provide immunity. Almost all adolescents and young adults are immune because of this. In the industrialized countries only about 40 percent of infants are infected. The virus is spread by close contact (this infection is often nicknamed "the kissing disease"), so during adolescence and young adulthood the 40 percent who were infected during infancy pass on the infection to the other 60 percent. In this age-group flu-like symptoms as well as swollen glands, jaundice, rashes and two or three weeks of weakness can result.

The AIDS virus is another that stays with a person for life. Fortunately most of the other examples have less devastating effects: we all carry some viruses, but usually we are blissfully unaware of the fact. Sometimes, though, the fact can be brought rather abruptly to our attention, as in the case of the varicella virus (which is distantly related to the Epstein-Barr virus).

The varicella virus is responsible for both chickenpox and shingles. Almost everyone has chickenpox once during childhood and never again. However, recovery from this illness does not mean that the virus has been cleared from the body; instead, it has become dormant in cells of the nervous system. Years later the infection may recur, this time as shingles – massed blisters on the skin above a group of inflamed nerves – with severe pain. The reason for the recurrence is probably that the immune response that developed during the original infection has gradually faded over the years. A reappearance of the virus in the body fluids boosts the immune response, so that the shingles disappear as the virus is once more brought under control.

How often should immunizations be renewed?

Vaccines work on the principle that dead organisms or weakened strains of them will raise a person's immunity to the level it would be if they had been infected by live, fully dangerous ones. In order to be effective, a vaccine should be given long enough in advance of exposure to the infection to give the body time to generate an immune response. Usually two or three weeks is long enough. One notable exception to this rule is the rabies vaccine, which can be effective even after infection: this is because the virus responsible spreads slowly from its initial point of entry (an animal bite) before infecting the nervous system, where it does its major damage.

Some vaccines act not against the invading organism itself but against the poisons it produces. A prime example is the tetanus vaccine. The level of immunity must be kept high.

Although with some vaccines a single dose will provide immunity for life, in many cases a person must be immunized regularly: at least every 10 years for polio and at least every 5 years for tetanus. **LB**

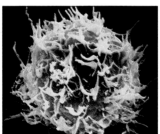

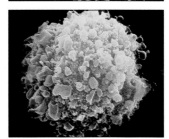

Infected with AIDS. TOP A foster mother cares lovingly for a child who was infected with the AIDS virus while still in her natural mother's womb. TOP RIGHT A healthy "T cell," an essential link in the chain of immune cells that fight infection, has a ragged appearance. BOTTOM RIGHT A T cell made ineffective by the AIDS virus has a rounder, smoother appearance. This one is magnified more than 3,000 times.

21 TIME TO HEAL

Injury and disease destroy large numbers of our cells. Whenever this happens, the body must react quickly to replace them or compensate for their loss. If the skin is wounded, the reaction produces visible signs – swelling, bruising and scarring. Similar healing processes occur unseen in almost every other kind of body tissue.

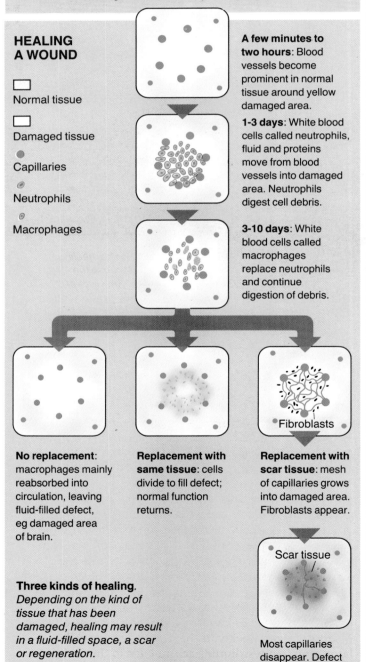

HEALING A WOUND

☐ Normal tissue

☐ Damaged tissue

• Capillaries

· Neutrophils

· Macrophages

A few minutes to two hours: Blood vessels become prominent in normal tissue around yellow damaged area.

1-3 days: White blood cells called neutrophils, fluid and proteins move from blood vessels into damaged area. Neutrophils digest cell debris.

3-10 days: White blood cells called macrophages replace neutrophils and continue digestion of debris.

Fibroblasts

No replacement: macrophages mainly reabsorbed into circulation, leaving fluid-filled defect, eg damaged area of brain.

Replacement with same tissue: cells divide to fill defect; normal function returns.

Replacement with scar tissue: mesh of capillaries grows into damaged area. Fibroblasts appear.

Scar tissue

Most capillaries disappear. Defect is filled with scar tissue produced by fibroblasts.

Three kinds of healing. *Depending on the kind of tissue that has been damaged, healing may result in a fluid-filled space, a scar or regeneration.*

PROVIDED that general health is good, the body's repair systems ensure that we recover quickly from the damage caused by most injuries and illnesses. Even with a very minor cut, healing begins as soon as the bleeding stops. Where possible, lost body cells are replaced with tissue of the same kind. If this is not possible, the damaged area is at least tidied. How long healing takes depends on factors such as the person's age and the extent and site of the damage.

How do our bodies repair damaged tissue?

Whenever tissues suffer disease or physical damage, large numbers of cells die. The body reacts with a standard sequence of countermeasures to clear the site of debris and, usually, to deal with the loss.

During the first few hours after cell loss occurs, the small blood vessels in nearby healthy tissue become gorged with blood; this is why, for example, sunburn or a sore, infected throat look red – inflamed. A little of the liquid part of the blood (the plasma) leaks through the walls of these vessels and into the affected tissues, which therefore swell up; the extra liquid can press on the local nerve endings to produce pain.

It is not only liquid that leaks through the walls of the minor blood vessels. Various blood cells emerge, including large numbers of a particular type of white blood cell called a neutrophil. Almost immediately after the tissues have been damaged, neutrophils start to appear; their numbers reach a peak at about 2-3 days. Neutrophils can clear away cell debris and ingest most forms of bacteria, and may cure any bacterial infection in the damaged area. Antibiotics reduce the numbers of bacteria, thus making the job of the neutrophils easier, but they are ineffective in viral infections (see *Ch 20*). Neutrophils are created on demand by specialized cells in the bone marrow.

The lifetime of a working neutrophil at a site of tissue damage is very short, only about one day. Many of them die at the site of the tissue damage, so that there is yet more debris to be cleared away. The body therefore has a second line of scavenger cells, macrophages, which have a longer lifetime. These reach the damaged area much later than the neutrophils. By about 10-14 days after the outbreak, the damaged area consists largely of liquid and macrophages. It is weak because the dead cells have been cleared away but replacements have yet to appear.

Sometimes the macrophages re-enter the blood circulation, so that only liquid is left in the damaged area. This is what happens when a substantial area of brain tissue is damaged in a stroke. Brain cells cannot reproduce to replace the dead cells, and so the function of that region of the brain is permanently impaired. Surrounding cells suffer damage but can recover.

▶ **The healing process is well underway** *by the time scabs have formed over the wound. The dry, hard scabs protect the tissue replacement that is going on below the surface. The bruising that occurred when blood leaked from damaged blood vessels into the surrounding tissue will fade over one or two weeks as the blood is reabsorbed into the circulation.*

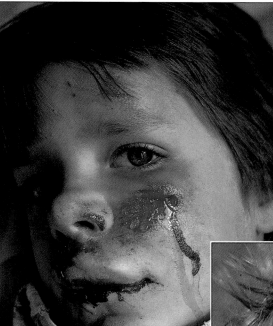

▲ **Immediately after falling from her bicycle,** *a girl's face is badly cut and scraped. To stem the bleeding, platelet cells in the blood must clump together to plug the wound. The chemical reactions they produce causes the protein fibrin to form a network of strands over the wound (this is the blood clot). Bleeding stops because red and white blood cells are trapped in the strands.*

◀ **After four weeks,** *healing is complete. Because the cuts were not deep enough to prevent the skin from rebuilding its tissues, the accident has left no scars. How long healing takes varies between individuals, depending on factors such as blood clotting tendencies. Youth and good health can speed up the process considerably.*

Which areas of the body heal fastest?

When there has been tissue damage, the ideal is that all the debris is cleared away and the dead cells are replaced by cells capable of performing exactly the same function. This occurs most rapidly in the areas of the body where the cells normally replace themselves fairly frequently: the skin, the inner lining of the stomach and bowel and so on. When there is damage to these tissues, they very rapidly produce a new population of cells which can take over the functions of those that have been lost.

For this to occur, however, it is important that there are enough living cells left in the region. Sunburn is a good example of the importance of this principle. Some hours after the skin has been exposed to an excessive amount of ultraviolet radiation from the sun, the skin becomes red (because the minor blood vessels are distended), swollen (because liquid from the blood vessels has leaked into the skin tissues) and painful (because the liquid is pressing on the skin's many nerve endings). If only a few skin cells have been destroyed these effects disappear very quickly. If the number of lost cells is large, and if excess liquid accumulates in the various skin layers, the skin blisters. When skin cells die, the skin peels.

There are usually plenty of cells left in the lower levels

of the skin to replace those that have been lost, so that within a few days there is a protective covering and not long afterward the original cells have been replaced by fully functional replicas. Should you suffer a very severe case of sunburn – perhaps through falling asleep under a sunlamp – you may not be so lucky. So many cells may have been destroyed that the survivors are incapable of generating enough new cells to replace the dead ones. In this event a skin graft may be required.

Why do some wounds scar?

In some areas of the body, cells reproduce only rarely, if at all. Here cell death has much more serious consequences. The lost cells – for example, heart muscle cells

that are destroyed by a heart attack – are replaced by scar tissue. Though this is strong and durable, it does not function in the same way that the original tissues did. Scar tissue also forms in the skin when deep cuts make it impossible for normal skin to rebuild from below. In small and in clean wounds, scar tissue starts to form after 1-2 days.

What happens is that large numbers of tiny blood vessels grow out – bud – from nearby blood vessels into the damaged area. These tiny blood vessels merge with each other to form a network through which blood can bring oxygen and vital nutrients, and through which liquid and any remaining macrophages can be reabsorbed. Special cells – fibroblasts – multiply rapidly in surrounding areas and migrate to the place where the

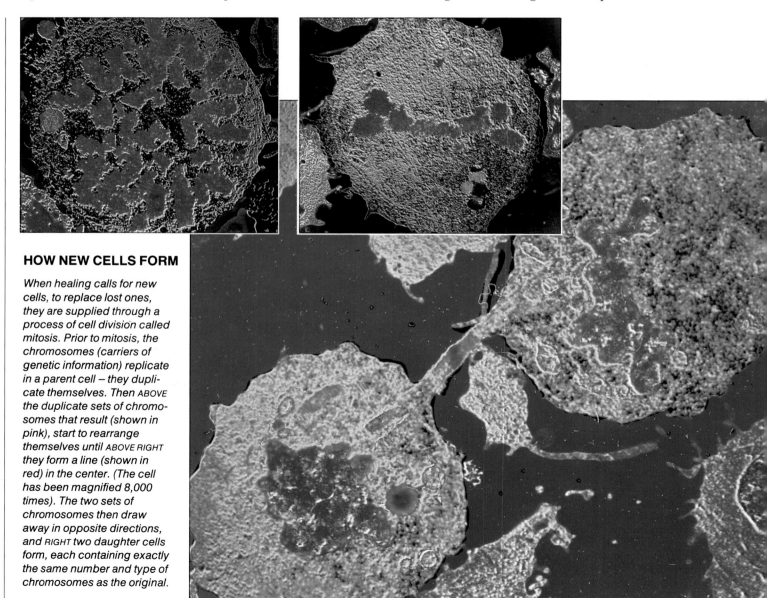

HOW NEW CELLS FORM

When healing calls for new cells, to replace lost ones, they are supplied through a process of cell division called mitosis. Prior to mitosis, the chromosomes (carriers of genetic information) replicate in a parent cell – they duplicate themselves. Then ABOVE the duplicate sets of chromosomes that result (shown in pink), start to rearrange themselves until ABOVE RIGHT they form a line (shown in red) in the center. (The cell has been magnified 8,000 times). The two sets of chromosomes then draw away in opposite directions, and RIGHT two daughter cells form, each containing exactly the same number and type of chromosomes as the original.

damage has occurred. These special cells produce a protein called collagen.

The fibers of collagen knit together to fill the hole in the damaged tissue. As soon as this happens, the fibroblasts stop producing collagen and most of the budded blood vessels retreat. The fibroblasts do not die, but remain where they are in case they are needed again. In time, the collagen fibers shuffle closer together, so that the scar gets smaller.

The time required for these processes varies a great deal. A clean flesh cut may be scarred over within days, but a broken bone may take months to heal. Further damage to the tissues – caused by renewed infection or by additional physical punishment – can delay healing enormously. AS

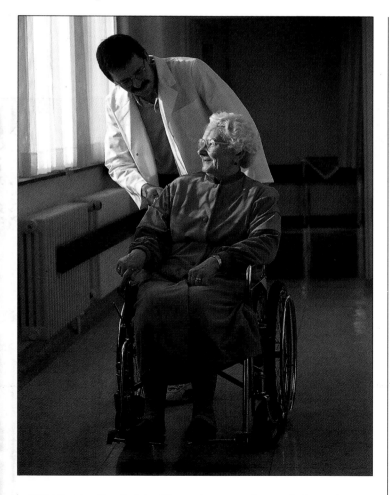

Effective healing in later life *is possible because of the renewal capacity of those body cells that can divide. Experiments have shown that there are limits to the number of cell divisions possible, but the limits are so high that our renewal capacity is much longer than a human lifetime. Cell replacement in some organs, such as the skin, decelerates as we age.*

What happens to damage repair in old age?

The ability to regenerate tissues and heal wounds stays with us throughout life, although the process becomes slower as we age. For example, the skin of older people is more easily torn and heals more slowly when cut. Another example is slower recovery from burns: a child aged under 14 with 50 percent of the skin area burned has a 50 percent chance of survival, but in people over 65 burns to only 9 percent of the skin area are sufficient to produce a 50 percent mortality rate.

The greatest influence on statistical differences in healing between young and old is not aging but the fact that more older people have generally poor health, and at any age poor health hampers healing. When elderly people urgently require surgery, they are often undernourished and possibly also they are suffering disease affecting the heart and lungs; when a limb is injured, its blood supply as a whole may be endangered because the person has atherosclerosis (hardening of the arteries – see *Ch2*). Another common ailment of age, diabetes (see *Ch18*), makes wounds more likely to become infected and can interfere with the healing process. The accumulation of fluid in the tissues, especially in the legs – for example, because of right-sided heart failure (see *Ch2*) – likewise makes infection more likely and healing slower.

Is surgery more dangerous in old age?

Those over 65 years of age account for one-quarter of all people admitted to surgical wards but for three-quarters of deaths in the aftermath of surgery – partly because these figures include older people requiring emergency surgery while suffering from diseases that impair recovery. Major elective surgery, as opposed to emergency surgery, however, holds little more danger for older people than for younger ones.

Today's older people have a far higher survival rate after surgery, in fact, than used to be the case. This is probably partly because more of them are fitter and better nourished than in previous generations.

Advances in anesthesia, surgical techniques and postoperative treatment of infection probably also contribute to surgeons' confidence of success with older patients. Operations like open-heart surgery can be extremely successful in people in their late seventies and early eighties, and less dramatic operations are performed routinely on people in even their late eighties. Total hip replacement, excision of part of the prostate gland and removal of cataracts from the eye followed by the implantation of an artificial lens are just three examples of everyday operations which can totally transform the life of an aged person. NC

Further Reading and Acknowledgments

FURTHER READING

READERS may want information about other aspects of a subject, or detail on particular topics that have aroused their interest. Some generally available books suggested for further reading are listed below.

1 The Beating Heart

Gardiner, J 1981 *The ECG – What Does it Tell?* Stanley Thornes, Cheltenham; Khan, G M 1987 *Heart Attacks, Hypertension and Heart Drugs* Rodale Press, Emmaus, PA; Silman, A J 1988 *You and Your Blood Pressure* Family Doctor Publications, British Medical Association, London.

2 The Life of the Heart

Becker, G L 1987 *Heart Smart. A Step-by-Step Guide to Reducing the Risk of Heart Disease* Simon and Schuster, New York; Piscatella, J C 1989 *Don't Eat Your Heart Out. The Guide to Eating for a Healthy Heart* Thorsons, Wellingborough; Portal, R W 1986 *Heart Attack: Prevention and Treatment* Family Doctor Publications, British Medical Association, London.

3 Breathing

Donaldson, J 1989 *Living with Asthma and Hay Fever* Penguin Books, London; Search, G and Denison, D M 1988 *Getting in Shape* New England Library, Sevenoaks, Kent; Sebel, P, Stoddart, D M, Waldhorn, R E, Waldmann, C S and Whitfield, P 1985 *Respiration. The Breath of Life* Torstar Books, New York.

4 Brainwaves

Chadwick, D and Usiskin, S 1987 *Living with Epilepsy* Macdonald Optima, London.

5 Biological Rhythms

Winfree, A T 1987 *The Timing of Biological Clocks* Scientific American Library, New York.

6 Sleep and Dreaming

Oswald, I and Adam, K 1983 *Get a Better Night's Sleep* Acro Publishing, New York.

7 Time and the Senses

Freeland, A 1989 *Deafness. The Facts* Oxford University Press, Oxford; Glasspool, M 1984 *Eyes. Their Problems and Treatments* Methuen Australia, North Ryde; Slater, R and Terry, M 1987 *Tinnitus. A Guide for Sufferers and Professionals* Croom Helm, Beckenham, Kent; Smith, J 1989 *Senses and Sensibilities* Wiley, New York.

8 Time and Physical Ability

Mayes, K 1987 *Brittle Bones and the Calcium Crisis. Osteoporosis – What It Is – Who It Affects – And What You Can Do to Prevent It* Grapevine, Wellingborough; Sayce, V and Fraser, I 1988 *Exercise Beats Arthritis* Thorsons, Wellingborough; Scully, P (ed) 1987 *Modern Gym Fitness* Guinness Books, Enfield, Middlesex.

9 Time for Digestion

Charlish, A and Gazzard, B 1988 *How to Cure Your Ulcer* Sheldon Press, London; Janowitz, H D 1987 *Your Gut Feelings. Prevention and Cure of Intestinal Problems* Oxford University Press, Oxford; Nicol, R 1989 *Coping Successfully With Your Irritable Bowel* Sheldon Press, London.

10 Keeping Fluids in Balance

Gartley, C B 1988 *Managing Incontinence. A Guide to Living with Loss of Bladder Control* Jameson Books, Ottawa, IL; Kilmartin, A 1980 *Cystitis: A Complete Self Help Guide* Hamlyn, London; Taguchi, Y 1988 *Private Parts. A Health Book for Men* Macdonald Optima, London.

11 Times of Fertility

Guillebaud, J 1987 *The Pill* Oxford University Press, Oxford; Stanway, A 1984 *Infertility. A Common-Sense Guide For the Childless* Thorsons, Wellingborough; Williams, W 1989 *It's Up to You: Overcoming Erection Problems* Thorsons, Wellingborough; 1987 *Your Body. A Woman's Guide to Her Sexual Health* Thorsons, Wellingborough, in association with the Marie Stopes Clinic.

12 The Menstrual Cycle

Dalton, K 1987 4th edn *Once a Month* Fontana, London; Harrison, M 1987 *Self-Help With PMS* Macdonald, London; Kingston, B 1984 *Lifting the Curse: How to Relieve Painful Periods* Sheldon Press, London; Wilson, R C D 1988 *Pre-Menstrual Syndrome. Diet Against It* Foulsham, Slough.

13 Time and Sexual Arousal

Hammond, D B 1987 *My Parents Never Had Sex: Myths and Facts of Sexual Aging* Prometheus Books, Buffalo, New York; Sandford, C E 1983 *Enjoy Sex in the Middle Years* Methuen Australia, North Ryde; Ward, B 1988 *Sex and Life* Macdonald Optima, London.

14 The Moment of Conception

Austin, C R and Short, R V (eds) 1986 2nd edn *Reproduction in Mammals: 5 Manipulating Reproduction* Cambridge University Press, Cambridge.

15 Nine Months of Pregnancy

Anderson, M 1984 *Pregnancy After Thirty* Faber and Faber, London; Bourne, G 1975 *Pregnancy* Pan Books, London.

16 Time of Birth

Balaskas, J 1983 *Active Birth* London University Paperbacks, London; Kitzinger, S 1989 *Breastfeeding Your Baby* Dorling Kindersley, London; Redshaw, M E, Rivers, R P A and Rosenblatt, D B 1985 *Born Too Early. Special Care For Your Preterm Baby* Oxford University Press, Oxford.

17 How Children Grow

Jolly, H 1985 *Book of Child Care. The Complete Guide for Today's Parents* The Leisure Circle, London; Leach, P 1983 *Babyhood* Penguin, Harmondsworth; Welford, H 1988 *The A-Z of Feeding in the First Year* Unwin Paperbacks, London.

18 How Adults Age

Brown, D S 1984 *Handle With Care. A Question of Alzheimer's* Prometheus Books, New York; Coni, N K, Davison, W and Webster, S G P 1984 *Ageing: the Facts* Oxford University Press, Oxford; Thomas, D J 1988 *Strokes and Their Prevention* Family Doctor Guides, British Medical Association, London; Tyndall, A 1986 *The Longevity Lifestyle. A Simple Program of Nutrition and Exercise for Prolonging the Prime of Your Life* Newcastle Publishing, North Hollywood, CA.

19 Abnormal Regeneration

Clyne, R 1989 *Cancer. Your Life, Your Choice* Thorsons, Wellingborough; Kushi, A and Esko, W 1988 *The Macrobiotic Cancer Prevention Cookbook, Towards Preventing and Controlling Cancer With Diet and Lifestyle* Avery, New York; Singer, A and Szarewski, A 1988 *Cervical Smear Test. What Every Woman Should Know* Macdonald Optima, London.

20 Times of Infection

British Medical Association 1989 *Infection Control* Edward Arnold, London; Crook, W G 1986 *The Yeast Connection. A Medical Breakthrough* Vintage Books, New York; Scott, A 1987 *Pirates of the Cell. The Story of Viruses from Molecule to Microbe* Blackwell, Oxford.

21 Time to Heal

The British Red Cross 1984 *Practical First Aid. The Basic Guide to Emergency Aid for Home, School and Work* Dorling Kindersley, London.

KEY TO PHOTOGRAPHERS

AB Alan Becker. **ABr** Dr Arnold Brody. **AHh** Alex Hubrich. **AHo** Alan Hobson. **AL** Dr Andrejs Liepins. **AMe** Abraham Menashe. **AP** Prof Aaron Polliack. **AS** Anthea Sieveking. **ASAT** Asa Thorensen. **ATs** Alexander Tsiaras. **BK** Barbara Kreve. **BS** Blair Seitz. **Ce** Cole. **CHi** Chip Hires. **CPr** Chris Priest. **CR** Co Rentmeeter. **CV** C Voigt. **DBar** David Barritt. **DFa** Don Fawcett. **DGG** Duclos-Guichard-Gouver. **DGn** David Gayon. **DHn** David Hurn. **DSk** David Strick. **EGe** Eric Grave. **FS** F Scianna. **FSa** Dr F Sauer. **GCo** Gene Cox. **GRo** Guido A Rossi. **GSe** Dr Garry Settles. **GV** Grey Villet. **HMo** Hank Morgan. **HS** Homer Sykes. **HSu** Harald Sund. **JdaC** Jérôme da Cunha. **JBu** Dr Jeremy Burgess. **JFr** John Freeman. **JJ** Prof J James. **JP** Jim Pickerell. **JPw** Judah Passow. **JS** John Sturrock. **JSt** James Stevenson **JWa** John Walsh. **LD** Larry Dale Gordon. **LM** Larry Mulvehill. **MaM** Mark Meyer. **MAn** Martin Anderson. **MCl** Mark Clarke. **MDo** Martin Dohrn. **MKa** Manfred Kage. **MN** Michael Nichols. **MSk** Marshall Sklar. **NB** Nancy Brown. **NDMcK** Nancy Durrell-McKenna. **NL** Norman Lomax. **PAr** Peter Arkell. **PAT** P A Tesman. **PPl** Philippe Plailly. **PSh** Paul Shambroom. **RB** René Burri. **RGC** Roger George Clark. **RKFS** Prof R K F Schiller. **RLt** Rory Lysaght. **SSa** Sebastiao Salgado Jr. **TS** Ted Spiegel. **Vl** Vloo. **WMo** W. Mohn. **YG** Yves Gellie. **ZG** Zao Grimberg.

PICTURE AGENCIES/SOURCES

B/C Blackstar/Colorific.
BM Biology Media.
C Colorific Photo Library Ltd, London, New York.
C/C Colorific/Contact.
CNRI Centre National des Recherches Iconographiques.
G/FSP Gamma/Frank Spooner Pictures, London.
H The Hutchison Library, London.
I Impact Photos, London.
JW John Watney Photo Library.
MPA Mashed Potato Archive.
MG Magnum Photos Ltd, London, Paris, New York.
N Network Photographers, London.
Né Nestlé.
NIBSC National Institute for Biological Standards and Control.
NMSB National Medical Slide Bank.
ONC Ohio Nuclear Corporation.
PF Petit Format, Paris.
PF/CSI/SLP Petit Format/CSI/Science Photo Library.
PP Picture Point Ltd.
R Rex Features Ltd, London.
SIU S I U.
SPL Science Photo Library, London.
SRG Sally and Richard Greenhill, London.
T Topham Picture Library, Kent.
TIB The Image Bank, London.
TIB/G+J The Image Bank/G and J Images, London.
USNIH US National Institute of Health.
V Viewfinder Colour Photo Library, Bristol.
Z Zefa, London.
Z/S Zefa/Stockmarket, London.

PICTURE LIST

Page number in **bold** type. Photographer's initials in parenthesis.

Frontmatter
2 Sunset (HSu) TIB.

Lifespan Health Chart
10 Fetal ultra sonography (ATs) SPL. **12** Reflex grip (JdaC) PF. **14** Ear examination (CP/MCl) SPL. **18** Measuring growth (TS) B/C. At dentist, SRG. **20** Ear examination (BS) SPL. **22-23** Breast examination. By kind permission of the Women's National Cancer Control Campaign. **24** Couple in bed (ZG) TIB. **30** Taking blood pressure, Z. **32** Stress test printout (JP) C. **34** Fitness room, Z.

1 The Beating Heart
39 Gamma camera scan of human heart (PPI) SPL. **44** ECG (MN) MG. **43** Parachuting from bridge, (RLt) V. **46** Injection, NMSB. **47** Portable defibrillator (DGn) The BOC Group PLC/SPL. **48** Emergency (LM) SPL.

2 The Life of the Heart
50-51 Fetal monitoring (AS) N. **52** Computer assisted image of heart, Z/S. **53** Businessmen, Milan (FS) MG. **55** Blocked arteries, CNRI/SPL. Open-heart surgery, USNIH/SPL. **57** Home checkup (PSh) SPL. **60** Man swimming, TIB. **61** Relaxing, T.

3 Breathing
63 Woman singing (CHi) G/FSP. Interior of bronchus, CNRI/SPL. Angiograph of right lung, CNRI/SPL. Alveolar sacs and bronchiole, CNRI/SPL. **64** Nurse and child, SIU/SPL. Deep sea diver (GRo) TIB. Pilot (MaM) C/C. **67** Boy sneezing, Z. Oak pollen (JBu) SPL. Pollen grain (JBu) SPL. **68** Asbestosis, CNRI/SPL. Macrophages (ABr) SPL. **69** Smoker's lung, (JSt) SPL. Healthy lung (JSt) SPL. **70** Blood cells, CNRI/SPL. **71** Swimmer, Z.

4 Brainwaves
72 Mapping the brain's electrical activity (ATs) SPL.

5 Biological Clocks
74 Nurse on night duty (LM) SPL. Girl relaxing, Z.

6 Sleep and Dreaming
79 Red goggles (MN) MG. Sleep graph (AHo) SPL. Eyes – REM from DREAMSTAGE Scientific Catalogue © J Allan Hobson, M D, and Hoffman La-Roche Inc. **83** Couple asleep in street (RB) MG.

7 Time and the Senses
85 Cat scan of skull ONC/SPL. **86** Sacré Coeur, Paris (Vision disorders) (MAn) MPA. **88** Wine tasting (SSa) MG. **90** Trawler (NL) I.

8 Time and Physical Ability
93 Fencing (AHh) TIB. **94** Synapses (EGe) SPL. Neuromuscular junction (DFa) SPL. Muscle tissue, CNRI/SPL. **95** Blood capillary (ASAT) SPL. Weight training (DSk) R. **96** Seoul Olympics, (DGG) G/FSP. **97** Rower (RGC). **99** Father and daughter (LD) TIB. **100** Dancers (CR) TIB. **101** Sun City, Arizona (DHn) MG.

9 Time for Digestion
103 Endoscope image of lining of stomach (RKFS) SPL. Small intestine (MSk) SPL. **106** Detailed interior of human colon, CNRI/SPL. False color X-ray of abdomen, CNRI/SPL. **108** Burping baby (AS) N. **109** Directors' lunch, Albert Hall, London (JS) N. Scanning electron micrograph of ulcer (JJ) SPL. **111** Brushing teeth (AS) N.

10 Keeping Fluids in Balance
112-3 Kidney tissue (MKa) SPL. **113** Drinking, Andromeda. **114** Collecting sweat (MDo) SPL. **115** X-ray, CNRI/SPL. **116** Kidney stone (FSa) Z. **117** Kidney dialysis, Z.

11 Times of Fertility
118 Ovarian follicle containing ripe ovum, PF/Né/SPL. Mature ovum, PF/CSI/SPL. **119** X-ray of female pelvis, CNRI/SPL. **121** Normal human sperms (JWa) SPL. Double headed sperm (JWa) SPL. Sperm showing two tails (JWa) SPL. **122** Laparoscopy (ATs) SPL. **123** In vitro fertilization, JW. Test-tube baby (HMo) SPL.

12 The Menstrual Cycle
127 Endometrium, CNRI/SPL. **131** Cervical mucus, JW. **134** Woman at breakfast, TIB/G+J. **135** Cyclists (AB) TIB.

14 The Moment of Conception
138 Actual moment of fertilization, PF/CSI/SPL. **139** Spermatozoid in uterus, JW. **139** Sperm and ovum, PF/CSI/SPL.

15 Nine Months of Pregnancy
141 Child listening to unborn baby (NDMcK) H. **145** Fetal Monitoring (AS) N. Ultrasound image, CNRI/SPL.

16 Time of Birth
148 Home birth, SRG. **150** Breast feeding, SRG. **151** Premature birth (ATs) SPL.

17 How Children Grow
152 Baby and mother (PAr) I. **152-3** Football (AS) N. **153** Girls (GV) C. **154** Bottle-fed baby (AS) N. **155** Top left (AS) N. Top center (AS) N. Top right (NB) TIB. Bottom left (AS) N. Bottom center (BK) TIB. Bottom right (AS) N. **156** Girl at cupboard (Vl) Z. **160** Girls (JFr) I. Teenagers (PAT) TIB. Young women (Ce) N. **163** Sextuplets (DBar) G/FSP.

18 How Adults Age
164 Young eye (MDo) SPL. Girls tanning (HS) I. **165** Old eye (MDo) SPL. **166** Hair treatment (YG) G/FSP. **167** Jogger (WMo) Z. **168** Brain cells (MKa) SPL. Painter, PP.

19 Abnormal Regeneration
171 Lymphocyte killer cell (AL) SPL. **174** Magnetic resonance image of abdomen, SPL. **175** "Hairy cell" leukemia (AP) SPL. Malignant teratoma of ovary (MKa) SPL.

20 Times of Infection
176 A sneeze (GSe) SPL. **177** Influenza virus, CNRI/SPL. Phagocytosis (GCo) SPL. **178** Lymphocyte, BM/SPL. **179** Toxoplasma, CNRI/SPL. **181** Child with AIDS (AMe) SPL. HIV infection, NIBSC/SPL.

21 Time to Heal
183 Injured child in stages of healing (3 pics), SRG. **184** Stages of division in the lymphocyte cell (3 pics), CNRI/SPL. **185** Lady in wheelchair (CV) Z.

Further Reading and Acknowledgments